Kentucky Pecan Pie,
page 312

Hunter-Style Chicken, page 184

Actually Delicious Turkey Burgers,
page 95

3

Peanut Butter Chip Chocolate Cookies, page 329, and Oatmeal-Toffee Cookies, page 331

all recipes
family favorites

Oxmoor
House®

ISBN: 0-8487-3010-0
Library of Congress Control Number: 2005929028
Printed in the United States of America
First Printing 2005

To order additional publications, call 1-800-765-6400.

For more books to enrich your life, visit
oxmoorhouse.com

Cover: Double-Chocolate Brownie Cake (page 295)

Allrecipes.com, Inc.
President: Bill Moore
Senior VP Development: Tim Hunt
Vice President Marketing: Esmée Williams
Senior Recipe Editor: Sydny Carter
Senior Food Editor: Jennifer Anderson
Recipe Editors: Emily Brune, Richard Kozel,
    Lesley Peterson, Britt Swearingen
Creative Direction: Yann Oehl, Jeff Cummings

Allrecipes.com, Inc.
400 Mercer Street, Suite 302
Seattle, WA 98109
(206) 292-3990
www.Allrecipes.com

Oxmoor House, Inc.
Editor in Chief: Nancy Fitzpatrick Wyatt
Executive Editor: Susan Carlisle Payne
Art Director: Cynthia Rose Cooper
Copy Chief: Allison Long Lowery

Allrecipes Family Favorites
Editor: McCharen Pratt
Copy Editor: Diane Rose
Editorial Assistants: Julie Boston, Shannon Friedmann,
    Terri Laschober
Senior Photographer: Jim Bathie
Senior Photo Stylist: Kay E. Clarke
Photo Stylist: Amy Wilson
Director, Test Kitchens: Elizabeth Tyler Luckett
Assistant Director, Test Kitchens: Julie Christopher
Test Kitchens Staff: Kristi Carter, Nicole Lee Faber,
    Kathleen Royal Phillips, Elise Weis, Kelley Self Wilton
Publishing Systems Administrator: Rick Tucker
Director of Production: Laura Lockhart
Production Assistant: Faye Porter Bonner

Contributors:
Designer: Carol Damsky
Indexer: Mary Ann Laurens
Photographers: Lee Harrelson, John O'Hagan
Photo Stylist: Missie Crawford

Table of Contents

Welcome from the Staff of Allrecipes!

Dear Friends:

Have you been searching for recipes that can stand the test of time—and satisfy a hungry family? Bringing your best to the dinner table every night can be hard, but a few family secrets can make mealtimes a pleasure. The millions of home cooks at **Allrecipes.com** have been sharing cherished recipes and tasteful traditions every day for over 8 years, and we've selected the best of their time-honored recipes here for you. For this all-new cookbook, we've gathered over 350 4- and 5-star recipes, all rated and reviewed by the online community at **Allrecipes.com.** We've organized them into a single book that will help you produce meals so delicious and comforting that every member of your family will become a proud member of the "clean-plate club"! Take a look at some of the features that make this book better than ever:

- **12 menus promise a variety of meals that guarantee a satisfied family every time. From *Quick & Easy* to *Make Ahead* to *Party Food,* we've got a menu for any occasion or schedule. Plus, every menu comes with a plan of attack to help you make the most of your time.**
- **To make finding the right recipe for the job even easier, we've created specific chapters that collect the best *Kid-Friendly* fare, *Brand-Name Classics,* and recipes that are sure to create memorable *Holidays.* Whenever you start to feel stumped in the kitchen, find solutions in these 3 bonus chapters.**
- **Tip boxes scattered throughout the book offer secrets to great cooking that are straight from the *Allrecipes.com* experts. Learn the culinary trick of brining a turkey (page 64), gain expertise on types of blue cheese (page 85), or get a little creative and make your own tortilla bowls (page 111). You'll find all this and much more inside.**
- **Valuable information such as prep time and cook time, a nutritional analysis, and the 4- or 5-star rating accompanies every recipe. You can use these tools to assist you in planning meals that are just right for you and your family.**
- **Every recipe comes with a review from a home cook at the *Allrecipes.com* website. These reviews let you know what to expect from the recipes, provide preparation tips, offer serving ideas, and suggest substitutions.**

Whether you've followed **Allrecipes.com** from the beginning or you're just now discovering this rich new recipe source, you'll find the best recipes for home cooking right here. After you've flipped through these pages, be sure to take your own favorite recipes and secret tricks to **Allrecipes.com** and share them with us. You just may have the perfect solution to someone's dinner dilemma!

Happy Cooking,

The Staff of Allrecipes

What is Allrecipes.com?

It's an interactive recipe swap that's helping over 10 million people effortlessly create family-pleasing meals.

Eight years ago, we created a place for home cooks to share their favorite recipes via the Internet. As word spread, others joined in, and in no time, **Allrecipes.com** grew into the world's largest community of home cooks—over 10 million strong—and became the number-one source for online recipes. On the website, recipes are posted for everyday home cooks to put them to the test and then rate and review them online.

About the recipes

Every recipe in this book includes a brief **comment from the contributor.** This may be a serving suggestion, details on where the recipe came from, or other valuable information about the dish. We always preserve the character of the contributed recipe, but we make slight changes where necessary to ensure consistency, accuracy, and completeness in the published version.

On **Allrecipes.com,** visitors post **recipe reviews,** and for this book, we've included the most helpful reviews alongside the recipes. Look for **"What other cooks have done"** in the box beside every recipe for these reviews that give serving suggestions and cooking tips.

Veterans of the website know to look not only to the **highest-rated, but also the most-rated recipes** when they're looking for winners. This means that lots of people have tried these recipes at home and rated them online. We've included the rating for each recipe. For this book, only 4- and 5-star recipes (out of a possible **5 stars**) were included. Once you've made a few of these recipes, go online and share your thoughts. Look on the next two pages for a list of the most rated and reviewed recipes from this book.

You may wonder why some of the recipe titles have **Roman numerals** attached to them, like Marinated Mushrooms II on page 156 or Snickerdoodles V on page 322. Contributors submit multiple recipes with these titles, so we assign them a number to help keep up with all the variations. In this book, you'll find only one of the variations—the highest-rated, most-reviewed version—but you can find all the different takes on classic recipes online.

Prep and cook times are included as a basic guide with each recipe to help you plan meals. Remember that these times are approximate. How fast you chop, the accuracy of your oven's temperature, the humidity, and other variations can affect your prep and cook time.

Need more information?

You'll find helpful tip boxes and charts throughout the book to help you with basic cooking and baking questions, and you can visit us online if you need more information. Check out the "Cooking Advice" section at **Allrecipes.com,** where you can browse through articles and step-by-step cooking tutorials.

Recipe Hall of Fame

Check out the all-star recipes with the most ratings and reviews from the website—the best of the best from this year's cookbook, Allrecipes Family Favorites. The following recipes received hundreds of ratings from the online community and come with the testimonials of home cooks everywhere who acclaim these as their all-time favorites. Listen to what people are saying about these great-tasting recipes.

▶ **Quick and Easy Alfredo Sauce** (page 27)
"I made this for a birthday party dinner I threw. It turned out creamy, yummy, and delicious, and it had my guests raving! I was a happy host who didn't have to spend tons of time or money on this dish. I'll definitely use this recipe time and time again! Thanks for sharing this classic."

▶ **Restaurant-Style Buffalo Chicken Wings** (page 31)
"These wings were awesome—nice and crispy and not over-poweringly spicy. I made them as directed, and they were perfect for my taste! This is my new 'stay-at-home' football party appetizer."

▶ **Cola Chops** (page 87)
"This recipe worked out well on a day when I didn't have ingredients in the house to make much of anything. Everyone thought this would be too sweet, but it was great. My family loved it."

▶ **Baked Teriyaki Chicken** (page 93)
"This was so good! I have had a hard time finding a teriyaki sauce in the store that I like, and now I can make my own. This is better than what they serve in restaurants, and it's so tender. I loved this and will be making it often."

▶ **Maple Salmon** (page 96)
"This was a truly delicious dish. The sweetness of the maple and the savory/salty flavor of the soy brought a different twist to salmon that I would never have thought to try. My husband and I thoroughly enjoyed it. I will cook this again, and I'll recommend it to my friends."

▶ **Apple Dip** (page 131)
"Excellent! This tastes wonderful and is so much better for you—and cheaper—than the store-bought dip. This only took a couple of minutes to whip up. So easy!"

▶ **Beef and Noodle Bake** (page 134)
"I smiled when I saw this recipe; it brought back memories. This is similar to what my husband introduced to me almost 19 years ago, the year we got married. It's quick and easy; sometimes we change it by using what is on hand. It's a good recipe for a quick meal."

▶ **Italian-Style Pork Chops** (page 134)
"I've always had trouble with pork chops. I never really knew how to make them, so mine usually came out dry. This, however, was an excellent dish. My husband and 3½-year-old loved it. It worked well with sweet potatoes and green beans. What a quick way to make dinner! This will be one of our usual items on the dinner menu."

11

Recipe Highlights

Every single recipe in Allrecipes Family Favorites *has a banner to help you identify favorite features. Here's a guide to all the banners scattered throughout the book. Look for them in the index for more help in finding the perfect recipe for your needs.*

Around-the-World Cuisine ▼

Open your mind and your palate with these recipes that feature exotic flavors from around the globe.

Blue Ribbon Winner ▼

Contributors share some of their special prizewinning fare from around the world.

Company is Coming ▼

When you need a meal to impress your guests, look for this banner to fill your entertaining needs.

Covered-Dish Favorite ▼

Whether it's a church potluck or a family reunion, you'll have the right dish to carry along.

Crowd-Pleaser ▼

These recipes yield enough for a large party and are fit for all kinds of celebrations.

5 Ingredients or Less ▼

Speed up your prep time with recipes that feature five ingredients or less, excluding salt, pepper, and water.

Freezer Fresh ▼

Fill your freezer with delicious dishes that hold up well to freezing and reheating for easy, ready meals.

From the Grill ▼

Add a little spice to backyard barbecuing with these new approaches to grilling your favorite meals.

From the Pantry ▼

You probably have everything you need to make these recipes that call for common pantry and fridge items.

Holiday Gift Giving ▼

Give a gift of the heart with these recipes for wonderful homemade gifts from your kitchen.

Hot & Spicy ▼

Hot and spicy fans can find their next indulgence here. Remember that you can adjust the seasonings to taste.

Kid-Friendly ▼

Pull out these recipes for surefire hits with little ones and adults alike. Everyone will clean their plates.

Make-Ahead ▼

For parties or weeknight meals, plan ahead and make life easier with recipes that can be made ahead.

Meatless Main Dish ▼

Looking for a break from meat and potatoes? These vegetarian delights will please even die-hard meat-eaters.

One-Dish Meal ▼

Dinner can't get much easier than a whole meal in one dish. You'll enjoy all the flavor without all the fuss.

Out-of-the-Ordinary ▼

Shake up things at the dinner table with recipes that turn everyday meals into extraordinary feasts.

Party Food ▼

Put on your party hat and get cooking. You'll set the mood for your next gathering with style.

Quick & Easy ▼

These recipes save the day when you're on the run and there are hungry mouths to feed.

Restaurant Fare ▼

Make standout dishes from your favorite restaurant at home with these classic recipes.

Slow-Cooker Creation ▼

Delicious dinners will be waiting on you when you use these slow-cooker concoctions.

Family-Favorite Menus

Who says planning meals can't be a pleasure? In this chapter, we offer a variety of menu ideas, from quick and easy weeknight dinners to hearty make-ahead fare. Meals for family fun and elegant occasions alike can be found here. For extra ease, we include prep plans with each menu. All that's left for you to do is enjoy!

A Meatless Dream

Light fare that's filling makes perfect sense for a quick lunch or casual dinner. The blooming onion appetizer will delight kids and adults alike, and an entrée from the grill takes almost no time to prepare. Round out the meal with greens and dressing from the grocery store and your favorite flavor of sherbet.

MENU PREP PLAN

1. Marinate portobellos and prepare Blooming Onion.

2. Cook Blooming Onion.

3. Grill portobellos; assemble rest of dish and broil.

4. Dress salad greens while the entrée broils.

5. Scoop sherbet after dinner.

RESTAURANT FARE ▶

Prep Time: 25 minutes

Cook Time: 10 minutes

Average Rating: ★★★★★

What other cooks have done:

"We gently opened the onion a little and then placed it, cut side down, into some simmering water for a minute. Afterwards, we placed it in an ice water bath for 3 minutes, and the onion bloomed nicely. To separate the petals during frying, we dry-dusted the onion with some flour mixed with the same spices the recipe called for and then dipped it into the batter and dusted it again. We got an awesome bloom."

MENU

Blooming Onion
Grilled Portobello and Mozzarella
mixed green salad
orange sherbet
Serves 4

Blooming Onion

Submitted by: **Joanne Bruck**
"A delicious onion is sliced to bloom and then breaded and deep-fried. The recipe for the dipping sauce is also included."

½	cup mayonnaise	1½	teaspoons salt
¾	tablespoon ketchup	1½	teaspoons cayenne pepper
2	tablespoons cream-style horseradish sauce	½	teaspoon ground black pepper
¼	teaspoon paprika	½	teaspoon garlic powder
¼	teaspoon salt	¼	teaspoon dried thyme
	Pinch ground black pepper	¼	teaspoon dried oregano
	Pinch cayenne pepper	⅛	teaspoon ground cumin
1	egg	1	large onion
1	cup milk	2	quarts vegetable oil for deep-frying
1	cup all-purpose flour		

1. To make the dipping sauce, combine mayonnaise, ketchup, horse-radish, paprika, ¼ teaspoon salt, pinch black pepper, and pinch cayenne pepper in a small bowl and refrigerate until ready to serve.
2. Beat egg and combine it with milk in a large bowl. In another bowl, combine flour, 1½ teaspoons salt, 1½ teaspoons cayenne pepper, ½ teaspoon black pepper, garlic powder, thyme, oregano, and cumin.
3. Cut approximately ¾ to 1 inch off of the top and bottom of the onion; remove skin. Remove the 1-inch diameter core from the middle of the onion. Using a large, sharp knife, slice down the center of the onion, cutting to, but not through, the bottom; turn at a right

angle and slice again. Keep slicing the sections in half, being careful not to cut to the bottom, until you have 16 sections. Gently spread the petals apart to make coating easier.

4. Dip the onion in the milk mixture and then coat well with the flour mixture. Separate the petals again and sprinkle the flour mixture between them. Once you have coated all of the petals well, dip the onion into the milk mixture and into the flour mixture again. Place in the refrigerator for at least 15 minutes.

5. Meanwhile, pour enough oil to cover the onion into a deep fryer or deep pot. Preheat the oil to 350°F (175°C).

6. Gently lower onion into hot oil, right side up. Fry for 10 minutes or until golden brown. Remove from oil and let drain on a rack or paper towels. Open the center of the onion wide so that you can put the small bowl of dipping sauce in the center. **Yield:** 4 servings.

Per serving: 787 calories, 8g protein, 33g carbohydrate, 70g fat, 2g fiber, 77mg cholesterol, 1261mg sodium

Grilled Portobello and Mozzarella

Submitted by: **Valerie Kasper**

"This is a simple and delicious appetizer or main course. Portobello mushrooms, red sauce, roasted red bell peppers, and mozzarella cheese make this a to-die-for dish."

4	portobello mushroom caps	1	(7 ounce) jar roasted red bell peppers, drained and sliced
½	(8 ounce) bottle Italian-style salad dressing	8	slices mozzarella cheese
1	(14 ounce) jar marinara sauce	½	teaspoon dried oregano
		½	teaspoon dried basil

1. Place the mushrooms and dressing in a large zip-top plastic bag. Seal and marinate for at least 15 minutes.

2. Lightly oil cold grill rack and preheat grill for medium-high heat. Heat the marinara sauce in a saucepan over medium heat; keep warm.

3. Cook the mushrooms on the prepared grill for 7 to 10 minutes on each side or until lightly toasted.

4. Preheat broiler.

5. Spread the bottom of a shallow baking dish or ovenproof plate with just enough marinara sauce to cover the bottom. Place mushrooms in the dish, bottom side up, and top with the peppers and remaining marinara sauce. Place 2 slices of cheese on each mushroom and sprinkle evenly with oregano and basil.

6. Broil in the preheated oven for 3 to 5 minutes or until the cheese is melted. Serve hot. **Yield:** 4 servings.

Per serving: 366 calories, 18g protein, 20g carbohydrate, 25g fat, 4g fiber, 32mg cholesterol, 1560mg sodium

◄ QUICK & EASY

Prep Time: 15 minutes

Marinate Time: 15 minutes

Cook Time: 25 minutes

Average Rating: ★★★★

What other cooks have done:

"Very tasty. I grilled the mushrooms on the stovetop first, and I used fresh mozzarella. I put a whole mushroom on a roll for a sandwich, and it turned out great. I'll make this again."

Blasé Gourmet

You can make an elegant meal in flash with this speedy menu. For a small, casual gathering of friends, share the simple flavors of a crunchy spring salad and an impressive pesto-encrusted salmon. Finish the meal with an indulgent make-ahead chocolate dessert.

MENU PREP PLAN

1. Prepare Chocolate Delight through layering step and store in refrigerator.

2. Chop and marinate vegetables.

3. Prepare and cook salmon.

4. Serve vegetables with salmon. Garnish Chocolate Delight before serving.

MENU

Stephan's Broiled Salmon Pesto
Easy Marinated Vegetables
Chocolate Delight
Serves 4

COMPANY IS COMING ▶

Prep Time: 10 minutes

Marinate Time: 15 minutes

Cook Time: 16 minutes

Average Rating: ★★★★★

What other cooks have done:

"Excellent. I made this for my folks, who thought it was exquisite. I made my own pesto, and I only needed about 1 cup for the fish. The crispy pesto melted in our mouths. I served it alongside a green salad and pasta tossed with the remaining pesto."

Stephan's Broiled Salmon Pesto

Submitted by: **Stephan Schwartz**
"Coat this salmon with a thick layer of pesto, sort of like icing on a cake. Then place coated side under the broiler, and the pesto will form a browned crust."

2	pounds salmon fillets	½	cup white wine
2	lemons	1½	cups pesto

1. Lightly oil a large baking pan. Place salmon in pan, skin side down. Run finger over flesh to make sure all bones have been removed. Use pliers to pull out any that remain. Squeeze juice from 1 lemon; pour juice and white wine over fish. Marinate 15 minutes.
2. Preheat broiler.
3. Coat the top side of the fish with a layer of pesto between ⅛ to ¼ inch thick, covering the surface of the fish.
4. Broil fish in the preheated oven about 9 inches from heat source for 8 to 10 minutes per inch of thickness or until fish flakes and flesh is opaque (pesto should form a heavily browned crust). Remove from the oven and set aside for a few minutes. Squeeze half of second lemon over fish. Slice remaining lemon half into thin slices. Place lemon slices on individual servings. **Yield:** 4 servings.

Per serving: 913 calories, 63g protein, 12g carbohydrate, 67g fat, 5g fiber, 164mg cholesterol, 851mg sodium

Easy Marinated Vegetables

Submitted by: **Chris**

"Serve these marinated vegetables as a salad or as an appetizer."

1½ cups broccoli florets
1½ cups cauliflower florets
1 green bell pepper, cut into 1 inch pieces
1 cucumber, peeled, seeded, and coarsely chopped
1 carrot, coarsely chopped
¼ cup Italian-style salad dressing

1. Bring a large pot of salted water to boil. Place the broccoli and cauliflower florets into the boiling water for 1 minute. Drain and rinse florets.

2. Combine broccoli, cauliflower, bell pepper, cucumber, carrot, and salad dressing in a medium mixing bowl. Cover and refrigerate the vegetables for 1 hour. **Yield:** 4 servings.

Per serving: 108 calories, 3g protein, 10g carbohydrate, 8g fat, 3g fiber, 0mg cholesterol, 143mg sodium

◀ MAKE-AHEAD

Prep Time: 10 minutes

Cook Time: 5 minutes

Chill Time: 1 hour

Average Rating: ★★★★☆

What other cooks have done:

"I thought this recipe was very good! Next time, I will blanch the carrots along with the broccoli and cauliflower. I added some artichoke hearts, and the combination was great!"

Chocolate Delight *(pictured on page 39)*

Submitted by: **Renee**

"For this wonderful trifle, chocolate cake is cubed and doused with coffee liqueur. This is the most delightful chocolate dessert you will ever taste!"

1 (18.25 ounce) package chocolate cake mix
1 cup coffee-flavored liqueur
2 (5.9 ounce) packages instant chocolate pudding mix
6 (1.4 ounce) chocolate-covered toffee bars, chopped
2 (12 ounce) containers frozen whipped topping, thawed
1 (1 ounce) square semisweet chocolate (optional)

1. Prepare chocolate cake according to package directions and bake in a 9x13 inch pan. Cool and cut into squares, leaving them in the pan; pour coffee-flavored liqueur over cake. Prepare pudding according to package directions.

2. In large trifle bowl or several small glass dishes, crumble half of cake. Top cake with half of chocolate pudding, a third of chopped candy bars, and 1 container of whipped topping. Repeat layers. Sprinkle with remaining chopped candy bars. If desired, use a vegetable peeler to shave chocolate curls from semisweet chocolate square; sprinkle shavings over top of desserts. Keep refrigerated until serving. **Yield:** 12 servings.

Per serving: 558 calories, 4g protein, 71g carbohydrate, 24g fat, 2g fiber, 12mg cholesterol, 489mg sodium

◀ MAKE-AHEAD

Prep Time: 15 minutes

Cook Time: 25 minutes

Average Rating: ★★★★★

What other cooks have done:

"Try this with chocolate-flavored whipped topping. I threw in some sliced fresh strawberries. Serve this with espresso for a real jolt!"

Let-Your-Hair-Down Holiday

This homestyle menu provides an easy, comforting solution to the post-holiday doldrums by allowing you to use your Thanksgiving leftovers to make the pot pie. Or cut the stress out of the season completely and serve this menu at your holiday table.

MENU PREP PLAN

1. Up to a day ahead, prepare Cranberry Gelatin Salad and Orange Fluff I. Store both in refrigerator.

2. Prepare Iced Tea II and chill.

3. Prepare and bake pot pie.

4. Steam green beans while pot pie bakes.

MENU

Turkey Pot Pie
steamed green beans
Cranberry Gelatin Salad
Iced Tea II
Orange Fluff I
Serves 8

Turkey Pot Pie *(pictured on page 37)*

Submitted by: **Linda**
"This is a perfect way to use up leftover turkey."

COVERED-DISH FAVORITE ▶

Prep Time: 20 minutes

Cook Time: 1 hour

Average Rating: ★★★★★

What other cooks have done:

"I was pressed for time, so I used frozen veggies (peas, carrots, and green beans), along with the fresh potatoes, onion, and celery. I also substituted chicken broth for more flavor. It was perfect. Definitely a keeper!"

1	(15 ounce) package refrigerated pie crusts	2	chicken bouillon cubes
¼	cup butter, divided	2	cups water
1	small onion, minced	3	potatoes, peeled and cubed
2	stalks celery, chopped	1½	cups cubed cooked turkey
2	carrots, diced	3	tablespoons all-purpose flour
3	tablespoons dried parsley	½	cup milk
1	teaspoon dried oregano Salt and ground black pepper to taste		

1. Preheat oven to 425°F (220°C).
2. Unroll bottom pie crust; place in a 10 inch pie plate and set aside.
3. Melt 2 tablespoons butter in a large skillet. Add the onion, celery, carrots, parsley, oregano, and salt and pepper to taste. Sauté vegetables until soft. Stir in the bouillon cubes and water. Bring mixture to a boil. Stir in the potatoes and cook until tender but still firm.
4. In a medium saucepan, melt remaining 2 tablespoons butter. Stir in turkey and flour. Add milk and heat through, stirring constantly. Stir turkey mixture into vegetable mixture and cook until thickened. Pour mixture into unbaked pie crust. Unroll the top crust and place

on top of filling. Flute edges and make 4 slits in the top crust to vent steam.

5. Bake in the preheated oven for 15 minutes. Reduce oven temperature to 350°F (175°C) and continue baking for 20 minutes or until crust is golden brown. **Yield:** 8 servings.

Per serving: 456 calories, 13g protein, 40g carbohydrate, 27g fat, 4g fiber, 38mg cholesterol, 682mg sodium

Cranberry Gelatin Salad

Submitted by: **Sharon Wolfe**
"Even people who don't like cranberry sauce like this tasty gelatin salad!"

1 (16 ounce) can jellied cranberry sauce	2 cups boiling water
1 (16.5 ounce) can pitted dark sweet cherries, drained	1 (6 ounce) package cherry-flavored gelatin
10½ ounces crushed pineapple with juice	1 cup chopped pecans (optional)

1. In a medium saucepan over low heat, melt the cranberry sauce.
2. Cut the cherries into pieces and add them to the melted sauce. Stir in the pineapple with its juice. Remove mixture from heat.
3. In a medium bowl, pour the boiling water over the gelatin. Stir until all the gelatin has dissolved.
4. Add the gelatin mixture to the cranberry mixture and stir. Stir in the nuts, if desired. Pour into an oiled 9x13 inch pan and chill until set. **Yield:** 12 servings.

Per serving: 211 calories, 3g protein, 37g carbohydrate, 7g fat, 2g fiber, 0mg cholesterol, 58mg sodium

◀ MAKE-AHEAD

Prep Time: 15 minutes

Cook Time: 10 minutes

Chill Time: 1 hour

Average Rating: ★★★★★

What other cooks have done:
"I have finally found my grandma's famous cranberry gelatin. My family was excited when they tried this recipe at our Thanksgiving dinner. Even friends who tried it were impressed by its taste."

Iced Tea II

Submitted by: **Sharon**
"This iced tea is fabulous—it tastes like the brand-name kind!"

| 8 | cups water | ¾ | cup white sugar |
| 3 | orange pekoe tea bags | ½ | cup lemon juice |

1. In a large saucepan, heat water to a rapid boil. Remove from heat and drop in the tea bags. Cover and let steep for 1 hour.
2. In a large pitcher, combine tea and sugar. Stir until sugar is dissolved; stir in lemon juice. Refrigerate until chilled. **Yield:** 8 servings.

Per serving: 76 calories, 0g protein, 20g carbohydrate, 0g fat, 0g fiber, 0mg cholesterol, 7mg sodium

Orange Fluff I

Submitted by: **D**
"This is a light and fruity orange dessert salad that is also cool and creamy."

2	(11 ounce) cans mandarin oranges, drained	2	(3 ounce) packages orange-flavored gelatin
1	(15 ounce) can crushed pineapple with juice	1	(16 ounce) container frozen whipped topping, thawed
1	(16 ounce) container cottage cheese		

1. Combine oranges, pineapple, and cottage cheese in a large bowl. Add gelatin and stir until well blended. Fold in whipped topping and refrigerate for at least 1 hour. **Yield:** 8 servings.

Per serving: 388 calories, 10g protein, 50g carbohydrate, 17g fat, 1g fiber, 9mg cholesterol, 302mg sodium

Friendly Feast

Indulge your friends with this mostly make-ahead menu that's sure to satisfy appetites as well as taste buds.

MENU

Mama's Balsamic Vinaigrette
salad greens
Porketta Roast
Cashew-Raisin Rice Pilaf
Strawberry Torte
Serves 6

MENU PREP PLAN

1. Up to a day ahead, prepare and chill Strawberry Torte. Prepare and chill vinaigrette.

2. Prepare Porketta Roast. While roast is in the oven, make pilaf.

3. Toss salad just before dinner.

Mama's Balsamic Vinaigrette

Submitted by: **SOSARA77**
"This is a wonderful vinaigrette that my mother invented. It's great as a dressing, but we also use it as a marinade for chicken and steamed veggies."

¾ cup extra virgin olive oil
¾ cup balsamic vinegar
1 clove garlic, crushed (or to taste)
½ teaspoon dried oregano
2 teaspoons prepared Dijon-style mustard
Pinch salt
Pinch freshly ground black pepper

1. Combine the olive oil, vinegar, garlic, oregano, mustard, salt, and pepper in a jar with a tight-fitting lid. Shake well before serving. Store in the refrigerator. **Yield:** 12 servings.

Per serving: 138 calories, 0g protein, 3g carbohydrate, 14g fat, 0g fiber, 0mg cholesterol, 57mg sodium

◄ FROM THE PANTRY
Prep Time: 10 minutes
Average Rating: ★★★★☆

What other cooks have done:
"This is a good and quick dressing! Nice and simple! I did add 1 more teaspoon of Dijon mustard to cut down the taste of the vinegar."

Porketta Roast *(pictured on page 40)*

Submitted by: **Dee**
"A spicy, tasty, and extremely moist boneless pork roast. This recipe uses a dry rub combination that you rub on the meat before you roast it. The blend includes dill seed, fennel seed, oregano, lemon pepper, garlic powder, and onion powder."

COMPANY IS COMING ▶

Prep Time: 15 minutes

Cook Time: 2 hours 40 minutes

Average Rating: ★★★★★

What other cooks have done:

"This is one of the best porketta recipes to date! Easy to make! Toss it in the slow cooker with potatoes and carrots, and you'll have a dinner everyone will enjoy!"

1	tablespoon dill seed	¼	teaspoon onion powder
1	tablespoon fennel seed	¼	teaspoon garlic powder
1	teaspoon dried oregano	4	pounds boneless pork roast
1	teaspoon lemon pepper		

1. Preheat oven to 325°F (165°C).
2. In a small bowl, combine the dill seed, fennel seed, oregano, lemon pepper, onion powder, and garlic powder. Mix well and apply to the roast. Place roast in a greased 10x15 inch roasting pan.
3. Bake in the preheated oven for 2 hours and 40 minutes or until a meat thermometer inserted into thickest part of pork registers 160°F (70°C). **Yield:** 6 servings.

Per serving: 571 calories, 62g protein, 1g carbohydrate, 34g fat, 1g fiber, 186mg cholesterol, 212mg sodium

Cashew-Raisin Rice Pilaf *(pictured on page 40)*

Submitted by: **Granny Loretta**
"Very good low-fat rice pilaf. This dish is delicious with both poultry and pork dishes."

COVERED-DISH FAVORITE ▶

Prep Time: 15 minutes

Cook Time: 50 minutes

Average Rating: ★★★★★

What other cooks have done:

"I recently prepared this recipe for a church group of 98 people! It scaled perfectly, and everybody loved it! I put it together the night before and put it in the refrigerator overnight to let the flavors blend. I toasted the cashews and added them at the last minute so they wouldn't get soggy."

¼	cup butter	¾	cup uncooked wild rice
1½	cups uncooked long-grain white rice	2	cups frozen green peas
1	chopped onion	1	(4 ounce) jar diced pimento, drained
1	cup chopped carrot	1	cup cashews
1	cup golden raisins	1	teaspoon salt
3	cups chicken broth		Ground black pepper to taste
1½	cups water, salted		

1. Melt butter in a large saucepan over medium-high heat. Sauté the long-grain rice, onion, carrot, and raisins for 3 to 5 minutes or until onion is tender. Pour in the broth and bring to a boil. Reduce heat to low, cover, and simmer for 20 to 25 minutes.
2. Meanwhile, in a saucepan, bring 1½ cups salted water to a boil. Add wild rice; reduce heat, cover, and simmer for 45 minutes. Drain and set aside.
3. When the raisin mixture is finished simmering and the wild rice is cooked, stir cooked wild rice, peas, pimento, cashews, salt, and pepper to taste into raisin mixture and heat through. **Yield:** 12 servings.

Per serving: 278 calories, 7g protein, 42g carbohydrate, 10g fat, 3g fiber, 0mg cholesterol, 596mg sodium

Strawberry Torte *(pictured on page 41)*

Submitted by: **Star Pooley**

"Light, fluffy, easy, and elegant! This recipe is from my mom."

1	(16 ounce) package frozen strawberries, thawed	2	teaspoons vanilla extract
1	tablespoon cornstarch	2	cups whipping cream
½	(8 ounce) package cream cheese, softened	2	(12 ounce) packages ladyfingers
¾	cup white sugar		Fresh strawberries

1. Strain strawberries, reserving juice for this recipe and pulp for other uses. In a saucepan, bring cornstarch and strawberry juice to a gentle boil. Remove from heat and let cool.

2. Whip together cream cheese, sugar, and vanilla.

3. In a separate bowl, beat whipping cream until stiff peaks form. Fold whipped cream into cream cheese mixture.

4. Arrange ladyfingers around sides and bottom of an 8 or 9 inch springform pan, standing ladyfingers lengthwise around sides of pan. Pour half of the cream cheese filling into the pan and place a layer of ladyfingers on top of filling. Pour remaining filling over ladyfingers.

5. Spread strawberry sauce over top of cake and place the fresh strawberries on top around outer edge. Refrigerate and remove from pan once thoroughly chilled. **Yield:** 12 servings.

Per serving: 514 calories, 9g protein, 56g carbohydrate, 29g fat, 1g fiber, 287mg cholesterol, 175mg sodium

◀ **MAKE-AHEAD**

Prep Time: 25 minutes

Cook Time: 7 minutes

Chill Time: 2 hours

Average Rating: ★★★★★

What other cooks have done:

"This recipe has a bit more oomph than strawberry shortcake but is not nearly as rich and dense as a cheesecake. This is exactly what a dessert should be—something sweet, but not something that's going to have you walking away from the table ready to explode."

Tropical Delight

Take a trip to the tropics with this variety of flavors. Everything can be made ahead of time, so you can plan this menu for casual dinner parties or for a family dinner after a busy day. If you'd like, you can save the fruit salad for dessert and serve the entrée with a quick green salad instead.

MENU PREP PLAN

1. Up to a day ahead, prepare and freeze ice cream.

2. Start kielbasa in the slow cooker.

3. Up to 6 hours before serving, prepare fruit salad and store in refrigerator.

4. Prepare rice and serve with kielbasa and fruit salad.

MENU

Island Kielbasa in a Slow Cooker
white rice
Juicy Fruit Salad
Five-Ingredient Ice Cream
Serves 6

Island Kielbasa in a Slow Cooker

Submitted by: **Denise**
"My mother gave this recipe to me. This dish is always a big hit at parties and potlucks. You'll never have to bring home any leftovers!"

SLOW-COOKER CREATION ▶

Prep Time: 10 minutes

Cook Time: 6 hours

Average Rating: ★★★★★

What other cooks have done:

"I only used 1 pound of kielbasa, and I cut the brown sugar down to 1 cup. I added 1 finely chopped green bell pepper and 1 tablespoon soy sauce. Also, I used crushed pineapple instead of pineapple chunks. I served this over white rice."

2 pounds kielbasa sausage, sliced into ½ inch pieces	2 cups brown sugar
2 cups ketchup	1 (8 ounce) can pineapple chunks, undrained

1. Place the sausage, ketchup, sugar, and pineapple in a slow cooker and mix together.
2. Cook on High for 1 hour; reduce heat to Low and cook for 4 to 5 hours or until sausage is cooked through. **Yield:** 6 servings.

Per serving: 871 calories, 22g protein, 108g carbohydrate, 41g fat, 2g fiber, 101mg cholesterol, 2606mg sodium

Juicy Fruit Salad

Submitted by: **Bobbie**

"It's the pineapple syrup combined with the juice of the orange that makes this fruit salad taste delectable!"

1 (8 ounce) can pineapple chunks with juice, drained and juice reserved	1 orange, peeled, diced, and juice reserved
1 apple, peeled, cored, and diced	1 banana, sliced
	1 cup seedless green grapes, halved

1. In a large bowl, toss together the pineapple, apple, orange, banana, and grapes. Add the juice from the pineapple and orange and chill until ready to serve. **Yield:** 6 servings.

Per serving: 106 calories, 1g protein, 27g carbohydrate, 0g fat, 3g fiber, 0mg cholesterol, 1mg sodium

◄ 5 INGREDIENTS OR LESS

Prep Time: 5 minutes

Chill Time: 25 minutes

Average Rating: ★★★★☆

What other cooks have done:

"My friend's mother used to make this whenever I would come over for dinner. She used a can of mandarin oranges. As a secret ingredient, she would sprinkle a little instant vanilla pudding on top of the salad. I went home and told my mother about it, and this has become a staple whenever either of us makes a fruit salad."

Five-Ingredient Ice Cream

Submitted by: **Alisha**

"It takes only five ingredients to make this fabulously creamy family-pleaser. Before freezing, you can also add crushed sandwich cookies, nuts, chocolate chips, coconut, or other favorites."

½ cup cold milk	⅛ teaspoon salt
1 tablespoon vanilla extract	2 cups whipping cream
1 (14 ounce) can sweetened condensed milk	

1. In a medium bowl, stir together cold milk, vanilla, condensed milk, and salt. Set aside.

2. In a large bowl, beat whipping cream with an electric mixer until stiff peaks form. Fold milk mixture into whipped cream.

3. Pour into a shallow 2 quart dish; cover and freeze for 4 hours, stirring once after 2 hours or when edges start to harden. Serve or store in an airtight container in the freezer for up to 10 days.

Yield: 6 servings.

Per serving: 504 calories, 8g protein, 39g carbohydrate, 36g fat, 0g fiber, 133mg cholesterol, 172mg sodium

◄ MAKE-AHEAD

Prep Time: 5 minutes

Freeze Time: 4 hours

Average Rating: ★★★★☆

What other cooks have done:

"I made this with my 3-year-old, and we had a great time, not to mention a very tasty treat at the end! We added crushed chocolate cookies and crushed peppermint candy, which covered up the sweetened condensed milk flavor. Also, we used 2½ cups of half-and-half instead of the milk and whipping cream (didn't whip the half-and-half). We just put it in an electric ice cream maker, which made the recipe even easier. The final product was smooth and creamy."

Easy Elegance

For any occasion you want to share with someone special, look to this menu to make the night carefree. With a quick-cooking entrée and side and a make-ahead dessert sauce, you'll have plenty of time to relax and enjoy the meal.

MENU PREP PLAN

1. Up to a day ahead, prepare Toffee Sauce. Cool and store in refrigerator.

2. Cook pasta while you prepare Alfredo Sauce; keep warm.

3. Prepare and cook pork chops. Serve with pasta and Alfredo Sauce.

4. Reheat Toffee Sauce in microwave and serve with pound cake.

MENU

Pork Chops Stuffed with Smoked Gouda and Bacon

Quick and Easy Alfredo Sauce

hot fettuccine

bakery pound cake

Toffee Sauce

Serves 2

Pork Chops Stuffed with Smoked Gouda and Bacon (pictured on page 42)

Submitted by: **Darla C.**
"Easy and elegant enough for the in-laws. When filling the chops, be sure not to stuff them too much."

FROM THE GRILL ▶

Prep Time: 15 minutes

Cook Time: 24 minutes

Average Rating: ★★★★★

What other cooks have done:

"I broiled the chops in the oven on Low for about 8 minutes on each side. I used thick boneless cuts, and they were beautiful and tasty. I will definitely make these again. Next time, I will maybe brush a bit of hoisin sauce on the pork after it has cooked."

2 ounces smoked Gouda cheese, shredded	2 (2¼ inch thick) center cut bone-in pork chops
4 slices bacon, cooked and crumbled	1 teaspoon olive oil
¼ cup chopped fresh parsley	¼ teaspoon salt
⅛ teaspoon ground black pepper	Ground black pepper to taste

1. Lightly oil cold grill rack and preheat grill for medium heat.
2. In a small bowl, combine cheese, bacon, parsley, and ⅛ teaspoon black pepper.
3. Lay 1 chop flat on a cutting board. With a sharp knife held parallel to the board, cut a pocket into the pork, going all the way to the bone, but leaving the sides intact. Stuff cheese mixture into pocket and close with a toothpick. Brush meat with oil and season with salt and black pepper to taste. Repeat with remaining chop.
4. Cook on the prepared grill for 12 minutes on each side or until pork is done (be careful not to overcook). **Yield:** 2 servings.

Per serving: 404 calories, 36g protein, 1g carbohydrate, 28g fat, 0g fiber, 117mg cholesterol, 880mg sodium

Quick and Easy Alfredo Sauce

Submitted by: **Dawn Carter**

"I experimented with these ingredients until I found a quick, cheap, and easy Alfredo sauce combination. The secret is cream cheese!"

½	cup butter	1½	cups grated Parmesan cheese
1	(8 ounce) package cream cheese	⅛	teaspoon ground black pepper
2	teaspoons garlic powder		
2	cups milk		

1. Melt butter in a medium nonstick saucepan over medium heat. Add cream cheese and garlic powder, stirring with a wire whisk until smooth. Add milk, a little at a time, whisking to smooth out lumps. Whisk in Parmesan and pepper. Remove from heat when sauce reaches desired consistency. Sauce will thicken rapidly; thin with milk if mixture seems thick. Toss with hot pasta to serve. **Yield:** 4 servings.

Per serving: 659 calories, 26g protein, 10g carbohydrate, 58g fat, 0g fiber, 167mg cholesterol, 1253mg sodium

Toffee Sauce *(pictured on page 43)*

Submitted by: **Annette**

"This is a great sauce for topping cakes, as it thickens when it cools. You can also serve it warm over ice cream or place it in a fondue pot over low heat and dip apples, pears, pineapple, strawberries, bananas, and orange wedges into it."

½	cup butter	1	(14 ounce) can sweetened condensed milk
2	cups packed brown sugar	1	teaspoon vanilla extract
1	cup light corn syrup		
2	tablespoons water		

1. In a medium saucepan over medium heat, melt butter. Stir in brown sugar, corn syrup, water, and condensed milk. Cook and stir until thickened. Remove from heat and stir in vanilla. Store leftovers in an airtight container in the refrigerator; reheat in microwave on Medium for 30 seconds. **Yield:** 20 servings.

Per serving: 233 calories, 2g protein, 45g carbohydrate, 6g fat, 0g fiber, 19mg cholesterol, 100mg sodium

◀ RESTAURANT FARE

Prep Time: 5 minutes

Cook Time: 5 minutes

Average Rating: ★★★★★

What other cooks have done:

"This is the best sauce I have ever had. I've used it over pasta, in lasagna, as a pizza sauce, and in tuna casserole! I get so many compliments for this sauce—no matter how I use it. I love it just the way it is, but I have also made it with less milk when I wanted a thicker sauce. I've also added more garlic to make it a garlicky pizza sauce. I will probably use this recipe forever."

◀ HOLIDAY GIFT GIVING

Prep Time: 10 minutes

Cook Time: 5 minutes

Average Rating: ★★★★★

What other cooks have done:

"I made this sauce for my family's Christmas Eve fruit fondue. It was a huge hit! My brothers devoured it. It was especially wonderful with pears and apples."

Bountiful Breakfast

For the most important meal of the day, start off ahead of the game by making breakfast the night before. Take your pick of either classic French toast or all-in-one Breakfast Pies to make ahead. The baked apple side dish will need to wait until morning to be assembled, so you can enjoy the aroma of baking apples while you treat yourself to French toast or Breakfast Pies!

MENU PREP PLAN

1. The night before, prepare and cook Breakfast Pies or assemble French toast. Store in refrigerator.

2. In the morning, bake French toast or reheat pies in microwave.

3. Prepare apples. Bake while enjoying French toast or pies.

MENU

Skiers' French Toast
or
Breakfast Pies
Simple Baked Apples
Serves 8 to 10

Skiers' French Toast

Submitted by: **Pat**
"Prepare this baked French toast that makes its own syrup the night before and then bake it in the morning. This is great for a crowd at breakfast before heading up to the slopes!"

MAKE-AHEAD ▶

Prep Time: 15 minutes

Chill Time: overnight

Cook Time: 45 minutes

Average Rating: ★★★★★

What other cooks have done:

"I used store-bought sliced cracked wheat bread instead of the unsliced white bread. I also buttered the baking dish before putting any ingredients in it. Everyone loved it, and my sister-in-law took the recipe home with her so she could try it herself."

2	tablespoons light corn syrup		5	eggs
½	cup butter		1½	cups milk
1	cup packed brown sugar		1	tablespoon vanilla extract
1	(1 pound) loaf unsliced white bread with crust trimmed		¼	teaspoon salt

1. Combine light corn syrup, butter, and sugar in a saucepan; simmer over medium heat until syrupy. Pour mixture into a 9x13 inch pan.
2. Slice bread into 12 to 16 slices; place over the syrup in pan. Layer slices if necessary.
3. Beat together the eggs, milk, vanilla, and salt. Pour over bread. Cover pan with plastic wrap and refrigerate overnight.
4. Preheat oven to 350°F (175°C).
5. Bake in the preheated oven, uncovered, for 45 minutes. Cut into squares. Invert and serve. **Yield:** 8 servings.

Per serving: 445 calories, 10g protein, 62g carbohydrate, 18g fat, 1g fiber, 168mg cholesterol, 574mg sodium

Breakfast Pies

Submitted by: **Jeanne**

"These individual breakfast pies can be made ahead of time and microwaved to reheat as needed. They make great finger food for the little ones. I fix hash browns and gravy as side dishes for the adults. This recipe is always a huge hit!"

¾ pound ground pork sausage
⅛ cup minced onion
⅛ cup minced green bell pepper
1 (12 ounce) can refrigerated biscuit dough
3 eggs, beaten
3 tablespoons milk
½ cup shredded colby-Monterey Jack cheese

1. Preheat oven to 400°F (200°C).
2. In a large, deep skillet over medium-high heat, combine sausage, onion, and green bell pepper. Cook until sausage is evenly browned. Drain, crumble, and set aside.
3. Separate the dough into 10 individual biscuits. Flatten each biscuit out; line bottom and sides of 10 greased muffin cups. Evenly distribute sausage mixture between the cups. Mix together the eggs and milk and divide between the cups. Sprinkle tops with shredded cheese.
4. Bake in the preheated oven for 18 to 20 minutes or until filling is set. **Yield:** 10 servings.

Per serving: 303 calories, 10g protein, 16g carbohydrate, 22g fat, 1g fiber, 91mg cholesterol, 669mg sodium

◄ KID-FRIENDLY

Prep Time: 20 minutes

Cook Time: 20 minutes

Average Rating: ★★★★★

What other cooks have done:

"I make these every Easter for brunch, and they are a huge hit! Leftovers reheat nicely. I recommend using the larger muffin pans (the kind that make 6 jumbo muffins). That way, you can add extra toppings without worrying about anything overflowing. You will need to increase the bake time if you do this."

Simple Baked Apples

Submitted by: **Kathar**

"This is a family standard. We have these apples at least once a week during the winter. The spices, nuts, and raisins can be interchanged or omitted depending upon your tastes. This serves as a great breakfast, side dish, or dessert."

6 apples, peeled, cored, and sliced
½ cup white sugar
3 tablespoons all-purpose flour
½ teaspoon ground cinnamon
½ teaspoon ground nutmeg
¼ teaspoon ground cloves
½ cup raisins
½ cup chopped walnuts
½ cup whole milk

1. Preheat oven to 350°F (175°C). Grease a 2 quart casserole dish.
2. Place apples in a large bowl. In a separate small bowl, mix together sugar, flour, cinnamon, nutmeg, and cloves. Stir spice mixture into apples until evenly distributed. Fold in raisins and walnuts. Spoon into prepared dish. Pour milk evenly over apple mixture.
3. Bake in the preheated oven for 45 minutes to 1 hour or until soft and bubbly. Allow to cool slightly before serving. **Yield:** 12 servings.

Per serving: 141 calories, 2g protein, 27g carbohydrate, 4g fat, 3g fiber, 1mg cholesterol, 6mg sodium

◄ CROWD-PLEASER

Prep Time: 30 minutes

Cook Time: 1 hour

Average Rating: ★★★★★

What other cooks have done:

"This recipe was delicious and easy to make. I scaled the recipe to serve 20. I also added a package of sweetened dried cranberries and a crumb topping made of a little cinnamon, equal parts flour and white sugar, and enough butter to make the dough come together and form crumbs."

Game Night

On the night of the big game, spread your table with classic munchies and a decadent dessert. Your guests will love making their own roast beef sandwiches, so set out a wide array of condiments for them to enjoy.

MENU PREP PLAN

1. Up to a day ahead, bake brownies.

2. The night before or morning of, assemble Italian beef, add to slow cooker, and start slow cooker.

3. An hour before, prepare bean spread and store in refrigerator.

4. Prepare and cook wings.

5. Slice or shred beef. Arrange menu items on buffet and let guests serve themselves.

> ### MENU
>
> **Festive Bean Spread with tortilla chips**
> **Restaurant-Style Buffalo Chicken Wings**
> **Italian Beef in a Bucket**
> **hoagie rolls**
> **supermarket vegetable tray**
> **Caramel Brownies III**
> *Serves 10 to 12*

Festive Bean Spread

Submitted by: **Lisa Garchow**

"This bean spread with a Mexican taste makes a wonderful appetizer. It looks very festive with the red and green toppings, and it's easy to put together. Your guests will be asking for the recipe, so keep it handy! Substitute a 3-cup package of shredded taco cheese blend for the two cheeses if you'd like."

MAKE-AHEAD ▶

Prep Time: 10 minutes

Chill Time: 1 hour

Average Rating: ★★★★★

What other cooks have done:

"What a hit! I warmed the dip in the microwave to melt the cheese. Everyone seemed to prefer it that way. I've also made a nondairy version by using soy cheese and tofu sour cream, and nobody knew the difference!"

1	(16 ounce) can refried beans	2	cups shredded Cheddar cheese
1	cup salsa	1	cup shredded Monterey Jack cheese
1	teaspoon ground cumin		
½	teaspoon garlic powder	2	tomatoes, chopped
1	pint sour cream	1	bunch green onions, chopped
1	(1.25 ounce) package taco seasoning mix		

1. Mix together beans, salsa, cumin, and garlic powder and spread on a large, flat serving dish in a thin layer about ½ inch thick.
2. Mix together sour cream and taco seasoning and spread over bean layer.
3. Sprinkle Cheddar cheese and Monterey Jack cheese over sour cream layer; top with chopped tomatoes and green onions.
4. Cover with plastic wrap and chill for about 1 hour. Serve cold with tortilla chips. **Yield:** 18 servings.

Per serving: 170 calories, 7g protein, 9g carbohydrate, 12g fat, 2g fiber, 32mg cholesterol, 407mg sodium

Restaurant-Style Buffalo Chicken Wings *(pictured on page 38)*

Submitted by: **Kelly**
"This recipe is similar to the hot wings recipe served at a popular restaurant chain. You'll surely love these."

	Oil for deep-frying	1	cup all-purpose flour
½	cup butter	½	teaspoon paprika
½	cup hot sauce	½	teaspoon cayenne pepper
	Dash ground black pepper	½	teaspoon salt
	Dash garlic powder	20	chicken wings

1. Heat oil in a deep fryer to 375°F (190°C). The oil should be just deep enough to cover wings entirely, about an inch or so deep. Combine the butter, hot sauce, black pepper, and garlic powder in a small saucepan over low heat. Stir together and heat until butter is melted and mixture is well blended. Remove from heat and reserve sauce for serving.

2. In a small bowl, mix together the flour, paprika, cayenne pepper, and salt. Place chicken wings in a large nonporous glass dish or bowl and sprinkle flour mixture over them until they are evenly coated.

3. Fry coated wings in hot oil for 10 to 15 minutes or until parts of wings begin to turn brown. Remove from heat, place wings in a serving bowl, add hot sauce mixture, and stir together.

Yield: 10 servings.

Per serving: 363 calories, 19g protein, 9g carbohydrate, 28g fat, 0g fiber, 100mg cholesterol, 326mg sodium

◀ RESTAURANT FARE

Prep Time: 15 minutes

Cook Time: 15 minutes

Average Rating: ★★★★★

What other cooks have done:

"We loved these—especially my husband, who is picky about his wings. (If we go to a restaurant and he doesn't like their wings, he won't go back!) I added a tablespoon of ketchup to thicken the sauce, a splash of vinegar, and a splash of vodka for a little extra zip. Delicious! I think the extra ingredients I added made them turn out more like our favorite restaurant's wings."

Italian Beef in a Bucket

Submitted by: **Cheryl Gross**

"Try this Italian beef that's prepared with pantry ingredients. This is wonderful for football parties! Adjust seasonings according to how spicy you like it. I serve this on sub rolls with mozzarella cheese."

3½ pounds rump roast, cut in half
1 (12 ounce) jar pickled mixed vegetables
1 (16 ounce) jar pepperoncini salad peppers
1 (0.7 ounce) package dry Italian-style salad dressing mix
1 (10.5 ounce) can beef broth

1. Place roast in a 3½ quart slow cooker; add the pickled mixed vegetables, pepperoncini salad peppers, salad dressing mix, and beef broth. Stir to blend. Cook on High for 1 hour; reduce heat to Low and cook for 8 hours.

2. To serve, remove roast from the slow cooker. If necessary, slice it for sandwiches, but it usually just falls apart. Place the pickled vegetables and pepperoncini in a bowl to serve along with the meat.

Yield: 12 servings.

Per serving: 300 calories, 27g protein, 3g carbohydrate, 19g fat, 1g fiber, 81mg cholesterol, 1187mg sodium

Table Matters

A successful party is usually one that features plenty of food and a well-stocked fridge. For casual affairs, a buffet is the most popular style of meal service, especially for large groups. Set the buffet on a dining table or other surface, such as a chest, kitchen counter, or sideboard, that will accommodate a stack of dinner plates and serving dishes of food. Since your guests will serve themselves, arrange the buffet using these tips:

• Place serving dishes in an arrangement that allows for easy circulation and traffic flow.

• Set the buffet near the kitchen so dishes are easy to refill.

• If a dish is to be served over rice, place the rice first in line. If guests are to assemble their own sandwiches, place buns and condiments first in line.

• Place any dressings and sauces close to the dishes they complement.

• Serve desserts at one end of the buffet or place them on a serving cart.

• Arrange beverages on a side table or serve them from a tray after your guests are seated.

For more information, visit **Allrecipes.com**

Caramel Brownies III *(pictured on page 38)*

Submitted by: **Mary Lewno**

"This is an older recipe that makes wonderful chocolate brownies with a chewy caramel layer in the middle."

1 (14 ounce) package individually wrapped caramels, unwrapped
⅓ cup evaporated milk
1 (18.25 ounce) package chocolate cake mix
¾ cup butter, melted
⅓ cup evaporated milk
1 cup semisweet chocolate chips

1. Preheat oven to 350°F (175°C). In a heavy saucepan, combine caramels and ⅓ cup evaporated milk. Cook over low heat, stirring constantly until smooth; set aside. Grease a 9x13 inch pan.
2. In a large bowl, stir together the cake mix, melted butter, and ⅓ cup evaporated milk until dough holds together. Press half of the dough into the prepared pan, reserving the rest.
3. Bake in the preheated oven for 10 minutes. Remove from the oven and sprinkle the chocolate chips over the crust; pour the caramel mixture evenly over the chips. Crumble the remaining dough over the caramel layer and return to the oven.
4. Bake for 15 to 18 more minutes. Cool in refrigerator to set the caramel before cutting into bars. **Yield:** 24 brownies.

Per serving: 249 calories, 3g protein, 34g carbohydrate, 13g fat, 1g fiber, 18mg cholesterol, 267mg sodium

◄ RESTAURANT FARE

Prep Time: 10 minutes

Cook Time: 30 minutes

Average Rating: ★★★★

What other cooks have done:

"Very rich and delicious, not to mention super easy! I think I will make this recipe again and play with it some (not that it needs it!). I might try adding some peanuts or coconut (or both!). I served these with vanilla ice cream, and I think my sweet tooth was in chocolate heaven."

Crowd-Pleasin' Cajun Creation

Light a fire on the dinner table with a spicy main dish; a salad and cornbread provide cooling flavors for overheated taste buds. You can even turn to this Louisiana-inspired menu for an at-home Mardi Gras celebration. Napkins, plates, and cups in shades of purple, green, and gold help bring the Big Easy to the dinner table.

MENU PREP PLAN

1. Up to 2 days ahead, prepare and chill salad dressing.

2. Prepare gumbo. While gumbo simmers, start cornbread.

3. Prepare and dress salad greens. Serve gumbo with warm wedges of cornbread.

MENU

salad greens
Batman's Best Caesar Dressing
Amusement Park Cornbread
Boudreaux's Zydeco Stomp Gumbo
Serves 8

Batman's Best Caesar Dressing

Submitted by: **John Marshall**
"This fast, easy, creamy Caesar salad dressing is also an excellent marinade for chicken or fresh seafood. This is best when allowed to sit in the refrigerator for a day or two so the flavors have time to develop."

MAKE-AHEAD ▶

Prep Time: 15 minutes

Average Rating: ★★★★☆

What other cooks have done:

"Yum! Much tastier than store-bought dressing. I didn't have any anchovy paste or Parmesan cheese on hand, so I put in a rounded teaspoon of kosher salt and substituted Pecorino Romano cheese. I also added freshly ground black pepper and a rounded teaspoon of sugar."

1½	cups olive oil	2	tablespoons anchovy paste
1	tablespoon red wine vinegar	½	teaspoon ground mustard
¼	cup lemon juice	4	cloves garlic, crushed
1	tablespoon Worcestershire sauce	3	tablespoons sour cream
		½	cup grated Parmesan cheese

1. In a food processor or blender, combine the olive oil, vinegar, lemon juice, Worcestershire sauce, anchovy paste, mustard, garlic, sour cream, and Parmesan cheese. Process until smooth. Pour into a glass container, seal, and refrigerate until ready to use. **Yield:** 2 cups.

Per serving: 165 calories, 1g protein, 1g carbohydrate, 18g fat, 0g fiber, 4mg cholesterol, 243mg sodium

Amusement Park Cornbread

Submitted by: **Trish**

"This is a delicious cornbread that will transport you to a magic kingdom of flavor. This recipe can also be used for cornbread muffins."

⅔ cup white sugar
1 teaspoon salt
⅓ cup butter, softened
1 teaspoon vanilla extract
2 eggs

2 cups all-purpose flour
1 tablespoon baking powder
¾ cup cornmeal
1⅓ cups milk

1. Preheat oven to 400°F (200°C). Lightly grease an 8 inch skillet.
2. In a large bowl, beat together sugar, salt, butter, and vanilla until creamy. Stir in eggs, 1 at a time, beating well after each addition. In a separate bowl, mix together flour, baking powder, and cornmeal. Stir flour mixture into egg mixture alternately with the milk. Beat well until blended.
3. Bake in the preheated oven for 20 minutes or until golden brown. Serve warm. **Yield:** 8 servings.

Per serving: 329 calories, 7g protein, 52g carbohydrate, 10g fat, 2g fiber, 77mg cholesterol, 593mg sodium

◄ QUICK & EASY

Prep Time: 10 minutes

Cook Time: 20 minutes

Average Rating: ★★★★★

What other cooks have done:

"I made this cornbread into muffins for Thanksgiving; a double batch yielded about 3 dozen large muffins. They were a huge hit with all of my guests, and they were gone in no time flat with lots of praise all around. Excellent choice for a sweet cornbread!"

Mardi Gras Meal

If the name "Carnival" doesn't ring the old holiday bell, it's possible you've heard of the French equivalent of Carnival—Mardi Gras. When Fat Tuesday rolls around, kick off a day dedicated to fun, feasting, and famously raucous parties, using this menu as a starting point.

Carnival is the overarching name for the holiday that can encompass the days or weeks leading to Lent. During Carnival, (historically) Christians rid their houses of indulgent foods—like meats, eggs, fats, and alcohol—and any indulgent practices before Lent officially begins. Over the years, Carnival has extended beyond the boundaries of religion and country and become universally celebrated. America's most famous celebration takes place in New Orleans, Louisiana. The streets of New Orleans are transformed into a sea of costumed revelers; people and music literally pour out of every cobblestoned inch of the French Quarter (ground zero for Mardi Gras celebration). It's widely recognized that there is no better party than Mardi Gras, and people flock from all around the world to take part in the incredible festivities.

If you can't make the journey to New Orleans for Mardi Gras, plan your own celebration. All you need are some Louisiana Cajun–inspired recipes, dance music, and a healthy appetite. Cajun classics you're family will surely love include barbecued chicken, crawfish étouffée, gumbo, and dirty rice. For dessert, pick up a king cake at your supermarket's bakery section. The green, purple, and yellow icing make it the perfect dessert to top off a Mardi Gras menu.

- Tammy Weisberger
For more information, visit **Allrecipes.com**

Boudreaux's Zydeco Stomp Gumbo

Submitted by: **Lupe Boudreaux & Jason Parks**

"Dis is da toe-curlin' Texi-Cajun hybrid of a classic dish. It'll put a smile on everyone's face that's eatin' it. Throw on some Zydeco music and serve on a bed of rice with cornbread and a cold beer. Whew, doggie!"

1	tablespoon olive oil	1	sweet onion, sliced
1	cup coarsely chopped raw chicken	1	(10 ounce) can diced tomatoes with green chile peppers, undrained
½	pound pork sausage links, thinly sliced	2	tablespoons chopped fresh red chile peppers
1	cup olive oil	1	bunch fresh parsley, chopped
1	cup all-purpose flour	¼	cup Cajun seasoning
2	tablespoons minced garlic	1	pound shrimp, peeled and deveined
3	quarts chicken broth		
1	(12 ounce) can or bottle beer		
6	stalks celery, diced		
4	roma (plum) tomatoes, diced		

1. Heat oil in a medium skillet over medium-high heat; cook chicken in oil until chicken is no longer pink and juices run clear. Stir in sausage and cook until evenly browned. Drain and set aside.

2. In a large, heavy saucepan over medium heat, blend olive oil and flour to create a roux. Stir constantly until browned and bubbly. Mix in garlic and cook about 1 minute.

3. Gradually stir chicken broth and beer into roux mixture. Bring to a boil and mix in celery, tomatoes, sweet onion, diced tomatoes with green chile peppers, red chile peppers, parsley, and Cajun seasoning. Reduce heat, cover, and simmer about 40 minutes, stirring often.

4. Mix chicken, sausage, and shrimp into the broth mixture. Cook, stirring frequently, about 20 minutes. **Yield:** 10 servings.

Per serving: 454 calories, 23g protein, 19g carbohydrate, 31g fat, 2g fiber, 99mg cholesterol, 2095mg sodium

Turkey Pot Pie, page 18

Restaurant-Style Buffalo Chicken Wings, page 31

Caramel Brownies III, page 33

Chocolate Delight, page 17

Porketta Roast, page 22,
and Cashew-Raisin Rice
Pilaf, page 22

Strawberry Torte, page 23

Pork Chops Stuffed with Smoked Gouda
and Bacon, page 26, and Quick and Easy
Alfredo Sauce, page 27

Toffee Sauce, page 27

Chocolate Cupcakes, page 48

Tortilla Rollups IV and Pickle Rollups,
page 47

Munchie Party

Guaranteed kid-friendly, these portable treats are perfect for a summer party by the pool, a tailgate party, or any occasion that calls for pick-up party food. If the weather doesn't cooperate, take the munchies inside for a day of watching movies and playing games. For a birthday party, celebrate the guest of honor by making the punch his or her favorite color—just change the flavor of gelatin!

MENU

Green Punch
Guilt-Free Snack Mix
Tortilla Rollups IV
Pickle Rollups
Chocolate Cupcakes
Serves 20

MENU PREP PLAN

1. Up to a day ahead, prepare and bake cupcakes. Prepare punch, but don't add ginger ale. Store punch in refrigerator.

2. On the day of the party, assemble rollups. Store in refrigerator. Prepare snack mix.

3. Up to 20 minutes before party, add ginger ale to punch.

Green Punch

Submitted by: **Alena**
"This is a green-colored punch that tastes wonderful. Great for Saint Patrick's Day or whenever you feel like drinking something green!"

2 (3 ounce) packages lime-flavored gelatin	2 cups white sugar
1 quart hot water	4½ cups cold water
1 (46 ounce) can pineapple juice, chilled	2 liters ginger ale, chilled
2 (12 ounce) cans frozen orange juice concentrate, thawed	

1. In a large saucepan, dissolve gelatin in 1 quart hot water. Cool.
2. When gelatin is cool, pour into a large punch bowl. Stir in pineapple juice, orange juice concentrate, sugar, and 4½ cups cold water. Pour in ginger ale just before serving. **Yield:** 20 servings.

Per serving: 234 calories, 2g protein, 58g carbohydrate, 0g fat, 0g fiber, 0mg cholesterol, 40mg sodium

◄ **MAKE-AHEAD**

Prep Time: 5 minutes

Other: 30 minutes

Average Rating: ★★★★★

What other cooks have done:
"This can get a little thick towards the bottom of the punch bowl, so you may want to run the pineapple juice through a sieve to keep the pulp out. And definitely use pulp-free orange juice."

Guilt-Free Snack Mix

Submitted by: **Sara**

"Here's a simple party or trail mix that doesn't contain chocolate or tons of salt! This is great to munch on under any circumstances. Play with the ingredients until you get the combination you like best."

KID-FRIENDLY ▶

Prep Time: 10 minutes

Average Rating: ★★★★☆

What other cooks have done:

"I loved the taste and nutritional value of this mix. If you're making this for a party, don't make it too far ahead of time, or the cereal will get soggy."

4	cups crispy corn cereal squares	¼	cup yogurt-covered raisins
1	cup dried mixed fruit, coarsely chopped	⅓	cup chopped mixed nuts
		⅔	cup banana chips

1. In a medium bowl, mix together crispy corn cereal squares, dried mixed fruit, yogurt-covered raisins, mixed nuts, and banana chips. Store in sealed airtight containers. **Yield:** 25 servings.

Per serving: 74 calories, 1g protein, 13g carbohydrate, 3g fat, 1g fiber, 1mg cholesterol, 64mg sodium

Kid's Corner

When the kids are out of school, those lazy, hazy days of summer call for special summer foods. This menu is easily adapted to any summertime occasion—from a pool party to a summer sports league party. For example, stick candles in the cupcakes for a birthday party or add red and blue candies to the snack mix for a 4th of July party. Keep your littlest party guests in the forefront of the festivities with a selection of games and activities to keep them entertained.

A Mess Is Best

A good rule of thumb is "if it's messy, kids will love it," and one party game that's guaranteed to be a hit is a variation on the classic pie-eating contest: a cupcake-eating contest. This contest can be run one of two ways. The first is to allow a prescribed amount of time for all of the competitors to eat as many cupcakes as they can stomach. The second is a one-cupcake-per-person affair where each competitor is given one cupcake to eat, and the first person to finish their cupcake wins! To make the cupcake-eating contest even more challenging, tie the competitors' hands behind their backs for the entire contest. (Be sure to have lots of fresh napkins on hand!) To set up the contest, line the cupcakes up on a picnic table and sit one competitor in front of each. Do not allow anyone to begin eating until everyone is told to get ready, get set, and GO!

- Tammy Weisberger

For more information, visit **Allrecipes.com**

Tortilla Rollups IV *(pictured on page 44)*

Submitted by: **Doreen**

"These rollups are always a huge hit with the kids as well as the adults. A creamy, cheesy salsa mixture provides the filling. These are easy to make and can be prepared in advance."

1	(8 ounce) package cream cheese, softened	1	cup chunky salsa
1	(8 ounce) container sour cream	1½	cups shredded Cheddar cheese
1	(1 ounce) package dry fiesta-style Ranch salad dressing mix	10	(10 inch) flour tortillas

1. In a medium bowl, mix the cream cheese, sour cream, fiesta-style Ranch salad dressing mix, chunky salsa, and Cheddar cheese. Spread mixture evenly onto the tortillas. Roll up tortillas and chill until ready to serve.

2. To serve, slice the chilled tortillas into ¾ inch slices and arrange on a large serving platter. **Yield:** 25 servings.

Per serving: 178 calories, 5g protein, 18g carbohydrate, 9g fat, 1g fiber, 21mg cholesterol, 334mg sodium

◄ **MAKE-AHEAD**

Prep Time: 15 minutes

Average Rating: ★★★★☆

What other cooks have done:

"These were a big hit at my party. I added thinly shredded lettuce, minced onion, and chopped black olives. Layering these items worked as effectively as adding them to the mixture."

Pickle Rollups *(pictured on page 44)*

Submitted by: **Carol Datillo**

"Here's a quick finger food that everybody loves, and you can vary the meat according to your taste. My friends like salami or corned beef best."

1	(8 ounce) package cream cheese, softened	2	whole dill pickles, quartered lengthwise
16	ounces sliced pastrami		

1. Spread cream cheese evenly over meat slices to cover. Place a pickle piece on 1 end of each meat slice and roll up the meat. Repeat with remaining ingredients. Chill until ready to serve.

2. To serve, cut into ¾ inch pieces and arrange on a large serving platter. **Yield:** 20 servings.

Per serving: 162 calories, 6g protein, 2g carbohydrate, 15g fat, 0g fiber, 46mg cholesterol, 610mg sodium

◄ **PARTY FOOD**

Prep Time: 10 minutes

Average Rating: ★★★★☆

What other cooks have done:

"I have made these several times for school and family functions, and they have always been eaten up! I've used light cream cheese and a variety of meats—ham, honey ham, turkey, and chicken. I haven't used pastrami because my family does not like it. My kids just love these."

Chocolate Cupcakes *(pictured on page 43)*

Submitted by: **ladan miller**

"Chocolate cupcakes are the ultimate party food. Make some for your next gathering, and your guests will rave!"

QUICK & EASY ▶

Prep Time: 15 minutes

Cook Time: 17 minutes

Average Rating: ★★★★☆

What other cooks have done:

"I tried this recipe today, and I thought these were really rather tasty! I made an addition of my own (some raspberry-flavored semisweet chocolate chips), and the cupcakes were wonderful. These were easy to make, too, so I will definitely be making these again!"

1⅓	cups all-purpose flour	1½	cups white sugar
2	teaspoons baking powder	2	eggs
¼	teaspoon baking soda	¾	teaspoon vanilla extract
¾	cup unsweetened cocoa powder	1	cup milk
⅛	teaspoon salt	1	(16 ounce) can frosting (optional)
¼	cup butter		

1. Preheat oven to 350°F (175°C). Line muffin pans with paper liners.

2. Sift together the flour, baking powder, baking soda, cocoa, and salt. Set aside.

3. In a large bowl, cream together the butter and sugar until light and fluffy. Add the eggs, 1 at a time, beating well after each addition; stir in the vanilla. Add the flour mixture alternately with the milk; beat well. Fill the muffin cups half full.

4. Bake in the preheated oven for 15 to 17 minutes or until a tooth-pick inserted into center of a cupcake comes out clean. Frost with your favorite frosting when cool, if desired. **Yield:** 30 cupcakes.

Per cupcake (unfrosted): 84 calories, 2g protein, 16g carbohydrate, 2g fat, 1g fiber, 18mg cholesterol, 65mg sodium

Casserole Comfort

Treat your family to a meal so comforting, you'll want to wear your pajamas to dinner. A hearty version of macaroni and cheese pairs with a delicious twist on an often-overlooked veggie. Make the pudding ahead of time so that dessert will be a breeze.

MENU

Canadian Bacon Macaroni and Cheese
Roasted Brussels Sprouts
Best Rolls Ever!
Butterscotch Pudding I
Serves 3 to 4

MENU PREP PLAN

1. Up to a day ahead, prepare and bake rolls. Cook pudding; cool and store in refrigerator.

2. Prepare and roast Brussels sprouts.

3. While Brussels sprouts roast, prepare and cook macaroni and cheese.

Canadian Bacon Macaroni and Cheese

Submitted by: **Roxy**
"Macaroni and cheese mixed with tomatoes and Canadian bacon—cheesy, eh?!"

1 cup elbow macaroni	1 cup canned tomatoes, half-drained
6 slices Canadian-style bacon	
2 tablespoons butter	1 cup shredded Cheddar cheese
2½ tablespoons all-purpose flour	

1. Bring a large pot of lightly salted water to a boil. Add macaroni and cook for 8 to 10 minutes or until al dente; drain.
2. While macaroni is cooking, cook bacon in a medium skillet until crisp; drain on paper towels. Cut into bite-size pieces.
3. Melt butter in a large saucepan over medium-low heat. Stir in flour; stir in tomatoes and let sauce thicken, stirring occasionally. When sauce reaches desired thickness, stir in cheese until melted. Stir in cooked macaroni and bacon and heat through. Serve hot.
Yield: 3 to 4 servings.

Per serving: 439 calories, 23g protein, 34g carbohydrate, 23g fat, 2g fiber, 59mg cholesterol, 955mg sodium

◄ KID-FRIENDLY

Prep Time: 15 minutes

Cook Time: 30 minutes

Average Rating: ★★★★★

What other cooks have done:

"I added a few things to give this a bit more zip. I stirred some ground mustard into the butter/flour mixture. When I fried the bacon, I added some minced garlic and finely diced onion. Then I added salt to taste to the final mixture, which really brought all of the flavors together."

Roasted Brussels Sprouts

Submitted by: **JAQATAC**

"This recipe is from my mother. It may sound strange, but this dish is really good and very easy to make. The Brussels sprouts should be brown with a bit of black on the outside when done. They taste sweet and salty at the same time! Any leftovers can be reheated or just eaten cold from the fridge."

1½	pounds Brussels sprouts, ends trimmed and yellow leaves removed	1	teaspoon kosher salt
		½	teaspoon freshly ground black pepper
3	tablespoons olive oil		Kosher salt (optional)

1. Preheat oven to 400°F (200°C).
2. Place Brussels sprouts, olive oil, 1 teaspoon kosher salt, and pepper in a large zip-top plastic bag. Seal tightly; shake to coat. Pour into a shallow roasting pan or baking sheet with edges and place on center oven rack.
3. Roast in the preheated oven for 30 to 45 minutes, shaking pan every 5 to 7 minutes for even browning. Reduce heat if necessary to prevent burning. Brussels sprouts should be dark brown when done. Add additional kosher salt, if desired. Serve immediately.
Yield: 6 servings.

Per serving: 104 calories, 3g protein, 10g carbohydrate, 7g fat, 3g fiber, 0mg cholesterol, 338mg sodium

Best Rolls Ever!

Submitted by: **Cara A. Austin**

"This yeast-roll recipe uses self-rising flour for the most airy, delicious rolls ever! The secret to these light rolls is not punching down or heavily kneading the dough. Plus, the self-rising flour gives these rolls an added lift."

2	cups water	3	(0.25 ounce) packages active dry yeast
1	cup butter		
1	cup white sugar	1	teaspoon salt
2	eggs	7½	cups self-rising flour, divided
½	cup water		Butter, melted
1	teaspoon white sugar		

1. In a large microwave-safe bowl, combine 2 cups water and 1 cup butter. Microwave on High for about 2 minutes.
2. In a separate bowl, mix 1 cup sugar and eggs.
3. In a microwave-safe cup, microwave ½ cup water on High for 30 seconds. Add 1 teaspoon sugar; add yeast and stir to dissolve.
4. Add egg mixture to butter mixture; add salt. Add in yeast mixture. Stir in 7 cups flour, adding more flour if necessary. Mix well and cover; let rise in the refrigerator overnight.
5. Turn dough out onto a floured surface; do not punch down. Cover and let dough come to room temperature. Lightly knead in just

enough extra flour to make dough easy to handle.

6. Preheat oven to 400°F (200°C). Lightly grease baking sheets.

7. Shape into rolls and place on prepared baking sheets. Cover and let rest 30 minutes or until doubled in size.

8. Bake in the preheated oven for 25 minutes or until tops are golden. Remove from oven; brush immediately with melted butter. **Yield:** 2 dozen rolls.

Per roll: 248 calories, 5g protein, 38g carbohydrate, 9g fat, 1g fiber, 38mg cholesterol, 678mg sodium

Butterscotch Pudding I

Submitted by: **Mary Ann Armstrong**
"This recipe makes a good pudding or pie filling."

1	cup dark brown sugar	2	cups milk
³⁄₈	cup cornstarch	1	teaspoon vanilla extract
½	teaspoon salt	¼	cup butter
2	eggs, beaten		

1. In a 1 quart saucepan over medium-low heat, stir together sugar, cornstarch, and salt. Stir in eggs and milk and cook, stirring constantly, until mixture thickens enough to coat the back of a metal spoon. Stir in vanilla and butter. Let cool briefly and serve warm or chill in refrigerator until ready to serve. **Yield:** 4 servings.

Per serving: 456 calories, 7g protein, 71g carbohydrate, 16g fat, 0g fiber, 147mg cholesterol, 523mg sodium

◀ MAKE-AHEAD

Prep Time: 10 minutes

Cook Time: 20 minutes

Average Rating: ★★★★☆

What other cooks have done:

"I used ¾ cup loosely packed light brown sugar and decreased the butter to 2 tablespoons. To keep lumps to a minimum, stir with a slotted wooden spoon or whisk. I recommend removing the mixture from the heat before adding the vanilla and butter. This pudding is highly addictive, so beware!"

New Year's Dinner

Begin a tradition of kicking off the New Year sans stress with this good-luck make-ahead menu. Black-eyed peas, long believed in the South to bring luck when eaten on the first day of the year, are especially tasty in chowder, and the pick-up appetizers make this menu appropriate for a casual gathering. Add a leafy green salad to ensure financial success in the year to come!

MENU PREP PLAN

1. Up to a day ahead, prepare and cook chowder; cool and store in refrigerator. Prepare vinaigrette for salad and store in refrigerator.

2. Prepare cherry tomatoes; store in refrigerator. Cook eggs for salad; let cool.

3. Prepare Herbed Cheese Puffs.

4. Cook bacon for salad; assemble salad.

5. Heat individual bowls of chowder and sprinkle with bacon before serving.

MENU

Creamy Shrimp-Stuffed Cherry Tomatoes
Spinach Salad II
Black-Eyed Pea Chowder
Herbed Cheese Puffs
Serves 6

Creamy Shrimp-Stuffed Cherry Tomatoes

Submitted by: **DeltaQueen50**
"A make-ahead appetizer that looks very pretty on the plate."

MAKE-AHEAD ▶

Prep Time: 45 minutes

Average Rating: ★★★★☆

What other cooks have done:

"I made these for a wedding shower, and everyone loved them. I added bacon to the mixture. If you turn the tomatoes stem down and cut off the bottoms, scooping out the insides, they won't roll around on your plate."

2 pints cherry tomatoes	2 teaspoons prepared horseradish
½ pound cooked shrimp, peeled and deveined	1 teaspoon lemon juice
1 (8 ounce) package cream cheese, softened	Salt and ground black pepper to taste
¼ cup mayonnaise	¼ cup chopped fresh parsley
¼ cup grated Parmesan cheese	

1. Cut the top off each cherry tomato and scoop out the pulp. Place the tomatoes upside down on paper towels to drain.
2. In a food processor, mix the shrimp, cream cheese, mayonnaise, Parmesan cheese, horseradish, and lemon juice. Season with salt and pepper to taste. Blend until smooth.
3. Using a pastry bag, pipe the shrimp mixture into the cherry tomatoes. Garnish with parsley and refrigerate until ready to serve.
Yield: 16 servings.

Per serving: 103 calories, 5g protein, 2g carbohydrate, 8g fat, 1g fiber, 46mg cholesterol, 128mg sodium

Spinach Salad II

Submitted by: **Dee J**

"This delicious salad uses eggs, bacon, spinach, onion, and an oil and lemon juice dressing."

4	eggs	6	tablespoons vegetable oil
8	slices bacon	3	tablespoons lemon juice
1	(10 ounce) package fresh spinach	2	cloves garlic, minced
1	small onion, chopped		Salt and ground black pepper to taste

1. Place eggs in a saucepan and cover with cold water. Bring water to a boil; cover, remove from heat, and let stand for 10 to 12 minutes. Remove eggs; cool, peel, and chop.
2. Place bacon in a large, deep skillet. Cook over medium-high heat until evenly browned. Drain, crumble, and set aside.
3. In a large bowl, combine eggs, bacon, spinach, and onion.
4. In a small bowl, whisk together the oil, lemon juice, garlic, and salt and pepper to taste. Pour over salad and toss well to coat.
Yield: 6 servings.

Per serving: 397 calories, 9g protein, 4g carbohydrate, 39g fat, 2g fiber, 167mg cholesterol, 352mg sodium

◀ QUICK & EASY

Prep Time: 10 minutes

Stand Time: 12 minutes

Cook Time: 5 minutes

Average Rating: ★★★★★

What other cooks have done:

"Very nice recipe. I used soy bacon and decreased the oil a little bit. It was just amazing."

Black-Eyed Pea Chowder

Submitted by: **Brenda**

"This is great for a cold winter's night. This chowder works best when prepared the night before and reheated the next day."

1	pound diced bacon	1	(14.5 ounce) can beef consommé
1	cup chopped celery	1	(29 ounce) can diced tomatoes
1	cup chopped onion		
1	cup chopped green bell pepper		
1	(15.5 ounce) can black-eyed peas, undrained		

1. In a large saucepan over medium-high heat, sauté the bacon until crisp. Drain bacon and set aside, reserving about 4 tablespoons drippings in pan. Add the celery, onion, and green bell pepper to the pan and sauté for 10 minutes or until tender.
2. Add the peas, consommé, and tomatoes and allow to heat through, about 15 more minutes. Top servings with bacon. **Yield:** 6 servings.

Per serving: 564 calories, 19g protein, 21g carbohydrate, 44g fat, 5g fiber, 51mg cholesterol, 6593mg sodium

◀ FREEZER FRESH

Prep Time: 10 minutes

Cook Time: 35 minutes

Average Rating: ★★★★★

What other cooks have done:

"I added about 1 pound of peeled shrimp for added flavor, and it took this chowder over the top! I also doubled the recipe and froze some for later; it was even better the second time around."

Herbed Cheese Puffs

Submitted by: **Kaylee**

"Filled with a savory cheese and herb mixture, these puffy biscuits are simple and delicious, and they make a great party appetizer."

Prep Time: 10 minutes

Cook Time: 12 minutes

Average Rating: ★★★★★

What other cooks have done:

"These were excellent. I like the texture of phyllo pastry better than canned biscuits, so I put the filling in mini muffin tins that were lined with phyllo. I also substituted ½ cup cream cheese and ½ cup mayo for the whole cup of mayo."

1	(4 ounce) package grated Parmesan cheese	2	teaspoons minced fresh oregano
4	ounces Romano cheese, grated	1	bunch green onions, chopped
1	cup mayonnaise	1	clove garlic, minced
2	teaspoons minced fresh basil	1	(12 ounce) can refrigerated biscuit dough

1. Preheat oven to 375°F (190°C). Lightly grease a large baking sheet.
2. In a medium bowl, mix together Parmesan cheese, Romano cheese, mayonnaise, basil, oregano, green onions, and garlic.
3. Separate refrigerated dough into individual biscuits. Separate each biscuit vertically into 3 pieces. Spread 1 tablespoon cheese mixture on each piece. Arrange pieces in a single layer on prepared baking sheet.
4. Bake in the preheated oven for 10 to 12 minutes or until puffed and golden brown. Serve warm. **Yield:** 15 servings.

Per serving: 242 calories, 7g protein, 12g carbohydrate, 19g fat, 1g fiber, 22mg cholesterol, 552mg sodium

Home for the Holidays

*In a season made for sharing meals and memories,
offer your friends and family the classic dishes that
have graced holiday dinner tables for generations.
These are recipes that will be part of your
celebrations for years to come.*

Amazingly Good Eggnog

Submitted by: **NATALIESMOM**

"It's taken me several years to perfect this recipe. Now everyone asks, 'When are you making the eggnog?' This uses cooked eggs for safety, and you can use more or less rum to taste. It's a bit of work to make, but it's well worth it. You'll never buy store-bought eggnog again!"

MAKE-AHEAD ▶

Prep Time: 20 minutes

Cook Time: 10 minutes

Cool Time: 1 hour

Chill Time: overnight

Average Rating: ★★★★★

What other cooks have done:

"Wow, I never realized eggnog could actually taste good. Just like the author says, this is nothing like the store-bought stuff. I put in only 1 cup of rum, and it was plenty for me. I'd suggest starting with a little rum and letting the eggnog chill. You can always add more later. It takes a while for the rum flavor to blend in completely."

4	cups milk	1½	cups white sugar
5	whole cloves	2½	cups light rum
½	teaspoon vanilla extract	4	cups half-and-half
1	teaspoon ground cinnamon	2	teaspoons vanilla extract
12	egg yolks	½	teaspoon ground nutmeg

1. Combine milk, cloves, ½ teaspoon vanilla, and cinnamon in a large saucepan and slowly bring to a boil over low heat.

2. In a large bowl, combine egg yolks and sugar. Whisk together until fluffy. Whisk hot milk mixture slowly into the eggs. Pour mixture into saucepan. Cook over medium heat, stirring constantly, for 3 minutes or until thick (do not allow mixture to boil). Strain to remove cloves and let cool for about 1 hour.

3. Stir in rum, half-and-half, 2 teaspoons vanilla, and nutmeg. Refrigerate overnight before serving. **Yield:** 12 servings.

Per serving: 471 calories, 8g protein, 33g carbohydrate, 22g fat, 0g fiber, 272mg cholesterol, 82mg sodium

Grandmother's Punch

Submitted by: **Angie V.**

"My grandmother found this recipe, and she makes it every year at Christmas. It's a family favorite, and kids love it."

PARTY FOOD ▶

Prep Time: 10 minutes

Average Rating: ★★★★★

What other cooks have done:

"We made this for Thanksgiving. I didn't use the full amount of sugar; I used ½ cup white sugar and ½ cup artificial sweetener. Also, I used diet ginger ale to cut down on the sugar. It worked out very well."

2	(0.13 ounce) packages unsweetened strawberry-flavored drink mix	2	(6 ounce) cans frozen pineapple juice concentrate, thawed
2½	cups white sugar	1	liter ginger ale
4	quarts cold water	½	gallon orange sherbet
2	(6 ounce) cans frozen orange juice concentrate, thawed	3	oranges, sliced

1. In a large punch bowl, combine drink mix, sugar, and water. Stir until sugar is dissolved. Stir in orange juice concentrate and pineapple juice concentrate. Just before serving, stir in ginger ale and add sherbet and orange slices. **Yield:** 20 servings.

Per serving: 306 calories, 2g protein, 74g carbohydrate, 2g fat, 1g fiber, 5mg cholesterol, 67mg sodium

Bisschopswijn

Submitted by: **Else**

"Bisschopswijn, meaning 'bishop's wine,' is the Dutch version of the German Gluehwein, a hot drink for snowy holidays that makes you glow inside. Don't drink this if you have to drive tonight! Each household has its own variety; this is the one my Dutch neighbors used to make for Christmas and New Year's Eve when I was a child in Amsterdam."

1	(750 milliliter) bottle red wine	1	teaspoon ground cinnamon
½	cup white sugar	1	orange
		8	whole cloves

1. In a large saucepan over medium-low heat, combine wine, sugar, and cinnamon. Cut the orange in half. Push the cloves into the outside of the orange halves and place the halves in the wine.
2. Heat slowly over low heat for about 30 minutes or until steaming (do not let boil). Serve in warm glasses. **Yield:** 8 servings.

Per serving: 55 calories, 0g protein, 14g carbohydrate, 0g fat, 0g fiber, 0mg cholesterol, 7mg sodium

◄ AROUND-THE-WORLD CUISINE

Prep Time: 5 minutes

Cook Time: 30 minutes

Average Rating: ★★★★★

What other cooks have done:

"This recipe is a traditional drink for New Year's Eve. Use a stick of cinnamon instead of ground; it's easy to remove, and it smells and tastes better. Don't use cheap or young wine because it turns into vinegar easily."

Hot Spiced Cranberry Cider

Submitted by: **Michele O'Sullivan**

"Make some memories with the aromas of cinnamon, cloves, and lemon mingled with hot apple-cranberry cider. If desired, float a fresh lemon slice in each cup."

2	quarts apple cider (8 cups)	4	cinnamon sticks
6	cups cranberry juice	1½	teaspoons whole cloves
¼	cup packed brown sugar	1	lemon, thinly sliced

1. In a large pot, combine apple cider, cranberry juice, brown sugar, cinnamon sticks, cloves, and lemon slices. Bring to a boil, reduce heat, and simmer for 15 to 20 minutes. Remove cinnamon, cloves, and lemon slices with a slotted spoon. Serve hot. **Yield:** 14 servings.

Per serving: 157 calories, 1g protein, 39g carbohydrate, 0g fat, 0g fiber, 0mg cholesterol, 4mg sodium

◄ QUICK & EASY

Prep Time: 15 minutes

Cook Time: 25 minutes

Average Rating: ★★★★★

What other cooks have done:

"The initial flavor is sweet, but then this cider has a 'kick'—a zesty, tangy after-bite. It will really warm you up. The aroma is fabulous, too. I had trouble chasing the cloves out of the final mixture, so I poured it through a mesh strainer into a pitcher. Problem solved!"

Gingerbread Coffee

Submitted by: **Jennifer**
"This drink was inspired by a gingerbread latte I had at a local coffee shop."

COMPANY IS COMING ▶

Prep Time: 20 minutes

Chill Time: 10 minutes

Average Rating: ★★★★★

What other cooks have done:

"My husband and I made this to sip while we decorated our Christmas tree. We've decided to make it a tradition! The molasses mixture can be kept on hand for visitors over the holidays."

½	cup molasses	6	cups hot brewed coffee
¼	cup brown sugar	1	cup half-and-half
½	teaspoon baking soda	1½	cups sweetened whipped
1	teaspoon ground ginger		cream
¾	teaspoon ground cinnamon	1	teaspoon ground cloves

1. In a small bowl, mix together molasses, brown sugar, baking soda, ginger, and cinnamon until well blended. Cover and refrigerate for at least 10 minutes.

2. Add about ¼ cup coffee to each of 6 cups. Stir about a tablespoon of the spice mixture into each cup until dissolved. Fill each cup to within an inch of the top with coffee. Stir in half and half to taste and garnish with whipped cream and ground cloves. **Yield:** 6 servings.

Per serving: 194 calories, 2g protein, 30g carbohydrate, 8g fat, 0g fiber, 26mg cholesterol, 159mg sodium

Festive Holiday Beverages

The goose is roasting, the cookies are baked, and the table is set. But what's this? Feeling a bit parched? You deserve to quench that thirst with something appropriately festive and delicious. Champagne, wine, and juice are good standbys, but you can't have Christmas without classic flavors like creamy eggnog or mulled cider.

Hot, Hot, Hot!

Curl up in front of the fire and get cozy. Warm drinks will stick to your ribs. Plus, heating the spice-filled liquids that make up hot holiday beverages has an added benefit—the aroma produced will spread throughout your home. When preparing hot drinks for a party, it's a good idea to set up your coffeemaker. Fill the pitcher with your favorite hot holiday beverage and turn the heat on low. Guests can serve themselves, and your stove will be free for other uses.

Cold Classics

Punches come in all shapes and sizes for all of your celebratory needs. Frosty, fizzy, or foamy? It all depends on your tastes and your locale. Many punches use ice cream to keep them cold, but you can also freeze a portion of your favorite beverage recipe into cubes or other shapes. The flavored ice will help your punch maintain its chill without diluting it.

For more information, visit **Allrecipes.com**

Kosher Salt-Encrusted Prime Rib Roast

Submitted by: **Holly**

"Be sure to remove the coating before slicing this prime rib roast. You will be amazed at the juiciness and incredible flavor of the meat."

2	cups coarse kosher salt, divided	1	tablespoon ground black pepper
4	pounds prime rib roast	1	tablespoon seasoning salt

1. Preheat oven to 210°F (100°C).

2. Cover the bottom of a roasting pan with a layer of kosher salt. Place the roast, bone side down, on the salt layer. Season the meat with the ground black pepper and seasoning salt; cover meat completely with kosher salt.

3. Roast in the preheated oven for 4 to 5 hours or until a meat thermometer inserted into thickest part of roast registers 145°F (65°C). Remove from oven and let rest for 30 minutes. Remove all the salt from the roast before serving. **Yield:** 6 servings.

Per serving: 787 calories, 43g protein, 1g carbohydrate, 67g fat, 0g fiber, 162mg cholesterol, 1208mg sodium

◀ 5 INGREDIENTS OR LESS

Prep Time: 10 minutes

Cook Time: 5 hours

Stand Time: 30 minutes

Average Rating: ★★★★★

What other cooks have done:

"This was not salty at all. We stuck garlic cloves in the roast for a little extra flavoring. This smelled so wonderful while cooking. The pan drippings mixed with red wine made a nice dipping sauce. We served the roast with homemade sourdough bread, baked potatoes, salad, and red wine."

Roasted Rack of Lamb *(pictured on page 77)*

Submitted by: **Jennine**

"I have had this recipe for a long time, and I always enjoy making it. You can use beef or pork instead of lamb."

½ cup fresh breadcrumbs
2 tablespoons minced garlic
2 tablespoons chopped fresh rosemary
1 teaspoon salt
¼ teaspoon ground black pepper
2 tablespoons olive oil
1 (8 bone) rack of lamb, trimmed and frenched, cut in half

1 teaspoon salt
1 teaspoon ground black pepper
2 tablespoons olive oil
1 tablespoon prepared Dijon-style mustard
Fresh rosemary sprigs (optional)

1. Move oven rack to center position. Preheat oven to 450°F (230°C).
2. In a large bowl, combine breadcrumbs, garlic, rosemary, 1 teaspoon salt, and ¼ teaspoon pepper. Add 2 tablespoons olive oil to form a paste. Set aside.
3. Season the lamb all over with 1 teaspoon salt and 1 teaspoon pepper. Heat 2 tablespoons olive oil in a large, heavy ovenproof skillet over high heat. Sear lamb for 1 to 2 minutes on all sides. Let rest. Brush lamb with the mustard. Roll in breadcrumb mixture until evenly coated. Cover the ends of the bones with aluminum foil to prevent charring. Arrange the lamb, bone side down, in the skillet.
4. Roast lamb in the preheated oven for 17 minutes or until a meat thermometer inserted into thickest part of lamb registers desired temperature, 145°F (65°C) for medium rare. Let lamb rest at least 10 minutes, loosely covered, before carving between the ribs. Garnish with fresh rosemary, if desired. **Yield:** 4 servings.

Per serving: 757 calories, 37g protein, 6g carbohydrate, 64g fat, 0g fiber, 161mg cholesterol, 1446mg sodium

Rita's Sweet Holiday Baked Ham

Submitted by: **Lysa Hollly Rita**

"My mom's always made this ham recipe for the holidays and for my birthday. This is made with maraschino cherries, sliced pineapple, brown sugar, honey, and more yummy ingredients. You'll love this ham dinner. It's not just for the holidays—it's great any time of year!"

1   cup maple syrup
1   cup orange juice
1   cup ginger ale
½   cup packed brown sugar
½   cup honey
1   (10 ounce) jar maraschino cherries, halved, divided, and juice reserved

1   (12 pound) fully cooked bone-in ham
1   (15.25 ounce) can pineapple slices in juice, drained

1. Preheat oven to 350°F (175°C).
2. In a medium bowl, mix together the maple syrup, orange juice, ginger ale, brown sugar, and honey. Stir in the juice from the maraschino cherries and half of the cherries. Score the outer edge of the ham with a sharp knife in a diamond pattern (cuts should be about ¼ inch deep).
3. Place the ham into an oven bag and carefully pour the juice mixture over it, keeping all of the juice in the bag. Place the pineapple slices on top of the ham and secure with toothpicks. Place remaining cherries into the centers of the rings and secure with toothpicks. Tie the end of the bag closed with the ties provided, place in a large roasting pan, and cut a few small slits in the top of the oven bag.
4. Bake in the preheated oven for 2 hours or until a meat thermometer inserted into thickest part of ham registers 160°F (70°C). Remove ham from bag to a serving plate and let stand for 10 minutes before carving. **Yield:** 24 servings.

Per serving: 657 calories, 39g protein, 28g carbohydrate, 42g fat, 0g fiber, 164mg cholesterol, 112mg sodium

◄ CROWD-PLEASER

Prep Time: 20 minutes

Cook Time: 2 hours

Stand Time: 10 minutes

Average Rating: ★★★★★

What other cooks have done:
"My husband and I had Christmas dinner for our parents and family in our home for the first time this year. All 11 of our guests loved this ham. I caught my husband smuggling some into the fridge to save for his lunches. He had to hurry because everyone kept picking at it. This recipe will become our tradition for Christmas dinner."

Easter Breakfast Casserole

Submitted by: **Stephanie**
"Everyone looks forward to this every Easter because it's so delicious!"

COVERED-DISH FAVORITE ▶

Prep Time: 25 minutes

Cook Time: 1 hour 25 minutes

Average Rating: ★★★★★

What other cooks have done:

"I got rave reviews for this one! I added red bell pepper and mushrooms and used a combination of sausage and bacon. I like this recipe because it has a solid base, which allows you to add anything you like. It will always be great!"

1	pound bacon	¼	cup diced onion
8	eggs	¼	cup diced green bell pepper
2	cups milk	1	(16 ounce) package frozen
3	cups shredded Cheddar cheese		hash brown potatoes, thawed

1. Preheat oven to 350°F (175°C). Lightly grease a 7x11 inch baking dish.

2. Place bacon in a large, deep skillet. Cook over medium-high heat until evenly browned. Drain and crumble.

3. In a large bowl, beat together eggs and milk. Mix in bacon, cheese, onion, and bell pepper. Stir in hash browns. Pour mixture into prepared baking dish and cover with aluminum foil.

4. Bake in the preheated oven for 45 minutes. Uncover and bake for 30 more minutes or until eggs have set. **Yield:** 12 servings.

Per serving: 426 calories, 17g protein, 10g carbohydrate, 38g fat, 1g fiber, 200mg cholesterol, 526mg sodium

Clark's Quiche

Submitted by: **Clark Hamblen**

"This recipe makes two 9-inch pies. This is great because if you only make one you will hate yourself the next day when there are no leftovers. This quiche microwaves well the next day. In fact, most people say that the flavors have blended and are better on the second day. This is a great gift to give to a friend or relative. It freezes well when covered with aluminum foil."

½ pound thick sliced bacon
1 (10 ounce) package frozen chopped spinach, thawed
2 tablespoons olive oil
1 onion, finely diced
½ pound fresh mushrooms, finely diced
2 cups finely diced smoked ham
1 (8 ounce) container sour cream
   Salt and ground black pepper to taste
2 (9 inch) unbaked pie crusts

8 ounces Monterey Jack cheese, shredded
8 ounces Cheddar cheese, shredded
4 ounces Parmesan cheese, grated
8 eggs
1½ cups half-and-half
1 tablespoon dried parsley
   Salt and ground black pepper to taste

◀ FREEZER FRESH

Prep Time: 15 minutes

Cook Time: 1 hour 10 minutes

Stand Time: 10 minutes

Average Rating: ★★★★★

What other cooks have done:

"The best quiche yet! I lined the bottom of a 9x13 inch glass baking dish with crescent roll dough because I couldn't find pie crusts deep enough to hold the recipe. This is a wonderful way to make this quiche for a party because it's easy to cut into little squares."

1. Preheat oven to 375°F (190°C).

2. Place bacon in a large, deep skillet. Cook over medium-high heat until evenly browned. Drain, crumble, and set aside. Cook spinach according to package instructions. Allow to cool and squeeze dry.

3. Heat olive oil in skillet over medium heat. Sauté onion in oil until soft and translucent. Stir in mushrooms and cook for 2 minutes or until soft. Stir in ham and cooked bacon. Remove from heat.

4. In a large bowl, combine spinach, sour cream, and salt and pepper to taste. Divide and spread evenly in pie crusts. Layer with bacon mixture. Mix together Monterey Jack, Cheddar, and Parmesan cheeses and sprinkle over pies. Whisk together eggs, half-and-half, and parsley. Season egg mixture with salt and pepper to taste and pour over pies. Place pies on a baking sheet.

5. Bake on middle rack in the preheated oven for 40 minutes or until tops are puffed and golden brown. Remove from oven and let stand for 5 to 10 minutes. **Yield:** 16 servings.

Per serving: 449 calories, 21g protein, 15g carbohydrate, 34g fat, 2g fiber, 168mg cholesterol, 1066mg sodium

Turkey Brine

Submitted by: **SHERI GAILEY**
"This is a tasty brine for any poultry. It will make your bird very juicy, and your gravy will be to die for! This is enough brine for a 10 to 18 pound turkey."

MAKE-AHEAD ▶

Prep Time: 5 minutes

Cook Time: 15 minutes

Average Rating: ★★★★★

What other cooks have done:

"This made the best turkey I've ever eaten! The flavor was fantastic; the meat was very moist and tender. There was enough brine so that I could soak the turkey in a huge pot in the refrigerator overnight. My mom was impressed!"

1	gallon vegetable broth		1	tablespoon dried sage
1	cup sea salt		1	tablespoon dried thyme
1	tablespoon crushed dried		1	tablespoon dried savory
	rosemary		1	gallon ice water

1. In a large pot, combine vegetable broth, sea salt, rosemary, sage, thyme, and savory. Bring to a boil, stirring frequently, until salt is dissolved. Remove from heat and let cool to room temperature.
2. When the broth mixture is cool, pour it into a clean 5 gallon bucket. Stir in the ice water. **Yield:** 2 gallons.

Nutrient Analysis Note: Nutrient analysis is not available for this recipe; the amount of brine absorbed will vary depending on the size of your poultry and the amount of time it is immersed in the brine.

Note: To marinate and roast a turkey using this recipe, wash and dry the turkey. Remove turkey innards. Place the turkey, breast down, into the brine, making sure the brine fills the turkey's cavity and covers the turkey. Refrigerate overnight. Remove the turkey carefully, draining off the excess brine; pat dry. Discard excess brine. Cook the turkey as desired, reserving the drippings for gravy. Keep in mind that brined turkeys cook 20 to 30 minutes faster, so watch the temperature gauge.

Brining a Turkey

When you hear the word "brine," you probably think of the salty liquid that gives pickles or other vegetables their tangy flavor. However, soaking poultry or meat in a brine prior to cooking is an old-fashioned technique to enhance flavor and juiciness that's becoming popular again. If you use a cooler to brine your bird, your refrigerator will be freed up for all of your other holiday foods.

Roasting a Better Bird

If you already have a favorite turkey recipe, consider adding a step to brine your bird. When you taste the juicy results, you'll know it was worth the extra step! If you don't have a favorite recipe, try the brine by itself. The process imparts plenty of flavor on its own. Need more convincing?

Take a look at these benefits of brining:
• The salty soak provides a tenderness cushion for the breast meat, so even if it overcooks by 10 degrees or so, it remains moist.
• The meat of a brined bird tastes pleasantly seasoned, which eliminates the need to season the bird before and after roasting.
• Because the turkey sits overnight in a tub of salted water, brining also ensures that all parts of the turkey are at the same temperature.
• The turkey meat absorbs water during the brining process. Water is a heat conductor and therefore expedites cooking. A brined bird cooks faster by about 20 to 30 minutes.
For more information, visit **Allrecipes.com**

Easy Herb-Roasted Turkey

Submitted by: **Lisa Hamm**

"This is an easy and delicious recipe for a turkey that is perfectly browned on the outside and tender and juicy on the inside!"

1	(12 pound) whole turkey	1	teaspoon salt
¾	cup olive oil	½	teaspoon ground black pepper
2	tablespoons garlic powder		
2	teaspoons dried basil	2	cups water
1	teaspoon ground sage		

1. Preheat oven to 325°F (165°C). Clean turkey, discarding giblets and organs, and place in a roasting pan with a lid.

2. In a small bowl, combine olive oil, garlic powder, dried basil, ground sage, salt, and pepper. Using a basting brush, apply the mixture to the outside of the uncooked turkey. Pour water into the bottom of the roasting pan and cover it with the lid.

3. Bake in the preheated oven for 3 to 3½ hours or until a meat thermometer inserted into thickest part of a thigh registers 180°F (82°C). Remove from oven and allow to stand for about 30 minutes before carving. **Yield:** 16 servings.

Per serving: 597 calories, 68g protein, 1g carbohydrate, 34g fat, 0g fiber, 198mg cholesterol, 311mg sodium

◄ CROWD-PLEASER

Prep Time: 15 minutes

Cook Time: 3 hours 30 minutes

Stand Time: 30 minutes

Average Rating: ★★★★★

What other cooks have done:

"This Thanksgiving, I will be making this turkey for the third time. Last year, the turkey was so good that I was asked to make it for Christmas. A month before Thanksgiving this year, I was receiving phone calls from folks who wanted to make sure that I would prepare the same turkey again!"

Four Seasons Enchiladas

Submitted by: **Janice Elder**

"Nice and spicy! Even the children will enjoy leftover turkey in this recipe. It's quick, too! Great topped with black olives, green onions, and tomatoes. Leftover ham would also be excellent in this dish."

Prep Time: 15 minutes

Cook Time: 21 minutes

Average Rating: ★★★★★

What other cooks have done:

"I used leftover pork roast and black beans in this recipe; it was absolutely delicious."

1 (4 ounce) can chopped green chile peppers, drained	8 (8 inch) flour tortillas
4 ounces cream cheese, softened	1 (16 ounce) jar salsa
½ teaspoon ground cumin	1 (16 ounce) can chili beans, undrained
2 cups chopped cooked turkey	1 cup shredded Monterey Jack cheese

1. Preheat oven to 350°F (175°C). Lightly grease a 9x13 inch baking dish.

2. In a medium bowl, mix chile peppers, cream cheese, and cumin. Stir in chopped turkey.

3. Microwave the tortillas on High for 1 minute or until the tortillas are softened. Spread about 2 heaping tablespoons of the chile pepper mixture on each tortilla and roll up. Place the rolled tortillas, seam side down, in a single layer in the prepared baking dish.

4. In a medium bowl, combine the salsa and beans. Spoon the mixture over the enchiladas. Sprinkle with cheese.

5. Bake in the preheated oven for 20 minutes or until bubbly and lightly browned. **Yield:** 8 servings.

Per serving: 388 calories, 23g protein, 42g carbohydrate, 15g fat, 5g fiber, 55mg cholesterol, 1036mg sodium

Vegetable and Feta Latkes

Submitted by: **Edna**

"There are great for a change of latke pace! Terrific for Hanukkah parties when you want to give your friends a little extra flavor."

2½	cups grated zucchini		Salt and ground black
1	cup peeled, shredded potatoes			pepper to taste
1	cup shredded carrots	¾	cup matzo meal or flour
½	teaspoon salt	½	cup chopped fresh parsley
3	eggs, lightly beaten	½	cup crumbled feta cheese
		¼	cup vegetable oil

1. Place the zucchini, potatoes, and carrots in a colander; cover with paper towels or cheesecloth and squeeze out as much moisture as possible. Sprinkle ½ teaspoon salt over the vegetables and let them drain for 15 minutes. Squeeze vegetables again in paper towels.
2. In a large mixing bowl, combine vegetables, eggs, and salt and pepper to taste. Mix well. Stir in matzo meal or flour, parsley, and feta. Form mixture into pancakes.
3. Heat vegetable oil in a large frying pan. Place cakes in hot oil and fry until golden brown on both sides, 2 to 3 minutes per side. Add more oil as needed. Drain fried latkes on paper towels.
Yield: 6 servings.

Per serving: 226 calories, 8g protein, 17g carbohydrate, 15g fat, 2g fiber, 117mg cholesterol, 377mg sodium

◄ OUT-OF-THE-ORDINARY

Prep Time: 20 minutes

Stand Time: 15 minutes

Cook Time: 6 minutes per batch

Average Rating: ★★★★★

What other cooks have done:

"These are as good as they sound, and they're well worth the time. I added an extra ¼ cup of matzo meal to make up for using very large eggs, and I added about ⅓ cup shredded onion. Perfect. I served them with a dollop of sour cream."

Crunchy Green Bean Casserole

Submitted by: **Becky Twitchell**

"This is my own variation of the old tried-and-true string bean casserole. My family has loved this for years, and now my daughter makes it for her family."

FROM THE PANTRY ▶

Prep Time: 10 minutes

Cook Time: 45 minutes

Average Rating: ★★★★★

What other cooks have done:

"My husband is not a fan of any casserole, but he loved this. I used frozen cut green beans. This recipe is a good twist on the original when you want something different—but still traditional—for a holiday meal."

4	slices bacon	¾	cup milk
1	(10.75 ounce) can condensed cream of mushroom soup	2	(15 ounce) cans green beans, drained
1	(8 ounce) can water chestnuts, drained and chopped		Ground black pepper to taste
		1⅓	cups French-fried onions

1. Preheat oven to 350°F (175°C).

2. Place bacon in a large, deep skillet. Cook over medium-high heat until evenly browned. Drain, crumble, and set aside.

3. In a 1½ quart casserole dish, mix together the bacon, soup, water chestnuts, milk, green beans, and pepper to taste.

4. Bake in the preheated oven for 30 minutes or until heated through.

5. Stir and top with French-fried onions. Bake for 5 more minutes or until onions are golden brown. **Yield:** 6 servings.

Per serving: 533 calories, 5g protein, 36g carbohydrate, 40g fat, 3g fiber, 15mg cholesterol, 1330mg sodium

Cheesy Potato Kugel

Submitted by: **Mindy**

"Potato kugel is a delicious traditional Jewish dish. It is served at any meal. I can't imagine a Jewish celebration without a kugel!"

COVERED-DISH FAVORITE ▶

Prep Time: 30 minutes

Cook Time: 1 hour 10 minutes

Average Rating: ★★★★★

What other cooks have done:

"It took me only 10 minutes to prepare this. I did everything in the food processor—shredding the cheese and potatoes and chopping the onion. Also, I had to cover it with foil during the last 20 minutes to prevent excessive browning. I also added a teaspoon of ground mustard for extra flavor."

3	pounds peeled, shredded potatoes	5	tablespoons olive oil
4	eggs	1	onion, chopped
	Salt and ground black pepper to taste	2½	cups shredded Cheddar cheese

1. Preheat oven to 350°F (175°C). Grease a 9x5 inch loaf pan.

2. Place potatoes in a colander and squeeze out moisture.

3. In a large bowl, combine eggs, salt and pepper to taste, oil, and onion. Add potatoes and cheese and mix well. Pour mixture into prepared loaf pan.

4. Bake in the preheated oven for 1 hour. Increase heat to 450°F (230°C) and bake for 5 to 10 more minutes or until browned. Serve hot. **Yield:** 12 servings.

Per serving: 262 calories, 10g protein, 22g carbohydrate, 15g fat, 3g fiber, 96mg cholesterol, 175mg sodium

Scrumptious Sweet Potato Casserole

Submitted by: **Cindy**

"This recipe is a family favorite for holiday dinners. It's requested even by those who don't eat sweet potatoes!"

3 cups cooked, mashed sweet potatoes	2 eggs, lightly beaten
⅔ cup white sugar	1 cup packed light brown sugar
¼ cup butter, softened	1 cup chopped pecans
1 teaspoon vanilla extract	½ cup all-purpose flour
½ cup milk	¼ cup butter, softened

1. Preheat oven to 350°F (175°C). Lightly grease a 9x9 inch baking dish.

2. In a large bowl, stir together sweet potatoes, white sugar, ¼ cup butter, vanilla, milk, and eggs. Mix well. Pour mixture into prepared baking dish.

3. In a medium bowl, combine brown sugar, chopped pecans, flour, and ¼ cup butter. Mix well. Sprinkle over sweet potato mixture.

4. Bake in the preheated oven for 25 to 30 minutes. **Yield:** 9 servings.

Per serving: 465 calories, 5g protein, 63g carbohydrate, 23g fat, 4g fiber, 81mg cholesterol, 159mg sodium

◄ CROWD-PLEASER

Prep Time: 10 minutes

Cook Time: 30 minutes

Average Rating: ★★★★★

What other cooks have done:

"I made this for Thanksgiving dinner. It received very high praise. I used two 40 ounce cans of sweet potatoes, drained well. That cut the prep time in half."

Rice Stuffing with Apples, Herbs, and Bacon *(pictured on page 78)*

Submitted by: **redheadedmystery**
"This is by far the best stuffing recipe I have ever had. I have made it for the last three Thanksgivings, and everyone has raved about it. It is unique, and the flavors are so delicious! Serve this for Thanksgiving, and your guests will be asking for the recipe."

COMPANY IS COMING ▶

Prep Time: 25 minutes

Cook Time: 1 hour 12 minutes

Average Rating: ★★★★★

What other cooks have done:

"This recipe immediately became a family favorite and has been used for the past three years at Thanksgiving. In fact, I had to give the recipe to a friend."

3½	cups water, divided	1	cup uncooked long-grain white rice
1	(6 ounce) package uncooked wild rice	1¾	cups currants
⅓	pound bacon (8 slices)	¾	cup dried cherries
3	cups diced onion	¾	cup dried cranberries
3	cups diced celery	½	cup dried apricots, chopped
¼	cup fines herbes	1	cup diced, unpeeled apples
1	(14 ounce) can low-fat, low-sodium chicken broth	½	cup chopped parsley

1. In a medium saucepan over medium heat, bring 1½ cups water to a boil. Stir in wild rice. Cover, reduce heat, and simmer for 40 minutes.
2. Meanwhile, place bacon in a large, deep skillet. Cook over medium heat until evenly browned. Drain bacon, reserving drippings; crumble and set aside.
3. In the reserved bacon drippings, sauté onions and celery. Cook until very soft, about 12 minutes. Stir in herbes.
4. Stir remaining water, broth, white rice, currants, cherries, cranberries, apricots, and apples into the wild rice. Continue cooking for 20 minutes or until wild rice and white rice are tender.
5. In a large bowl, mix the bacon and the onion mixture into the rice mixture. Season with the parsley. **Yield:** 12 servings.

Per serving: 326 calories, 7g protein, 58g carbohydrate, 8g fat, 7g fiber, 8mg cholesterol, 185mg sodium

Apple-Raisin French Toast Strata

Submitted by: **Terrie**

"A simple but elegant way to make a fast breakfast. Put this together the night before and bake while you're getting ready in the morning. Serve with lots of extra maple syrup! You may also add extra raisins."

1 (1 pound) loaf cinnamon-
   raisin bread, cubed
1 (8 ounce) package cream
   cheese, diced
1 cup peeled, diced apples

8 eggs
2½ cups half-and-half
6 tablespoons butter, melted
¼ cup maple syrup

1. Lightly grease a 9x13 inch baking dish. Arrange half of cubed bread in the bottom of the dish. Sprinkle cream cheese evenly over the bread and top with apples. Top with remaining bread.
2. In a large bowl, beat the eggs with half-and-half, butter, and maple syrup. Pour over the bread mixture. Cover with plastic wrap, pressing down so that all bread pieces are soaked. Refrigerate at least 2 hours.
3. Preheat oven to 325°F (165°C).
4. Bake in the preheated oven for 45 minutes. Let stand for 10 minutes before serving. **Yield:** 12 servings.

Per serving: 357 calories, 10g protein, 29g carbohydrate, 23g fat, 2g fiber, 196mg cholesterol, 323mg sodium

◄ MAKE-AHEAD
Prep Time: 20 minutes
Chill Time: 2 hours
Cook Time: 45 minutes
Stand Time: 10 minutes
Average Rating: ★★★★★
What other cooks have done:
"Instead of using a fresh apple, I had a bag of roasted apples in the freezer, and I took some apples out of there. I chopped them up before adding; because the apples were already spiced, I think that added a lot of flavor."

The Brunch Crunch

You've gotten through all of your holiday preparations with flying colors and have even managed to keep your family well fed and happy. Now you've reached the zero hour: Your house is full of relatives, and the big holidays are upon you! Then you realize with alarm that it's not enough to clean the house for your guests, give them a place to sleep, and prepare an elaborate holiday dinner—you have to feed them breakfast, too! Thankfully, there are plenty of wonderful, festive breakfasts you can throw together in a jiffy when the time comes or whip up ahead of time and freeze. Add coffee, juice, and some fresh fruit, and everyone, the chef included, will be scrumptiously nourished and ready to celebrate a joyful holiday!

Taking a Shortcut

Breakfast pastries that use cake mix or refrigerator biscuits cut down on prep time, so you can have home-baked treats in no time at all. Coffee cakes, bun cakes, and pull-apart cakes are all easily assembled using these cheats. Classics that you make from scratch, such as scones, biscuits, and muffins, can usually be made ahead and then frozen. When the holidays start creeping up, just make a batch or two of your family's favorites to store in the freezer. Then on busy mornings, you can thaw the treats at room temperature. Dry breakfast mixes like granola can be made in bulk and stored in the pantry. For more information, visit **Allrecipes.com**

Gingerbread Waffles with Hot Chocolate Sauce

Submitted by: **Michele O'Sullivan**

"Yummy and delicious. These extraordinary waffles are flavored with molasses and spices. Topped with homemade chocolate sauce, they are perfect for a special breakfast treat."

KID-FRIENDLY ▶

Prep Time: 25 minutes

Cook Time: 10 minutes per waffle

Average Rating: ★★★★★

What other cooks have done:

"To serve with these waffles, I make a nutmeg sauce with ½ cup white sugar, 1½ tablespoons all-purpose flour, salt, ¼ teaspoon nutmeg, 1 cup boiling water, 1½ tablespoons butter, and 1 teaspoon vanilla. Combine all dry ingredients in a saucepan. Add boiling water, stirring constantly. Cook over low heat until thick and smooth. Remove from heat; add butter and vanilla."

1 cup light molasses
½ cup butter
1½ teaspoons baking soda
½ cup milk
1 egg, lightly beaten
2 cups all-purpose flour
1½ teaspoons ground ginger
½ teaspoon ground cinnamon
½ teaspoon salt
2 cups boiling water
1 cup white sugar
2 tablespoons cornstarch
½ cup unsweetened cocoa powder
1 teaspoon salt
2 teaspoons vanilla extract
2 tablespoons butter

1. In a small saucepan, heat molasses and ½ cup butter until almost boiling. Remove from heat and let cool slightly. Stir in baking soda, milk, and egg.

2. Preheat a waffle iron.

3. In a large bowl, sift together flour, ginger, cinnamon, and salt. Make a well in the center and pour in the molasses mixture. Mix until smooth.

4. Spray preheated waffle iron with cooking spray. Pour batter onto hot waffle iron. Cook until golden brown.

5. In a saucepan, combine water, 1 cup sugar, cornstarch, cocoa powder, and 1 teaspoon salt. Cook over medium heat, stirring constantly, until mixture comes to a boil. Remove from heat and add vanilla and 2 tablespoons butter; stir until smooth. Serve with hot waffles.

Yield: 6 servings.

Per serving: 651 calories, 8g protein, 111g carbohydrate, 22g fat, 4g fiber, 89mg cholesterol, 1130mg sodium

Sweet Potato Pound Cake

Submitted by: **Anne McCullough**

"This light, fine-textured cake is excellent for the holiday season."

3   cups all-purpose flour
2   teaspoons baking powder
1   teaspoon ground cinnamon
½   teaspoon baking soda
½   teaspoon ground nutmeg
¼   teaspoon salt
1   cup butter, softened
2   cups white sugar
2   cups mashed, cooked
    sweet potatoes

1   teaspoon vanilla extract
4   eggs
1   cup sifted confectioners'
    sugar
3   to 5 teaspoons orange juice
2   tablespoons grated orange
    zest (optional)

1. Preheat oven to 350°F (175°C). Grease and flour a 10 inch tube pan.

2. Sift together flour, baking powder, cinnamon, baking soda, nutmeg, and salt. Set aside.

3. In a large mixing bowl, cream together butter and white sugar until light and fluffy. Add mashed sweet potatoes and vanilla. Beat until well blended. Add eggs, 1 at a time (the batter will look curdled). Add flour mixture to potato mixture. Beat on low speed until combined. Pour batter into prepared tube pan.

4. Bake in the preheated oven for about 1 hour and 20 minutes or until a toothpick inserted into center of cake comes out clean. Cool cake for 20 minutes in the pan and then invert onto a serving plate.

5. Meanwhile, in a small bowl, combine confectioners' sugar with 3 to 5 teaspoons orange juice to achieve drizzling consistency. Spoon over warm cake and sprinkle with orange zest, if desired.

Yield: 14 servings.

Per serving: 414 calories, 5g protein, 66g carbohydrate, 15g fat, 2g fiber, 96mg cholesterol, 312mg sodium

◀ COMPANY IS COMING

Prep Time: 20 minutes

Cook Time: 1 hour 20 minutes

Cool Time: 20 minutes

Average Rating: ★★★★★

What other cooks have done:

"Loved it! This cake came out very moist and tasted just like sweet potato pie. I mixed a little brown sugar, cinnamon, and nutmeg into the mashed sweet potatoes, and I used cake flour."

Bread Pudding with Whiskey Sauce III

Submitted by: **Emily**
"This bread pudding is absolutely delicious!"

CROWD-PLEASER ▶

Prep Time: 15 minutes

Cook Time: 45 minutes

Average Rating: ★★★★★

What other cooks have done:

"This recipe is absolutely the best; everyone raved about it. I cut the whiskey amount in half and served the pudding warm with vanilla ice cream on the side."

6	eggs, lightly beaten	1	(1 pound) loaf bread, cut into 1 inch cubes
1½	cups white sugar		
4	cups milk	½	cup golden raisins
1	cup whipping cream	1½	cups white sugar
1	tablespoon vanilla extract	¾	cup butter
½	tablespoon ground cinnamon	¾	cup corn syrup
		½	cup whiskey

1. Preheat oven to 300°F (150°C). Lightly grease a medium baking dish.

2. In a medium bowl, whip together eggs and 1½ cups sugar. Mix in milk, whipping cream, vanilla extract, and cinnamon. Whip until smooth.

3. Arrange bread cubes in prepared dish and top with golden raisins. Cover with the whipped mixture. Allow the bread to become saturated with the mixture.

4. Bake in the preheated oven for 45 minutes or until lightly browned.

5. Meanwhile, mix 1½ cups sugar, butter, and corn syrup in a medium saucepan over low heat. Remove from heat when thoroughly blended and whisk in the whiskey. Serve warm over bread pudding.

Yield: 12 servings.

Per serving: 643 calories, 10g protein, 94g carbohydrate, 24g fat, 1g fiber, 171mg cholesterol, 426mg sodium

Christmas Cornflake Wreath Cookies

Submitted by: **Sharon P.**

"These cookies look like little Christmas wreaths and are great fun for the kids. People always look at these suspiciously, but once they try them, they can't get enough. This recipe is easily halved."

4	cups miniature marshmallows	½	teaspoon almond extract
½	cup butter	½	teaspoon vanilla extract
1	teaspoon green food coloring	4	cups cornflakes cereal
		1	(2.25 ounce) package red cinnamon candies

1. Microwave marshmallows and butter on High for 2 minutes. Stir and microwave for 2 more minutes. Stir until smooth. (This can be done in a double boiler instead of a microwave, if desired.)
2. Add food coloring, almond extract, vanilla, and cornflakes and mix quickly. Drop by spoonfuls onto greased wax paper and decorate with 3 red cinnamon candies each.
3. Let cool and transfer with lightly greased fingers to a lightly greased serving tray. **Yield:** 3 dozen cookies.

Per cookie: 117 calories, 1g protein, 15g carbohydrate, 6g fat, 0g fiber, 17mg cholesterol, 177mg sodium

◀ **KID-FRIENDLY**

Prep Time: 20 minutes

Cook Time: 4 minutes

Average Rating: ★★★★★

What other cooks have done:

"I buttered a big bowl, added the cornflakes, and then poured the warm mixture over the flakes, stirring with a buttered spoon. You have to work fast once you pour the marshmallow mixture over the cornflakes because the mixture becomes sticky as it cools. I refrigerated the cookies for a faster setting. These are really fun holiday treats; they get raves in my house."

Butter Snow Flakes

Submitted by: **Linda**

"These wonderful spritz cookies made with cinnamon freeze very well."

2¼	cups all-purpose flour	1	cup white sugar
¼	teaspoon salt	1	egg yolk
¼	teaspoon ground cinnamon	1	teaspoon vanilla extract
1	cup butter, softened	1	teaspoon orange zest
1	(3 ounce) package cream cheese, softened		

1. Preheat oven to 350°F (175°C).
2. Sift together the flour, salt, and cinnamon; set aside.
3. In a medium bowl, cream together butter and cream cheese. Add sugar and egg yolk; beat until light and fluffy. Stir in the vanilla and orange zest. Gradually blend in the dry ingredients. Fill a cookie press or pastry bag with dough and form cookies on ungreased baking sheets.
4. Bake in the preheated oven for 12 to 15 minutes or until the cookies are golden brown on the peaks and on the bottoms. Remove immediately to wire racks to cool. **Yield:** 6 dozen cookies.

Per cookie: 52 calories, 1g protein, 6g carbohydrate, 3g fat, 0g fiber, 11mg cholesterol, 30mg sodium

◀ **HOLIDAY GIFT GIVING**

Prep Time: 15 minutes

Cook Time: 15 minutes per batch

Average Rating: ★★★★★

What other cooks have done:

"I broke my cookie press and had to improvise and came out with the best cookies ever! I rolled the dough into balls and rolled those in coconut. I made a thumbprint in the middle of each and filled it with strawberry jam."

Easter Eggs

Submitted by: **Joan Zaffary**

"If you want to wow your family with extra special Easter eggs, this is the recipe for you! These are peanut butter and coconut cream eggs dipped in chocolate. They are delicious and beautiful!"

HOLIDAY GIFT GIVING ▶

Prep Time: 30 minutes

Freeze Time: 3 hours

Cook Time: 2 minutes

Average Rating: ★★★★★

What other cooks have done:

"After taking these to a church luncheon, I was inundated with compliments! I doubled the butter, which made the filling much smoother. I made vanilla, chocolate, and butter-pecan fillings. (For butter-pecan filling, I used butter pecan flavoring and about ½ cup well-chopped pecans for a third of the filling mixture.) All of the flavors were a big success!"

2	pounds confectioners' sugar	12	ounces peanut butter
¼	pound butter, softened	1	pound flaked coconut
1	(8 ounce) package cream cheese, softened	4	cups semisweet chocolate chips
2	teaspoons vanilla extract	2	tablespoons shortening

1. In a mixing bowl, combine sugar, butter, cream cheese, and vanilla. Divide the batter in half and place each half in separate bowls. Stir peanut butter into one of the bowls and coconut into the other.
2. Using your hands, mold the dough into egg shapes and arrange on baking sheets. Place the eggs in the freezer until frozen.
3. Microwave the chocolate and shortening together on High until melted, stirring every 30 seconds. Dip the eggs into the chocolate until coated. Place the eggs on baking sheets lined with wax paper and return to the freezer to harden. After the chocolate has hardened, store the eggs in the refrigerator. **Yield:** 5 dozen eggs.

Per egg: 226 calories, 3g protein, 25g carbohydrate, 14g fat, 2g fiber, 4mg cholesterol, 59mg sodium

Melt-In-Your-Mouth Toffee

Submitted by: **Ruth Denton**

"This is the easiest, best toffee I have ever made. Everyone who tries it wants the recipe."

5 INGREDIENTS OR LESS ▶

Prep Time: 10 minutes

Cook Time: 20 minutes

Average Rating: ★★★★☆

What other cooks have done:

"This recipe is wonderful! Don't be afraid to cook the sugar mixture over lower heat than the recipe calls for. I've had it burn using a family member's range, which ran hotter than my own. A way to tell if it's burning in the beginning is to watch it for a few minutes once you've stopped stirring it. If very dark bubbles start to pop up in the center, the heat's too high. The center bubbles should have more of a light amber color than a darker brown color."

1	pound butter	1	cup chopped walnuts
1	cup white sugar	2	cups semisweet chocolate chips
1	cup packed brown sugar		

1. In a heavy saucepan, combine butter, white sugar, and brown sugar. Cook over medium heat, stirring constantly, until mixture boils. Boil to hard crack stage, 300°F (150°C), without stirring. Remove from heat.
2. Pour nuts and chocolate chips into a 9x13 inch baking dish. Pour hot mixture over the nuts and chocolate. Let the mixture cool; break into pieces before serving. **Yield:** 48 servings.

Per serving: 153 calories, 1g protein, 14g carbohydrate, 11g fat, 1g fiber, 21mg cholesterol, 80mg sodium

Roasted Rack of Lamb, page 60

Rice Stuffing with Apples, Herbs, and Bacon,
page 70

Actually Delicious
Turkey Burgers, page 95

Apple-Stuffed Chicken Breast,
page 90

Quick Country Cupboard Soup,
page 99

Light & Luscious

Collected here are the robust recipes your family will never know are good for them. These dishes are full of flavor—but not full of all the fat and calories normally associated with home cooking.

Emily's Famous Onion Dip

Submitted by: **Emily B.**

"This onion dip is a hit with all of my friends. Sometimes I throw in some fresh herbs from the garden. To make this really low in fat, use fat-free plain yogurt. This is a perfect dip for potato chips or veggie sticks."

2	tablespoons butter	½	teaspoon white vinegar
1	small onion, finely chopped		Salt and ground black
2	cups plain yogurt		pepper to taste

1. Melt butter in a skillet over medium heat. Sauté onion in butter until tender and lightly browned.

2. Transfer onion to a serving bowl and stir in yogurt and vinegar. Season with salt and pepper to taste. Refrigerate for at least 1 hour or overnight before serving to blend flavors. **Yield:** 16 servings.

Per serving: 34 calories, 2g protein, 3g carbohydrate, 2g fat, 0g fiber, 6mg cholesterol, 60mg sodium

Texas Caviar with Avocado

Submitted by: **Kim Lawn**

"A delicious party dip with peas, tomatoes, onion, and lots of diced avocado. Take one bite and you won't leave the bowl. Serve with 'scoop' tortilla chips."

2	(15.5 ounce) cans black-eyed peas, rinsed and drained	½	cup chopped jalapeño pepper
2	tomatoes, chopped	1	cup Italian-style salad dressing
1	medium sweet onion, chopped		Cayenne pepper to taste
		2	avocados, peeled, pitted, and chopped

1. In a large bowl, mix black-eyed peas, tomatoes, sweet onion, jalapeño pepper, Italian-style salad dressing, and cayenne pepper to taste. Stir in avocado just before serving. **Yield:** 32 servings.

Per serving: 79 calories, 2g protein, 6g carbohydrate, 6g fat, 2g fiber, 0mg cholesterol, 141mg sodium

Baked Pork Spring Rolls

Submitted by: **Rayna**

"An exciting blend of pork, vegetables, and seasonings is sealed inside wrappers and then baked until crisp. Delicious and crunchy—without any deep-frying!"

½ pound ground pork	2 teaspoons grated fresh ginger root
1 cup finely shredded cabbage	1½ teaspoons minced garlic
¼ cup finely shredded carrot	1 teaspoon chili sauce
2 green onions, thinly sliced	1 tablespoon cornstarch
2 tablespoons chopped fresh cilantro	1 tablespoon water
½ teaspoon sesame oil	12 (7 inch square) spring roll wrappers
1½ teaspoons oyster sauce	4 teaspoons vegetable oil

1. Preheat oven to 425°F (220°C).

2. Place pork in a medium saucepan. Cook over medium–high heat until evenly browned. Remove from heat and drain.

3. In a medium bowl, mix together pork, cabbage, carrot, green onions, cilantro, sesame oil, oyster sauce, ginger, garlic, and chili sauce.

4. Mix cornstarch and water in a separate small bowl.

5. Place approximately 1 tablespoon of the pork mixture in the center of each spring roll wrapper. Roll wrappers around the mixture, folding edges inward to close. Brush wrapper seams with cornstarch mixture to seal.

6. Arrange spring rolls in a single layer on a medium baking sheet. Brush with vegetable oil.

7. Bake in the preheated oven for 20 minutes or until hot and lightly browned. For crispier spring rolls, turn after 10 minutes.

Yield: 12 servings.

Per serving: 154 calories, 7g protein, 20g carbohydrate, 5g fat, 1g fiber, 15mg cholesterol, 200mg sodium

◄ AROUND-THE-WORLD CUISINE

Prep Time: 25 minutes

Cook Time: 25 minutes

Average Rating: ★★★★

What other cooks have done:

"I love these. They are pretty simple to make, and they're great served with a ramen stir-fry. They are like low-fat egg rolls. I did not have a few items on hand (oyster sauce, cilantro, chili sauce), and they still turned out great. I will definitely make these again."

Pumpkin Fluff Dip

Submitted by: **Tiera Lesley**

"This creamy vanilla-pumpkin dip is delicious served with graham crackers. I like the cinnamon graham crackers best, but you can decide for yourself."

1 (5 ounce) package instant vanilla pudding mix
1 (15 ounce) can pumpkin
1 teaspoon pumpkin pie spice
1 (16 ounce) container frozen whipped topping, thawed

1. In a large bowl, mix together instant vanilla pudding mix, pumpkin, and pumpkin pie spice. Fold in thawed frozen whipped topping. Chill until ready to serve. **Yield:** 32 servings (4 cups).

Per serving: 65 calories, 0g protein, 8g carbohydrate, 4g fat, 0g fiber, 0mg cholesterol, 99mg sodium

5 INGREDIENTS OR LESS ▶

Prep Time: 5 minutes

Average Rating: ★★★★★

What other cooks have done:

"My youngest son loves anything made with pumpkin, so I let him make this with my guidance. Easy as pie! It tasted great with gingersnaps, apple slices, and graham crackers. Pumpkin Fluff Dip is his contribution to our Thanksgiving table from this year on."

Sweet Pea Mockamole

Submitted by: **CACTUSUE**

"Delicious and slightly sweet dip to serve with tortilla chips, crackers, or fresh veggies."

1 cup frozen green peas, thawed and drained
3 tablespoons chopped onion
1 teaspoon ground cumin
1 large clove garlic, chopped
1 tablespoon lemon juice
1 tablespoon olive oil
½ teaspoon crushed red pepper flakes (or to taste)
Salt and ground black pepper to taste

1. Combine the peas, onion, cumin, and garlic in a blender or food processor. Process until smooth. Add lemon juice and olive oil and process just until blended. Season with red pepper flakes and salt and black pepper to taste. Blend for just a few more seconds and transfer to a serving bowl. **Yield:** 12 servings.

Per serving: 23 calories, 1g protein, 2g carbohydrate, 1g fat, 1g fiber, 0mg cholesterol, 15mg sodium

HOT & SPICY ▶

Prep Time: 10 minutes

Average Rating: ★★★★☆

What other cooks have done:

"This was delicious! I made it for a party, and nobody knew that it wasn't 'authentic' guacamole. I used less red pepper flakes, and it still packed quite a punch. I think I will use even less the next time I make it. The 'heat' seems to grow the longer the dip sits. I can't wait to make a layered taco dip and use this in place of guacamole."

Blue Cheese and Pear Tartlets

Submitted by: **BOLLIVEB**

"These tasty hot appetizers take little time to prepare but will impress your guests!"

1 (2.1 ounce) package mini phyllo tart shells
4 ounces blue cheese, crumbled
1 ripe pear, peeled, cored, and chopped
2 tablespoons light cream
Ground black pepper to taste

1. Preheat oven to 350°F (175°C).
2. Bake phyllo shells according to package directions. Set aside to cool.
3. Meanwhile, mix together blue cheese, pear, and cream. Season to taste with pepper. Spoon mixture into cooled shells.
4. Bake in the preheated oven for 5 to 8 minutes. Serve warm.
Yield: 15 servings.

Per serving: 60 calories, 2g protein, 5g carbohydrate, 4g fat, 0g fiber, 7mg cholesterol, 116mg sodium

◄ QUICK & EASY

Prep Time: 10 minutes

Cook Time: 13 minutes

Average Rating: ★★★★★

What other cooks have done:

"Very good! I took these to a dinner party, and they were a big hit. I had too much filling for one package of phyllo tarts, so I saved the extra filling for the next day. Next time, I will decrease the amount of filling by using less blue cheese."

Choosing a Blue

Because it packs a potent punch, a little blue cheese goes a long way. All blue cheeses are treated with molds that form blue or green veins throughout. These molds give the cheeses their characteristic strong flavors and aromas. Aging is an important part of the manufacturing of blue cheese; the longer it's aged, the stronger the flavor. It's this distinctive flavor of blue cheese that drives people to love it or hate it. There are several varieties of this cheese; use the guide below to help you select the perfect cheese for your palate.

Domestic blues: Generally white with delicate blue marbling. Texture varies from creamy to crumbly. Subtle, sharp flavor. Many regional variations.

Danish blue (Danablu): White to yellowish with greenish-blue veins. Soft, crumbly consistency, but can be sliced or spread. Mellow to tangy in flavor.

Gorgonzola: White to light straw color with tendril-like green mottling. Soft, moist consistency. Made from whole cow's milk. Highly developed aroma that ranges from mild to pungent. Piquant flavor.

Roquefort: Creamy white with blue-green marbling. Made from sheep's milk; red sheep emblem on package. Semi-soft; can be salty. Sharp flavor.

Stilton: Creamy white to ivory in color with blue veins radiating from center. Made from cow's milk. Rich, creamy, almost buttery. Natural rough crust. Dense but crumbly. Melts well.

For more information, visit **Allrecipes.com**

Mongolian Beef I

Submitted by: **Onemina**

"A simple but spicy dish with beef, carrots, and green onions. Serve over rice for a very filling meal."

AROUND-THE-WORLD CUISINE ▶

Prep Time: 20 minutes

Cook Time: 10 minutes

Stand Time: 10 minutes

Average Rating: ★★★★☆

What other cooks have done:

"I cannot think of a word to describe how good this is. My husband and I couldn't stop eating this. We had leftovers the next day, and the meal was even better. I tripled the sauce ingredients, as my husband and I like a lot of sauce that we can put over rice. I will make this over and over and over."

1 teaspoon sesame seeds	½ teaspoon white sugar
1 tablespoon soy sauce	1 teaspoon crushed red
1 tablespoon cornstarch	pepper flakes
2 cloves garlic, minced	2 tablespoons vegetable oil,
1 pound beef round steak, cut	divided
into thin strips	2 carrots, thinly sliced
¾ cup water	1 bunch green onions, cut
2 tablespoons soy sauce	into 2 inch pieces, white
2½ teaspoons cornstarch	and green parts divided

1. In a dry skillet over medium heat, toast sesame seeds for 1 to 2 minutes or until the seeds begin to turn golden brown; set aside.

2. In a medium bowl, mix together 1 tablespoon soy sauce, 1 tablespoon cornstarch, and minced garlic. Stir in beef strips. Let stand for at least 10 minutes.

3. In a separate small bowl, mix together water, 2 tablespoons soy sauce, 2½ teaspoons cornstarch, sugar, red pepper flakes, and sesame seeds; set aside.

4. Heat 1 tablespoon oil in a wok or skillet over high heat. Cook beef, stirring constantly, in hot oil for 1 minute; remove and set aside. Heat remaining 1 tablespoon oil in the same pan. Sauté carrots and white part of green onions for 2 minutes. Stir in green part of green onions and sauté for 1 minute. Stir in sesame seed mixture and beef. Cook, stirring constantly, until sauce boils and thickens.

Yield: 6 servings.

Per serving: 155 calories, 11g protein, 9g carbohydrate, 9g fat, 2g fiber, 18mg cholesterol, 429mg sodium

Bubble 'n' Squeak

Submitted by: **Doreen Friesen**

"Cabbage, bacon, ham, onion, and potatoes make up this tasty, easy dish. This is a great way to get the kids to eat cabbage. Using leftovers makes this main dish especially quick to make. I recommend using a good nonstick pan. Serve with ketchup, if desired."

½	medium head cabbage, sliced	3	cups potatoes, baked and thinly sliced
3	slices bacon, diced	½	teaspoon paprika
1	onion, thinly sliced		Salt and ground black pepper to taste
1	cup cubed cooked ham		
1	tablespoon butter		

1. In a medium saucepan, cook cabbage in a small amount of water for about 5 minutes or until tender. Drain and set aside.
2. In a well-seasoned cast-iron or nonstick skillet, cook bacon and onion until onion is soft and bacon is cooked. Add ham and cook until heated through. Add butter and mix in the cooked cabbage and potatoes. Season with paprika and salt and pepper to taste. Cook until browned on bottom; turn and brown again. **Yield:** 6 servings.

Per serving: 164 calories, 8g protein, 19g carbohydrate, 7g fat, 3g fiber, 22mg cholesterol, 399mg sodium

◄ AROUND-THE-WORLD CUISINE

Prep Time: 15 minutes

Cook Time: 15 minutes

Average Rating: ★★★★★

What other cooks have done:

"Very good! I used packaged shredded cooked potatoes and packaged cubed ham, and I chopped my own onion and cabbage. Everyone loved this and asked for the recipe. I used a nonstick pan and had just enough room to turn it. It didn't really get brown, but it didn't matter. I liked it with hot sauce. I served it with jalapeño cheese."

Cola Chops

Submitted by: **Chiara Wine**

"Easy Southern main dish."

8	pork chops, trimmed	1	cup ketchup
1	cup cola-flavored carbonated beverage	4	tablespoons brown sugar

1. Preheat oven to 350°F (175°C).
2. Place pork chops in a 9x13 inch baking dish. In a small bowl, mix together the cola and ketchup. Pour over chops. Sprinkle chops with brown sugar.
3. Bake in the preheated oven, uncovered, for about 1 hour or until pork is cooked through and a meat thermometer inserted into thickest part of pork registers 160°F (70°C). **Yield:** 8 servings.

Per serving: 204 calories, 20g protein, 18g carbohydrate, 6g fat, 0g fiber, 59mg cholesterol, 408mg sodium

◄ 5 INGREDIENTS OR LESS

Prep Time: 15 minutes

Cook Time: 1 hour

Average Rating: ★★★★☆

What other cooks have done:

"These were so good! You can't beat the simplicity. Even my daughter said this dish was delicious. I can definitely see myself making this again. I might use the same recipe to prepare ribs."

Pork Chops with Apples, Onions, and Sweet Potatoes

Submitted by: **Ashbeth**

"This is so easy, so good, and so versatile! I've used pork chops (with and without bones), pork loin, and pork roast in this recipe. You can sprinkle the brown sugar, pepper, and salt on the different layers or all at the end, as mentioned in the recipe. Play around with the brown sugar and spices to your taste."

4	pork chops, trimmed	3	tablespoons brown sugar
	Salt and ground black pepper to taste	2	teaspoons freshly ground black pepper
2	onions, sliced into rings	1	teaspoon salt
2	sweet potatoes, sliced		
2	apples, peeled, cored, and sliced into rings		

1. Preheat oven to 375°F (190°C).
2. Season pork chops with salt and pepper to taste and arrange in a medium ovenproof skillet. Top pork chops with onions, sweet potatoes, and apples. Sprinkle with brown sugar. Season with 2 teaspoons pepper and 1 teaspoon salt.
3. Bake in the preheated oven, covered, for 1 hour or until sweet potatoes are tender and a meat thermometer inserted into thickest part of pork registers 160°F (70°C). **Yield:** 4 servings.

Per serving: 325 calories, 13g protein, 42g carbohydrate, 12g fat, 5g fiber, 45mg cholesterol, 754mg sodium

Cuban Shredded Pork

Submitted by: **Lisa**

"This is a popular Cuban pork dish known as Lechon Asado. *My version is a shortcut. The pork is simmered in a broth until tender, and then it's shredded. This is traditionally served with black beans and rice."*

1	pint water	2	tablespoons olive oil
1	lime, juiced	1	large onion, halved and thinly sliced
1	sprig fresh thyme		
8	black peppercorns	3	cloves garlic, peeled and sliced
1	tablespoon garlic powder (or to taste)		
		1	lime, juiced
1	tablespoon onion powder	¼	cup chopped fresh cilantro
	Salt to taste		
1½	pounds boneless pork chops, trimmed		

1. In a large saucepan, combine water, juice of 1 lime, thyme sprig, peppercorns, garlic powder, onion powder, and salt to taste. Bring mixture to a boil. Add pork chops; reduce heat to medium-low and simmer for 1 to 1½ hours or until meat is very tender. Add more water as necessary to keep chops covered.

2. Turn off heat and let the chops rest in the broth for 30 minutes. Remove chops from broth and shred, removing excess fat; set aside.

3. In a large frying pan, heat olive oil over medium-high heat. Add the shredded pork and fry until it is almost crisp, about 5 minutes. Add the onion and garlic and continue to cook until the onion is just tender yet slightly crisp, about 10 more minutes. Add the juice of 1 lime; mix thoroughly and toss with cilantro. **Yield:** 5 servings.

Per serving: 203 calories, 19g protein, 8g carbohydrate, 11g fat, 1g fiber, 43mg cholesterol, 103mg sodium

Pleasant Pork Chops

Submitted by: **Clyde Patterson**

"When I was a bachelor cooking for two other roommates, this dinner of pork chops simmered with spices in a sour cream and onion sauce was a feast for us! We all really liked it."

1	onion, chopped	1	bay leaf
1	clove garlic, minced	¾	cup chicken broth
3	tablespoons butter	1	cup sour cream
6	pork chops, trimmed	2	teaspoons paprika
	Salt and ground black		
	pepper to taste		

1. In a skillet, sauté onion and garlic in hot butter. Remove from skillet. Sprinkle pork chops with salt and pepper to taste. Brown chops in skillet; drain.

2. Reduce heat; add bay leaf and chicken broth. Cook, covered, over low heat for 1 hour. Transfer chops to a serving plate and keep hot.

3. Bring remaining liquid in skillet to a boil; cook until reduced by half. Add the sour cream, onion-garlic mixture, and paprika, blending thoroughly. Heat through but don't boil. Remove bay leaf. Pour over pork chops and serve. **Yield:** 6 servings.

Per serving: 263 calories, 16g protein, 4g carbohydrate, 21g fat, 0g fiber, 69mg cholesterol, 226mg sodium

◀ FROM THE PANTRY

Prep Time: 15 minutes

Cook Time: 1 hour 15 minutes

Average Rating: ★★★★★

What other cooks have done:

"I am convinced there is no better way to prepare pork chops than this. I stick to the recipe, and the pork is perfect every time. It's very important to reduce the liquid, or it will turn out too thin. I serve this with Parmesan-mashed red potatoes and steamed veggies; the sauce can go over everything! My family requests this one all the time; it's our all-time favorite."

Apple-Stuffed Chicken Breast

(pictured on page 79)

Submitted by: **Behr Kleine**

"This is a great dish for the fall. Golden Delicious, Granny Smith, Newtown Pippin, Rome Beauty, or Winesap apples may be used."

COMPANY IS COMING ▶

Prep Time: 21 minutes

Cook Time: 26 minutes

Average Rating: ★★★★★

What other cooks have done:

"This was wonderful. I used more than ½ cup Fuji apples, and I really stuffed the chicken breast rolls to the max. I used apple juice instead of wine for the gravy. Tonight when I heated up the leftovers, I thinned out the cold gravy with apple juice and a bit of evaporated fat-free milk. I really liked the creaminess the milk added and will make it that way next time. I will also sauté some onions for the filling next time."

½ cup chopped apple	¼ cup dry white wine
¼ cup shredded Cheddar cheese	¼ cup water
2 tablespoons Italian-style breadcrumbs	1 tablespoon water
2 skinless, boneless chicken breast halves	1½ teaspoons cornstarch
1 tablespoon butter	1 tablespoon chopped fresh parsley

1. Combine apple, cheese, and breadcrumbs. Set aside.

2. Flatten chicken breasts between sheets of wax paper to ¼ inch thickness. Place apple mixture evenly in the center of each chicken breast; roll up each breast. Secure with toothpicks.

3. Melt butter in a 7 inch skillet over medium heat. Brown stuffed chicken breasts in butter. Add wine and ¼ cup water. Cover. Simmer for 15 to 20 minutes or until chicken is no longer pink and juices run clear.

4. Transfer chicken to a serving platter. Combine 1 tablespoon water and cornstarch; stir into juices in pan. Cook and stir until thickened. Pour gravy over chicken and top with parsley. **Yield:** 2 servings.

Per serving: 348 calories, 44g protein, 12g carbohydrate, 13g fat, 1g fiber, 129mg cholesterol, 441mg sodium

Sweet-and-Sour Chicken III

Submitted by: **Sallie**

"This version of the Asian-style favorite includes carrots, bell pepper, garlic, and pineapple. The requisite soy sauce and vinegar add the sour to the sweet, and voilà! Serve over hot cooked rice, if desired."

1	pound skinless, boneless chicken breast halves, cubed	1	clove garlic, minced
2	tablespoons vegetable oil	1	tablespoon cornstarch
½	cup sliced green bell pepper	¼	cup soy sauce
½	cup sliced red bell pepper	1	(8 ounce) can pineapple chunks, with juice
1	cup carrot strips	1	tablespoon vinegar
		1	tablespoon brown sugar
		½	teaspoon ground ginger

1. In a large skillet over medium-high heat, brown chicken in oil. Add green bell pepper, red bell pepper, carrot, and garlic and stir-fry for 1 to 2 minutes.

2. In a small bowl, combine cornstarch and soy sauce and mix together; pour mixture into the skillet, along with the pineapple and its juice, vinegar, brown sugar, and ginger. Stir together and bring just to boil.

Yield: 4 servings.

Per serving: 260 calories, 24g protein, 21g carbohydrate, 9g fat, 2g fiber, 59mg cholesterol, 972mg sodium

◀ QUICK & EASY

Prep Time: 10 minutes

Cook Time: 10 minutes

Average Rating: ★★★★★

What other cooks have done:

"I really liked this recipe. I have had a hard time finding sweet-and-sour recipes that I like. I added ketchup. I also had only half a can of pineapple juice, so I made up the difference with mango juice; it added a nice subtle flavor. I also added bean sprouts and cabbage. They added a great crispy texture. I will be using this recipe again."

Cherry-Chicken Lettuce Wraps

Submitted by: **Barry**

"Crisp lettuce leaves make a crunchy and refreshing wrapper for a teriyaki chicken mixture."

PARTY FOOD ▶

Prep Time: 15 minutes

Cook Time: 10 minutes

Average Rating: ★★★★★

What other cooks have done:

"Delicious! I used romaine lettuce to give the wraps a little extra crunch. I also added water chestnuts and spicy red pepper–garlic sauce for some kick. My husband loved these!"

2	tablespoons vegetable oil, divided		2	tablespoons teriyaki sauce
1	tablespoon minced fresh ginger root		1	tablespoon honey
1¼	pounds skinless, boneless chicken breast halves, cut into bite-size pieces		1	pound dark sweet cherries, pitted and halved
			1½	cups shredded carrot
			½	cup chopped green onions
2	tablespoons rice vinegar		⅓	cup toasted sliced almonds
			12	lettuce leaves

1. Heat 1 tablespoon oil in a large skillet over medium-high heat. Add ginger and chicken and sauté until chicken is no longer pink and juices run clear, about 7 to 10 minutes. Set aside.

2. In a large bowl, whisk together remaining 1 tablespoon oil, vinegar, teriyaki sauce, and honey. Add chicken mixture, cherries, carrot, green onions, and almonds; toss together.

3. Spoon chicken mixture evenly onto the center of each lettuce leaf; roll up leaf around filling and serve. **Yield:** 6 servings.

Per serving: 283 calories, 25g protein, 22g carbohydrate, 11g fat, 4g fiber, 55mg cholesterol, 129mg sodium

Baked Teriyaki Chicken

Submitted by: **Marian Collins**
"A much-requested chicken recipe! Easy to double for a large group. Delicious!"

1	tablespoon cornstarch	1	clove garlic, minced
1	tablespoon cold water	½	teaspoon ground ginger
½	cup white sugar	¼	teaspoon ground black
½	cup soy sauce		pepper
¼	cup cider vinegar	12	skinless chicken thighs

1. Preheat oven to 425°F (220°C). Lightly grease a 9x13 inch baking dish.
2. In a small saucepan over low heat, combine the cornstarch, cold water, sugar, soy sauce, vinegar, garlic, ginger, and pepper. Let simmer, stirring frequently, until sauce thickens and bubbles.
3. Place chicken in prepared baking dish. Brush chicken with the sauce. Turn pieces over and brush again.
4. Bake in the preheated oven for 30 minutes. Turn pieces over and bake for 30 more minutes or until chicken is no longer pink and juices run clear. Brush with sauce every 10 minutes during cooking.
Yield: 6 servings.

Per serving: 277 calories, 25g protein, 21g carbohydrate, 10g fat, 0g fiber, 88mg cholesterol, 1296mg sodium

◄ OUT-OF-THE-ORDINARY

Prep Time: 30 minutes

Cook Time: 1 hour 10 minutes

Average Rating: ★★★★★

What other cooks have done:
"What a wonderful recipe! We have never cared for bottled teriyaki sauce, so I'm very pleased that I found this. The only thing I added was some crushed red pepper flakes, and that really lit it up. I'm anxious to try the sauce on grilled salmon; I think that would be wonderful."

Chicken Jambalaya I

Submitted by: **Suzanne**

"This is a one-skillet chicken and rice dish with veggies, herbs, and a slightly spicy kick!"

Prep Time: 10 minutes

Cook Time: 30 minutes

Average Rating: ★★★★★

What other cooks have done:

"I loved this dish. I got home from work and still had time to make this. One thing I added was a tiny little bit of Cajun pepper. The dish was nice and spicy; just make sure that if you do that, you have a glass of water handy when you eat it. I've made this dish a couple of times now, and I found that I could add or delete ingredients as I liked."

2	tablespoons butter	⅔	cup white rice
⅓	cup chopped celery	1	teaspoon dried thyme
¼	cup chopped onion	½	teaspoon garlic salt
¼	cup chopped green bell pepper	¼	teaspoon ground black pepper
1	(14.5 ounce) can diced tomatoes	½	teaspoon hot pepper sauce
		1	bay leaf
1½	cups low-sodium chicken broth	2	cups cubed cooked chicken

1. Melt butter in a large skillet over medium-low heat. Add celery, onion, and green bell pepper and sauté until tender. Stir in tomatoes, broth, rice, thyme, garlic salt, ground black pepper, hot pepper sauce, and bay leaf.

2. Bring to a boil; reduce heat, cover skillet, and simmer for about 20 minutes or until rice is tender. Stir in chicken and cook until heated through. Discard bay leaf and serve hot. **Yield:** 4 servings.

Per serving: 320 calories, 26g protein, 31g carbohydrate, 9g fat, 2g fiber, 75mg cholesterol, 1011mg sodium

Actually Delicious Turkey Burgers

(pictured on page 79)

Submitted by: **Trudi Davidoff**

"Turkey burgers are a delicious change of pace. Slap these moist patties on the grill for a special summer treat!"

2	egg whites	3	pounds ground turkey
¼	cup finely diced onion	¼	cup seasoned breadcrumbs
¼	cup chopped fresh parsley		Toppings: buns, lettuce,
2	cloves garlic, peeled and minced		tomato, prepared mustard (optional)
1	teaspoon salt		Pimento-stuffed olives
¼	teaspoon ground black pepper		(optional)

1. Lightly beat egg white in a large bowl. Beat in onion, parsley, garlic, salt, and pepper. Add turkey and breadcrumbs; mix thoroughly. Form into 10 patties.

2. Cook the patties in a medium skillet over medium heat, turning once, until a meat thermometer inserted into thickest part of turkey registers 180°F (85°C). Serve with toppings and garnish with olives, if desired. **Yield:** 10 burgers.

Per serving: 183 calories, 21g protein, 2g carbohydrate, 9g fat, 0g fiber, 90mg cholesterol, 377mg sodium

◀ KID-FRIENDLY

Prep Time: 20 minutes

Cook Time: 15 minutes

Average Rating: ★★★★★

What other cooks have done:

"I thought these were great. I added a little diced bell pepper to the patties and then topped the burgers with fat-free sour cream mixed with Greek spice. I put them on whole wheat buns. Yummy. Next time, I will add a piece of lettuce for crunch, as my meat-adoring hubby thought these were still a little too 'soft' in texture."

Make It Lean

When it comes to entrées, a good way to eat healthy is to purchase lean meats. Using a lean ground meat in your casseroles and burgers gives you great flavor with less fat and calories. However, when you're at the supermarket, read labels with a careful eye to make sure you know exactly what you're getting.

Talking Turkey

You'll see several types of ground turkey in the supermarket. The leanest (about 3 percent fat) is white meat only, with no skin. It's labeled "ground turkey breast." Regular "ground turkey" is made from white and dark meat with some skin and is about 10 percent fat (similar to ground round). Frozen ground turkey is usually all dark meat with skin and is 15 percent fat, similar to ground sirloin.

Here's the Beef

Ground beef labels can be quite confusing. Some ground beef is labeled by cut (chuck, sirloin, or round), while some is labeled by percent fat to percent lean. The maximum fat content in any ground beef is 30 percent (70 percent lean). Look for labels that tell the amount of percent fat to percent lean—then there will be no guessing about which has the least fat. Or choose a whole piece of chuck, sirloin, or round and ask the person behind the meat counter to trim and grind it for you. Here's how the percentages stack up:
- Ground chuck: 20 percent fat
- Ground sirloin: 15 percent fat
- Ground round: 11 percent fat

For more information, visit **Allrecipes.com**

Maple Salmon

Submitted by: **starflower**

"This is the best and most delicious salmon recipe, and it's very easy to prepare. I love maple in everything, so I put this together one night. My husband totally loved it; he did not like salmon that much until he had this."

COMPANY IS COMING ▶

Prep Time: 10 minutes

Chill Time: 30 minutes

Cook Time: 20 minutes

Average Rating: ★★★★★

What other cooks have done:

"This is a really brilliant recipe that works for chicken as well as salmon. I actually flip the ratio of syrup to soy, as it is a bit too sweet for me otherwise. The sauce cooks up really nicely and mixes in well with roasted vegetables."

¼ cup maple syrup
2 tablespoons soy sauce
1 clove garlic, minced
¼ teaspoon garlic salt
⅛ teaspoon ground black pepper
1 pound salmon

1. In a small bowl, mix the maple syrup, soy sauce, garlic, garlic salt, and pepper.
2. Place salmon in a shallow baking dish and coat with the maple syrup mixture. Cover and chill 30 minutes, turning once.
3. Preheat the oven to 400°F (200°C).
4. Bake in the preheated oven for 20 minutes or until fish flakes easily with a fork. **Yield:** 4 servings.

Per serving: 65 calories, 23g protein, 14g carbohydrate, 12g fat, 0g fiber, 67mg cholesterol, 639mg sodium

Get Started with Salmon

Salmon's distinctive color, exceptional flavor, and incredible versatility make it one of the most popular varieties of fish. Salmon is also naturally tender and cooks quickly. It even provides a hedge for beginning cooks—its high fat content keeps it moist even when overdone. In fact, salmon stays moist when cooked by almost any method—you can pan-fry, grill, roast, steam, poach, or smoke it.

Good Fat?

Don't let the high fat content that makes salmon so flavorful and forgiving worry you. Salmon is high in monounsaturated and polyunsaturated fats—those that don't raise blood cholesterol levels. Perhaps even more important is that salmon is high in omega-3 fats, a type of polyunsaturated fat that guards against heart disease. In addition, salmon delivers a healthy dose of other nutritional pluses: It's high in protein, vitamin E, vitamin B, and the minerals iron, magnesium, and zinc. Serve salmon with low-fat sides, such as rice, couscous, or potatoes, and you'll bring the fat percentage way down.

Wild at Heart

Most of what you'll find at the supermarket is farmed Atlantic salmon. The peak season for wild salmon is April to October, while farmed salmon is available year-round. Taste is a good indicator of whether a salmon is wild or farmed. Wild salmon has a greater range of flavors, from rich, distinctive king salmon to delicately flavored pink. The flavor of farmed salmon will vary depending on the feed mixture each farm uses, but the end result is usually a midrange mild taste.

For more information, visit **Allrecipes.com**

Roasted Red Pepper and Tomato Soup

Submitted by: **Carol Crane**

"On a cold winter's night, this soup hits the spot. Serve with warm cornbread and salad. Or go Mexican and serve with taco toppings. For an even lighter soup, this is also delicious without the sour cream."

2	teaspoons olive oil, divided		Salt and ground black pepper to taste
3	red bell peppers		Pinch cayenne pepper
1	onion, chopped		Dash hot pepper sauce (optional)
2	cloves garlic, minced		
4	large tomatoes, peeled, seeded, and chopped	2	tablespoons butter
1½	teaspoons dried thyme	1½	tablespoons all-purpose flour
2	teaspoons paprika		
⅛	teaspoon white sugar	6	tablespoons sour cream
6	cups chicken broth		

◄ RESTAURANT FARE

Prep Time: 15 minutes

Cook Time: 1 hour 25 minutes

Stand Time: 15 minutes

Average Rating: ★★★★

What other cooks have done:
"This was very good. To make it more creamy, I pureed a can of cannellini beans with the soup."

1. Preheat broiler.

2. Rub 1 teaspoon oil on bell peppers and broil in the preheated oven until blackened, turning to blacken all sides. Put bell peppers into a paper bag and fold edges over to seal. Let rest for 15 minutes; peel bell peppers. Core and seed bell peppers; discard peel, core, and seeds. Chop bell peppers. Reserve one-third of chopped bell pepper; set aside.

3. Heat remaining 1 teaspoon olive oil over medium heat. Add onion and garlic and cook until soft but not brown, about 5 minutes. Stir in tomato, remaining two-thirds of chopped bell pepper, thyme, paprika, and sugar. Cook over medium-low heat until all the juices have evaporated, about 25 minutes.

4. Stir in chicken broth, salt and black pepper to taste, cayenne pepper, and hot sauce, if desired. Bring to a boil, decrease heat, and simmer, partially covered, for 25 minutes or until vegetables are tender.

5. Strain soup, reserving broth. Place solids in a blender or food processor and process until fairly smooth. Add puree back into broth.

6. Melt butter and stir in the flour; cook for 1 minute. Stirring slowly, add the broth mixture. Add reserved one-third of chopped bell pepper and bring to a boil. Reduce heat and simmer 10 minutes.

7. Ladle into bowls and add 1 tablespoon of sour cream to each bowl.

Yield: 6 servings.

Per serving: 171 calories, 8g protein, 15g carbohydrate, 10g fat, 3g fiber, 17mg cholesterol, 828mg sodium

Stuffed Pepper Soup IV

Submitted by: **Kate**

"An easy soup that tastes like stuffed peppers. This can be a full meal in one bowl, but it's also great with warm bread and a salad."

ONE-DISH MEAL ▶

Prep Time: 10 minutes

Cook Time: 55 minutes

Average Rating: ★★★★★

What other cooks have done:

"This tasted just like my mom's stuffed peppers (one of my favorite meals growing up), and this was so quick and easy compared to the all-day affair of preparing and cooking a stuffed pepper meal! The only thing I'll do differently next time I make this is to add a little extra bell pepper for my own personal taste."

1 pound lean ground sirloin	¼ teaspoon dried thyme
1 green bell pepper, chopped	¼ teaspoon dried sage
1 cup finely diced onion	Salt and ground black pepper to taste
1 (29 ounce) can diced tomatoes	2 cups water
1 (15 ounce) can tomato sauce	1 cup white rice
1 (14 ounce) can chicken broth	

1. In a large stockpot, brown ground sirloin. Drain fat and add bell pepper and onion. Cook until onion is translucent but not brown.

2. Add tomatoes, tomato sauce, broth, thyme, sage, and salt and black pepper to taste. Cover and simmer for 30 to 45 minutes, until bell pepper is tender.

3. Meanwhile, in another saucepan, bring 2 cups water to a boil and add rice. Cook until rice is tender; add to soup. Heat through and serve. **Yield:** 6 servings.

Per serving: 273 calories, 20g protein, 39g carbohydrate, 5g fat, 4g fiber, 41mg cholesterol, 875mg sodium

Quick Country Cupboard
Soup *(pictured on page 80)*

Submitted by: **Kat Board**

"A family favorite recipe that is very quick when time is short and leftovers are plenty. This may also be made in a slow cooker. I like to add zucchini, peas, corn, or any leftover 'soup-friendly' veggie."

1	teaspoon vegetable oil	2	tablespoons white sugar
½	pound skinless, boneless chicken breast halves, cut into 1 inch cubes	4	cups water
		1	(28 ounce) can crushed tomatoes
1	cup thinly sliced carrots	1	teaspoon Italian seasoning
1	cup diced potatoes	1	teaspoon hot pepper sauce
1	small zucchini, diced	½	teaspoon ground black pepper
1	cup green peas		
1	cup corn kernels	½	cup seashell pasta
2	(1 ounce) packages dry onion soup mix		

1. In a large stockpot, heat oil over medium heat; add chicken and brown lightly.

2. Stir in carrots, potatoes, zucchini, peas, corn, onion soup mix, sugar, water, tomatoes, Italian seasoning, hot pepper sauce, and black pepper. Stir frequently.

3. Bring to a boil; reduce heat and cook, covered, for 20 minutes. Add pasta and cook, covered, for 10 minutes or until pasta is tender.

Yield: 6 servings.

Per serving: 238 calories, 16g protein, 41g carbohydrate, 2g fat, 6g fiber, 22mg cholesterol, 1052mg sodium

◀ **HOT & SPICY**

Prep Time: 15 minutes

Cook Time: 38 minutes

Average Rating: ★★★★☆

What other cooks have done:

"An easy soup to make that has great flavor! Perfect comfort food. I use elbow pasta instead of seashell pasta; it works out well. This soup freezes nicely, too."

Pasta e Fagioli II

Submitted by: Kathy

"Wonderful Italian veggie soup! My parents had this while in Rome, and they convinced the chef to give them the recipe."

CROWD-PLEASER ▶

Prep Time: 20 minutes

Cook Time: 1 hour 10 minutes

Average Rating: ★★★★★

What other cooks have done:

"This soup was good. I added fresh parsley and, more importantly, a Parmesan cheese rind. The rind made all the difference—it really rounded out the flavors."

½	cup chopped onion	1	tablespoon dried parsley
1	small carrot, grated	2	teaspoons dried basil
¼	cup chopped celery	⅛	teaspoon cayenne pepper
1	clove garlic, minced	1	tablespoon distilled white
¼	pound prosciutto, finely		vinegar
	chopped	2	teaspoons white sugar
1	tablespoon olive oil		Salt and ground black
6	cups chicken broth		pepper to taste
3	cups tomato juice	1	(16 ounce) package ditalini
2	cups red beans		pasta

1. In a large stockpot, sauté onion, carrot, celery, garlic, and prosciutto in olive oil until onion is transparent.

2. Add chicken broth, tomato juice, red beans, parsley, basil, cayenne pepper, vinegar, and sugar and season with salt and black pepper to taste. Simmer for 1 hour.

3. Meanwhile, fill a separate stockpot three-fourths full of water and bring to a boil. Add pasta and cook until tender; drain.

4. Place desired amount of pasta into separate serving bowls and ladle soup on top. **Yield:** 12 servings.

Per serving: 258 calories, 12g protein, 40g carbohydrate, 6g fat, 5g fiber, 8mg cholesterol, 723mg sodium

Winter Lentil Vegetable Soup

Submitted by: **Cecile Leverman**

"This soup has very little fat, is cheap and easy to make, and tastes delicious. Our family practically lives on it in the winter, and I usually double the recipe. Sprinkle grated Cheddar on top, if desired. If you can't hang around long enough for this to cook, put it in a slow cooker."

½	cup red or green lentils	1	clove garlic, crushed
1	cup chopped onion	1	teaspoon salt
1	stalk celery, chopped	½	teaspoon ground black pepper
2	cups shredded cabbage		
1	(28 ounce) can whole peeled tomatoes, chopped	¼	teaspoon white sugar
		½	teaspoon dried basil
2	cups chicken broth	½	teaspoon dried thyme
3	carrots, chopped	¼	teaspoon curry powder

1. Place the lentils in a stockpot or a Dutch oven and add water to twice the depth of the lentils. Bring to a boil; reduce heat and simmer for about 15 minutes. Drain and rinse lentils; return them to the pot.
2. Add onion, celery, cabbage, tomatoes, chicken broth, carrots, and garlic to the pot and season with salt, pepper, sugar, basil, thyme, and curry powder. Simmer for 1½ to 2 hours or to desired tenderness.
Yield: 6 (1 cup) servings.

Per serving: 118 calories, 7g protein, 22g carbohydrate, 1g fat, 8g fiber, 0mg cholesterol, 948mg sodium

◄ OUT-OF-THE-ORDINARY

Prep Time: 20 minutes

Cook Time: 2 hours 20 minutes

Average Rating: ★★★★★

What other cooks have done:

"This was a big hit with everyone in my family. It was very easy. It's the sort of meal where anything goes—you can throw in just about any kind of vegetable. I'm not usually a big lentil or vegetable soup fan, but this was surprisingly good. The leftovers were good for lunch the next day, too."

Cozy Cottage Beef Stew

Submitted by: **Cat**

"This is a delicious blend of tender beef and vegetables, with just the right amount of thick, flavorful broth to tie everything together. Add a loaf of crusty bread for a perfect meal when you're on the run or for sitting down together and sharing the day's events. This can also be reheated in the microwave."

SLOW-COOKER CREATION ▶

Prep Time: 20 minutes

Cook Time: 6 hours

Average Rating: ★★★★☆

What other cooks have done:

"This recipe was a big hit in my home! The flavors blended really well, and it was even better when reheated a few days later. It was easy and quick to put together. My husband sopped up every last drop with his bread and took another portion to work the next day for lunch. A keeper for sure!"

¾ pound beef stew meat, cut into 1 inch cubes
2 onions, diced
3 cloves garlic, minced
1 large stalk celery, minced
2 carrots, finely chopped
¼ pound green beans, cut into 1 inch pieces
8 ounces fresh mushrooms, coarsely chopped
3 potatoes, peeled and diced
1 (14.5 ounce) can crushed tomatoes
1 (8 ounce) can tomato sauce
1 bay leaf
½ teaspoon ground black pepper
½ teaspoon dried thyme
¼ teaspoon dried marjoram
2 (14 ounce) cans fat-free chicken broth
½ cup all-purpose flour
2 (10.5 ounce) cans beef consommé

1. In a slow cooker, combine beef, onion, garlic, celery, carrot, green beans, mushrooms, and potatoes. Pour in the tomatoes and tomato sauce. Season with bay leaf, pepper, thyme, and marjoram. Stir together chicken broth and flour. Pour chicken broth mixture and beef consommé into slow cooker and stir.

2. Cover and cook on Low for 6 hours. Remove bay leaf before serving. **Yield:** 8 servings.

Per serving: 273 calories, 22g protein, 28g carbohydrate, 8g fat, 4g fiber, 37mg cholesterol, 743mg sodium

Momma OB's Chicken Chili

Submitted by: **Betty O'Brien**

"This is my version of chicken chili. It was thrown together for work, and everyone loved it."

½ tablespoon olive oil
2 pounds skinless, boneless chicken breast halves, cubed
1 tablespoon Italian seasoning, divided
2 (28 ounce) cans whole peeled tomatoes
1 (16 ounce) can chili beans, rinsed and drained

1 (15 ounce) can kidney beans, rinsed and drained
1 (1.25 ounce) package chili seasoning mix
1 (4 ounce) can diced green chile peppers
1 onion, minced
3 cloves garlic, minced
½ cup water

1. Heat oil in a skillet over medium heat and add the chicken and half of the Italian seasoning. Cook, stirring frequently, until chicken is no longer pink and juices run clear.

2. Place the remaining Italian seasoning, tomatoes, chili beans, kidney beans, chili seasoning, chile peppers, onion, garlic, and water in a slow cooker. Stir in chicken and juices.

3. Cover and cook on High for 3 hours. **Yield:** 8 servings.

Per serving: 269 calories, 33g protein, 28g carbohydrate, 3g fat, 6g fiber, 66mg cholesterol, 785mg sodium

◀ SLOW-COOKER CREATION

Prep Time: 15 minutes

Cook Time: 3 hours 10 minutes

Average Rating: ★★★★★

What other cooks have done:

"I wanted to find a chicken chili recipe, and I stumbled onto this one. It was very easy and exceptionally good. I liked that it wasn't too spicy. The leftovers were even better the next day!"

Black Bean Chili

Submitted by: **Jane Dagenhart**
"This chili is best when prepared with fresh vegetables, but it's still delicious with canned or frozen veggies. Serve this by itself or over rice."

1	tablespoon olive oil	1	cup fresh corn kernels
1	onion, chopped	1	teaspoon ground black pepper
2	red bell peppers, seeded and chopped	1	teaspoon ground cumin
1	jalapeño pepper, seeded and minced	1	tablespoon chili powder
10	fresh mushrooms, quartered	2	(15 ounce) cans black beans, rinsed and drained
6	roma (plum) tomatoes, diced	1½	cups chicken broth
		1	teaspoon salt

1. Heat oil in a large saucepan over medium-high heat. Sauté the onion, red bell peppers, jalapeño, mushrooms, tomatoes, and corn in oil for 10 minutes or until the onion is translucent. Season with black pepper, cumin, and chili powder. Stir in the black beans, chicken broth, and salt. Bring to a boil.

2. Remove 1½ cups of the soup to a blender or food processor; puree and stir back into the soup. Serve hot. **Yield:** 8 servings.

Per serving: 167 calories, 9g protein, 28g carbohydrate, 3g fat, 10g fiber, 0mg cholesterol, 901mg sodium

Brand-Name Classics

Turn to your favorite convenience products to create delicious home-cooked meals with ease. These trusted brands have their own food traditions to share with your family.

Herb and Garlic Cheese Spread

Submitted by: **McCormick® & Company**

"This savory herb-flavored cheese spread, highlighted with garlic, is incredibly easy to prepare and can be made up to a week in advance of your party."

MAKE-AHEAD ▶

Prep Time: 10 minutes

Chill Time: 2 hours

Average Rating: ★★★★★

What other cooks have done:

"This is absolutely delicious melted on top of a grilled steak. I also use it on hot sandwiches. Sometimes we just eat it spread on crackers for a quick snack. Very yummy and easy to make."

1   (8 ounce) package cream cheese, softened
½   cup butter, softened
¾   teaspoon McCORMICK® Dill Weed
½   teaspoon McCORMICK® Thyme Leaves
¼   teaspoon McCORMICK® Oregano Leaves
¼   teaspoon McCORMICK® Garlic Powder
¼   teaspoon McCORMICK® Ground Black Pepper
¼   teaspoon McCORMICK® Season-All® Seasoned Salt

1. Combine all ingredients in food processor or mixer. Mix until well blended. Cover and refrigerate at least 2 hours or up to 1 week. **Yield:** 11 (2 tablespoon) servings.

Per serving: 146 calories, 2g protein, 1g carbohydrate, 16g fat, 0g fiber, 45mg cholesterol, 173mg sodium

Cheddary Artichoke Snacks

Submitted by: **Kraft® Foods**

"Try this fun and easy appetizer."

RESTAURANT FARE ▶

Prep Time: 10 minutes

Cook Time: 3 minutes

Average Rating: ★★★★★

What other cooks have done:

"My husband and I loved this recipe. It was so delicious, and we thought that it looked and tasted like an appetizer you would order in a restaurant! I used sun-dried tomato-basil-and-garlic-Parmesan bread for an extra kick."

20   (½-inch) slices French bread, toasted
1   (6 ounce) jar marinated artichoke hearts, drained and chopped
¼   cup sliced roasted red bell peppers
2   tablespoons sliced green onion
1   (10 ounce) package CRACKER BARREL® Extra Sharp Cheddar Cheese, cut into 20 slices
Sliced roasted red bell pepper and green onion (optional)

1. Preheat broiler.
2. Top toast slices with artichokes, ¼ cup bell pepper, green onions, and cheese. Place on a baking sheet.
3. Broil in the preheated oven for 2 to 3 minutes or until cheese begins to melt. Garnish with additional sliced red bell pepper and green onion, if desired. **Yield:** 20 servings.

Per serving: 130 calories, 5g protein, 14g carbohydrate, 6g fat, 1g fiber, 15 mg cholesterol, 270mg sodium

Layered Artichoke and Cheese Spread

Submitted by: **McCormick® & Company**

"Layered Artichoke and Cheese Spread makes an attractive addition to your holiday table. Artichoke hearts, cheese, chives, dill weed, and garlic make a great combination."

1	(14 ounce) can water-packed artichoke hearts, drained	¼	cup olive oil
1	tablespoon fresh lemon juice	1	cup grated Parmesan cheese McCORMICK® Ground Black Pepper to taste
2	tablespoons McCORMICK® Freeze-Dried Chives	⅛	teaspoon salt
1	teaspoon McCORMICK® Dill Weed	2	(8 ounce) containers whipped cream cheese
½	teaspoon McCORMICK® Garlic Powder	⅓	cup roasted red bell peppers, drained, patted dry, and chopped

1. Finely chop artichokes in food processor. Add lemon juice, chives, dill weed, and garlic powder; pulse to combine. With motor running, add olive oil in a steady stream until combined. Add Parmesan, black pepper to taste, and salt; pulse to combine.

2. Layer ingredients in each of 2 (1½ cup) glass bowls as follows: half of 1 cream cheese tub, one-fourth of bell peppers, half of artichoke mixture, half of remaining cream cheese tub, and one-fourth of bell peppers. Cover and refrigerate at least 2 hours or up to 1 week.

Yield: 36 (2 teaspoon) servings.

Per serving: 75 calories, 2g protein, 2g carbohydrate, 7g fat, 1g fiber, 17mg cholesterol, 184mg sodium

◀ PARTY FOOD

Prep Time: 30 minutes

Chill Time: 2 hours

Average Rating: ★★★★★

What other cooks have done:

"A luscious cheese spread—the layering of the artichoke and herb mixture with the cream cheese makes this recipe a delight for the palate. I used pickled red pepper (a commercial product with a touch of red wine vinegar), which further enhanced the flavors. Wonderful on crackers or stuffed in celery. A hands-down hit at a New Year's gathering."

Double Peanut Snack Mix

Submitted by: **The J.M. Smucker Company**

"This easy snack made with cereal squares and JIF® Peanut Butter is sure to satisfy anyone's sweet tooth. A great munchie for a movie night!"

4 cups sweet shredded oat cereal	½ cup JIF® Creamy Peanut Butter
1 cup peanuts	1 teaspoon ground cinnamon
½ cup butter or margarine	

1. Preheat oven to 350°F (175°C).

2. In a large bowl, combine cereal and peanuts.

3. In small saucepan over low heat, stir butter or margarine, JIF® peanut butter, and cinnamon until butter and JIF® are melted. Stir until blended.

4. Slowly pour over cereal mixture, mixing well.

5. Spread mixture in a 9x13 inch pan.

6. Bake in the preheated oven for 10 to 12 minutes, stirring occasionally. Cool before serving. **Yield:** 8 servings.

Per serving: 392 calories, 11g protein, 26g carbohydrate, 30g fat, 5g fiber, 31mg cholesterol, 297mg sodium

Black Bean Pinwheels

Submitted by: **Kraft® Foods**

"Try this fun and easy appetizer."

4 ounces (½ of 8 ounce package) PHILADELPHIA® Cream Cheese, softened	¼ teaspoon onion salt
	1 cup canned black beans, rinsed and drained
½ cup KRAFT® Shredded Monterey Jack Cheese with Jalapeño Peppers or KRAFT® Shredded Monterey Jack Cheese	3 TACO BELL® HOME ORIGINALS® Flour Tortillas
¼ cup sour cream	1 (16 ounce) jar TACO BELL® HOME ORIGINALS® Thick 'N Chunky Salsa

1. Mix cheeses, sour cream, and onion salt at medium speed with an electric mixer until well blended.

2. Place beans in a food processor container fitted with a steel blade or blender container; cover. Process until smooth. Spread a thin layer of beans evenly on each tortilla; spread cheese mixture over beans.

3. Roll up tortillas tightly. Wrap individually in plastic wrap. Refrigerate 30 minutes. Cut ends from rolls; discard. Cut each roll into 5 slices. Serve with salsa. **Yield:** 15 servings.

Per serving: 90 calories, 4g protein, 8g carbohydrate, 5g fat, 2g fiber, 15mg cholesterol, 130mg sodium

Black Olive and Goat Cheese Croustade

Submitted by: **Lindsay® Olives**

"Let store-bought pizza dough make you look like a kitchen pro! A delicious spread of Lindsay® Black Ripe Pitted Olives and sautéed leeks, topped with goat cheese and fresh herbs, makes for impressive party fare without the fuss."

1	teaspoon unsalted butter	3	ounces crumbled goat cheese
¼	cup diced leeks	1	teaspoon chopped fresh thyme
¼	cup diced LINDSAY® Black Ripe Pitted Olives	1	teaspoon chopped fresh oregano
1	(10 ounce) can refrigerated pizza dough		

1. Preheat oven to 400°F (200°C). Line a baking sheet with parchment paper; lightly grease parchment paper.
2. Heat butter in a small sauté pan over medium heat. Add leeks and cook for 3 to 4 minutes or until soft. Remove from heat and stir in olives. Set aside.
3. Cut pizza dough into 20 (½ ounce) pieces. Shape into 2 inch circles and place on prepared baking sheet.
4. Bake in the preheated oven for 7 to 8 minutes.
5. Remove from oven and spread each disk with olive mixture. Top with goat cheese and bake for 5 to 7 more minutes. Sprinkle with fresh herbs just before serving. **Yield:** 8 servings.

Per serving: 145 calories, 6g protein, 18g carbohydrate, 6g fat, 1g fiber, 10mg cholesterol, 321mg sodium

◄ PARTY FOOD
Prep Time: 20 minutes
Cook Time: 20 minutes
Average Rating: ★★★★☆
What other cooks have done:
"I was in a rush to make an appetizer that I could take to a holiday potluck. This appetizer was so easy to make, and the other guests were so impressed that many of them asked me for the recipe. This dish is a keeper!"

Strawberry Lemonade

Submitted by: **Kraft® Foods**

"You'll be delighted with this favorite from Kraft®."

6	cups cold water, divided	1	cup strawberry halves
1	(2.2 ounce) tub CRYSTAL LIGHT® Lemonade or Pink Lemonade Flavor Low Calorie Soft Drink Mix		

1. Place 2 cups water, drink mix, and strawberries in a blender; cover. Blend on high speed until smooth. Pour into a large plastic or glass pitcher. Stir in remaining 4 cups water. Serve over ice cubes. **Yield:** 7 (1 cup) servings.

Per serving: 10 calories, 0g protein, 2g carbohydrate, 0g fat, 1g fiber, 0mg cholesterol, 5mg sodium

◄ 5 INGREDIENTS OR LESS
Prep Time: 5 minutes
Average Rating: ★★★★★
What other cooks have done:
"I am always looking for ways to add fruit into my family's diet, and this is great. Both my kids and my husband love it. This is a refreshing drink on a hot day, and it's especially good served with barbecue."

Herb-Marinated London Broil

Submitted by: **McCormick® & Company**

"This marinade imparts a tantalizing herb flavor to a grilled London broil. Thinly slice any leftover steak for French-dip sandwiches or serve the steak slices over a Caesar salad."

FROM THE GRILL ▶

Prep Time: 5 minutes

Marinate Time: 30 minutes

Cook Time: 21 minutes

Average Rating: ★★★★★

What other cooks have done:

"I seared the outside of the meat and then turned the grill down just a tad to cook the meat the rest of the way. The steak was juicy and perfect. I boiled the leftover marinade for 1 minute and rubbed it on asparagus that we grilled as a side. It was so good!"

½ cup dry red wine

¼ cup olive oil

2 teaspoons Worcestershire sauce

2 teaspoons McCORMICK® Italian Seasoning

1½ teaspoons McCORMICK® Garlic Powder

1 teaspoon McCORMICK® Season-All® Seasoning Salt

1 teaspoon McCORMICK® Coarse Grind Black Pepper

1 London broil or top round steak (about 1 inch thick)

1. Combine wine, olive oil, Worcestershire sauce, and seasonings in a large zip-top plastic bag. Place steak in bag and seal. Turn bag gently to distribute marinade. Refrigerate 30 minutes or up to 3 hours for a stronger flavor, turning bag occasionally.

2. Preheat grill for medium heat.

3. Remove steak from marinade; reserving marinade. Bring marinade to a boil and boil for 1 minute. Grill steak, brushing with reserved marinade, 8 to 10 minutes per side or until desired doneness. Discard leftover marinade. Cut into thin slices across the grain.

Yield: 6 servings.

Per serving: 257 calories, 26g protein, 9g carbohydrate, 13g fat, 0g fiber, 72mg cholesterol, 178mg sodium

Texas Grilled Steak

Submitted by: **McCormick® & Company**
"Excite your taste buds with the robust flavor of Texas Grilled Steak, served thinly sliced, in warm tortillas."

1½ pounds flank steak	Flour tortillas
1 tablespoon olive oil	Salsa
1 tablespoon McCORMICK® Chili Powder	Shredded Cheddar cheese
	Sour cream
¼ teaspoon McCORMICK® Oregano Leaves	
2 tablespoons lime juice	

1. Brush steak with oil.
2. Combine the next 3 ingredients to make a paste. Rub paste over steak and refrigerate overnight
3. Preheat grill or broiler.
4. Cook on the preheated grill or broil in the preheated oven for 20 minutes or to desired doneness.
5. Thinly slice steak. Wrap steak in warm flour tortillas. Serve with salsa, Cheddar cheese, and sour cream. **Yield:** 6 servings.

Per serving: 417 calories, 33g protein, 24g carbohydrate, 21g fat, 1g fiber, 70mg cholesterol, 600mg sodium

◄ FROM THE GRILL

Prep Time: 5 minutes

Marinate Time: overnight

Cook Time: 20 minutes

Average Rating: ★★★★★

What other cooks have done:

"I used this recipe to make fajitas for lunch. I added some garlic powder, and they turned out very well."

Tortilla Talk

Both corn and flour tortillas are a familiar sight these days. They are found as easily in countless Mexican dishes, such as enchiladas, tacos, and burritos, as they are in sandwich rollups, southwestern lasagnas, and other fusion recipes.

The differences between corn and flour tortillas are few. Corn tortillas are made from ground corn flour called masa; they have a coarser texture and are smaller than flour tortillas. Flour tortillas, made from wheat flour, are whiter, have a smoother texture, and are larger than corn tortillas. Both can be found prepackaged in the refrigerator section of most supermarkets. Make this convenient food a part of your pantry for delicious meals that are quick and easy.

Get creative with your tortillas and try forming them into bowls to hold salads. Place a tortilla over an inverted 10 ounce custard cup coated with cooking spray. Bake at 400°F (200°C) for 10 minutes or until crisp. Cool the tortilla cup completely on a wire rack before filling with salad.

If you have any leftover tortillas after making a recipe, don't throw them away. Cut them into triangles or thin strips and fry or bake them to top a salad or soup, or sprinkle them over your favorite casserole.

For more information, visit **Allrecipes.com**

Individual Meat Loaves *(pictured on facing page)*

Submitted by: **McCormick® & Company**

"Perfectly seasoned Individual Meat Loaves are time-savers for a weeknight family meal."

What other cooks have done:

"This was a hit with the family, especially my wife, who got a night off from cooking. It was simple and good enough to make every week. I followed the recipe exactly, except when the loaves had about a minute left to cook, I put American cheese on top of them to melt. This was a definite hit with busy parents and hungry kids."

1	egg
2	pounds lean ground beef
1	cup ketchup, divided
1	cup soft breadcrumbs
2	tablespoons McCORMICK® Parsley Flakes
2	tablespoons McCORMICK® Minced Onion
1	teaspoon McCORMICK® Ground Mustard

½ teaspoon McCORMICK® Season-All® Seasoned Salt

½ teaspoon McCORMICK® Basil Leaves

½ teaspoon McCORMICK® Oregano Leaves

1. Preheat oven to 375°F (190°C).

2. Combine first 8 ingredients, reserving ¼ cup ketchup. Mix thoroughly; shape into 8 loaves. Place in a lightly greased 9x13 inch pan.

3. Combine reserved ¼ cup ketchup, basil, and oregano; set aside.

4. Bake in the preheated oven for 30 minutes or until internal temperature reaches 165°F (75°C). Spoon sauce evenly over loaves. Bake 10 more minutes. **Yield:** 8 servings.

Per serving: 329 calories, 26g protein, 19g carbohydrate, 16g fat, 1g fiber, 104mg cholesterol, 613mg sodium

Individual Meat Loaves

Chicken and Artichoke Pizza with Fresh
Tomatoes, page 120

Cookies 'n' Creme Fudge,
page 127

Baked Chicken Nuggets,
page 136

Roast Chicken with Potato, Olives, and Greek Seasoning

Roast Chicken with Potato, Olives, and Greek Seasoning *(pictured on facing page)*

Submitted by: **McCormick® & Company**

"Chef Suzanne Goin of Lucques in Los Angeles uses Greek Seasoning to add an authentic Greek taste to a roast chicken dinner including roasted potatoes and onions, plus spinach and olives, highlighted with feta cheese."

4 tablespoons McCORMICK® Gourmet Collection™ Greek Seasoning, divided	2 tablespoons olive oil
2 tablespoons butter, softened	⅓ cup pitted kalamata or black olives
1 (3 to 4 pound) whole chicken	¼ teaspoon salt
2 lemons, cut in half	¼ teaspoon McCORMICK® Gourmet Collection™ Coarse Grind Black Pepper
1 medium red onion, cut into wedges	6 ounces fresh spinach, rinsed and patted dry (optional)
6 small Yukon gold potatoes, each cut into 6 wedges	2 ounces feta cheese, crumbled

1. Preheat oven to 375°F (190°C).

2. Mix 2 tablespoons Greek Seasoning with butter. Rub three-fourths of butter mixture under chicken skin (breasts and legs) and rub remaining mixture on the outside of chicken. Sprinkle 1 tablespoon Greek seasoning over outside of chicken and stuff 3 lemon halves inside the chicken cavity.

3. Combine onion, potato, olive oil, and remaining tablespoon Greek seasoning. Place chicken in a roasting pan and arrange potato mixture around chicken.

4. Roast in the preheated oven for 1¼ to 1½ hours.

5. Remove chicken from oven; let rest 10 minutes. Transfer vegetables to a large skillet. Add olives, salt, and pepper. Cook 1 to 2 minutes over low heat. Toss in spinach just before serving, if desired. Cook 1 to 2 minutes or until leaves wilt. Remove from heat; gently stir in feta and juice of remaining lemon half. Remove vegetables to a large platter. Carve chicken and serve over vegetables. **Yield:** 6 servings.

Per serving: 490 calories, 37g protein, 26g carbohydrate, 28g fat, 5g fiber, 118mg cholesterol, 555mg sodium

◄ COMPANY IS COMING

Prep Time: 10 minutes

Cook Time: 1 hour 35 minutes

Stand Time: 10 minutes

Average Rating: ★★★★★

What other cooks have done:

"Wonderful dish for entertaining. I used Swiss chard instead of spinach because that's what I had in the fridge. It gave the veggies more 'bite.' Also, I cooked the chicken, breast side down, covered with foil for the first hour, and then I removed the foil. I brushed some melted butter on top during the last 15 minutes to make the chicken brown."

Chipotle Roasted Chicken with Potatoes

Submitted by: **McCormick® & Company**

"The distinctive smoky-sweet flavor and heat of the chipotle chile pepper, a dried and smoked jalapeño, is much sought after by those who love Mexican cooking. Savor the authentic flavors in this rub for roasted chicken and enjoy this easy-to-use form of chipotle chiles."

1½ teaspoons McCORMICK® Gourmet Collection™ Chipotle Chile Pepper

1 teaspoon McCORMICK® Gourmet Collection™ Paprika

1 teaspoon McCORMICK® Gourmet Collection™ Oregano Leaves

1 teaspoon McCORMICK® Gourmet Collection™ Garlic Salt

½ teaspoon McCORMICK® Gourmet Collection™ Ground Cumin

1½ pounds small (1½ to 2 inch) red or white potatoes, quartered

1 tablespoon vegetable oil

2 teaspoons brown sugar

1 (3 pound) chicken, quartered

1 tablespoon chopped fresh cilantro

1. Preheat oven to 400°F (200°C). Line a jellyroll pan with aluminum foil and spray with cooking spray.

2. Combine chipotle chile pepper, paprika, oregano, garlic salt, and cumin. In a large bowl, toss potatoes with oil and 1 teaspoon of the spice mixture. Mix brown sugar with remaining spice mixture and set aside.

3. Rub chicken pieces on both sides with brown sugar mixture, rubbing a little under the skin as well. Arrange chicken, skin side up, on half of pan. Arrange potatoes, in a single layer, on other half of pan. Loosely cover chicken and potatoes with aluminum foil.

4. Bake in the preheated oven for 40 minutes; remove foil covering chicken and potatoes. Turn and rearrange potatoes. Bake, uncovered, 20 more minutes or until a meat thermometer inserted into thickest part of a chicken thigh registers 180°F (80°C) and potatoes are tender. Garnish with cilantro. **Yield:** 4 servings.

Per serving: 664 calories, 60g protein, 34g carbohydrate, 32g fat, 4g fiber, 182mg cholesterol, 428mg sodium

Peach-Pepper Chicken

Submitted by: **The J.M. Smucker Company**

"You'll love this delightful dish of pan-fried chicken pieces in an Asian-inspired peach sauce. Using Smucker's® Peach Preserves makes this an easy weeknight dinner."

1	(3 to 4 pound) chicken, cut into serving pieces
½	teaspoon salt
¼	cup butter or margarine
¾	cup SMUCKER'S® Peach Preserves
1	medium onion, sliced
1	tablespoon lemon juice
½	teaspoon ground ginger
1	medium green, red, or yellow bell pepper, cut into strips
1	teaspoon cornstarch
2	tablespoons water
	Hot cooked rice

1. Sprinkle chicken with salt.

2. Melt butter in a large skillet. Add chicken pieces and brown lightly on all sides.

3. Stir together SMUCKER'S® preserves, onion, lemon juice, ginger, and bell pepper. Pour over chicken; cover and simmer 25 minutes.

4. Blend cornstarch with water. Stir into mixture and cook until sauce is slightly thickened. Serve with rice. **Yield:** 4 servings.

Per serving: 718 calories, 43g protein, 44g carbohydrate, 41g fat, 1g fiber, 154mg cholesterol, 523mg sodium

◄ KID-FRIENDLY

Prep Time: 10 minutes

Cook Time: 35 minutes

Average Rating: ★★★★★

What other cooks have done:

"My 12-year-old son had to cook for a school project, and he chose this recipe. We used boneless chicken breasts and red bell peppers instead of green. We used jarred peaches as a garnish. This was delicious, quick, and easy!"

Chicken and Artichoke Pizza with Fresh Tomatoes *(pictured on page 114)*

Submitted by: **Tyson Foods**
"Make a delicious gourmet pizza at home in less time than it takes for delivery. Serve with a tossed salad."

QUICK & EASY ▶

Prep Time: 15 minutes

Cook Time: 25 minutes

Average Rating: ★★★★★

What other cooks have done:

"I added a box of chopped frozen spinach, thawed and drained, and a 4 ounce container of feta cheese. I brushed a homemade crust with melted butter and minced garlic and prebaked it. Then I layered the spinach, tomatoes and basil, chicken and artichokes, and feta cheese and mozzarella on the crust. Better than anything in a gourmet restaurant!"

2	TYSON® Fresh Boneless, Skinless Chicken Breasts
1	(6 ounce) jar marinated artichoke hearts, undrained
1	large clove garlic, minced
1	(14 ounce) prebaked pizza crust
4	roma (plum) tomatoes, sliced
½	teaspoon dried basil leaves
1½	cups shredded mozzarella cheese

1. Preheat oven to 425°F (220°C). Wash hands.
2. Cut chicken breasts into ¾ inch pieces. Wash hands and cutting board. Drain artichoke hearts, reserving liquid. Coarsely chop artichoke hearts.
3. Place artichoke liquid in a large nonstick skillet and bring to boil over medium-high heat. Cook until most of liquid has evaporated, about 1 minute. Add chicken and garlic to skillet. Cook chicken 3 to 5 minutes or until done and internal temperature reaches 170°F (75°C). Stir in artichoke hearts. Remove from heat.
4. Place pizza crust on a baking sheet; top evenly with tomato slices. Top with chicken mixture; sprinkle with basil. Top with cheese.
5. Bake in the preheated oven for 12 to 17 minutes or until hot and cheese is melted. Cut pizza into wedges. Refrigerate leftovers.

Yield: 6 servings.

Per serving: 177 calories, 21g protein, 6g carbohydrate, 8g fat, 2g fiber, 49mg cholesterol, 262mg sodium

Smucker's® Chicken Salad with Wild Rice, Pecans, Grapes, and Orange Dressing

Submitted by: **The J.M. Smucker Company**

"A simple orange marmalade dressing—made with Smucker's® Sugar Free Orange Marmalade, raspberry vinegar, and orange rind—gives this salad a fresh spring taste."

CRISCO® Cooking Spray
4 (4 ounce) skinless, boneless chicken breasts
3½ cups cooked wild rice
1 cup red or green grapes
1 cup sliced green onions
¼ cup chopped pecans, toasted (optional)
1 tablespoon grated orange rind
1 cup SMUCKER'S® Sugar Free Orange Marmalade
⅓ cup raspberry vinegar
¼ teaspoon salt
⅛ teaspoon ground black pepper
Lettuce leaves (optional)

1. Preheat oven to 450°F (230°C). Coat an 11x17 inch baking dish with CRISCO® cooking spray.

2. Spray a large skillet with cooking spray; heat over medium–high heat until hot. Add chicken; cook 2 minutes on each side or until lightly browned. Place chicken in prepared dish.

3. Bake in the preheated oven for 20 minutes or until cooked through. Remove chicken; cool and cut into ¼ inch strips.

4. In a large bowl, combine chicken, rice, grapes, green onions, and, if desired, pecans. Toss well and set aside. In a small bowl, combine orange rind and next 4 ingredients; stir well. Pour over chicken mixture; toss well. Serve salad at room temperature on lettuce-lined plates, if desired. **Yield:** 7 servings.

Per serving: 245 calories, 19g protein, 37g carbohydrate, 5g fat, 3g fiber, 38mg cholesterol, 133mg sodium

◄ COVERED-DISH FAVORITE

Prep Time: 15 minutes

Cook Time: 24 minutes

Average Rating: ★★★★★

What other cooks have done:

"I made this recipe as a main dish, and I served it cold—excellent on a hot day. I liked the contrasting flavors. I did not have wild rice, so I used three brown-and-wild rice pouches; also, I did not have enough pecans, so I added some crushed cashew nuts. Everything worked well. Next time, I'll increase the amount of raspberry vinegar to make more dressing, and perhaps I'll add more grapes."

Turnaround Turkey and Rice

Submitted by: **McCormick® & Company**

"By using leftover cooked turkey, this recipe not only tastes great but is also quick enough for a weeknight treat."

QUICK & EASY ▶

Prep Time: 10 minutes

Cook Time: 17 minutes

Average Rating: ★★★★★

What other cooks have done:

"I loved this! The yummy turkey and gravy stew tasted great over white rice. This is nothing fancy, but it's great comfort food."

2 tablespoons butter	¼ cup milk
2 stalks celery, chopped	2 tablespoons all-purpose flour
1 small onion, chopped	1 teaspoon McCORMICK® Season-All® Seasoned Salt
1 cup cooked turkey, cut into cubes	
1½ cups water	Hot cooked rice
1 (0.87 ounce) package McCORMICK® Turkey Gravy Mix	

1. In a saucepan, melt butter over medium heat. Add celery and onion and cook for 5 minutes or until tender, stirring occasionally. Add cooked turkey.
2. Blend water, Gravy Mix, milk, flour, and Season-All; pour over turkey mixture. Stir. Bring to a boil. Reduce heat and simmer 5 minutes. Serve over rice. **Yield:** 4 servings.

Per serving: 164 calories, 12g protein, 9g carbohydrate, 8g fat, 1g fiber, 43mg cholesterol, 490mg sodium

Shrimp with Red Curry and Basil

Submitted by: **McCormick® & Company**

"This quick and easy shrimp recipe, created by Chef Paul Kahan of the Blackbird in Chicago, has a gentle Asian flavor. The addition of just ½ cup sour cream blends the flavors perfectly."

COMPANY IS COMING ▶

Prep Time: 15 minutes

Cook Time: 12 minutes

Average Rating: ★★★★☆

What other cooks have done:

"I love this recipe. I add some cornstarch to thicken the sauce, and I also add more sugar because I like it sweeter. I often throw in some snow peas; the bright green makes the dish more pleasing to the eye."

1 tablespoon butter	1 teaspoon fresh lime juice
2 pounds large shrimp, peeled and deveined (32 to 40 shrimp)	4 large fresh basil leaves, rolled lengthwise and thinly sliced
2 green onions, thinly sliced	1 teaspoon salt
2 cloves garlic, thinly sliced	1 teaspoon white sugar
1 cup white wine	½ cup sour cream
1½ teaspoons McCORMICK® Gourmet Collection™ Red Curry Powder	Hot cooked rice or noodles

1. In a large nonstick skillet, melt butter over medium heat. Add shrimp, green onions, and garlic; sauté 3 minutes.
2. Stir in wine. Cover and cook on high heat 2 to 3 minutes or until shrimp turn pink. Remove shrimp and keep warm.

3. Add red curry powder, lime juice, basil, salt, sugar, and sour cream to skillet. Simmer 2 minutes over low heat. Return shrimp to pan. Warm gently. Serve over rice or noodles. **Yield:** 6 servings.

Per serving: 255 calories, 32g protein, 4g carbohydrate, 9g fat, 0g fiber, 244mg cholesterol, 645mg sodium

1-2-3 Vegetable Chili

Submitted by: **Kraft® Foods**
"A delicious, satisfying recipe that the whole family will enjoy."

1   (28 ounce) can tomatoes, undrained, cut up
1   (16 ounce) jar TACO BELL® HOME ORIGINALS© Thick 'N Chunky Salsa
1   (15 ounce) can black beans, rinsed and drained
1   (10 ounce) package frozen whole kernel corn
1   cup halved zucchini slices
1   teaspoon chili powder
1   (8 ounce) package KRAFT® 2% Milk Shredded Reduced Fat Mild Cheddar Cheese, divided

1. Mix tomatoes with their liquid, salsa, beans, corn, zucchini, and chili powder in a saucepan over medium-high heat. Bring to a boil.
2. Reduce heat to low; simmer 10 minutes, stirring occasionally.
3. Sprinkle 2 tablespoons cheese onto bottom of each serving bowl; top with chili. Sprinkle each serving with an additional 2 tablespoons cheese. **Yield:** 8 servings.

Per serving: 230 calories, 14g protein, 30g carbohydrate, 7g fat, 7g fiber, 20mg cholesterol, 760mg sodium

◀ QUICK & EASY

Prep Time: 10 minutes

Cook Time: 15 minutes

Average Rating: ★★★★★

What other cooks have done:
"This is the best chili I have ever had! It's so delicious, and it's perfect for vegetarians. I made a few modifications. I added a package of veggie crumbles, an extra can of black beans, about an extra cup of zucchini, and lots more chili powder (you can add to suit your taste)."

Pasta Rustica

Submitted by: **Lindsay® Olives**

"Lindsay® Black Olives or Lindsay® Green Ripe Select Olives—or even a mixture of both—are tossed into Pasta Rustica, bringing together the flavors of sweet bell pepper, mellow olive oil, and spicy pepper flakes. Finish with Parmesan cheese and enjoy!"

COMPANY IS COMING ▶

Prep Time: 25 minutes

Cook Time: 30 minutes

Average Rating: ★★★★☆

What other cooks have done:

"Very good. I added extra bacon and cut down on the oil. Be generous with the crushed red pepper flakes, garlic, and parsley (and the capers, too!). I may add chicken and extra Parmesan cheese next time."

1	pound rotini or fusilli pasta
6	slices bacon
½	cup extra virgin olive oil
2	medium onions, chopped
1	red bell pepper, chopped
¼	cup chopped parsley
4	cloves garlic, minced
½	teaspoon crushed red pepper flakes
1	(28 ounce) can roma (plum) tomatoes, undrained and coarsely chopped
½	cup LINDSAY® Black Ripe Pitted Olives or LINDSAY® Green Ripe Select Olives, sliced and drained
2	tablespoons capers, drained
½	teaspoon dried oregano
	Salt to taste (optional)
½	cup grated Parmesan cheese

1. Cook pasta according to package directions. Meanwhile, place bacon in a large, deep skillet; cook over medium-high heat until evenly browned. Drain bacon on paper towels; cut into ½ inch pieces.
2. Discard bacon drippings from skillet; add oil. Cook onions in oil over medium heat 5 minutes, stirring occasionally. Add bell pepper, parsley, garlic, and pepper flakes; cook 2 minutes. Add tomatoes and bacon; simmer 10 minutes, stirring occasionally. Stir in olives, capers, and oregano; simmer 2 minutes. Season to taste with salt, if desired.
3. Drain pasta; toss with sauce and Parmesan cheese. **Yield:** 6 servings.

Per serving: 607 calories, 18g protein, 69g carbohydrate, 29g fat, 5g fiber, 14mg cholesterol, 764mg sodium

Pumpkin Cake with Orange Glaze

Submitted by: **The J.M. Smucker Company**
"Break out the Bundt pan! This intoxicating pumpkin spice cake is drizzled with a sweet orange glaze and topped with nuts."

Cake:
- 2 cups boiling water
- ½ cup raisins
- 2 cups white sugar
- 1 cup Butter Flavor CRISCO® Shortening, melted
- 1 (16 ounce) can solid-pack pumpkin (not pumpkin pie filling)
- 4 eggs
- 2 cups PILLSBURY BEST® All-Purpose Flour
- 1 tablespoon ground cinnamon
- 2 teaspoons baking powder
- 1 teaspoon baking soda
- 1 teaspoon ground ginger
- ¾ teaspoon salt
- ¼ teaspoon ground cloves

Orange Glaze:
- 1 cup confectioners' sugar
- ¾ teaspoon grated orange rind
- 4 teaspoons orange juice
  Chopped walnuts

◀ CROWD-PLEASER
Prep Time: 18 minutes
Cook Time: 50 minutes
Cool Time: 20 minutes
Average Rating: ★★★★★

What other cooks have done:
"This is a great cake. I didn't add the raisins or the walnuts. I did add a teaspoon of vanilla, which I think added just a little punch. The glaze is very good, with just a hint of orange, and it adds moistness to the cake, although the cake doesn't really need it. I served this as part of my Thanksgiving meal, and my family loved it!"

1. Preheat oven to 350°F (175°C). Grease a 10 inch Bundt pan with Butter Flavor CRISCO®. Flour lightly.
2. Pour boiling water over raisins in a colander. Drain. Press lightly to remove excess water.
3. In a large bowl, combine white sugar, melted CRISCO® Shortening, pumpkin, and eggs in a large bowl. Beat at medium-high speed with an electric mixer 5 minutes.
4. Combine flour, cinnamon, baking powder, baking soda, ginger, salt, and cloves in a medium bowl. Add to pumpkin mixture, 1 cup at a time, beating at low speed after each addition until blended. Stir in raisins with a spoon. Pour into prepared pan.
5. Bake in the preheated oven for 40 to 50 minutes or until a toothpick inserted into center comes out clean. Cool 15 to 20 minutes before removing from pan. Place cake, top side up, on a wire rack. Cool completely. Place cake on a serving plate.
6. Combine confectioners' sugar, orange rind, and orange juice in a small bowl. Stir with a spoon to blend. Spoon over top of cake, letting excess glaze run down sides. Sprinkle with chopped nuts before glaze hardens. **Yield:** 12 servings.

Per serving: 470 calories, 5g protein, 70g carbohydrate, 20g fat, 3g fiber, 71mg cholesterol, 407mg sodium

Banana Crunch Parfaits

Submitted by: **Kraft® Foods**

"Delight your family tonight with this scrumptious dessert from Kraft®."

5 INGREDIENTS OR LESS ▶

Prep Time: 5 minutes

Average Rating: ★★★★★

What other cooks have done:

"I love this recipe. I mixed peach and piña colada yogurts with the whipped topping and also added cream cheese and a teaspoon of vanilla. I used fruit salad instead of pineapple. It was great."

1 (8 ounce) container low-fat yogurt, any variety	1 banana, sliced
1 (8 ounce) container COOL WHIP® FREE Whipped Topping, thawed and divided	1 (20 ounce) can pineapple chunks, drained
	1 cup POST SELECTS® BANANA NUT CRUNCH® Cereal

1. Stir yogurt and half of the whipped topping in a large bowl until smooth. Alternately layer yogurt mixture, banana slices, pineapple chunks, cereal, and remaining whipped topping in 6 parfait glasses; repeat layers. **Yield:** 6 servings.

Per serving: 220 calories, 3g protein, 48g carbohydrate, 4g fat, 2g fiber, 5mg cholesterol, 80mg sodium

Cherry Cheese Pie

Submitted by: **Eagle Brand®**

"Cherry pie filling tops a chilled, creamy cheesecake."

MAKE-AHEAD ▶

Prep Time: 5 minutes

Chill Time: 4 hours

Average Rating: ★★★★★

What other cooks have done:

"I have used this recipe for 20 years. It is fast, and the pie always tastes wonderful. Plus, the recipe never fails! I have substituted fat-free cream cheese, but it makes a softer pie."

1 (8 ounce) package cream cheese, softened	1 teaspoon vanilla extract
1 (14 ounce) can EAGLE BRAND® Sweetened Condensed Milk (NOT evaporated milk)	1 (8 or 9 inch) baked pie crust or graham cracker crust
⅓ cup lemon juice	1 (21 ounce) can cherry pie filling, chilled

1. In a large bowl, beat cream cheese until fluffy. Gradually beat in EAGLE BRAND® until smooth. Stir in lemon juice and vanilla.
2. Pour into crust; chill 4 hours or until set. Top with cherry pie filling before serving. Store leftovers covered in refrigerator.
Yield: 8 servings.

Per serving: 430 calories, 4g protein, 38g carbohydrate, 19g fat, 1g fiber, 32mg cholesterol, 226mg sodium

JIF® Irresistible Peanut Butter Cookies

Submitted by: **The J.M. Smucker Company**
"The classic peanut butter cookie is made even more irresistible with JIF® Peanut Butter!"

1¼ cups firmly packed light brown sugar	1 tablespoon vanilla extract
¾ cup JIF® Peanut Butter	1 egg
½ cup Butter Flavor CRISCO® Stick	1¾ cups sifted all-purpose flour
3 tablespoons milk	¾ teaspoon baking soda
	¾ teaspoon salt

1. Preheat oven to 375°F (190°C).
2. Combine brown sugar, JIF® Peanut Butter, Butter Flavor CRISCO®, milk, and vanilla in a large bowl. Beat at medium speed with an electric mixer until well blended. Add egg. Beat just until blended.
3. Combine flour, baking soda, and salt. Add to creamed mixture and beat at low speed. Mix just until blended.
4. Drop by rounded tablespoonfuls 2 inches apart onto ungreased baking sheets. Flatten slightly in a crisscross pattern with tines of a fork.
5. Bake in the preheated oven for 7 to 8 minutes per batch or until set and just beginning to brown (do not overbake). Cool 2 minutes on baking sheets. Remove cookies to wire rack to cool completely.
Yield: 2 dozen cookies.

Per cookie: 166 calories, 3g protein, 20g carbohydrate, 8g fat, 1g fiber, 9mg cholesterol, 158mg sodium

◀ CROWD-PLEASER

Prep Time: 10 minutes

Cook Time: 8 minutes per batch

Average Rating: ★★★★★

What other cooks have done:
"I've been looking for this recipe! These cookies are really chewy and yummy. Full of peanut butter flavor! I like to dip the tines of a fork in sugar and then make the crisscrosses. Don't overbake!"

Cookies 'n' Creme Fudge *(pictured on page 115)*

Submitted by: **Eagle Brand®**
"Creme-filled chocolate cookies are great in this white chocolate fudge."

3 (6 ounce) packages white chocolate baking squares	⅛ teaspoon salt
1 (14 ounce) can EAGLE BRAND® Sweetened Condensed Milk (NOT evaporated milk)	2 cups coarsely crushed chocolate creme-filled sandwich cookies

1. Line a 8x8 inch pan with aluminum foil. Lightly grease foil.
2. In a heavy saucepan over low heat, melt chocolate squares with EAGLE BRAND® and salt. Remove from heat; stir in crushed cookies. Spread evenly into prepared pan. Chill 2 hours or until firm.
3. Turn fudge onto cutting board; peel off foil and cut into squares. Store leftovers covered in refrigerator. **Yield:** 36 servings.

Per serving: 143 calories, 2g protein, 18g carbohydrate, 7g fat, 0g fiber, 9mg cholesterol, 74mg sodium

◀ HOLIDAY GIFT GIVING

Prep Time: 10 minutes

Cook Time: 10 minutes

Chill Time: 2 hours

Average Rating: ★★★★☆

What other cooks have done:
"This delicious recipe was very easy, and I say this as a first-time fudge maker! It turned out good enough to give away as Christmas presents."

Peanut Butter Marshmallow Bars

Submitted by: The J.M. Smucker Company

"An already yummy peanut butter brownie is topped with more JIF® Peanut Butter. Toasted marshmallows and chocolate syrup take it over the top!"

¼ cup firmly packed light brown sugar
½ cup Butter Flavor CRISCO® All-Vegetable Shortening
½ cup JIF® Extra Crunchy Peanut Butter
¼ cup white sugar
1 egg
1¼ cups PILLSBURY BEST® All-Purpose Flour
1 teaspoon baking powder
¼ teaspoon salt
½ cup JIF® Creamy Peanut Butter
4 cups miniature marshmallows
½ cup chocolate-flavored syrup

1. Preheat oven to 350°F (175°C). Grease a 9x13 inch baking dish.
2. For cookie base, combine brown sugar, shortening, JIF® Extra Crunchy Peanut Butter, white sugar, and egg in a large bowl. Beat at medium speed with electric mixer until well blended.
3. In a separate bowl, combine flour, baking powder, and salt. Add gradually to creamed mixture at low speed. Beat until well blended. Cover and refrigerate for 15 minutes. Press chilled cookie base into prepared dish.
4. Bake in the preheated oven for 20 minutes or until light brown (do not overbake). Cool 2 to 3 minutes.
5. For topping, place JIF® Creamy Peanut Butter in a microwave-safe measuring cup. Microwave at High for 1 minute. Pour over baked surface of cookie base. Spread to cover. Cover with marshmallows. Drizzle chocolate syrup over marshmallows. Return to oven. Bake 5 minutes or until marshmallows are light brown (do not overbake). Loosen from sides of dish with a knife. Remove dish to a wire rack. Cool completely before cutting into squares with a sharp knife.
Yield: 2 dozen bars.

Per bar: 194 calories, 4g protein, 24g carbohydrate, 10g fat, 1g fiber, 9mg cholesterol, 103mg sodium

Top 15
Kid-Friendly Recipes

Got picky eaters? These 15 recipes will have everyone smiling at the dinner table, Mom and Dad included. Turn to these mealtime miracles when you need a recipe that's guaranteed to please.

Ants on a Log

Submitted by: **Michele O'Sullivan**

"This is a fun snack that kids can make. It consists of artfully arranged celery, peanut butter, and raisins."

5 stalks celery	¼ cup raisins
½ cup peanut butter	

1. Cut the celery stalks in half. Spread with peanut butter. Sprinkle with raisins. **Yield:** 5 servings.

Per serving: 184 calories, 7g protein, 13g carbohydrate, 13g fat, 3g fiber, 0mg cholesterol, 156mg sodium

Way Easy Pizza Sauce/Breadstick Dip

Submitted by: **Dan**

"A simple tomato sauce for creating instant pizza snacks! Use as a dip for breadsticks or spread over warm French bread. Melt some cheese on top to complete the pizza experience."

1 (8 ounce) can tomato sauce	1 teaspoon minced garlic
1 (6 ounce) can tomato paste	½ teaspoon garlic salt
¼ teaspoon dried oregano	¼ teaspoon minced fresh
¼ teaspoon white sugar	parsley

1. In a medium bowl, mix all ingredients. **Yield:** 16 servings.

Per serving: 14 calories, 1g protein, 3g carbohydrate, 0g fat, 1g fiber, 0mg cholesterol, 225mg sodium

Apple Dip

Submitted by: **Rachel**

"This was a childhood treat. I was craving it, so I called my nanny, and she gave the recipe to me. It tastes like caramel. Enjoy with slices of apples for a healthy snack. Be creative—you can add peanut butter, nuts, or chocolate sauce."

1 (8 ounce) package cream cheese, softened	½ cup packed brown sugar
	1 tablespoon vanilla extract

1. In a medium bowl, combine cream cheese, brown sugar, and vanilla. Mix well until all of the brown sugar has been blended into the cream cheese. Add additional brown sugar, if necessary, to reach desired thickness. **Yield:** 4 servings.

Per serving: 273 calories, 4g protein, 20g carbohydrate, 20g fat, 0g fiber, 62mg cholesterol, 173mg sodium

◀ 5 INGREDIENTS OR LESS

Prep Time: 5 minutes

Average Rating: ★★★★

What other cooks have done:

"Very good and simple dip! I used strawberry-flavored cream cheese, and I doubled the recipe for a party. It got rave reviews! Very good the next morning on toast and bagels."

Kids in the Kitchen

The exclamation "don't play with your food!" may roll off your tongue as readily as your children's own names because you've repeated the phrase so many times. But when the complaints of boredom begin to roll in, maybe you should reconsider the rule. Inviting kids into the kitchen to make their own snacks and meals—and even letting them play with their food in the process—can spark a lifelong interest in cooking and in trying new foods, not to mention that it will keep them occupied during those long, hot afternoons. Many simple recipes are easy enough for kids to try. Just remember to take over any duties that involve knives or high heat until the kids are old enough to do those things themselves (but always under supervision).

Freezer Fun

We've never met a kid whose eyes didn't light up when presented with any sort of sweet frozen treat. It's easy and fun (not to mention economical) to let kids make their own frozen pops. They can invent their own flavors—from plain frozen orange, apple, or grape juice to fantastic concoctions of mashed strawberries and bananas mixed with pineapple juice. You can also freeze yogurt or pudding to make creamy, no-drip pops. If you don't have popsicle molds, you can improvise with small paper or plastic cups. Fill each cup almost to the top, stretch a piece of plastic wrap over the top, and then poke a wooden popsicle stick or plastic spoon through it. The plastic wrap will keep the stick in place until the pops are frozen.

Pudding Paintings

The kids' jaws will drop when you set them down at the table and let them fingerpaint with pudding! Make a few different flavors of pudding in different colors—vanilla, chocolate, butterscotch, and pistachio will give them a good variety—and then cover the table with a plastic tablecloth. Set out bowls of pudding along with some dishes of edible decorations, such as pretzel sticks, raisins, chocolate chips, dried apricots, and shredded coconut. Give each child a large sheet of wax paper to use as a "canvas," and then just let the kids go to it.

- Jennifer Anderson

For more information, visit **Allrecipes.com**

Kid's Favorite Meatballs

Submitted by: **Jen**

"This easy recipe is perfect for a young cook. It's so delicious that any kid will love it! This dish goes very well with garlic mashed potatoes and a vegetable side dish. For a shortcut, I use frozen precut peppers and onions."

FREEZER FRESH ▶

Prep Time: 30 minutes

Cook Time: 1 hour 10 minutes

Average Rating: ★★★★☆

What other cooks have done:

"I loved how easy it was to make these very tasty meatballs. Use only lean meat to combat greasiness. This recipe works well with chicken soup with star-shaped noodles, and my daughter thought having stars on her meatballs was fun."

1	tablespoon butter	½	cup water
1	cup chopped green bell pepper	1	pound ground beef
1	cup chopped onion	1	egg
1	(10.75 ounce) can condensed tomato soup	2	tablespoons milk
1	(10.5 ounce) can condensed chicken and rice soup	2	slices bread

1. Melt butter in a large saucepan over medium heat. Sauté green bell pepper and onion for 5 minutes or until tender. Stir in the tomato soup, chicken and rice soup, and water and bring to boil. Reduce heat to low and simmer.

2. Meanwhile, in a medium bowl, combine the ground beef, egg, and milk. Break the bread into very small pieces and add to the meat mixture. Mix together well.

3. Shape the meat mixture into meatballs and drop them into the soup mixture. Continue to simmer over low heat, uncovered, for 45 minutes to 1 hour. Stir occasionally but be very careful not to break the meatballs. **Yield:** 6 servings.

Per serving: 364 calories, 17g protein, 18g carbohydrate, 25g fat, 2g fiber, 108mg cholesterol, 743mg sodium

Taco Casserole

Submitted by: **Debi Van Name**

"My family loves Mexican food, and I love easy meals. This recipe is both. Serve with a salad for a complete dinner."

8	ounces macaroni	1	cup crushed tortilla chips
1	pound lean ground beef	½	cup shredded Cheddar cheese
½	cup chopped onion	½	cup shredded Monterey Jack cheese
1	(10.75 ounce) can condensed tomato soup	¼	cup chopped green onions
1	(14.5 ounce) can diced tomatoes	½	cup sour cream (optional)
1	(1.25 ounce) package taco seasoning mix		

1. Preheat oven to 350°F (175°C). Lightly grease a 9x13 inch baking dish.
2. Cook pasta in a large pot of boiling water until al dente. Drain.
3. In a large skillet, cook ground beef and chopped onion over medium heat until browned. Mix in tomato soup, diced tomatoes, and taco seasoning mix. Stir in cooked pasta.
4. Spoon beef mixture into prepared dish. Sprinkle crushed tortilla chips and shredded cheeses on top.
5. Bake in the preheated oven for 30 to 35 minutes or until cheeses melt. Sprinkle with chopped green onions; serve with sour cream, if desired. **Yield:** 8 servings.

Per serving: 304 calories, 18g protein, 28g carbohydrate, 13g fat, 2g fiber, 49mg cholesterol, 458mg sodium

◄ CROWD-PLEASER

Prep Time: 25 minutes

Cook Time: 55 minutes

Average Rating: ★★★★★

What other cooks have done:

"My picky eaters ate this up! I used a can of diced tomatoes with jalapeños, and it wasn't too hot for the kids. I also put some cheese under the chips and some on top. And I only baked it for 20 minutes, which was plenty of time to melt the cheese."

Beef and Noodle Bake

Submitted by: **Elizabeth Nell**

"Kids cannot get enough of this easy and yummy dish."

1 pound ground beef
2 cups elbow macaroni
4 cups pasta sauce
12 ounces processed cheese, sliced

1. Preheat oven to 375°F (190°C). Lightly grease a 9x13 inch baking dish.
2. Brown the ground beef in a large skillet over medium-high heat; set aside. Cook macaroni according to package directions; drain and set aside.
3. In a prepared dish, layer one-third each of the macaroni, ground beef, pasta sauce, and cheese; repeat layers twice.
4. Bake in the preheated oven for 30 minutes or until top layer of cheese is bubbly. **Yield:** 5 servings.

Per serving: 580 calories, 37g protein, 56g carbohydrate, 23g fat, 4g fiber, 83mg cholesterol, 1945mg sodium

Italian-Style Pork Chops

Submitted by: **Marilyn**

"When I make these chops, I always have to make extra. Everyone has to eat more than they need. These are great with a salad. The chops are baked in a crispy, buttery coating in the oven."

3 cups crushed saltine crackers
2 cups grated Parmesan cheese
1 tablespoon Italian seasoning
¼ teaspoon garlic powder
6 pork chops
1 cup butter, melted

1. Preheat oven to 425°F (220°C). Lightly grease a 9x13 inch baking dish.
2. In a medium bowl, combine the crushed saltines, Parmesan cheese, Italian seasoning, and garlic powder; mix together well.
3. Dip the chops in the melted butter and then dredge each chop in the cracker mixture, coating all sides thoroughly. Place the chops in prepared dish.
4. Bake in the preheated oven for 30 to 40 minutes or until a meat thermometer inserted into thickest part of pork registers 160°F (70°C). **Yield:** 6 servings.

Per serving: 711 calories, 37g protein, 27g carbohydrate, 50g fat, 1g fiber, 168mg cholesterol, 1437mg sodium

Bacon-Wrapped Chicken

Submitted by: **Anna Henson**

"I often make these chicken breasts ahead and freeze them, leaving only the sauce to make. This is delicious served over wide egg noodles. So wrap up your chicken in a bacon slice and smile, smile, smile!"

4 skinless, boneless chicken breast halves	½ cup mayonnaise
½ (8 ounce) package cream cheese, cut into 4 slices	½ cup milk
	1 teaspoon lemon juice
1 teaspoon chopped fresh chives, divided	¼ teaspoon ground black pepper
4 slices bacon	Pinch salt
1 (10.75 ounce) can condensed cream of chicken soup	

1. Preheat oven to 325°F (165°C). Lightly grease a 9x13 inch baking dish.

2. Pound the chicken breasts until flat. Put a slice of cream cheese and ¼ teaspoon chopped chives in the middle of each breast half and roll up. Wrap each rolled breast with 1 slice of bacon and secure with toothpicks. Place in prepared dish.

3. In a medium bowl, combine condensed soup, mayonnaise, milk, lemon juice, pepper, and salt. Mix until smooth and pour over chicken.

4. Bake in the preheated oven for 1 hour or until chicken is no longer pink and juices run clear. **Yield:** 4 servings.

Per serving: 667 calories, 35g protein, 9g carbohydrate, 54g fat, 0g fiber, 143mg cholesterol, 1232mg sodium

◀ RESTAURANT FARE

Prep Time: 25 minutes

Cook Time: 1 hour

Average Rating: ★★★★★

What other cooks have done:

"I cooked and crumbled the bacon and added it to the stuffing mixture. I used reduced-fat garlic-and-herb cream cheese. I added 1 teaspoon each of garlic powder and onion powder and added ½ cup chopped ham. For the sauce, I used light mayo and omitted the lemon juice. My family loved this recipe."

Chicken-Fried Chicken

Submitted by: **Cassie Wicks**

"A fun chicken recipe the kids can help prepare. They love crushing the crackers. It doesn't matter if the measurements aren't perfect—just wing it!"

RESTAURANT FARE ▶

Prep Time: 15 minutes

Cook Time: 20 minutes

Average Rating: ★★★★★

What other cooks have done:

"I dredge the chicken pieces in flour first so the egg has something to stick to, and I omit the flour from the breading mixture. Use just the potato flakes if you're in a hurry. This makes a light and tasty breading that my whole family loves."

30	saltine crackers	½	teaspoon ground black pepper
2	tablespoons all-purpose flour	1	egg, lightly beaten
2	tablespoons dry potato flakes	¼	cup vegetable oil
1	teaspoon seasoning salt	6	skinless, boneless chicken breast halves

1. Place crackers in a large zip-top plastic bag; seal bag and crush crackers until they are coarse crumbs. Add flour, potato flakes, seasoning salt, and pepper to bag and mix well.
2. Beat egg in a shallow dish or bowl; heat oil in a large skillet over medium heat.
3. Dredge chicken, 1 breast half at a time, in beaten egg. Place in bag with crumb mixture; seal bag and shake to coat.
4. Cook coated chicken in hot oil in skillet over medium heat, turning frequently, for 15 to 20 minutes or until golden brown and juices run clear. **Yield:** 6 servings.

Per serving: 321 calories, 29g protein, 14g carbohydrate, 16g fat, 1g fiber, 107mg cholesterol, 422mg sodium

Baked Chicken Nuggets *(pictured on page 115)*

Submitted by: **Teresa**

"A Parmesan crust lifts these chicken nibbles above the ordinary. Serve alone or with an array of dipping sauces."

QUICK & EASY ▶

Prep Time: 15 minutes

Cook Time: 20 minutes

Average Rating: ★★★★☆

What other cooks have done:

"Wow! What a simple and fast, yet great, recipe! My boyfriend loved it. To add extra flavor, I used kosher salt and a little garlic powder. I definitely will make this again for us and guests."

4	skinless, boneless chicken breast halves	1	teaspoon salt
1	cup Italian-seasoned breadcrumbs	1	teaspoon dried thyme
½	cup grated Parmesan cheese	1	tablespoon dried basil
		½	cup butter, melted

1. Preheat oven to 400°F (200°C). Lightly grease a baking sheet.
2. Cut chicken breasts into 1½ inch pieces. In a medium bowl, mix together the breadcrumbs, cheese, salt, thyme, and basil.
3. Dip chicken pieces into the melted butter; coat with the breadcrumb mixture. Place well-coated chicken pieces on prepared baking sheet in a single layer. Bake in the preheated oven for 20 minutes. **Yield:** 6 servings (32 nuggets).

Per serving: 365 calories, 32g protein, 15g carbohydrate, 19g fat, 1g fiber, 112mg cholesterol, 1208mg sodium

Quick and Easy Tuna Casserole

Submitted by: **Jennie Ridgeway**
"This recipe is perfect for the busy mom!"

1	(12 ounce) package egg noodles	1	onion, chopped
2	cups frozen green peas	10	slices American processed cheese
2	(10.75 ounce) cans condensed cream of mushroom soup		Ground black pepper to taste
2	(6 ounce) cans tuna, drained		

1. Bring a large pot of water to a boil. Add noodles and frozen peas. Cook until noodles are al dente; drain well.

2. Add soup, tuna, onion, processed cheese, and pepper to pasta and peas. Stir constantly until all of the ingredients are well mixed and heated through and the cheese has melted. **Yield:** 5 servings.

Per serving: 701 calories, 43g protein, 72g carbohydrate, 26g fat, 5g fiber, 125mg cholesterol, 1840mg sodium

◄ **COVERED-DISH FAVORITE**

Prep Time: 5 minutes

Cook Time: 25 minutes

Average Rating: ★★★★☆

What other cooks have done:

"My roommates all had midterms, so I wanted to give them a little taste of home. I gave this one a try because it looked good and didn't take a long time to cook. Everyone loved it! I substituted Monterey Jack cheese for American, and I added sautéed mushrooms and garlic to the pasta mixture. I also sprinkled some garlic powder on top after everything was combined."

Easy Vegetable Pot Pie

Submitted by: **Karen C. Greenlee**
"This pie takes only a few minutes of preparation time. The filling is made using a can of soup and a can of mixed vegetables combined with a little thyme. The kids are sure to love this savory dish."

1	(15 ounce) package refrigerated pie crusts, thawed	½	cup milk
1	(10.75 ounce) can condensed cream of potato soup	½	teaspoon dried thyme
		½	teaspoon ground black pepper
1	(15 ounce) can mixed vegetables, drained	1	egg, lightly beaten (optional)

1. Preheat oven to 375°F (190°C). Fit 1 pie crust into the bottom of a 9 inch pie plate.

2. In a medium bowl, combine potato soup, mixed vegetables, milk, thyme, and black pepper.

3. Spoon filling into bottom pie crust. Cover with top crust and crimp edges to seal. Cut slits into top crust and brush crust with beaten egg, if desired.

4. Bake in the preheated oven for 40 minutes. Remove from oven and cool for 10 minutes before serving. **Yield:** 6 servings.

Per serving: 385 calories, 6g protein, 41g carbohydrate, 22g fat, 4g fiber, 41mg cholesterol, 934mg sodium

◄ **RESTAURANT FARE**

Prep Time: 5 minutes

Cook Time: 40 minutes

Cool Time: 10 minutes

Average Rating: ★★★★☆

What other cooks have done:

"This was really good! Instead of using canned mixed veggies, I put fresh carrots, broccoli, and zucchini in the blender and chopped them up. I added those and a can of corn to the filling. Everyone loved it. My son sprinkled cheese over his, and he went back for seconds!"

Potato Casserole II

Submitted by: **Bea**

"This easy, kid-pleasing casserole is a delicious main or side dish."

MEATLESS MAIN DISH ▶

Prep Time: 15 minutes

Cook Time: 1 hour

Average Rating: ★★★★★

What other cooks have done:

"This was awesome! It even does well when reheated. We had a little left over, since it makes so much. We stuck it back in the oven the next night, and it was just as good. I will make this again for sure!"

½ cup chopped onion
1 pint sour cream
1 (10.75 ounce) can condensed cream of chicken soup
2 cups shredded Cheddar cheese

Salt and ground black pepper to taste
1 (2 pound) package frozen hash brown potatoes, thawed
2 cups crushed potato chips
½ cup melted butter

1. Preheat oven to 350°F (175°C). Lightly grease a 9x13 inch baking dish.

2. In a large bowl, combine onion, sour cream, soup, cheese, and salt and pepper to taste. Press the excess water out of the hash browns and add to soup mixture; mix well. Transfer to prepared dish. Sprinkle potato chips on top and drizzle with butter.

3. Bake in the preheated oven for 45 minutes to 1 hour or until golden brown. **Yield:** 7 servings.

Per serving: 649 calories, 16g protein, 42g carbohydrate, 56g fat, 3g fiber, 102mg cholesterol, 880mg sodium

Crazy Cake

Submitted by: **Amy Parsons**

"This cake, which was popular during the Depression, does not have eggs in it. Frost with your favorite icing."

3	cups all-purpose flour	¾	cup vegetable oil
2	cups white sugar	2	tablespoons distilled white vinegar
1	teaspoon salt		
2	teaspoons baking soda	2	teaspoons vanilla extract
½	cup unsweetened cocoa powder	2	cups cold water

1. Preheat oven to 350°F (175°C).

2. Sift together flour, sugar, salt, baking soda, and cocoa into an ungreased 9x13 inch pan. Make 3 wells in flour mixture. Pour oil into the first well, vinegar into the second, and vanilla into the third. Pour cold water over all and stir well with a fork.

3. Bake in the preheated oven for 30 to 40 minutes or until a toothpick inserted into center of the cake comes out clean. Frost with your favorite icing. **Yield:** 18 servings.

Per serving (cake only): 250 calories, 3g protein, 40g carbohydrate, 10g fat, 1g fiber, 0mg cholesterol, 271mg sodium

◄ CROWD-PLEASER

Prep Time: 15 minutes

Cook Time: 40 minutes

Average Rating: ★★★★★

What other cooks have done:

"Great recipe. I made cupcakes from this recipe for my daughter's birthday party. Some of her friends have dairy allergies, and this recipe allowed them to enjoy cake along with the other kids. I used a nondairy white icing made from confectioners' sugar and shortening, and I topped it with rainbow sprinkles. The cupcakes were a hit!"

Snack Attack

Afternoon snacks help kids battle the grumpy after-school monster inside by supplying them with the energy to carry them through the afternoon. Whether your child comes straight home after school and dives into homework or spends the after-school hours immersed in sports and other extracurricular activities, it's important to make sure that he or she eats an energy-filled snack. Store-bought snacks are often very expensive, and they tend to be packed with sugar, fat, salt and preservatives. Spend some time making your own snacks; they taste better and are better for your kids.

Carry-Along Energy Boosters

When you know your kids will spend the immediate after-school hours away from home, be sure to stock their backpacks with a snack well suited for after-school consumption. Homemade granola bars, muffins, nut and snack mixes, crackers, and slices of bread packed with nutritious fruits (such as banana) or veggies (such as carrot or zucchini) are all easy to make. And don't forget convenient resealable bags that can be quickly stuffed with baby carrots, raisins, celery, radishes, or seasonal fruits.

At-Home Energy Boosters

In addition to all of the snacks kids can take with them, there's a large assortment of treats that can be made on the spot or premade and popped in the oven to serve hot. Smoothies, mini pizzas, and crunchy salads can be thrown together quickly and easily. Hot dips can be assembled ahead of time and heated when the kids get home, as can mini sandwiches made on heat-and-serve dinner rolls—just combine your child's favorite varieties of cheeses and sandwich meats. No matter what your kids like to snack on, giving them the fuel they need in the afternoon will ensure strong bodies and brains all day long.

- Tammy Weisberger

For more information, visit **Allrecipes.com**

Dirt Cake II

Submitted by: **Kym**

"Kids love dirt. This can be served in a large flowerpot or two small flowerpots."

RESTAURANT FARE ▶

Prep Time: 15 minutes

Chill Time: 3 hours

Average Rating: ★★★★☆

What other cooks have done:

"Exceptional! I made a triple batch of this recipe for a big party and served it in a big children's plastic bucket with little plastic hand shovels. It was a huge hit! To reduce the calories a little, I used light margarine, Neufchâtel cheese instead of cream cheese, light whipped topping, and fat-free milk. Everyone has been asking me for the recipe. I will definitely make this again!"

1	(20 ounce) package cream-filled chocolate sandwich cookies
¼	cup butter, softened
1	(8 ounce) package cream cheese, softened
1	cup confectioners' sugar
1	teaspoon vanilla extract
2	(3.9 ounce) packages instant chocolate pudding mix
3	cups milk
1	(12 ounce) container frozen whipped topping, thawed
24	gummi worms

1. Put the cookies in a food processor and process until they become fine crumbs. Set aside.
2. In a large bowl, combine the butter, cream cheese, confectioners' sugar, and vanilla. Beat at low speed with an electric mixer to combine; then beat on medium speed until smooth. Add the chocolate pudding mix and milk. Beat on low speed to combine.
3. Fold the whipped topping into the pudding mixture with a rubber spatula.
4. Press one-third of the cookie crumbs into the bottom of an ungreased 9x13 inch pan. Layer one-third of the pudding mixture over cookie crumbs. Repeat layers twice.
5. Tuck the ends of gummi worms in the cookie "dirt." Chill for at least 3 hours before serving. Cut into 24 squares or serve with a clean garden trowel or a toy sand shovel if serving in a flowerpot.

Yield: 24 servings.

Per serving: 288 calories, 4g protein, 38g carbohydrate, 14g fat, 1g fiber, 18mg cholesterol, 337mg sodium

Appetizers & Beverages

*When friends stop by or company comes for dinner,
you want to have something flavorful and fun for
them to nibble. Whether you're looking for a little treat
or a big thirst-quencher, we've got just the thing.*

Garlic-Feta Dip

Submitted by: **KATEZ21**

"For serious garlic lovers, start with two cloves of garlic in this creamy, tangy dip and add more if you can handle it. This is totally addictive. Serve with toasted pita wedges and raw vegetables."

1	cup crumbled feta cheese	¼	teaspoon salt
½	cup sour cream	¼	teaspoon ground black
½	cup plain yogurt		pepper
2	cloves garlic, peeled		

1. Combine feta cheese, sour cream, yogurt, and garlic in the container of a food processor or blender. Pulse briefly until garlic is minced. Spoon into a serving dish and season with salt and pepper. **Yield:** 8 servings.

Per serving: 125 calories, 6g protein, 3g carbohydrate, 10g fat, 0g fiber, 35mg cholesterol, 443mg sodium

Uncle Howie's Favorite Artichoke Dip

Submitted by: **Barb Wilson**

"Serve this cheesy, creamy dip loaded with artichokes and garlic with toasted French bread slices for a fantastic appetizer. To serve the dip hot, transfer to a medium baking dish and heat at 375°F (190°C) for 20 minutes or until bubbling and slightly browned."

1	(8 ounce) package cream cheese, softened	2	cloves garlic, pressed
		1	chopped red bell pepper
2	(6.5 ounce) jars marinated artichoke hearts, drained and chopped	½	cup shredded Swiss cheese
		½	cup mayonnaise
		⅓	cup sliced green onions

1. In a medium bowl, mix all ingredients. **Yield:** 40 servings.

Per serving: 66 calories, 1g protein, 1g carbohydrate, 6g fat, 0g fiber, 11mg cholesterol, 72mg sodium

Tzatziki

Submitted by: **Teina P**

"This is truly a wonderful Greek accompaniment to many meals, especially meats. It's also great as a dip for veggies and pita bread. This is something I made with my mom while growing up. To save time, you can buy strained yogurt at Greek groceries and specialty shops. Adjust the amount of garlic to taste. Opa!"

32	ounces plain yogurt
1	large English cucumber, peeled and shredded
5	cloves garlic, minced
3	tablespoons white vinegar
¼	cup extra virgin olive oil
	Salt to taste

1. Place a cheesecloth securely over a medium bowl. Place the yogurt over the cheesecloth. Refrigerate and strain the yogurt 6 hours or overnight.
2. Press the cucumber and garlic between paper towels to drain as much excess liquid as possible.
3. In a large bowl, mix together the yogurt, cucumber, garlic, vinegar, olive oil, and salt. Stir until thickened. Chill until ready to serve.
Yield: 32 servings.

Per serving: 35 calories, 2g protein, 2g carbohydrate, 2g fat, 0g fiber, 2mg cholesterol, 20mg sodium

◄ MAKE-AHEAD

Prep Time: 20 minutes

Chill Time: 6 hours

Average Rating: ★★★★☆

What other cooks have done:

"I served this at a dinner party with warm pita bread. It was a hit! Using a food processor made this appetizer easy. If you buy a low-water-content yogurt, you won't need to drain it over cheesecloth."

Bonnie's Fruit Dip

Submitted by: **Bonnie**

"This fruit dip is served at all of our family get-togethers. It's enjoyed by all!"

1	(8 ounce) package cream cheese, softened
½	cup sour cream
½	cup whipping cream, whipped
¼	cup packed brown sugar
¼	cup white sugar
1	tablespoon maple syrup
1	teaspoon vanilla extract

1. In a mixing bowl, combine all ingredients. Mix until smooth. Serve immediately or chill until ready to serve. **Yield:** 10 servings.

Per serving: 165 calories, 2g protein, 14g carbohydrate, 12g fat, 0g fiber, 34mg cholesterol, 83mg sodium

◄ KID-FRIENDLY

Prep Time: 15 minutes

Average Rating: ★★★★★

What other cooks have done:

"I hollowed out a cantaloupe and a grapefruit and placed the dip inside. Let the cream cheese and whipped cream reach room temperature and soften. Blend those first. Slowly add the white sugar; then slowly blend in the brown sugar, stopping to mash out any lumps with a fork. Then add the maple syrup."

Best Spinach Dip Ever

Submitted by: **Shawna**

"This is my dad's recipe. A flavorful spinach mixture fills a tasty bread bowl. My entire family loves it! Your family will love it, too."

PARTY FOOD ▶

Prep Time: 15 minutes

Chill Time: overnight

Average Rating: ★★★★★

What other cooks have done:

"I baked my own bread for the bread bowl. When it was cool, I traced the lip of a small glass bowl in the top of the bread with a knife and then cut the hole out. I set the bowl containing the spinach dip in the center of the bread bowl so that the bread wouldn't get soggy during the evening. This made the clean-up much easier."

1 cup mayonnaise
1 (16 ounce) container sour cream
1 (1.8 ounce) package dry leek soup mix
1 (4 ounce) can water chestnuts, drained and chopped
½ (10 ounce) package frozen chopped spinach, thawed and drained
1 (1 pound) round loaf sourdough bread

1. In a medium bowl, mix together mayonnaise, sour cream, dry leek soup mix, water chestnuts, and chopped spinach. Chill for 6 hours or overnight.

2. Remove top and interior of sourdough bread. Fill bread bowl with dip, reserving removed bread. Tear removed bread into chunks for dipping. **Yield:** 24 servings.

Per serving: 167 calories, 3g protein, 12g carbohydrate, 12g fat, 1g fiber, 14mg cholesterol, 288mg sodium

Hoagie Dip

Submitted by: **C. Schuster**

"This mouth-watering dip tastes like a hoagie!"

OUT-OF-THE-ORDINARY ▶

Prep Time: 15 minutes

Average Rating: ★★★★★

What other cooks have done:

"I added balsamic vinaigrette to the dip, and everyone loved it. This is a nice change from the typical fare that appears at every party. I will definitely make this again."

½ pound cooked ham, thinly sliced
½ pound Genoa salami, thinly sliced
1 pound processed American cheese, sliced
2 cups mayonnaise
2 teaspoons dried oregano
1 onion, chopped
½ head iceberg lettuce, shredded
2 tomatoes, diced
12 hoagie rolls, torn into pieces

1. Tear the ham, salami, and American cheese into small pieces. Place in a large bowl.

2. In a medium bowl, blend the mayonnaise and oregano. Mix the mayonnaise mixture into the ham mixture, ½ cup at a time, until meats and cheese are well coated. Mix in the onion.

3. Just before serving, mix in the lettuce and tomatoes. Serve with hoagie roll pieces for dipping. **Yield:** 16 servings.

Per serving: 560 calories, 19g protein, 27g carbohydrate, 42g fat, 2g fiber, 67mg cholesterol, 1093mg sodium

Fantastic Mexican Dip

Submitted by: **Bumblebee**

"This recipe was given to me by my sister-in-law. This always goes fast! Cream cheese as the base of the dip makes it extra thick and scoopable, while seasoned beef and vegetables make it extra filling and tasty! Serve with tortilla chips and enjoy."

2	pounds lean ground beef	1	(16 ounce) package shredded Cheddar cheese
1	(16 ounce) jar taco sauce	1	cup shredded lettuce
1	(16 ounce) container sour cream	1	tomato, cubed
1	(8 ounce) package cream cheese, softened	2	green onions, sliced
1	(1 ounce) package taco seasoning mix	1	(2 ounce) can sliced black olives, drained

1. Crumble ground beef in a large, deep skillet. Cook over medium-high heat until evenly browned; drain. Mix in the taco sauce and set aside.
2. In a large bowl, mix the sour cream, cream cheese, and taco seasoning mix. Spread the mixture into a medium serving dish.
3. Layer the beef mixture over the sour cream mixture. Sprinkle with Cheddar cheese and lettuce. Top with tomato, green onions, and black olives. **Yield:** 64 servings.

Per serving: 99 calories, 5g protein, 2g carbohydrate, 8g fat, 0g fiber, 25mg cholesterol, 141mg sodium

◀ CROWD-PLEASER

Prep Time: 20 minutes

Cook Time: 10 minutes

Average Rating: ★★★★★

What other cooks have done:

"I add refried beans, green chiles, and lots of garlic to the meat layer, and it's fabulous. I've even made it with ground chicken and ground pork, and it's all been good. I cut the amount of meat to about 1 pound, and it makes plenty. Definitely try this."

Baby Shower Raspberry Dip

Submitted by: **Heather Maxwell**

"This easy, sweet dip is excellent on a fruit platter. I usually serve this dip at baby showers because it has a lovely pastel pink color. The taste can easily be altered by using your choice of extract. Also, the dip is thick enough that it can be used as a tea-sandwich filling."

1	cup sour cream	½	cup white sugar
1	(8 ounce) package Neufchâtel cheese, softened	1	tablespoon raspberry extract
		½	cup fresh raspberries

1. Combine the sour cream, Neufchâtel cheese, white sugar, and raspberry extract in a medium bowl. With an electric mixer, blend until smooth. Chill for about 30 minutes. Garnish with fresh raspberries. **Yield:** 24 servings.

Per serving: 62 calories, 1g protein, 5g carbohydrate, 4g fat, 0g fiber, 11mg cholesterol, 42mg sodium

◀ COMPANY IS COMING

Prep Time: 5 minutes

Chill Time: 30 minutes

Average Rating: ★★★★★

What other cooks have done:

"Yum! Perfect consistency and tasted like a light cheesecake. I used strawberry extract because I couldn't find raspberry, so I garnished the dip with sliced strawberries instead."

Bologna Salad Sandwich Spread I

Submitted by: **LaDonna**

"A girlfriend's mom made this spread years ago for our Teen Club luncheon back in Iowa in the 50s. I asked her to tell my mom how to make it. I made the recipe for my kids while they were growing up, and they still love it. Sweet relish and eggs round out the flavor of bologna in this simple but delicious spread. The amount of egg, salad dressing, and relish can be adjusted to taste."

5 INGREDIENTS OR LESS ▶

Prep Time: 20 minutes

Cook Time: 2 minutes

Stand Time: 12 minutes

Chill Time: 3 hours

Average Rating: ★★★★☆

What other cooks have done:

"My mother used to make this for me for sandwiches. Instead of salad dressing, she used mayonnaise. I, also, have been feeding this to my family for years. It's just so good! Great on crackers, too."

4 eggs	1 (16 ounce) jar creamy salad
1 (16 ounce) package	dressing
bologna	1 cup sweet pickle relish

1. Place eggs in a medium saucepan and cover with cold water. Bring water to a boil and immediately remove from heat. Cover and let stand for 10 to 12 minutes. Remove eggs; cool, peel, and chop eggs.
2. Grind bologna and eggs in a meat grinder with a medium blade.
3. In a large bowl, mix bologna mixture with creamy salad dressing and sweet pickle relish. Refrigerate 2 to 3 hours or until chilled.
Yield: 48 servings (3 tablespoons per serving).

Per serving: 79 calories, 2g protein, 3g carbohydrate, 7g fat, 0g fiber, 26mg cholesterol, 216mg sodium

Party Shortcut

Appetizer parties are a fun, stress-free way to entertain, and a tray of miniature sandwiches can transform a simple gathering into a special occasion. Most of your favorite dips and spreads can double as sandwich fillings, so you can use familiar recipes to create these party favorites.

To get a head start on your celebration, stir up several kinds of spreads and store them in the refrigerator. Then follow these tips for creating picture-perfect party sandwiches.
• Freeze the bread before filling.
• Cover the sandwiches with damp paper towels until all are assembled; then wrap them individually with plastic wrap and store them in the refrigerator up to 1 day before serving.
• Garnish the sandwiches, if desired, and arrange them on trays just before serving.

No Time to Cook

If you're in a real hurry, turn to one of the quick fixes below.
• Dress up a plain block of cream cheese with pepper jellies. For a sweeter taste, serve the cheese with gingersnaps instead of crackers.
• For a hearty appetizer, chicken fingers are always a favorite. Buy them in the deli section of the grocery store; add a bowl of honey mustard or another dipping sauce for a tasty treat.
• Many grocery stores have a scrumptious selection of cheese and bread. Choose some different flavors of each and arrange on a plate or in a basket. Consider adding some grapes, apples, or other fruit to the mix.
For more information, visit **Allrecipes.com**

Aunt Phyllis' Magnificent Cheese Ball

Submitted by: **Natalie K.**

"This recipe is fantastic! Every time I take this somewhere, people ask me for the recipe. For the cheese sauce mix, you can use half of an envelope of dry cheese mix from a macaroni and cheese boxed mix, if you'd like."

2 (8 ounce) packages cream cheese, softened	2 tablespoons thinly sliced green onions
½ cup butter, softened	1 tablespoon lemon juice
1 tablespoon instant Cheddar cheese sauce mix	1 teaspoon dried parsley
2 cups shredded Cheddar cheese	½ cup chopped walnuts (or to taste)

1. In a medium mixing bowl, blend cream cheese and butter. Stir in cheese sauce mix, Cheddar cheese, green onions, lemon juice, and parsley. Shape mixture into 2 large balls or logs and roll them in chopped walnuts. Refrigerate until ready to serve. **Yield:** 10 servings.

Per serving: 375 calories, 10g protein, 3g carbohydrate, 37g fat, 1g fiber, 98mg cholesterol, 436mg sodium

◀ **MAKE-AHEAD**

Prep Time: 10 minutes

Average Rating: ★★★★★

What other cooks have done:

"This is a cheese ball I like to make and have in the fridge for holiday visitors. It's easy to put this on a tray and serve with crackers and a glass of wine! Makes a great gift, too."

Chocolate Chip Cheese Ball

Submitted by: **Kim**

"A sweet switch from the usual cheese ball. Serve with graham crackers or chocolate wafers."

1 (8 ounce) package cream cheese, softened	¼ teaspoon vanilla extract
½ cup butter, softened	¾ cup miniature semisweet chocolate chips
¾ cup confectioners' sugar	¾ cup finely chopped pecans
2 tablespoons brown sugar	

1. In a medium bowl, beat together cream cheese and butter until smooth. Mix in confectioners' sugar, brown sugar, and vanilla. Stir in chocolate chips. Cover and chill for 2 hours.
2. Shape chilled cream cheese mixture into a ball. Cover with plastic wrap and chill for 1 hour.
3. Roll the cheese ball in finely chopped pecans before serving.
Yield: 32 servings.

Per serving: 106 calories, 1g protein, 7g carbohydrate, 9g fat, 1g fiber, 15mg cholesterol, 51mg sodium

◀ **OUT-OF-THE ORDINARY**

Prep Time: 20 minutes

Chill Time: 3 hours

Average Rating: ★★★★★

What other cooks have done:

"I tried a variation on this recipe. I added raspberry flavoring I got from the cake-decorating section of a craft store to the cream cheese. Then I rolled the cheese ball in chopped white chocolate morsels. It was a huge success! When served on chocolate wafers, it had a taste similar to a Black Forest cake. You can also serve it with graham crackers or vanilla wafers."

Caramel Snack Mix

(pictured on facing page)

Submitted by: **Trish Bennett**

"This is the most requested item I bring to the office. It has become the Christmas gift of choice from my kitchen."

HOLIDAY GIFT GIVING ▶

Prep Time: 10 minutes

Cook Time: 1 hour 2 minutes

Average Rating: ★★★★★

What other cooks have done:

"I added a teaspoon each of cinnamon and vanilla, as well as some candy-coated chocolate pieces. These really added a little something! For faster cooling, divide this into two pans after removing it from the oven."

½	cup butter	1	cup chopped pecans
¾	cup white corn syrup	1	cup almonds
1	cup packed brown sugar		
1	(12 ounce) package crispy corn and rice cereal		

1. Preheat oven to 275°F (135°C). Spray a large roasting pan with cooking spray.
2. In a medium-size microwave-safe bowl, mix butter, white corn syrup, and brown sugar. Microwave on High for 2 minutes or until butter melts.
3. Place the cereal, pecans, and almonds in a large paper bag. Pour in the melted butter mixture; shake gently until the cereal and nuts are coated. Place mixture in prepared pan.
4. Bake in the preheated oven for 1 hour, stirring every 15 minutes. Let cool, stirring occasionally to prevent large clumps from forming. **Yield:** 20 servings.

Per serving: 262 calories, 3g protein, 37g carbohydrate, 13g fat, 2g fiber, 12mg cholesterol, 205mg sodium

Cheddar Pennies

Submitted by: **Adrienne Anderson**

"My mother and I have made these delicious Cheddar penny cookies for years, and they are just as good now as they were when I was young."

BLUE RIBBON WINNER ▶

Prep Time: 20 minutes

Cook Time: 25 minutes

Average Rating: ★★★★☆

What other cooks have done:

"I used my hands to knead the dough so it would form a ball. I made mine the size of 50-cent pieces and baked them for 20 minutes. I used Cajun spice, since I didn't have any cayenne pepper, and I added real bacon bits; the pennies were fantastic! I entered them in our state fair and won first place!"

2	cups sifted all-purpose flour	1½	cups shredded Cheddar cheese
	Pinch salt		
	Pinch cayenne pepper	½	cup butter, melted

1. Preheat oven to 325°F (165°C). Lightly grease a large baking sheet.
2. In a medium bowl, mix together the flour, salt, and cayenne pepper. Stir in the Cheddar cheese and melted butter to form a firm dough. Roll pieces of dough into ropes as big around as a penny. Slice into ¼ inch slices. (If dough is too soft, it can be chilled until firm.) Place slices 1 inch apart on the prepared baking sheet.
3. Bake in the preheated oven for 20 to 25 minutes or until the bottoms of the pennies are lightly toasted and the tops are firm. Cool pennies completely before serving. Store in an airtight container at room temperature. **Yield:** 35 servings.

Per serving: 69 calories, 2g protein, 6g carbohydrate, 4g fat, 0g fiber, 12mg cholesterol, 68mg sodium

Caramel Snack Mix

Delicious Healthy Strawberry
Shake, page 163

White Sangria, page 165

Ali's Amazing Bruschetta,
page 154

Chicken and Broccoli Braid,
Page 158

Cucumber and Olive Appetizers

Cucumber and Olive Appetizers

(pictured on facing page)

Submitted by: **Gwena Hedlund**

"I got this recipe from one of my cooking classes in college. These are an 'old-fashioned' type of appetizer, but they make a beautiful display on the plate. I never take any home with me because these disappear quickly."

1	large cucumber	1	(1 pound) loaf cocktail rye bread
1	(3 ounce) package cream cheese, softened	15	pimento-stuffed green olives, sliced
¼	cup blue cheese salad dressing		

1. Using a citrus stripper or the tines of a fork, score the unpeeled cucumber lengthwise on all sides. Slice the cucumber into ¼ inch thick rounds.

2. In a small bowl, combine cream cheese and blue cheese salad dressing. Spread cheese mixture on rye bread slices. Top each with a slice of cucumber and a slice of olive. **Yield**: 10 servings.

Per serving: 189 calories, 5g protein, 23g carbohydrate, 9g fat, 2g fiber, 11mg cholesterol, 507mg sodium

◄ PARTY FOOD

Prep Time: 15 minutes

Average Rating: ★★★★★

What other cooks have done:

"After peeling and seeding the cucumber, I chopped up it and the olives and added them to the cream cheese mixture. It was a hit spread on rye bread!"

Sarah's Salsa

Submitted by: **Sarah**

"This easy recipe for salsa is made in a blender. It's a staple at my house (and my friends' houses, too). Remember, you can always add ingredients to taste. This is good on just about anything."

2	(14.5 ounce) cans diced tomatoes, undrained	⅓	cup fresh cilantro leaves
1½	(10 ounce) cans diced tomatoes with green chile peppers, undrained	½	large yellow onion, quartered
2	tablespoons lemon juice	3	drops hot pepper sauce
1	fresh jalapeño pepper, quartered	1	clove garlic, minced

1. In a blender, combine all ingredients. Blend to desired consistency. Chill until ready to serve. **Yield:** 32 servings.

Per serving: 9 calories, 0g protein, 2g carbohydrate, 0g fat, 0g fiber, 0mg cholesterol, 95mg sodium

◄ QUICK & EASY

Prep Time: 15 minutes

Average Rating: ★★★★★

What other cooks have done:

"This is the best salsa I've ever had! My husband and I don't like really chunky salsa, and this is perfect because it can be blended to our liking. I love cilantro and garlic, so this was perfect for me. I added an extra clove of garlic and a little more hot pepper sauce."

Roasted Garlic

Submitted by: **Viviane**

"Roasted garlic is great served with bread, crackers, or apples. People can peel off a clove of the garlic and literally squeeze the garlic out of its shell onto their bread or cracker. Delicious!"

5 INGREDIENTS OR LESS ▶

Prep Time: 5 minutes

Cook Time: 1 hour

Average Rating: ★★★★★

What other cooks have done:

"This is so good! It's very easy to make, and it's delicious on French bread with some olive oil. I use this recipe and add the garlic to my mashed potatoes as well."

10	medium heads garlic	3	tablespoons olive oil

1. Preheat oven to 400°F (200°C).
2. Arrange heads of garlic on a baking sheet. Sprinkle garlic with olive oil.
3. Bake in the preheated oven for 40 minutes to 1 hour or until garlic is soft and squeezable. Remove, cool, and serve. **Yield:** 15 servings.

Per serving: 79 calories, 2g protein, 12g carbohydrate, 3g fat, 1g fiber, 0mg cholesterol, 6mg sodium

Ali's Amazing Bruschetta

(pictured on page 150)

Submitted by: **Alison**

"This bruschetta will turn out every time you make it. Use small slices of bread for a unique appetizer or serve as a side with Italian dishes."

RESTAURANT FARE ▶

Prep Time: 15 minutes

Cook Time: 10 minutes

Cool Time: 5 minutes

Average Rating: ★★★★★

What other cooks have done:

"We enjoyed this immensely! I added some finely minced garlic and let the tomato mixture sit in the refrigerator for several hours to allow the flavors to develop. My husband wants me to make just the topping as a salad."

2	large tomatoes, coarsely chopped	2	teaspoons chopped fresh parsley
½	sweet onion, chopped	½	(1 pound) loaf Italian bread, cut into 1 inch slices
2	tablespoons olive oil		
1	tablespoon chopped fresh oregano	¼	cup freshly grated Parmesan cheese
1	teaspoon chopped fresh basil		Fresh basil sprig (optional)

1. Preheat oven to 400°F (200°C).
2. In a medium bowl, combine tomatoes, onion, olive oil, oregano, basil, and parsley. Place bread slices on a baking sheet and top with tomato mixture. Sprinkle with Parmesan.
3. Bake in the preheated oven for 8 to 10 minutes or until bottom of bread is browned. Allow to cool for 5 minutes before serving. Garnish with basil sprig, if desired. **Yield:** 6 servings.

Per serving: 178 calories, 6g protein, 23g carbohydrate, 7g fat, 2g fiber, 3mg cholesterol, 305mg sodium

Italian Torte

Submitted by: **Elaine**

"This wonderful mix of pesto, sun-dried tomatoes, and cream cheese is formed into an attractive tortelike dome. You can't go wrong with this recipe."

3	ounces sun-dried tomatoes	1	clove garlic, minced
2	(8 ounce) packages cream cheese, softened	10	slices provolone cheese
		8	ounces pesto

1. Bring a small saucepan of water to boil. Turn off heat. Place sun-dried tomatoes in the water and cover. Let stand for 5 minutes. Drain and finely chop tomatoes.

2. In a medium bowl, mix cream cheese and garlic.

3. Line a medium bowl or loaf pan with a large piece of dampened cheesecloth. Layer with one-third of the provolone cheese. Spread with half of the pesto. Pour in half of the cream cheese and garlic mixture. Layer with half of the sun-dried tomatoes. Layer with half of remaining provolone, remaining pesto, remaining cream cheese and garlic mixture, and remaining sun-dried tomatoes. Top with remaining provolone cheese.

4. Pull cheesecloth around the layered mixture and gently press into bowl or loaf pan to mold and remove excess oil. Chill 3 to 4 hours. Remove cheesecloth and turn torte upside down onto a large dish to serve. **Yield:** 32 servings.

Per serving: 124 calories, 5g protein, 3g carbohydrate, 11g fat, 1g fiber, 24mg cholesterol, 232mg sodium

◀ AROUND-THE-WORLD CUISINE

Prep Time: 20 minutes

Cook Time: 5 minutes

Chill Time: 4 hours

Average Rating: ★★★★★

What other cooks have done:

"I substituted goat cheese for the provolone, and it was really good! I also ground up pine nuts and sprinkled them over the top just before serving."

Spicy Rye Rounds

Submitted by: **Kristen Edwards-Good**

"This is a recipe that my mother loved to use at the holidays. It is quick and easy, and it can be prepared in advance. Enjoy this; it tastes great!"

1	pound lean ground beef	1	(1 pound) loaf sliced cocktail rye bread
1	pound spicy Italian sausage		
1	pound processed cheese, cubed		

1. Preheat oven to 325°F (165°C).

2. In a large skillet, brown ground beef and sausage. After beef and sausage are browned, add cheese, stirring until ingredients are combined. Spoon 1 tablespoon of the mixture onto each piece of rye bread. Arrange topped bread slices on a baking sheet.

3. Bake in the preheated oven for 5 to 7 minutes. **Yield:** 8 servings.

Per serving: 676 calories, 35g protein, 32g carbohydrate, 45g fat, 2g fiber, 122mg cholesterol, 1375mg sodium

◀ FREEZER FRESH

Prep Time: 10 minutes

Cook Time: 12 minutes

Average Rating: ★★★★★

What other cooks have done:

"I used homemade rye bread that had been cut into little squares. I froze them ahead of time and popped them in the oven for 7 to 8 minutes. They were crispy and hot, and not a one was left, so I'd say everyone enjoyed them!"

Homemade Refrigerator Pickles

Submitted by: **Diana**

"Just pickles! These are easy to make, and they're a great way to use vegetables from the garden."

1	cup distilled white vinegar	1	cup sliced onion
1	tablespoon salt	1	cup sliced green bell peppers
2	cups white sugar		
6	cups sliced cucumbers		

1. In a medium saucepan over medium heat, bring vinegar, salt, and sugar to a boil. Boil until the sugar has dissolved, about 10 minutes.
2. Place the cucumbers, onions, and green bell peppers in a large bowl. Pour the vinegar mixture over the vegetables. Transfer to sterile containers and store in the refrigerator up to 1 month.
Yield: 64 servings.

Per serving: 27 calories, 0g protein, 7g carbohydrate, 0g fat, 0g fiber, 0mg cholesterol, 109mg sodium

Marinated Mushrooms II

Submitted by: **Cristi White**

"This recipe was handed down to me from my grandma. Little mushrooms are marinated in a zesty mixture. They're great for buffet-style gatherings. They keep well for a long time in the fridge, or you may can them and store them in the cupboard."

⅓	cup red wine vinegar	1	tablespoon brown sugar
⅓	cup olive oil	2	cloves garlic, peeled and crushed
1	small onion, thinly sliced		
1	teaspoon salt	1	pound small fresh button mushrooms
2	tablespoons dried parsley		
1	teaspoon ground mustard		

1. In a medium saucepan, mix red wine vinegar, olive oil, onion, salt, parsley, mustard, brown sugar, and garlic. Bring to a boil. Reduce heat. Stir in mushrooms. Simmer for 10 to 12 minutes, stirring occasionally. Transfer to sterile containers and chill until ready to serve.
Yield: 16 servings.

Per serving: 55 calories, 1g protein, 3g carbohydrate, 5g fat, 1g fiber, 0mg cholesterol, 148mg sodium

Party Franks

Submitted by: **Ann Marie**

"This is a very old sweet-and-sour cocktail recipe; I remember looking forward to it as a kid at my mom's holiday parties. Don't ever tell what's in the sauce until after your guests have tasted it (otherwise, they'll never try it). Serve with toothpicks; keep warm with a fondue pot."

1 (8 ounce) jar grape jelly	1 pound cocktail wieners
1 (8 ounce) jar yellow mustard	

1. In a medium saucepan over medium heat, mix the grape jelly and mustard. When the mixture begins to bubble, stir in the cocktail wieners. Reduce heat and simmer until ready to serve.
Yield: 8 servings.

Per serving: 257 calories, 8g protein, 21g carbohydrate, 16g fat, 1g fiber, 36mg cholesterol, 874mg sodium

◀ **5 INGREDIENTS OR LESS**

Prep Time: 5 minutes

Cook Time: 15 minutes

Average Rating: ★★★★☆

What other cooks have done:

"I like these wrapped in crescent dough (each triangle cut in half lengthwise) and baked until golden brown. After cooking, dip them in the jelly and mustard mixture or in duck sauce mixed with hot mustard."

Gyoza

Submitted by: **Meridith**

"I learned this recipe for gyoza while living in Japan. They're great hot or cold, and they may be eaten plain or with the dipping sauce. Any ground meat may be substituted for pork."

1 tablespoon sesame oil	1 (10 ounce) package won ton wrappers
2 cups chopped cabbage	1 tablespoon vegetable oil
¼ cup chopped onion	¼ cup water
1 clove garlic, chopped	¼ cup soy sauce
¼ cup chopped carrot	2 tablespoons rice vinegar
½ pound ground pork	
1 egg	

1. Heat sesame oil in a large skillet over medium–high heat. Mix in cabbage, onion, garlic, and carrot. Cook and stir until cabbage wilts. Mix in ground pork and egg. Cook until pork is evenly browned and egg is no longer runny.
2. Place approximately 1 tablespoon of the cabbage and pork mixture in the center of each won ton wrapper. Fold wrappers in half over filling and seal edges with moistened fingers.
3. Heat vegetable oil in a large skillet over medium–high heat.
4. In the heated vegetable oil, cook gyoza, in batches, approximately 1 minute per side until lightly browned. Drain off oil and wipe skillet clean. Heat ¼ cup water in skillet. Add gyoza and allow to steam until the water evaporates.
5. In a small bowl, mix soy sauce and rice vinegar. Serve as a dipping sauce with gyoza. **Yield:** 10 servings.

Per serving: 184 calories, 8g protein, 19g carbohydrate, 9g fat, 1g fiber, 40mg cholesterol, 548mg sodium

◀ **AROUND-THE-WORLD CUISINE**

Prep Time: 40 minutes

Cook Time: 20 minutes

Average Rating: ★★★★★

What other cooks have done:

"This is very similar to our family recipe, though we don't use an egg. You can assemble gyoza and then freeze them in a single layer on a baking sheet. Once frozen, transfer them to zip-top bags. This helps with the amount of last-minute prep work. You can also fry them using more oil and omitting the addition of water, so they will be more like egg rolls."

Chicken and Broccoli Braid

(pictured on page 151)

Submitted by: **Kelly Grimes**

"This beautiful braided crescent roll with chicken and broccoli inside is as impressive as it is easy."

2	cups diced cooked chicken	2	tablespoons slivered almonds, toasted
1	cup chopped fresh broccoli	¼	cup diced onion
½	cup chopped red bell pepper	2	(8 ounce) packages refrigerated crescent roll dough
1	clove garlic, crushed		
1	cup shredded Cheddar cheese	1	egg white, beaten
½	cup mayonnaise		
2	tablespoons fresh dill weed		
¼	teaspoon salt		

1. Preheat oven to 375°F (190°C).
2. In a large bowl, toss together chicken, broccoli, red bell pepper, garlic, cheese, mayonnaise, dill weed, salt, almonds, and onion.
3. Unroll crescent roll dough and lay flat on a medium baking sheet. Pinch together perforations to form a single sheet of dough. Using a knife or scissors, cut 1 inch wide strips in towards the center, starting on the long sides. (There should be a solid strip about 3 inches wide down the center, with the cut strips forming a fringe down each side.) Spread the chicken mixture along the center strip. Fold the side strips over chicken mixture, alternating strips from each side. Pinch or twist to seal. Brush braided dough with the egg white.
4. Bake in the preheated oven for 25 to 28 minutes or until golden brown. **Yield:** 6 servings.

Per serving: 578 calories, 27g protein, 36g carbohydrate, 36g fat, 4g fiber, 103mg cholesterol, 754mg sodium

Beverage Cubes

Submitted by: **Erin**

"Everyone has a favorite drink that is always in the fridge, but don't you hate it when your ice cubes melt and make your drink watery? Here's a simple solution. Use your favorite noncarbonated beverage to make ice cubes—fruit juice, coffee, and prepared drink mix all work well. I prefer tea."

| 2 | cups brewed black tea, chilled |

1. Pour tea into an ice cube tray and freeze. Pop out a few whenever you're ready for a tall, cool drink. **Yield:** 12 cubes.

Per cube: 1 calorie, 0g protein, 0g carbohydrate, 0g fat, 0g fiber, 0mg cholesterol, 1mg sodium

Flavored Milk Syrup

Submitted by: **Leo M. Lalande**

"This quick and easy recipe for making delicious syrups for flavoring milk is a great alternative to those boring old chocolate or strawberry milk syrups. Make any flavor you like. You can also mix this syrup with carbonated water for a fruit-flavored soda."

2 cups white sugar
1 cup water
1 (0.13 ounce) package
    unsweetened fruit-
    flavored drink mix

1. In a saucepan over medium-high heat, combine sugar and water. Cook, stirring often, until mixture comes to a boil. Boil for 30 seconds to 1 minute. Remove from heat and allow to cool. Stir in drink mix.
2. To serve, stir 1 tablespoon syrup (or to taste) into 8 ounces milk.
Yield: 16 servings.

Per serving: 97 calories, 0g protein, 25g carbohydrate, 0g fat, 0g fiber, 0mg cholesterol, 8mg sodium

◀ **5 INGREDIENTS OR LESS**

Prep Time: 5 minutes

Cook Time: 5 minutes

Average Rating: ★★★★

What other cooks have done:

"We use this syrup in water rather than milk. I keep it in empty plastic bottles with pouring spouts that nondairy creamer comes in."

Cran-Dandy Cooler

Submitted by: **Bea**

"A carbonated cranberry and pineapple drink makes a very refreshing cooler."

1 (4 ounce) jar maraschino
    cherries
2 cups cranberry juice
1 cup pineapple juice
1 cup orange juice
2 tablespoons lemon juice
1 (12 ounce) can or bottle
    ginger ale
1 orange, sliced

1. Drain cherries, reserving juice. Set cherries aside for garnish.
2. In a gallon pitcher, combine cranberry juice, pineapple juice, orange juice, lemon juice, and cherry juice. Just before serving, slowly add ginger ale; stir to blend. Serve over ice in cups or glasses. Garnish with reserved cherries and orange slices. **Yield:** 8 servings.

Per serving: 110 calories, 1g protein, 27g carbohydrate, 0g fat, 1g fiber, 0mg cholesterol, 7mg sodium

◀ **KID-FRIENDLY**

Prep Time: 10 minutes

Average Rating: ★★★★

What other cooks have done:

"I made this for Christmas Eve so the kids would have a fun drink. I served it over ice with a maraschino cherry garnish, and they loved it. Even the adults went back for seconds."

Cherry Limeade I

Submitted by: **CindyM**

"This is extra tart cherry limeade. To reduce the tartness, stir in an additional bottle of lemon-lime soda."

2 (12 ounce) cans frozen limeade concentrate

1 (2 liter) bottle lemon-lime flavored carbonated beverage

1 (10 ounce) jar maraschino cherries, drained and juice reserved

1 lime

1. Pour limeade concentrate into a large pitcher. Mix in lemon-lime beverage. Stir in reserved cherry juice. Squeeze juice from lime into mixture; slice lime and set aside. Stir well and serve over ice. Garnish with cherries and lime slices. **Yield:** 12 servings.

Per serving: 234 calories, 0g protein, 62g carbohydrate, 0g fat, 1g fiber, 0mg cholesterol, 19mg sodium

Italian Cream Soda

Submitted by: **Darien Q**

"A watermelon- and passion fruit-flavored Italian cream soda."

1 cup carbonated water

1½ tablespoons passion fruit-flavored syrup

1½ tablespoons watermelon-flavored syrup

2 tablespoons half-and-half

1. Fill a tall glass half full with ice. Fill glass two-thirds full with carbonated water. Pour in passion fruit- and watermelon-flavored syrups; float half-and-half on top. Stir when ready to drink. **Yield:** 1 serving.

Per serving: 190 calories, 1g protein, 42g carbohydrate, 4g fat, 0g fiber, 11mg cholesterol, 89mg sodium

Honey-Lemon Tea

Submitted by: **COOKIN*KTH**

"This is my favorite tea; my dad used to make it for me all the time. It's sweet and tangy. Great for soothing sore throats!"

1 cup water	1 teaspoon white sugar
2 teaspoons honey	(or to taste)
1 teaspoon fresh lemon juice	

1. Pour water into a mug. Add honey; microwave on High for 1 minute and 30 seconds. Stir in lemon juice, mixing until honey is dissolved. Stir in sugar. **Yield:** 1 serving.

Per serving: 63 calories, 0g protein, 17g carbohydrate, 0g fat, 0g fiber, 0mg cholesterol, 8mg sodium

◄ FROM THE PANTRY

Prep Time: 3 minutes

Cook Time: 1 minute 30 seconds

Average Rating: ★★★★☆

What other cooks have done:

"Lemon tea is the best thing for a sore throat. It's so soothing. I prefer it without the sugar, though. I get the best results from rolling two lemons on the counter, juicing them, and then sticking a slice of the lemon in the water."

Hot Cranberry Tea

Submitted by: **Terra Spickerman**

"A sentimental favorite. My mother and I made this when I was 7 years old, and it's been a part of our holiday tradition ever since. A fun recipe to make with the kids. A slow cooker will keep it warm while serving."

3½ quarts water	2 oranges, juiced
1 (12 ounce) package cranberries	2 lemons, juiced
	12 whole cloves
2 cups white sugar	2 cinnamon sticks

1. In a large pot, combine water and cranberries. Bring to a boil, reduce heat, and simmer for 30 minutes. Add sugar, orange juice, lemon juice, cloves, and cinnamon sticks. Cover and steep for 1 hour. Strain tea and serve hot. **Yield:** 14 servings.

Per serving: 141 calories, 1g protein, 37g carbohydrate, 0g fat, 3g fiber, 0mg cholesterol, 10mg sodium

◄ MAKE-AHEAD

Prep Time: 5 minutes

Cook Time: 30 minutes

Stand Time: 1 hour

Average Rating: ★★★★☆

What other cooks have done:

"This is a beautiful rosy color, which is very attractive! I refrigerated the leftovers. It's delicious cold, and I think the flavor of the spices came through even better the second day."

Iced Mochas

Submitted by: **Wendy Cain**

"All of my friends rave about these frosty drinks. I pour my leftover coffee into ice cube trays and keep them on hand all the time. You can make fun squiggly designs on the insides of glasses with chocolate syrup before pouring the mochas. Top with whipped cream."

1½	cups cold coffee	¼	cup chocolate syrup
2	cups milk	¼	cup white sugar

1. Pour coffee into an ice cube tray. Freeze until solid, or overnight.
2. In a blender, combine coffee ice cubes, milk, chocolate syrup, and sugar. Blend until smooth. Pour into glasses and serve.
Yield: 4 servings.

Per serving: 163 calories, 5g protein, 31g carbohydrate, 3g fat, 0g fiber, 10mg cholesterol, 76mg sodium

FROM THE PANTRY ▶

Prep Time: 5 minutes

Freeze Time: overnight

Average Rating: ★★★★★

What other cooks have done:

"I use a simple syrup (1 part water and 1 part sugar, boiled together) instead of the white sugar. It makes a smoother drink. The syrup will keep just fine in the refrigerator."

Blueberry Cream Slushy

Submitted by: **GoldilocksMail**

"My husband and I went crazy over a blueberry smoothie at a local café. This is our attempt to recreate it, but we actually like this better than the original!"

1	cup frozen blueberries	1	cup vanilla yogurt
1	cup frozen strawberries	2	teaspoons white sugar
1	cup pineapple and orange juice blend	6	ice cubes

1. Place the blueberries, strawberries, juice, yogurt, and sugar in the container of a blender. Process until smooth. Add ice cubes and process until ice is small enough to fit through a straw but large enough to crunch on. Pour into glasses and drink through straws.
Yield: 2 servings.

Per serving: 261 calories, 7g protein, 56g carbohydrate, 2g fat, 4g fiber, 6mg cholesterol, 98mg sodium

FREEZER FRESH ▶

Prep Time: 5 minutes

Average Rating: ★★★★☆

What other cooks have done:

"This is so good that I can't get enough! If you have some left over, put it in the freezer. Thaw it out for an hour or so and put it back in the blender when you want a quick treat. It's just as good."

Delicious Healthy Strawberry Shake

(pictured on page 150)

Submitted by: **Melissa Anaya**
"My mom used to make this for me when I was a kid. I loved it then, and I still love it, especially on hot days."

2	cups milk	1	cup frozen strawberries
1	tablespoon honey		Fresh strawberries
1	teaspoon vanilla extract		

1. In a blender, combine milk, honey, vanilla, and frozen strawberries. Blend until smooth. Pour into glasses and serve Garnish with fresh strawberries. **Yield:** 2 servings.

Per serving: 186 calories, 9g protein, 27g carbohydrate, 5g fat, 2g fiber, 20mg cholesterol, 124mg sodium

◄ KID-FRIENDLY
Prep Time: 5 minutes
Average Rating: ★★★★★

What other cooks have done:
"Add an extra tablespoon each of honey and vanilla and an extra ¼ cup of sugar, and it becomes even more delicious. Make it for yourself or for your kids!"

Mint Tea Punch

Submitted by: **MCBartKO**
"Tea, mint, sugar, and orange and lemon juices make this a quick, easy, and refreshingly delicious drink on a hot summer's day. This recipe was given to me by a true Southern lady. Goes great with Cajun or spicy foods. Every time I serve this, someone asks me for the recipe!"

4	regular-size tea bags	¼	cup lemon juice
12	fresh mint sprigs	5	cups cold water
3	cups boiling water	3	orange or lemon slices
1	cup white sugar		(optional)
1	cup orange juice		

1. Place tea bags and mint sprigs in a large pitcher. Pour boiling water over tea bags and allow to steep for about 8 minutes. Remove and discard tea bags and mint leaves, gently squeezing out any excess liquid. Stir in sugar until dissolved. Stir in orange juice and lemon juice. Pour cold water into the pitcher. Serve in glasses over ice. Garnish with orange or lemon slices, if desired. **Yield:** 10 servings.

Per serving: 94 calories, 0g protein, 24g carbohydrate, 0g fat, 0g fiber, 0mg cholesterol, 6mg sodium

◄ MAKE-AHEAD
Prep Time: 10 minutes
Average Rating: ★★★★★

What other cooks have done:
"I make several gallons of this every week during the summer months. My whole family loves it. For me, it has just the right blend of flavors."

Party Punch III

Submitted by: **Amy Coon**

"This punch is so extremely easy to make that a child could do it, yet it is so delicious. It is always served at our family gatherings, and my sisters, brother, and I all served it at our weddings."

1 (2 liter) bottle fruit punch, chilled
1 (64 ounce) bottle orange juice, chilled
1 (2 liter) bottle ginger ale, chilled

1. In a punch bowl, combine fruit punch and orange juice. Slowly pour ginger ale down the side of the bowl to retain carbonation. **Yield:** 48 servings.

Per serving: 50 calories, 0g protein, 12g carbohydrate, 0g fat, 0g fiber, 0mg cholesterol, 14mg sodium

Easy Punch

Submitted by: **Donna**

"I served this at my grandmother's 90th birthday party, and everyone wanted the recipe. Use any flavor of drink mix."

4 (0.13 ounce) packages unsweetened strawberry drink mix
2 (46 ounce) cans pineapple juice
3 cups white sugar
4 quarts water
2 liters ginger ale

1. In a large punch bowl, combine drink mix, pineapple juice, sugar, and water. Stir until dissolved. Stir in ginger ale. **Yield:** 50 servings.

Per serving: 91 calories, 0g protein, 23g carbohydrate, 0g fat, 0g fiber, 0mg cholesterol, 22mg sodium

White Sangría

(pictured on page 150)

Submitted by: **Shawna**

"A wonderful punch made with white wine and mango and orange slices. Peach schnapps, cognac, and ginger ale round out this summer party drink."

½ cup peach schnapps
½ cup cognac
¼ cup white sugar
4 oranges, sliced into rounds
2 mangoes, peeled and sliced

4 (750 milliliter) bottles dry white wine, chilled
1 liter ginger ale, chilled
Fresh orange wedges

1. In a pitcher, combine peach schnapps, cognac, sugar, sliced oranges, and sliced mangoes. Chill for at least 1 hour.

2. Pour fruit mixture into a large punch bowl. Stir in white wine and ginger ale. Garnish with fresh orange wedges. **Yield:** 32 servings.

Per serving: 205 calories, 0g protein, 13g carbohydrate, 0g fat, 0g fiber, 0mg cholesterol, 14mg sodium

◄ CROWD-PLEASER

Prep Time: 15 minutes

Chill Time: 1 hour

Average Rating: ★★★★☆

What other cooks have done:

"I made this for a party, and it was a huge hit. People kept saying they usually didn't like sangría or white sangría, but they liked this. I love white sangría because drinks always get spilled, and white doesn't stain. I left out the sugar, and it was definitely sweet enough. For a garnish, I loaded up on fruit—nectarines, grapes, oranges, mangoes, and more."

Dressed-Down Drinks

Every hostess needs a signature drink to serve her guests—something with a little bit of personality that's sure to please everyone. But what if your favorite recipe calls for alcohol? If you're itching to exercise your bartending muscles but worried that your beverage of choice will leave some partygoers out of the fun, don't fret. This substitution chart covers the main offenders. If one of your more spirited ingredients isn't listed below, keep in mind that many liqueurs have a fruit juice counterpart you can turn to.

ALCOHOL SUBSTITUTION CHART

ALCOHOL	SUBSTITUTION
Amaretto: 2 tablespoons	¼ to ½ teaspoon almond extract*
Bourbon or sherry: 2 tablespoons	1 to 2 teaspoons vanilla extract*
Brandy, fruit-flavored liqueur, port wine, rum, or sweet sherry: ¼ cup or more	Equal amount of unsweetened orange or apple juice plus 1 teaspoon vanilla extract or corresponding flavor
Brandy or rum: 2 tablespoons	½ to 1 teaspoon brandy or rum extract*
Grand Marnier or other orange-flavored liqueur: 2 tablespoons	2 tablespoons unsweetened orange juice concentrate or 2 tablespoons orange juice and ½ teaspoon orange extract
Kahlúa or other coffee- or chocolate-flavored liqueur: 2 tablespoons	½ to 1 teaspoon chocolate extract plus ½ to 1 teaspoon instant coffee dissolved in 2 tablespoons water
Wine, red: ¼ cup or more	Equal measure of red grape juice or cranberry juice
Wine, white: ¼ cup or more	Equal measure of white grape or apple juice or chicken broth

*Add water or apple juice to get the specified amount of liquid (when the liquid amount is crucial).

Daddy Charles's Spooley

Submitted by: **Alicia**

"This alcoholic fruit punch was concocted by my dad in the 60s. Looking at the ingredients, you'd never think that this would be good, but somehow you can't really taste the alcohol. Be careful, though—stand up after two glasses, and suddenly the floor looks all, well, spooley!"

1	(750 milliliter) bottle rum	3	(12 ounce) cans or bottles lemon-lime carbonated beverage
1	(750 milliliter) bottle Chianti wine		
⅓	cup lemon juice	1	(46 ounce) can fruit punch

1. In a gallon jug or punch bowl, combine rum, wine, lemon juice, and carbonated beverage. Add fruit punch to taste. Serve in red plastic cups. **Yield:** 24 servings.

Per serving: 146 calories, 0g protein, 13g carbohydrate, 0g fat, 0g fiber, 0mg cholesterol, 29mg sodium

PARTY FOOD ▶

Prep Time: 5 minutes

Average Rating: ★★★★★

What other cooks have done:

"I omitted the lemon juice, and I used a medium bottle of lemon-lime seltzer and a big bottle of ginger ale so my guests wouldn't get too 'spooley.' It was a hit."

Bourbolicious

Submitted by: **Katrina Wood**

"This great recipe for bourbon slush is originally from my friend's Kentucky cousins, and I renamed it at a recent dinner party. It's especially good made with citrus herbal tea."

1	(12 ounce) can frozen lemonade concentrate, thawed	1	cup white sugar
		1½	cups bourbon whiskey
1	(6 ounce) can frozen orange juice concentrate, thawed	2¼	cups brewed tea
		6	cups water

1. In a large pitcher, combine lemonade concentrate, orange juice concentrate, sugar, bourbon, tea, and water. Mix well and freeze overnight. **Yield:** 8 servings.

Per serving: 349 calories, 1g protein, 61g carbohydrate, 0g fat, 0g fiber, 0mg cholesterol, 5mg sodium

FREEZER FRESH ▶

Prep Time: 15 minutes

Freeze Time: overnight

Average Rating: ★★★★★

What other cooks have done:

"We make this recipe with brandy. We fill the glasses half full with this and then add a carbonated beverage the rest of the way. This makes it a really refreshing drink for the summer."

Entrées

No matter how you define comfort food, you're sure to find your all-time favorites here, from meatloaf to lasagna to baked chicken, plus some new ones. These dinnertime solutions, straight from the kitchens of moms and grandmoms, guarantee clean plates.

Kathy's Roast and Vegetables

Submitted by: **Jaque**

"This easy, delicious roast is made in a slow cooker with potatoes and carrots."

SLOW-COOKER CREATION ▶

Prep Time: 25 minutes

Cook Time: 9 hours 20 minutes

Average Rating: ★★★★★

What other cooks have done:

"Everyone loved this—even the kids! I added some sliced baby mushrooms, and I'll add more carrots next time. I used the mini bagged carrots to make this even easier."

1 (3 pound) chuck roast
Ground black pepper to
  taste
Garlic powder to taste
	1 (1 ounce) package dry
	  onion soup mix

1 tablespoon vegetable oil	5 carrots, peeled and sliced into 1 inch pieces

2 (10.75 ounce) cans
  condensed cream of
  mushroom soup
	6 small new potatoes, halved

1. Season roast with black pepper and garlic powder to taste. In a large pot, heat the oil over medium heat. Sear the roast on all sides until brown, about 20 minutes.
2. Mix together the mushroom soup and the onion soup mix in a slow cooker. Place roast in the slow cooker and arrange carrots and potatoes around the meat.
3. Cover and cook on High for 1 hour; reduce heat to Low and cook for 6 to 8 hours, stirring occasionally. **Yield:** 8 servings.

Per serving: 329 calories, 27g protein, 24g carbohydrate, 14g fat, 3g fiber, 72mg cholesterol, 988mg sodium

Yakatori

Submitted by: **Rayna**

"This traditional yakatori is made with beef. You can also make it with pork or chicken, but you will need to adjust the cooking time."

AROUND-THE-WORLD CUISINE ▶

Prep Time: 15 minutes

Marinate Time: 4 hours

Cook Time: 15 minutes

Average Rating: ★★★★★

What other cooks have done:

"I love to entertain, and this recipe is always a hit. These are the first to disappear from the table. I use half sesame oil and half vegetable oil in the marinade. The sesame oil adds a little more Asian flavor. I also make these with chicken breast strips that I have pounded flat with a meat mallet."

½ cup soy sauce	2 green onions, thinly sliced
2 tablespoons vegetable oil	1 clove garlic, minced
2 tablespoons lemon juice	½ teaspoon ground ginger
1 tablespoon sesame seeds	1 pound sirloin steak, cubed
2 tablespoons white sugar	

1. In a glass or plastic bowl, whisk together the soy sauce, oil, lemon juice, sesame seeds, sugar, green onions, garlic, and ginger.
2. Thread the meat onto skewers (if you are using wooden skewers, soak them in water 30 minutes first). Place the skewers in a glass or plastic container just large enough to hold them. Add the marinade, turning skewers to coat well. Cover and chill for at least 4 hours.
3. Preheat grill for high heat.
4. Brush grill rack with oil and place skewers on grill. Cook on the prepared grill for 10 to 15 minutes, turning kabobs occasionally. **Yield:** 4 servings.

Per serving: 366 calories, 24g protein, 11g carbohydrate, 25g fat, 1g fiber, 76mg cholesterol, 1884mg sodium

Marinated Flank Steak *(pictured on page 188)*

Submitted by: **Connie DiPianta**

"My friends just love this wonderful grilled flank steak recipe that I invented! My daughters think this is great, and it doesn't take long to grill. This also works well when the steak is sliced and used in fajitas."

½ cup vegetable oil
⅓ cup soy sauce
¼ cup red wine vinegar
2 tablespoons fresh lemon juice
1½ tablespoons Worcestershire sauce
1 tablespoon prepared Dijon-style mustard
2 cloves garlic, minced
½ teaspoon ground black pepper
1½ pounds flank steak
Fresh rosemary sprigs (optional)

1. In a medium bowl, mix the oil, soy sauce, vinegar, lemon juice, Worcestershire sauce, mustard, garlic, and ground black pepper. Place meat in a shallow glass dish. Pour marinade over the steak, turning meat to coat thoroughly. Cover and refrigerate for 6 hours.
2. Preheat grill for medium-high heat.
3. Oil the grill rack. Remove steak from marinade, discarding marinade. Grill meat for about 6 minutes per side or to desired doneness. Garnish with fresh rosemary sprigs, if desired **Yield:** 6 servings.

Per serving: 282 calories, 15g protein, 3g carbohydrate, 24g fat, 0g fiber, 33mg cholesterol, 957mg sodium

◀ FROM THE GRILL

Prep Time: 6 minutes

Marinate Time: 6 hours

Cook Time: 12 minutes

Average Rating: ★★★★★

What other cooks have done:

"I added some slices of sweet onion and red and yellow bell pepper to the marinade an hour before I was ready to grill. I put the vegetables in aluminum foil and cooked them on the grill as well; they took longer to cook than the steak, which we cooked to medium. I sliced the meat into thin strips and added vegetables, tortillas, cheese, sour cream, salsa, and guacamole to make fajitas. They were awesome!"

Steak Parmesan

Submitted by: **Mary Lynn**

"Here's a fairly simple recipe for something different to do with cubed steak. It involves breading meat and then combining it with your favorite spaghetti sauce. Serve over pasta with additional Parmesan cheese. A real family-pleaser!"

1 cup dry breadcrumbs	2 pounds cubed steak
½ cup grated Parmesan cheese	¼ cup vegetable oil
Salt and ground black pepper to taste	1 (32 ounce) jar spaghetti sauce

1. In a medium bowl, combine the breadcrumbs, Parmesan cheese, and salt and pepper to taste. Dredge steak in breadcrumb mixture.
2. Heat the oil in a large skillet over medium-high heat. Place the breaded meat in the oil and sauté for 5 to 10 minutes or until meat is well browned on both sides.
3. Drain excess oil and pour spaghetti sauce into skillet with steak. Reduce heat to low and simmer for 30 minutes. **Yield:** 8 servings.

Per serving: 382 calories, 29g protein, 19g carbohydrate, 20g fat, 2g fiber, 76mg cholesterol, 754mg sodium

Braciola I

Submitted by: **Michele O'Sullivan**

"Try this delicious meat dish served with your favorite tomato sauce. The top round steak just oozes with mozzarella and Parmesan cheeses. Serve over pasta."

1 pound top round steak	¼ cup raisins
6 ounces mozzarella cheese, sliced	Salt and ground black pepper to taste
4 teaspoons butter, divided	2 tablespoons olive oil
⅓ cup grated Parmesan cheese, divided	1 (32 ounce) jar spaghetti sauce
2 cloves garlic, minced	

1. Cut the steak into 4 pieces and pound each piece with a mallet or the side of a cleaver until thin. Place a slice of mozzarella cheese and 1 teaspoon of butter on each piece, sprinkle each piece evenly with Parmesan cheese, garlic, raisins, and salt and pepper to taste. Roll each piece tightly and tie securely with string.
2. Heat olive oil in a medium skillet over medium-high heat. Sauté each roll in the oil for 5 to 10 minutes or until browned on all sides.
3. Heat spaghetti sauce in a pot over low heat. Add rolls and simmer for 1 to 1½ hours or until tender. Remove from sauce and cool slightly. Remove the strings before serving. **Yield:** 4 servings.

Per serving: 628 calories, 40g protein, 27g carbohydrate, 40g fat, 4g fiber, 125mg cholesterol, 1357mg sodium

Chile Relleno Casserole

Submitted by: **Dorothy**

"This is a Mexican-style casserole made with hamburger meat and green chile peppers. It produces a much easier version of chile rellenos, which are simply stuffed chile peppers."

1	pound lean ground beef	4	eggs
1	onion, chopped	¼	cup all-purpose flour
2	(4 ounce) cans whole green chile peppers, drained	1½	cups milk
1½	cups shredded Cheddar cheese, divided		Salt and ground black pepper to taste

1. Preheat oven to 350°F (175°C).
2. In a large skillet over medium–high heat, combine the ground beef and onion and sauté for 5 to 10 minutes or until browned; drain excess fat.
3. Arrange 1 can of the chile peppers on the bottom of a 7x11 inch baking dish. Sprinkle with half of the cheese and top with the meat mixture. Sprinkle the meat mixture with the remaining cheese, followed by the remaining can of chile peppers.
4. In a medium bowl, combine the eggs, flour, and milk, whisking until smooth. Pour into the baking dish over the chile peppers. Season with salt and ground black pepper to taste.
5. Bake in the preheated oven for 45 to 50 minutes. Let cool for about 5 minutes before cutting. **Yield:** 5 servings.

Per serving: 513 calories, 33g protein, 13g carbohydrate, 36g fat, 1g fiber, 280mg cholesterol, 886mg sodium

◄ AROUND-THE-WORLD CUISINE

Prep Time: 15 minutes

Cook Time: 1 hour

Cool Time: 5 minutes

Average Rating: ★★★★★

What other cooks have done:

"Man, this was good! I added some salsa to the beef. I really thought this recipe was too simple to be good, but I was wrong. It was even better warmed up the next day."

Rempel Family Meatloaf

Submitted by: **Connie Rempel**

"Tired of boring old meatloaf? Well, give this one a try. My husband won't eat any other meatloaf but mine."

FROM THE PANTRY ▶

Prep Time: 10 minutes

Cook Time: 1 hour

Average Rating: ★★★★★

What other cooks have done:

"This recipe was so good that I actually got my stubborn son to eat meatloaf for the first time in his life! Next time, I may add a little drizzle of ketchup over the top of the meatloaf during the last 15 minutes of cooking, just because we usually like some sort of sauce with our meat."

1½	pounds lean ground beef	1	(1 ounce) package dry onion soup mix
½	cup crushed buttery round crackers	2	eggs, lightly beaten
¾	cup shredded Cheddar cheese	¼	cup ketchup
		2	tablespoons steak sauce

1. Preheat oven to 350°F (175°C).

2. In a large bowl, stir together ground beef, crushed crackers, Cheddar cheese, and onion soup mix until well combined. In a separate bowl, stir together eggs, ketchup, and steak sauce until smooth. Stir the egg mixture into the beef mixture, adding a little water if necessary. Shape into a loaf and place in a 9x5 inch loaf pan.

3. Bake in the preheated oven for 45 minutes to 1 hour or until no longer pink inside. **Yield:** 6 servings.

Per serving: 362 calories, 27g protein, 10g carbohydrate, 24g fat, 1g fiber, 152mg cholesterol, 808mg sodium

Taylor's Piroshki

Submitted by: **Taylor's Mommy**

"These piroshki are as authentic as you can get without traveling to Russia. I received the recipe from my Russian-language teacher in high school, and I have been making them ever since. The kids like them, too! They take a little time to roll out, but then doesn't anything 'authentic' take a little time?"

CROWD-PLEASER ▶

Prep Time: 30 minutes

Stand Time: 25 minutes

Rise Time: 45 minutes

Cook Time: 20 minutes

Average Rating: ★★★★★

What other cooks have done:

"The recipe does take a little time to make, but it's so simple, and it's absolutely worth the extra time. This recipe makes a really big batch. We still have a lot in the freezer, but I'm sure they won't last long!"

1½	pounds ground beef	1	cup milk
1	onion, finely chopped	3	eggs
1	teaspoon salt	½	cup vegetable oil
	Ground black pepper to taste	2	tablespoons white sugar
	Dried dill weed to taste	1	teaspoon salt
1	(0.25 ounce) package active dry yeast	4	cups all-purpose flour, divided
¼	cup warm water	3	cups oil

1. In a medium skillet over medium heat, cook the ground beef until evenly browned; drain. Stir in the onion and cook until onion is translucent. Sprinkle in salt and pepper and dill weed to taste. Set aside to cool.

2. Meanwhile, dissolve the yeast in ¼ cup warm water and place in a warm location until frothy, about 10 to 15 minutes. In a medium saucepan over low heat, warm the milk and gently whisk in the eggs, ½ cup oil, sugar, and salt. Remove from heat.

3. Place half the flour in a large mixing bowl and gradually stir in the milk mixture. Add the yeast solution alternately with the remaining flour, stirring after each addition. Mix well. Knead until the dough forms a ball and does not stick to the bowl, gradually adding more flour if necessary. Cover the bowl with a clean cloth. Set in a warm location and allow to rise until doubled in bulk.

4. Turn dough out onto a lightly floured surface. Pinch off pieces approximately the size of golf balls. Roll the pieces into disks about 3½ to 4 inches in diameter.

5. Fill center of each disk with a heaping tablespoon of the cooled meat mixture. Fold disks over the mixture and firmly pinch edges to seal. Arrange on a flat surface and allow to sit approximately 10 minutes.

6. In a large, heavy skillet or deep fryer, heat 3 cups oil to 375°F (190°C). Fry the piroshki in batches until golden brown on 1 side; gently turn and fry the other side. Remove and let drain on paper towels. **Yield:** 11 servings.

Per serving: 447 calories, 14g protein, 43g carbohydrate, 25g fat, 2g fiber, 74mg cholesterol, 478mg sodium

Surprise Burgers

Submitted by: **SunKissed31**

"These are my favorite burgers. The pineapple inside the burger adds a hint of sweetness, while the sauce adds some tang. Warning: The added sauce and pineapple makes for a mess with little ones!"

1	pound lean ground beef	½	cup brown sugar
4	pineapple rings	1	tablespoon prepared
½	cup ketchup		mustard

1. Preheat grill for high heat.

2. Divide the ground beef into 4 portions; form a patty around each pineapple ring so that none of the pineapple is showing. In a small saucepan over medium heat, mix together the ketchup, brown sugar, and mustard. Heat until sugar is dissolved. Set aside.

3. Cook burgers on the prepared grill for about 5 minutes per side or until well done. Spoon brown sugar sauce evenly over the burgers before serving. **Yield:** 4 servings.

Per serving: 407 calories, 20g protein, 47g carbohydrate, 16g fat, 1g fiber, 69mg cholesterol, 478mg sodium

◄ FROM THE GRILL

Prep Time: 15 minutes

Cook Time: 20 minutes

Average Rating: ★★★★★

What other cooks have done:

"My family said that this was the best burger variation they had ever tried. I topped the burgers with red onion and avocado."

Garlic Pork Roast

Submitted by: **Brandy**

"Quick and easy in the slow cooker and very good. Everyone enjoys it."

SLOW-COOKER CREATION ▶

Prep Time: 20 minutes

Cook Time: 6 hours 5 minutes

Average Rating: ★★★★☆

What other cooks have done:

"Oh my goodness, what a great recipe! I added 1 tablespoon crushed peppercorns, 1 teaspoon oregano, 1 teaspoon ground cumin, ½ teaspoon ground cloves, 1½ teaspoons cinnamon, and 1 teaspoon chipotle powder. This was a huge hit at our house!"

1 tablespoon vegetable oil	4 sweet potatoes, quartered
1 (2 pound) boneless pork roast	1 onion, quartered
Salt and ground black pepper to taste	6 cloves garlic
	1 (14 ounce) can chicken broth

1. Heat oil in a large, heavy skillet. Season roast with salt and pepper to taste; brown roast on all sides in oil.

2. In a slow cooker, layer sweet potatoes, onion, and garlic. Place browned roast on top of vegetables and pour in chicken broth.

3. Cover and cook on High for 1 hour; reduce to Low and cook for 4 to 5 hours. **Yield:** 4 servings.

Per serving: 633 calories, 50g protein, 36g carbohydrate, 31g fat, 3g fiber, 134mg cholesterol, 555mg sodium

Southwestern-Style Chalupas

Submitted by: **Eleta**

"This recipe came from my sister, who lives in Arizona. It is a very tasty blend of pork, beans, and spices served over corn chips. Try topping with cheese, peppers, salsa, sour cream, or any favorite taco topping. Everyone who tastes it asks for the recipe."

SLOW-COOKER CREATION ▶

Prep Time: 15 minutes

Cook Time: 8 hours

Average Rating: ★★★★☆

What other cooks have done:

"I loved this recipe. I used large tortilla chips instead of corn chips. Next time, I plan on adding some Spanish rice and guacamole to the tortillas. I included garlic. I also sliced up half an onion into large pieces so I could add the pieces to the slow cooker and remove them after cooking."

1 (4 pound) pork roast	1 teaspoon dried oregano
1 pound dried pinto beans	Salt and ground black pepper to taste
1 (4 ounce) can chopped green chile peppers	1 quart water
2 tablespoons chili powder	1 (16 ounce) package corn chips
2 teaspoons cumin seeds	

1. In a slow cooker, combine pork roast, pinto beans, chile peppers, chili powder, cumin seeds, oregano, salt and ground black pepper to taste, and 1 quart water. Cover and simmer on Low for 4 hours.

2. Shred meat, discarding any bones or fat. Cover and continue cooking for 2 to 4 more hours. Add more water if necessary.

3. Place corn chips on serving plates. Spoon pork mixture evenly over chips and serve with desired toppings. **Yield:** 8 servings.

Per serving: 685 calories, 45g protein, 68g carbohydrate, 27g fat, 15g fiber, 77mg cholesterol, 897mg sodium

Texas Pork Ribs

Submitted by: **Laura Walton**

"This is a prizewinning master recipe that can be used for pork spareribs, country-style ribs, or pretty much any other type of pork rib; simply increase the bake time for meatier cuts. Try using some wood chips on the barbecue. The smokier the grill, the better the ribs will taste!"

6	pounds pork spareribs	½	cup chopped onion
1½	cups white sugar	4	cups ketchup
¼	cup salt	3	cups hot water
2½	tablespoons ground black pepper	4	tablespoons brown sugar
3	tablespoons paprika		Cayenne pepper to taste
1	teaspoon cayenne pepper (or to taste)		Salt and ground black pepper to taste
2	tablespoons garlic powder	1	cup wood chips (optional)

1. Clean the ribs and trim away any excess fat. In a medium bowl, stir together the white sugar, ¼ cup salt, 2½ tablespoons ground black pepper, paprika, 1 teaspoon cayenne pepper, and garlic powder. Coat ribs liberally with spice mix. Place the ribs in 2 (10x15) inch roasting pans, piling 2 racks of ribs per pan. Cover and refrigerate ribs for at least 8 hours.

2. Preheat oven to 275°F (135°C).

3. Bake ribs in the preheated oven, uncovered, for 3 to 4 hours or until the ribs are tender and they nearly fall apart.

4. Remove 5 tablespoons of drippings from the bottom of the roasting pans and place in a skillet over medium heat. Cook onion in pan drippings until lightly browned and tender. Stir in ketchup and heat for 3 to 4 more minutes, stirring constantly. Mix in water and brown sugar and season to taste with cayenne pepper, salt, and ground black pepper. Reduce heat to low; cover and simmer for 1 hour, adding water as necessary to achieve desired thickness. Set sauce aside.

5. Preheat grill for medium-low heat. If using wood chips, soak chips in water for 30 minutes.

6. If desired, add soaked wood chips to the coals or to the smoker box of a gas grill. Lightly oil grill rack on the prepared grill. Place 2 racks of ribs at a time on the prepared grill so they are not crowded. Cook for 20 minutes, turning occasionally. Baste ribs with sauce during the last 10 minutes of grilling. **Yield:** 12 servings.

Per serving: 620 calories, 33g protein, 55g carbohydrate, 31g fat, 2g fiber, 127mg cholesterol, 3375mg sodium

◀ **BLUE RIBBON WINNER**

Prep Time: 30 minutes

Marinate Time: overnight

Cook Time: 5 hours 30 minutes

Average Rating: ★★★★★

What other cooks have done:

"These ribs were awesome! I skipped making the sauce because we were going to serve bottled barbecue sauce on the side, but after one taste of these tender, juicy ribs, we decided no sauce was needed! These will definitely appear on the menu often."

Pork Tenderloin alla Napoli

Submitted by: **DELTAQUEEN50**

"If you like the robust flavor of olives, tomatoes, and rosemary, this is the dish for you. I find using a cast-iron skillet works best."

AROUND-THE-WORLD CUISINE ▶

Prep Time: 15 minutes

Cook Time: 40 minutes

Average Rating: ★★★★★

What other cooks have done:

"I substituted evaporated milk for the whipping cream, and it was very rich. We served this over a small amount of whole wheat angel hair pasta, and the flavor was amazing. I could even see skipping the pork and using the sauce over pasta as a main dish for my vegetarian guests."

1 tablespoon olive oil	2 cloves garlic, minced
2 (¾ pound) pork tenderloins	½ teaspoon salt
2 roma (plum) tomatoes, seeded and chopped	¼ teaspoon ground black pepper
¼ cup chopped green olives	½ cup whipping cream
¼ cup dry white wine	Fresh rosemary sprigs (optional)
1 teaspoon chopped fresh rosemary	

1. Preheat oven to 400°F (200°C). Heat the oil in a cast-iron skillet over medium-high heat. Brown pork on all sides in the skillet.

2. Mix the tomatoes, olives, wine, rosemary, and garlic in a bowl. Pour over the pork. Season with salt and pepper.

3. Place skillet with pork in the preheated oven and bake 20 to 30 minutes or until a meat thermometer inserted into thickest part of pork registers 160°F (70°C).

4. Remove pork from skillet, leaving remaining tomato mixture and juices. Place skillet over medium heat and gradually mix in the cream. Bring to a boil, stirring constantly. Reduce heat to low and continue cooking 5 minutes or until thickened. Slice pork and drizzle with the cream sauce to serve. Garnish with fresh rosemary, if desired.

Yield: 6 servings.

Per serving: 223 calories, 19g protein, 2g carbohydrate, 14g fat, 0g fiber, 80mg cholesterol, 380mg sodium

Marinated Pork Tenderloin *(pictured on page 189)*

Submitted by: **Lisa**

"This slightly sweet marinade makes for the best-tasting pork you will ever have."

¼	cup soy sauce	1	teaspoon ground cinnamon
¼	cup packed brown sugar	2	tablespoons olive oil
2	tablespoons sherry		Pinch garlic powder
1½	teaspoons dried minced onion	2	(¾ pound) pork tenderloins

1. Place soy sauce, brown sugar, sherry, dried onion, cinnamon, olive oil, and garlic powder in a large zip-top plastic bag. Seal and shake to mix. Place pork in bag with marinade and seal. Refrigerate pork for 6 to 12 hours.
2. Preheat grill for high heat.
3. Lightly oil grill rack. Discard marinade and cook tenderloins on the prepared grill for 20 minutes or to desired doneness. Slice into medaillons and serve. **Yield:** 4 servings.

Per serving: 303 calories, 29g protein, 17g carbohydrate, 13g fat, 1g fiber, 79mg cholesterol, 1016mg sodium

◀ FROM THE GRILL

Prep Time: 10 minutes

Marinate Time: 6 hours

Cook Time: 20 minutes

Average Rating: ★★★★★

What other cooks have done:

"This was fantastic. I baked the pork at about 325°F (165°C) for about 30 minutes. I also boiled the leftover marinade from the bag and used it as a sauce for the tenderloin."

Honey Pork with Peppers

Submitted by: **Nancy Olsen**

"A friend gave me this recipe many years ago, and it has been a family favorite ever since. Serve over rice and add salad and bread for a hearty meal."

1½	pounds boneless pork loin, cut into 1 inch cubes	2	tablespoons red wine vinegar
2	tablespoons vegetable oil	½	teaspoon ground ginger
1	(0.75 ounce) package dry brown gravy mix	⅛	teaspoon garlic powder
1	cup water	1	onion, cut into wedges
¼	cup honey	1	green bell pepper, chopped
3	tablespoons soy sauce	1	red bell pepper, chopped

1. In a large skillet over medium heat, sauté pork in oil for about 15 minutes or until browned on all sides. Add gravy mix, water, honey, soy sauce, vinegar, ginger, and garlic powder. Mix well; reduce heat to low. Cover and simmer for 15 minutes or until sauce has thickened and pork is nearly done.
2. Add onion, green bell pepper, and red bell pepper to skillet; simmer for 15 more minutes or until all vegetables are tender.
Yield: 4 servings.

Per serving: 431 calories, 30g protein, 29g carbohydrate, 22g fat, 2g fiber, 83mg cholesterol, 1004mg sodium

◀ COMPANY IS COMING

Prep Time: 30 minutes

Cook Time: 45 minutes

Average Rating: ★★★★☆

What other cooks have done:

"Very good recipe. To prevent a watery sauce, make sure the oil is really hot before adding the pork. Boil the excess liquid to reduce it before adding the gravy mixture. I added fresh garlic instead of garlic powder. I sautéed the pork with it."

Creamy Potato-Pork Chop Bake

Submitted by: **Ter Denlinger**

"No one can resist these chops that are browned and then baked with hash browns, onion rings, and Cheddar cheese in a sour cream sauce. Very tasty and easy. I've even made it an 'all-in-one' dinner by adding a drained can of green beans to the potato mixture before pouring it into the baking dish. Hooray for spuds 'n' chops!"

COVERED-DISH FAVORITE ▶

Prep Time: 15 minutes

Cook Time: 50 minutes

Average Rating: ★★★★☆

What other cooks have done:

"This is an easy make-ahead meal that's also great to take to someone else. Be careful not to totally cook the chops on the stovetop—just brown them. They'll cook the rest of the way in the oven and come out nice and moist."

1	tablespoon vegetable oil	1	(20 ounce) package frozen hash brown potatoes, thawed
6	pork chops		
1	(10.75 ounce) can condensed cream of celery soup	1	cup shredded Cheddar cheese, divided
½	cup milk	1½	cups French-fried onions, divided
½	cup sour cream		
	Salt and ground black pepper to taste		

1. Heat oil in a large skillet over medium–high heat. Add pork chops and sauté until browned. Remove from skillet; drain on paper towels.
2. Preheat oven to 350°F (175°C).
3. In a medium bowl, mix together soup, milk, sour cream, and salt and pepper to taste. Stir in potatoes, ½ cup cheese, and ½ cup onions. Mix together; spread mixture in the bottom of a 9x13 inch baking dish. Arrange pork chops over potato mixture. Cover dish.
4. Bake in the preheated oven for about 40 minutes or until a meat thermometer inserted into thickest part of pork registers 160°F (70°C). Uncover; top with remaining cheese and onions and bake, uncovered, for 5 more minutes. **Yield:** 6 servings.

Per serving: 753 calories, 28g protein, 46g carbohydrate, 55g fat, 2g fiber, 95mg cholesterol, 1080mg sodium

World's Best Lasagna

Submitted by: **John Chandler**

"This takes a little work, but it is worth it."

1	pound sweet Italian sausage		1	tablespoon salt
¾	pound lean ground beef		¼	teaspoon ground black pepper
½	cup minced onion		4	tablespoons chopped fresh parsley, divided
2	cloves garlic, crushed		12	uncooked lasagna noodles
1	(28 ounce) can crushed tomatoes		1	(15 ounce) container ricotta cheese
2	(6 ounce) cans tomato paste		1	egg
2	(6.5 ounce) cans tomato sauce		½	teaspoon salt
½	cup water		¾	pound mozzarella cheese, sliced and divided
2	tablespoons white sugar		¾	cup grated Parmesan cheese, divided
1½	teaspoons dried basil			
½	teaspoon fennel seeds			
1	teaspoon Italian seasoning			

1. In a Dutch oven over medium heat, cook sausage, ground beef, onion, and garlic until well browned. Stir in crushed tomatoes, tomato paste, tomato sauce, and water. Stir in sugar, basil, fennel seeds, Italian seasoning, 1 tablespoon salt, pepper, and 2 tablespoons parsley. Simmer, covered, for about 1½ hours, stirring occasionally.

2. Meanwhile, bring a large pot of lightly salted water to a boil. Cook lasagna noodles in boiling water for 8 to 10 minutes. Drain noodles and rinse with cold water. In a mixing bowl, combine ricotta cheese with egg, remaining 2 tablespoons parsley, and ½ teaspoon salt.

3. Preheat oven to 375°F (190°C).

4. To assemble, spread 1½ cups of meat sauce in a 9x13 inch baking dish. Arrange 6 noodles lengthwise over meat sauce. Spread with half of the ricotta cheese mixture. Top with a third of mozzarella cheese slices. Spoon 1½ cups meat sauce over mozzarella and sprinkle with ¼ cup Parmesan cheese. Repeat layers and top with remaining mozzarella and Parmesan cheese. Cover with aluminum foil; to prevent sticking, either spray foil with cooking spray or make sure the foil does not touch the cheese.

5. Bake in the preheated oven for 25 minutes. Remove foil and bake for 25 more minutes. Cool for 15 minutes before serving.

Yield: 12 servings.

Per serving: 452 calories, 30g protein, 37g carbohydrate, 21g fat, 4g fiber, 88mg cholesterol, 1750mg sodium

◄ MAKE-AHEAD

Prep Time: 30 minutes

Cook Time: 2 hours 30 minutes

Cool Time: 15 minutes

Average Rating: ★★★★★

What other cooks have done:

"Being an Italian, I know lasagna, and this truly is the best lasagna I have ever eaten! I followed the recipe to a 'T,' and it was superb. I replaced the water with Merlot, replaced ½ pound sweet Italian sausage with ½ pound hot sausage, and added a bit more garlic because, well, that's just what we Italians do. At the end of cooking, I briefly browned the top of the cheeses by broiling. This not only made a spectacular dish, but it made a lovely presentation, too."

Cheesy Sausage-Zucchini Casserole

Submitted by: **Mandy**

"My mom made this recipe with the zucchini and tomatoes that flourished in our garden. It's my favorite casserole."

FREEZER FRESH ▶

Prep Time: 15 minutes

Cook Time: 1 hour 20 minutes

Average Rating: ★★★★★

What other cooks have done:

"This is so delicious that it has inspired my husband and me to start planning a garden! I increased the rice to 1 cup. The first time I made this, I accidentally purchased hot Italian sausage, which my husband loved. I couldn't handle so much spice, so I used medium the next time, and it was perfect."

½ cup uncooked white rice	1 (8 ounce) package
1 cup water	processed cheese, cubed
1 pound pork sausage	Pinch dried oregano
¼ cup chopped onion	Salt and ground black
4 cups cubed zucchini squash	pepper to taste
1 cup diced fresh tomato	
2 (4 ounce) cans sliced mushrooms, drained	

1. Combine rice and water in a small saucepan and bring to a boil. Reduce heat to low and simmer for about 20 minutes or until rice is tender. Remove from heat and set aside.

2. Preheat the oven to 325°F (165°C). Grease a 9x13 inch baking dish or a 2 quart casserole dish.

3. Cook sausage and onion in a large skillet over medium heat, stirring constantly, until evenly browned. Drain excess grease. Stir in zucchini and tomato and cook until tender. Stir in rice, mushrooms, and cheese. Season with oregano and salt and pepper to taste. Spread into prepared dish.

4. Bake in the preheated oven, uncovered, for 1 hour or until lightly browned and bubbly. **Yield:** 8 servings.

Per serving: 304 calories, 16g protein, 17g carbohydrate, 20g fat, 2g fiber, 50mg cholesterol, 966mg sodium

Spicy Mexican Torte

Submitted by: **Tsfoust**

"This is a great recipe that my husband loves to make—it's a whole meal in itself and is very simple to put together. Serve with salsa, sour cream, or guacamole, if desired."

1 pound chorizo sausage, casings removed, crumbled	8 (10 inch) flour tortillas
1 cup chopped onion	2 cups shredded pepper Jack cheese, divided
2 cloves garlic, finely chopped	1 (16 ounce) can refried beans, divided
1 (4 ounce) can chopped green chile peppers, drained	1 (7 ounce) jar roasted red bell peppers, drained

1. In a large skillet, cook chorizo, onion, and garlic over medium heat, stirring occasionally, until sausage is done. Drain off grease; stir in chiles, and set aside.

2. Preheat oven to 400°F (200°C). Lightly grease a 10 inch pie plate.

3. Place 2 tortillas in pie plate. Spread half of the sausage mixture over tortillas. Sprinkle with half of the cheese. Place 2 tortillas on top of cheese. Spread with beans. Place 2 tortillas over beans and place bell peppers over tortillas. Place 2 tortillas on top of bell peppers. Spread with remaining sausage mixture. Sprinkle with remaining cheese and cover.

4. Bake in the preheated oven for 40 minutes. Uncover and bake for 15 more minutes or until cheese is melted and center is hot. Cool for 10 minutes before cutting. **Yield:** 8 servings.

Per serving: 690 calories, 32g protein, 55g carbohydrate, 38g fat, 6g fiber, 89mg cholesterol, 1981mg sodium

◀ HOT & SPICY

Prep Time: 15 minutes

Cook Time: 1 hour

Cool Time: 10 minutes

Average Rating: ★★★★★

What other cooks have done:

"My very picky husband loved this! I used fat-free refried black beans, and since my husband doesn't like red bell peppers, I used thin slices of tomato instead. When we made this the next time, we added jalapeños instead of the green chiles to make it hotter."

Chungles Pasta

Submitted by: **Sarah and Annette**

"A pepperoni, olive, mushroom, and caper sauce tops a pound of your favorite pasta. An eclectic mix of ingredients makes a quick and satisfying pasta dish."

QUICK & EASY ▶

Prep Time: 20 minutes

Cook Time: 20 minutes

Average Rating: ★★★★★

What other cooks have done:

"This made a very tasty dinner! You can adjust this recipe to your taste. I added a little white wine to the sauce and tossed in some leftover diced tomatoes I had on hand. Next time, I think I'll try it with feta. You could add other things, such as artichokes or a different kind of sausage—it would be fun to experiment!"

2 tablespoons olive oil	2 tablespoons capers
1 clove garlic, crushed	Salt and ground black
1 onion, chopped	pepper to taste
½ cup sliced fresh mushrooms	1 pound pasta
1 large tomato, chopped	1 cup cubed smoked
1 cup kalamata olives, pitted and sliced	mozzarella cheese
⅓ cup sliced pepperoni sausage, cut into strips	

1. Heat the olive oil in a large skillet over medium-high heat. Add garlic, onion, and mushrooms and sauté until onion and mushrooms are tender.

2. Add the tomato, olives, pepperoni, capers, and salt and pepper to taste and simmer until heated through.

3. Meanwhile, bring a large pot of lightly salted water to a boil. Add pasta and cook for 8 to 10 minutes or until al dente; drain.

4. Add warm sauce to pasta and sprinkle with mozzarella cheese; mix well and serve immediately. **Yield:** 6 servings.

Per serving: 556 calories, 17g protein, 64g carbohydrate, 25g fat, 3g fiber, 24mg cholesterol, 1027mg sodium

Curried Honey-Mustard Chicken

Submitted by: **Priscilla**

"This is the best chicken recipe I have ever had. I am not normally a curry fan, but I love this recipe!"

⅓	cup butter, melted	4	teaspoons curry powder	
⅓	cup honey		Pinch cayenne pepper	
¼	cup prepared Dijon-style mustard	4	skinless, boneless chicken breast halves	

1. In a medium bowl, combine melted butter, honey, mustard, curry powder, and cayenne pepper. Mix well. Place chicken breasts in a 9x13 inch baking dish and pour honey mixture over chicken. Cover and place in refrigerator. Marinate for at least 4 hours or overnight.
2. Preheat oven to 375°F (190°C).
3. Bake chicken in the preheated oven, covered, for 10 minutes. Uncover and bake about 10 more minutes or until chicken is no longer pink and juices run clear. **Yield:** 4 servings.

Per serving: 377 calories, 29g protein, 26g carbohydrate, 19g fat, 1g fiber, 110mg cholesterol, 614mg sodium

◀ MAKE-AHEAD

Prep Time: 10 minutes

Marinate Time: 4 hours

Cook Time: 20 minutes

Average Rating: ★★★★★

What other cooks have done:

"I reduced the amount of honey and butter to ¼ cup each. I used 2½ teaspoons of red curry powder, which is a little stronger than yellow curry powder. I also added a pinch of cumin. Nice recipe!"

Crispy Herb-Baked Chicken *(pictured on page 187)*

Submitted by: **Diana Canterbury**

"The secret ingredient to the crispy coating is instant mashed potatoes."

⅔	cup dry potato flakes	¼	teaspoon dried rosemary	
⅓	cup grated Parmesan cheese	1	(3 pound) chicken, skin removed, cut into pieces	
1	teaspoon garlic salt			
¼	teaspoon dried thyme	½	cup butter, melted	

1. Preheat oven to 425°F (220°C). Grease or line a baking sheet or a 9x13 inch pan with aluminum foil.
2. In a medium bowl, combine potato flakes, Parmesan cheese, garlic salt, thyme, and rosemary. Stir until well mixed.
3. Dip chicken pieces into melted butter and roll in potato flake mixture to coat. Place in prepared pan.
4. Bake in the preheated oven for 45 minutes to 1 hour or until chicken is no longer pink and juices run clear. **Yield:** 4 servings.

Per serving: 567 calories, 60g protein, 7g carbohydrate, 32g fat, 1g fiber, 218mg cholesterol, 938mg sodium

◀ KID-FRIENDLY

Prep Time: 15 minutes

Cook Time: 1 hour

Average Rating: ★★★★☆

What other cooks have done:

"I like this recipe because it's quick and easy. I added some more spice to it by sprinkling some Italian seasoning and a dash of chili powder into the dry mixture."

Hunter-Style Chicken *(pictured on facing page)*

Submitted by: **Diane**

"Italian cooks call this Pollo Alla Cacciatora—*a variation on Chicken Cacciatore that's made with bacon for a twist and lots of flavor. Serve with pasta or roasted potatoes, if desired."*

COMPANY IS COMING ▶

Prep Time: 15 minutes

Cook Time: 45 minutes

Average Rating: ★★★★★

What other cooks have done:

"Very good! I made a few adjustments, though. First, I used some leftover pea pods instead of mushrooms (they added a little color). I also included plenty of garlic. Finally, I added some yellow bell peppers. It was incredible."

¼	cup olive oil	1	tablespoon chopped fresh basil
1	(3 pound) whole chicken, cut into pieces	1	teaspoon salt
6	slices bacon, diced		Freshly ground black pepper to taste
2	onions, chopped	1	cup white wine
1	cup fresh sliced mushrooms	1	pound tomatoes, diced
1	tablespoon chopped fresh parsley		

1. Heat oil in a large skillet. Brown chicken in hot oil and remove from skillet. Add bacon and sauté over medium heat for about 2 minutes.

2. Add onions and mushrooms and continue to sauté until onions are translucent. Return chicken to skillet; sprinkle with parsley, basil, salt, and pepper to taste. Add wine and tomato. Cover and simmer for 25 to 30 minutes, turning chicken once during cooking. Remove chicken from skillet and pour sauce over chicken. **Yield:** 4 servings.

Per serving: 942 calories, 55g protein, 9g carbohydrate, 72g fat, 2g fiber, 227mg cholesterol, 914mg sodium

Cranberry Chicken I

Submitted by: **Heather**

"This is an incredibly easy recipe—just mix it up before going to work and pop it in the oven when you get home in the evening. The sauce that forms while it bakes tastes great over rice."

5 INGREDIENTS OR LESS ▶

Prep Time: 15 minutes

Marinate Time: 8 hours

Cook Time: 1 hour

Average Rating: ★★★★☆

What other cooks have done:

"I got everything ready for this recipe before discovering I had no French dressing, so I used blue cheese dressing instead. It was delicious, and the tartness of the blue cheese went well with the sweetness of the cranberry sauce."

6	skinless, boneless chicken breast halves	1	(16 ounce) can jellied cranberry sauce
1½	(1 ounce) packages dry onion soup mix	1	cup French-style salad dressing

1. Place chicken breast halves in a glass casserole dish.

2. In a mixing bowl, combine soup mix, cranberry sauce, and French dressing. Pour over chicken. Cover with plastic wrap and refrigerate for at least 8 hours.

3. Preheat oven to 350°F (175°C). Remove plastic wrap from chicken and cover loosely with aluminum foil.

4. Bake in the preheated oven for 1 hour or until done. **Yield:** 6 servings.

Per serving: 481 calories, 28g protein, 40g carbohydrate, 22g fat, 1g fiber, 68mg cholesterol, 1087mg sodium

Hunter-Style Chicken

Roasted Chicken with Risotto and Caramelized
Onions, page 195

Crispy Herb-Baked Chicken,
page 183

Marinated Flank Steak, page 169, and
Onion Meat Relish, page 245

Marinated Pork Tenderloin,
page 177

Cajun Catfish Supreme,
page 199

Firecracker Grilled Alaska
Salmon, page 201

Fast and Easy Tofu Lo Mein,
page 208

Smoky Mountain Chicken

Submitted by: **Kellie Ledford**
"I usually serve this chicken with fries, potato wedges, or a baked potato."

4	skinless, boneless chicken breast halves
	Ground black pepper to taste
1	teaspoon garlic powder
1	teaspoon Italian-style seasoning
1	(18 ounce) bottle barbecue sauce
4	slices ham
4	slices Monterey Jack cheese
	Toppings: ¼ cup chopped tomato, ⅛ cup chopped green onions

1. Preheat oven to 350°F (175°C). Grease a 9x13 inch baking dish.
2. Place chicken in prepared dish. Season with pepper, garlic powder, and Italian-style seasoning.
3. Bake in the preheated oven for 20 to 30 minutes or until chicken is no longer pink and juices run clear.
4. Remove chicken from oven and cover with barbecue sauce. Layer each breast with a slice of ham and a slice of cheese. Return to oven and bake for 5 more minutes or until cheese is melted. Remove from oven and top with tomato and green onions. **Yield:** 4 servings.

Per serving: 402 calories, 42g protein, 18g carbohydrate, 17g fat, 2g fiber, 108mg cholesterol, 1646mg sodium

◀ FROM THE PANTRY
Prep Time: 15 minutes
Cook Time: 35 minutes
Average Rating: ★★★★☆
What other cooks have done:
"I make this dish as a sandwich. I pound the breasts until they're thin before seasoning them. After they're done, I put them on buns and garnish to suit individual tastes. I pair this with home fries and cole slaw."

Unbelievable Chicken

Submitted by: **Ruthie Crickmer**
"This unusual combination of common ingredients is fabulous! Everyone who tastes this asks me to share the recipe."

¼	cup cider vinegar
3	tablespoons prepared coarse-ground mustard
3	cloves garlic, minced
1	lime, juiced
½	lemon, juiced
½	cup brown sugar
1½	teaspoons salt
	Ground black pepper to taste
6	tablespoons olive oil
6	skinless, boneless chicken breast halves

1. In a large glass bowl or dish, mix together cider vinegar, mustard, garlic, lime juice, lemon juice, brown sugar, salt, and pepper. Whisk in the olive oil. Place chicken in the mixture. Cover and refrigerate for 8 hours or overnight.
2. Preheat grill for high heat.
3. Lightly oil the grill rack. Remove chicken from marinade; discard marinade. Cook chicken on the prepared grill for 6 to 8 minutes per side or until chicken is no longer pink and juices run clear.
Yield: 6 servings.

Per serving: 276 calories, 40g protein, 7g carbohydrate, 9g fat, 0g fiber, 99mg cholesterol, 457mg sodium

◀ FROM THE GRILL
Prep Time: 15 minutes
Marinate Time: overnight
Cook Time: 16 minutes
Average Rating: ★★★★☆
What other cooks have done:
"This marinade is delicious! I've made this recipe quite often, and I've never had leftovers. The tang of the citrus juices and the sweetness of the sugar are wonderful together. Be careful grilling because the sugar tends to burn quickly."

Chicken Jerusalem I

Submitted by: **Angela Bacon**

"This quick and easy recipe for chicken breasts baked with a creamy white wine sauce is one of my husband's favorites. The taste far exceeds the preparation, which makes it one of my favorites, too!"

5 INGREDIENTS OR LESS ▶

Prep Time: 10 minutes

Cook Time: 1 hour

Average Rating: ★★★★★

What other cooks have done:

"Excellent and easy recipe. I halved the Ranch dressing mix, and I sprinkled the chicken with paprika when serving for color. This is a big keeper! My guests raved about it."

6　skinless, boneless chicken breast halves
1　(10.75 ounce) can condensed cream of mushroom soup
1　(8 ounce) package cream cheese, softened
1　(1 ounce) package dry Ranch-style salad dressing mix
1¼　cups white wine

1. Preheat oven to 350°F (175°C).
2. Place chicken in a 9x13 inch baking dish. In a blender, combine the soup, cream cheese, dressing mix, and wine. Blend until smooth and pour over chicken.
3. Bake in the preheated oven for 1 hour or until chicken is no longer pink and juices run clear. **Yield:** 5 servings.

Per serving: 431 calories, 37g protein, 9g carbohydrate, 22g fat, 0g fiber, 132mg cholesterol, 1042mg sodium

Mediterranean Pasta

Submitted by: **Sara**

"Serve these chicken breast pieces flavored with bacon, artichoke hearts, and rosemary in a tomato sauce over a steaming bowl of linguine."

QUICK & EASY ▶

Prep Time: 15 minutes

Cook Time: 30 minutes

Average Rating: ★★★★★

What other cooks have done:

"This was super! I omitted the feta and used chopped green bell peppers instead of artichokes. I topped it with Parmesan, and voilà! This wasn't a saucy dish, but it was full of flavor."

1　(8 ounce) package linguine pasta
3　slices bacon
1　pound skinless, boneless chicken breast halves, cooked and diced
　Salt to taste
1　(14.5 ounce) can peeled and diced tomatoes, undrained
¼　teaspoon dried rosemary
⅔　cup pitted black olives
1　(6 ounce) can artichoke hearts, drained
⅓　cup crumbled feta cheese

1. Bring a large pot of lightly salted water to a boil. Add linguine and cook for 8 to 10 minutes or until al dente; drain.
2. Meanwhile, place bacon in a large, deep skillet over medium-high heat. Cook until evenly browned. Crumble and set aside.
3. Season chicken with salt. Add chicken to skillet with bacon drippings. Add tomatoes and rosemary and simmer for 20 minutes. Stir in olives and artichoke hearts and cook until heated through. Toss with pasta. Sprinkle with feta cheese and bacon. Serve warm. **Yield:** 4 servings.

Per serving: 645 calories, 45g protein, 51g carbohydrate, 29g fat, 5g fiber, 110mg cholesterol, 890mg sodium

Roasted Chicken with Risotto and Caramelized Onions *(pictured on page 186)*

Submitted by: **Michele O'Sullivan**

"Moist roasted chicken gets the royal treatment with caramelized onions, balsamic vinegar, and creamy risotto. Preparation is especially quick if you purchase a rotisserie chicken from a grocery store. Sprinkle a little grated Parmesan or Pecorino Romano on top before serving for a nice touch."

4 tablespoons olive oil, divided
1 onion, chopped
2 tablespoons balsamic vinegar
1½ cups uncooked Arborio rice
¼ cup dry white wine
4 cups chicken broth, divided

2 tablespoons butter
2 cups chopped cooked chicken breast
   Salt and ground black pepper to taste
2 tablespoons chopped fresh thyme (optional)
   Grated Parmesan cheese (optional)

1. Heat 2 tablespoons oil in a medium saucepan over medium heat. Stir in the onion and sauté for 15 to 20 minutes or until onion is dark golden brown. Remove from heat; stir in the balsamic vinegar and set aside.

2. Heat the remaining 2 tablespoons oil in a separate large skillet over medium heat. Stir in the rice and mix well. Heat for about 2 minutes; pour in the wine. Reduce heat to medium-low and start pouring in the broth about 1 cup at a time, waiting until broth is absorbed before adding more. Stir constantly until all of the broth is absorbed and the rice is al dente, about 20 minutes.

3. Stir in the reserved onion mixture and allow to heat through. Remove from heat and stir in the butter and chicken. Season with salt and pepper to taste. Garnish each serving with thyme, if desired. Sprinkle with Parmesan cheese, if desired. **Yield:** 4 servings.

Per serving: 783 calories, 45g protein, 76g carbohydrate, 29g fat, 2g fiber, 72mg cholesterol, 2858mg sodium

◄ COMPANY IS COMING

Prep Time: 15 minutes

Cook Time: 45 minutes

Average Rating: ★★★★★

What other cooks have done:

"I reduced the amount of vinegar. I added the onion mixture to the rice while the rice was cooking, rather than leaving it to stir in after the rice was done. At the very end, I added some whipping cream to finish the dish. The taste was excellent."

Chicken Hurry

Submitted by: **Liz Lambert**

"This is a quick and easy dish to make. Great for potlucks or family dinners. Or serve it cold the next day with a salad for a picnic. This sauce is also great on pork spareribs. Serve hot with rice and salad."

1	(3 pound) whole chicken, cut into pieces	¼	cup packed brown sugar
½	cup ketchup	1	(1 ounce) package dry onion soup mix
¼	cup water		

1. Preheat oven to 350°F (175°C). Lightly grease a 9x13 inch baking dish.

2. Place chicken pieces in a single layer in prepared dish.

3. In a medium bowl, combine ketchup, water, brown sugar, and dry soup mix. Carefully pour sauce over chicken, making sure that all of the pieces are covered.

4. Bake in the preheated oven, covered, for 1 hour. **Yield:** 6 servings.

Per serving: 556 calories, 43g protein, 17g carbohydrate, 34g fat, 1g fiber, 170mg cholesterol, 812mg sodium

Salsafied Chicken and Rice

Submitted by: **Jamey Corrin**

"Spice up any night at your dinner table with this delicious combination of chicken, salsa, and rice."

1	tablespoon olive oil	1	(14 ounce) can chicken broth
1	pound skinless, boneless chicken breast halves, cubed	1	(8 ounce) jar salsa
¼	teaspoon salt	2	cups instant rice
¼	teaspoon ground black pepper	2	cups shredded Cheddar cheese

1. Heat oil in a large skillet over medium-high heat. Season chicken with salt and pepper; brown chicken in oil until chicken is no longer pink and juices run clear.

2. Add broth and salsa to skillet and bring to a boil. Remove skillet from heat and stir in rice. Sprinkle cheese on top. Cover and let sit for 5 minutes before serving. **Yield:** 4 servings.

Per serving: 592 calories, 46g protein, 44g carbohydrate, 25g fat, 2g fiber, 125mg cholesterol, 1255mg sodium

Curried Coconut Chicken

Submitted by: **ROMA80**

"Curried chicken simmered in coconut milk and tomatoes makes for a mouth-watering hint of the tropics! Goes great with rice and vegetables."

2	pounds skinless, boneless chicken breast halves, cut into ½ inch chunks	½	onion, thinly sliced	
1	teaspoon salt (or to taste)	2	cloves garlic, crushed	
1	teaspoon ground black pepper (or to taste)	1	(14 ounce) can coconut milk	
1½	tablespoons vegetable oil	1	(14.5 ounce) can stewed, diced tomatoes	
2	tablespoons curry powder	2	tablespoons tomato paste	
		3	tablespoons white sugar	

1. Season chicken pieces with salt and pepper.

2. Heat oil and curry powder in a large skillet over medium-high heat for 2 minutes. Stir in onions and garlic and cook 1 minute. Add chicken, tossing lightly to coat with curry oil. Reduce heat to medium and cook for 7 to 10 minutes or until chicken is no longer pink and juices run clear.

3. Pour coconut milk, tomatoes, tomato paste, and sugar into the pan and stir to combine. Cover and simmer, stirring occasionally, for approximately 30 to 40 minutes. **Yield:** 6 servings.

Per serving: 378 calories, 32g protein, 18g carbohydrate, 21g fat, 3g fiber, 78mg cholesterol, 837mg sodium

◀ OUT-OF-THE-ORDINARY

Prep Time: 20 minutes

Cook Time: 53 minutes

Average Rating: ★★★★★

What other cooks have done:

"If you like curry, you have to try this! I skipped the tomato sauce and added just a bit more curry powder, as well as some potatoes and carrots. I will definitely make this again!"

Chicken and Bacon Shish Kabobs

Submitted by: **Angie**

"Tangy marinated chicken is wrapped in bacon and skewered with mushrooms and pineapple. Excellent for entertaining. These kabobs are a must-try! They can also be broiled instead of grilled if you're low on time."

FROM THE GRILL ▶

Prep Time: 30 minutes

Marinate Time: 1 hour

Cook Time: 21 minutes

Average Rating: ★★★★★

What other cooks have done:

"The flavor was great. I put red and yellow bell peppers and red onion into the marinade along with the chicken. I didn't use green onions, and I added extra honey. We will be having these kabobs again very soon."

¼ cup soy sauce	1 pound skinless, boneless chicken breast halves, cut into chunks
¼ cup cider vinegar	
2 tablespoons honey	
2 tablespoons vegetable oil	½ pound sliced thick-cut bacon, cut in half
2 green onions, minced	
10 large mushrooms, cut in half	1 (8 ounce) can pineapple chunks, drained

1. If using wooden skewers, soak skewers in water for 30 minutes.
2. In a large bowl, mix together soy sauce, cider vinegar, honey, vegetable oil, and green onions. Add mushrooms and chicken to mixture, stirring to coat. Cover and marinate in the refrigerator for at least 1 hour.
3. Preheat grill for high heat.
4. Wrap the chicken chunks with bacon and thread onto skewers alternately with mushroom halves and pineapple chunks. Boil remaining marinade in a small saucepan for 1 minute.
5. Lightly oil grill rack. Cook skewers on the prepared grill 15 to 20 minutes, brushing occasionally with boiled marinade, until bacon is crisp and chicken is no longer pink and juices run clear.

Yield: 6 servings.

Per serving: 241 calories, 18g protein, 15g carbohydrate, 12g fat, 1g fiber, 44mg cholesterol, 839mg sodium

Cajun Catfish Supreme *(pictured on page 190)*

Submitted by: **Lu Post**
"I entered this recipe into a large neighborhood Cajun-recipe contest and won first prize. It is an unusual but delicious way of preparing catfish."

1½   pounds catfish fillets, cut
        into strips
  2   teaspoons Cajun-style
        blackening seasoning
  ¼   cup mayonnaise
  ½   cup butter, divided
  1   cup sliced fresh mushrooms
  ½   cup chopped fresh parsley

  1   cup sliced green onions
  1   pound small, peeled shrimp
  2   (10.75 ounce) cans
        condensed cream of
        shrimp soup
        Fresh cilantro sprig
        (optional)

1. Sprinkle catfish with blackening seasoning. Spread catfish with mayonnaise. Place in a shallow dish, cover, and refrigerate for 1 hour.
2. Preheat oven to 375°F (190°C).
3. In a large skillet over medium-high heat, heat ¼ cup butter until it begins to sizzle. Sear the fish strips until golden, turning once. Transfer to a 9x13 inch baking dish and arrange fish in a single layer.
4. In the same skillet, sauté mushrooms in remaining ¼ cup butter until golden. Stir in parsley, green onions, and shrimp. Reduce heat to low; cook until shrimp are pink and tender. Stir in cream of shrimp soup and blend well. Ladle soup mixture over fish in baking dish.
5. Bake in the preheated oven for 15 minutes. Garnish with cilantro sprig, if desired. **Yield:** 6 servings.

Per serving: 494 calories, 34g protein, 10g carbohydrate, 37g fat, 1g fiber, 228mg cholesterol, 1338mg sodium

◀ BLUE RIBBON WINNER

Prep Time: 30 minutes

Marinate Time: 1 hour

Cook Time: 25 minutes

Average Rating: ★★★★★

What other cooks have done:
"This mouth-watering fish is incredibly tender, and the sauce is very good. I did make a few slight adjustments. I am not crazy about blackening seasoning, so I substituted Creole seasoning. I added some extra mushrooms and some half-and-half to add some richness. Cream of shrimp soup can be a little salty, and I found that this combination helped eliminate that."

Super Grouper

Submitted by: **Shirley**

"Here's a simple, delicious broiled grouper fillet recipe for all of you grouper groupies. Fillets that are 1 inch thick take about 12 to 14 minutes to cook properly. If using thinner fillets, reduce cooking time accordingly."

½ cup butter, melted	¼ teaspoon ground white pepper
2 tablespoons lemon juice	
¼ teaspoon garlic salt	2 pounds grouper fillets
½ teaspoon dried parsley	2 tablespoons mayonnaise
⅛ teaspoon paprika	⅛ teaspoon paprika

1. Preheat oven to 350°F (175°C). Line a pan with aluminum foil.
2. Combine melted butter and lemon juice in a small bowl. Brush 2 tablespoons mixture on the foil lining the pan.
3. Mix together garlic salt, parsley, paprika, and white pepper. Sprinkle spice mixture on both sides of fillets.
4. Bake fillets in the preheated oven until fish flakes easily with fork, about 12 to 14 minutes. Brush fillets with lemon-butter mixture and spread with mayonnaise. Sprinkle with paprika before serving.
Yield: 4 servings.

Per serving: 465 calories, 44g protein, 1g carbohydrate, 31g fat, 0g fiber, 150mg cholesterol, 481mg sodium

Grilled Fish Steaks

Submitted by: **Colleen**

"My husband is not much of a fish lover, but when I made this simple recipe with halibut, he very much enjoyed it."

1 clove garlic, minced	1 tablespoon fresh lemon juice
6 tablespoons olive oil	
1 teaspoon dried basil	1 tablespoon chopped fresh parsley
1 teaspoon salt	
1 teaspoon ground black pepper	2 (6 ounce) halibut fillets

1. In a stainless steel or glass bowl, combine garlic, olive oil, basil, salt, pepper, lemon juice, and parsley.
2. Place the halibut fillets in a shallow glass dish or zip-top plastic bag and pour the marinade over the fish. Cover or seal and place in the refrigerator for 1 hour, turning occasionally.
3. Preheat grill for high heat and lightly oil rack.
4. Remove halibut fillets from marinade, discarding marinade. Cook fillets on the prepared grill for 5 minutes per side or until fish flakes easily with a fork. **Yield:** 2 servings.

Per serving: 539 calories, 36g protein, 2g carbohydrate, 44g fat, 1g fiber, 55mg cholesterol, 1259mg sodium

Firecracker Grilled Alaska Salmon *(pictured on page 191)*

Submitted by: **Christine L.**

"Salmon usually does quite well unadorned, but a hot and sassy marinade makes this grilled salmon even more delicious. With lots of zippy ingredients like balsamic vinegar, crushed red pepper, ginger, and soy sauce, you can't go wrong."

8	(4 ounce) salmon fillets	2	cloves garlic, minced
¼	cup peanut oil	1½	teaspoons ground ginger
¼	cup soy sauce	2	teaspoons crushed red
¼	cup balsamic vinegar		pepper flakes
¼	cup green onions, chopped	1	teaspoon sesame oil
1	tablespoon brown sugar	½	teaspoon salt

1. Place salmon fillets in a medium glass dish. In a medium bowl, combine peanut oil, soy sauce, vinegar, green onions, brown sugar, garlic, ginger, red pepper flakes, sesame oil, and salt. Whisk together well and pour over fish. Cover and marinate fish in the refrigerator for 4 to 6 hours.

2. Preheat grill for high heat and lightly oil rack.

3. Cook the fillets on the prepared grill 5 inches from coals for 10 minutes per inch of thickness, measured at the thickest part, or until fish just flakes with a fork, turning fillets halfway through cooking time. **Yield:** 8 servings.

Per serving: 308 calories, 23g protein, 5g carbohydrate, 22g fat, 0g fiber, 63mg cholesterol, 656mg sodium

◄ HOT & SPICY

Prep Time: 20 minutes

Marinate Time: 4 hours

Cook Time: 20 minutes

Average Rating: ★★★★★

What other cooks have done:

"This is by far the best salmon recipe I've ever had. The marinade is awesome! If your red pepper flakes are not fresh, be sure to rub them between your fingers to activate the heat. Served with grilled veggies, this is a healthy meal that is truly something to look forward to."

Broiled Scallops

Submitted by: **Gail New**

"My husband thinks these scallops are better than any we have found in any restaurant."

1½	pounds bay scallops	2	tablespoons lemon juice
1	teaspoon garlic salt		Fresh basil (optional)
2	tablespoons butter, melted		

1. Preheat broiler.
2. Rinse scallops and place in a shallow baking pan. Sprinkle with garlic salt, melted butter, and lemon juice.
3. Broil in the preheated oven for 7 to 10 minutes or until scallops start to turn golden. Remove from oven and serve pan drippings on the side for dipping. Garnish with basil, if desired. **Yield:** 2 servings.

Per serving: 403 calories, 57g protein, 9g carbohydrate, 14g fat, 0g fiber, 142mg cholesterol, 1113mg sodium

Bacon-Wrapped Barbeque Shrimp

Submitted by: **Jan**

"This dish is spicy and wonderful and as close as I can get to a restaurant version that I am addicted to. Be sure and use large shrimp; the cooking time for the shrimp and the bacon is similar. If you do use medium shrimp, you might want to precook the bacon a little—overcooked shrimp are tough and rubbery and a real sin!"

16	large shrimp	2	teaspoons barbecue
8	slices bacon, halved		seasoning (or to taste)

1. Clean and devein the shrimp, if desired, leaving the tails intact. Wrap each shrimp with a half slice of bacon, securing with a toothpick.
2. Line a 15x10 inch jellyroll pan with aluminum foil and place baking rack in pan. Place the shrimp on the rack and sprinkle with barbecue seasoning to taste; turn shrimp and sprinkle with barbecue seasoning to taste. Set aside for 15 to 20 minutes. The bacon will turn from creamy white to a little opaque as the seasoning soaks in.
3. Preheat oven to 450°F (230°C).
4. Bake shrimp in the preheated oven for 7 to 10 minutes or until bacon is crisp and shrimp are pink and tender. **Yield:** 3 servings.

Per serving: 455 calories, 14g protein, 0g carbohydrate, 44g fat, 0g fiber, 107mg cholesterol, 600mg sodium

Shrimp and Crab Enchiladas

Submitted by: **Lisa L.**

"Enchiladas made with shrimp, crab, and Monterey Jack cheese have a Southwestern flair."

12 (12 inch) flour tortillas
2 cups Monterey Jack cheese, shredded and divided
1 (6 ounce) can crabmeat, drained
1 pound cooked medium shrimp, peeled and deveined
1 (20 ounce) can green enchilada sauce
1 (8 ounce) container sour cream
1 bunch green onions, chopped

1. Preheat oven to 350°F (175°C).
2. Lay tortillas on a flat surface. In the middle of each tortilla, place equal amounts of cheese, crab, and shrimp, reserving some cheese to sprinkle on top of the tortillas. Roll the tortillas to form enchiladas. Arrange side by side in a 9x13 inch pan.
3. Pour green enchilada sauce over all of the enchiladas, covering the enchiladas completely. Sprinkle the reserved cheese over the enchiladas. Cover.
4. Bake in the preheated oven for 30 minutes. Uncover and bake for 15 more minutes. Top enchiladas with sour cream and green onions to serve. **Yield:** 12 servings.

Per serving: 586 calories, 27g protein, 70g carbohydrate, 22g fat, 5g fiber, 120mg cholesterol, 811mg sodium

◀ CROWD-PLEASER

Prep Time: 15 minutes

Cook Time: 45 minutes

Average Rating: ★★★★★

What other cooks have done:

"This meal was quick and easy to make. I served the enchiladas with grape tomatoes and scallions tossed with lemon, cilantro, cayenne pepper, and salt. It was like eating at a restaurant. Next time, I'll use a 30 ounce can of green enchilada sauce. This is definitely a do-again meal!"

Fresh Tomato Pie

Submitted by: **Britt Terry**

"A great way to use surplus tomatoes from your garden. Tasty served warm or cold!"

PARTY FOOD ▶

Prep Time: 15 minutes

Cook Time: 36 minutes

Average Rating: ★★★★☆

What other cooks have done:

"This is delicious at room temperature. I used part mayonnaise and part sour cream. Also, I sautéed the onions in a little butter first. I used roma (plum) tomatoes because they have less pulp; definitely use the ripest tomatoes you can find."

1	(9 inch) pie crust, unbaked	¾	cup mayonnaise
1	yellow onion		Ground black pepper to taste
6	small ripe tomatoes		
⅓	cup shredded mozzarella cheese	2	teaspoons chopped fresh basil
⅓	cup grated Parmesan cheese	2	teaspoons chopped fresh oregano

1. Preheat oven to 350°F (175°C).

2. Bake the pie crust in the preheated oven for 8 to 10 minutes or until lightly browned.

3. Slice onion and place in the bottom of crust. Slice tomatoes and arrange over onions.

4. In a medium bowl, combine mozzarella cheese, Parmesan cheese, mayonnaise, pepper, basil, and oregano. Spread mixture evenly over tomatoes.

5. Bake in the preheated oven for 22 to 26 minutes or until golden brown. **Yield:** 8 servings.

Per serving: 289 calories, 5g protein, 15g carbohydrate, 24g fat, 2g fiber, 19mg cholesterol, 325mg sodium

Broccoli and Rice Stir-Fry

Submitted by: **Trisha Caudill**

"This makes a quick and tasty meal, but it can also be served as a side dish. You can modify this recipe to include any veggies you choose."

QUICK & EASY ▶

Prep Time: 5 minutes

Cook Time: 30 minutes

Average Rating: ★★★★☆

What other cooks have done:

"I ended up adding more soy sauce. I used a pack of frozen stir-fry vegetables I had in the freezer, and I added a little garlic."

3	cups water	3	green onions, diced
1½	cups uncooked long-grain rice	2	eggs, beaten
1	tablespoon vegetable oil	2	tablespoons soy sauce
1	(16 ounce) package frozen broccoli florets, thawed	½	teaspoon salt
		¼	teaspoon ground black pepper

1. In a saucepan, bring 3 cups water to a boil. Stir in rice. Reduce heat, cover, and simmer for 20 minutes.

2. Heat oil in a large skillet over medium heat. Sauté broccoli until tender-crisp and add green onions. Remove from skillet. Add eggs to skillet; stir constantly until cooked. Return broccoli mixture to pan. Stir in cooked rice, soy sauce, salt, and pepper. **Yield:** 4 servings.

Per serving: 363 calories, 13g protein, 63g carbohydrate, 7g fat, 5g fiber, 106mg cholesterol, 815mg sodium

Eggplant Burgers

Submitted by: **Irv Thomas**

"This is the veggie burger supreme—the easiest and most economical burger of all. A single medium-size eggplant, together with the usual trimmings, feeds a family of six. Use whatever types of cheese and burger toppings suit your family's taste."

1	eggplant, peeled and sliced into ¾ inch rounds
1	tablespoon butter
6	slices Monterey Jack cheese
6	hamburger buns, split
6	leaves lettuce
6	slices tomato
½	onion, sliced
½	cup dill pickle slices
1	(20 ounce) bottle ketchup
3	tablespoons mayonnaise
2	tablespoons prepared mustard

1. Place the eggplant slices on a plate and microwave on High for about 5 minutes or until the centers are cooked.

2. Melt butter in a large skillet over medium-high heat. Fry eggplant slices until lightly toasted on each side and place 1 slice of cheese over each eggplant slice. Cook until cheese has melted and remove from the skillet.

3. Place an eggplant slice on each hamburger bun bottom. Top each with lettuce, tomato, onion, and pickles as desired. Dress with ketchup, mayonnaise, and mustard as desired. Cover sandwiches with bun tops. **Yield:** 6 servings.

Per serving: 427 calories, 14g protein, 55g carbohydrate, 19g fat, 5g fiber, 29mg cholesterol, 1788mg sodium

◀ QUICK & EASY

Prep Time: 7 minutes

Cook Time: 10 minutes

Average Rating: ★★★★☆

What other cooks have done:

"These are great. Definitely try them with garlic mayo if your store has it—it is fantastic with eggplant. Red onion is great on these burgers, too. I make double burgers and put two eggplant slices on each bun. Also, the 5 minutes in the microwave was a bit much for mine, so try 1 to 2 minutes to start."

Spinach Casserole

Submitted by: **Dianna Rom**

"I use this as a main-dish casserole, side dish, or appetizer—whatever the occasion calls for. If desired, you may add one can of diced tomatoes and green chiles to the cheese-spinach mixture for a little zing."

COMPANY IS COMING ▶

Prep Time: 15 minutes

Cook Time: 20 minutes

Average Rating: ★★★★☆

What other cooks have done:

"This recipe is easy and fabulous. I used Cheddar cheese instead of processed cheese. The whole thing got rave reviews from everyone who ate it. This is an attractive dish. Also, I made it the night before a big luncheon, and it reheated nicely. After it had been cooked, I let it cool, covered it with foil, and then I refrigerated it overnight. I took it out of the fridge in the morning and let it come to room temperature. I warmed it up in the oven for 15 minutes or so. The phyllo browned at the edges, but otherwise, it was perfect."

2 (10 ounce) packages frozen chopped spinach, thawed and drained
8 ounces crumbled feta cheese
2 cups shredded mozzarella cheese
1 cup cubed processed cheese
1 cup melted butter, divided
2 tablespoons distilled white vinegar
½ teaspoon garlic powder
Salt and ground black pepper to taste
1 (16 ounce) package phyllo dough

1. Preheat oven to 425°F (220°C). Lightly grease a 2 quart casserole dish.

2. In a large bowl, combine the spinach, feta cheese, mozzarella cheese, processed cheese, ½ cup butter, vinegar, garlic powder, and salt and pepper to taste. Mix well and set aside.

3. Place a layer of phyllo dough in the bottom of the prepared dish. Spread the spinach and cheese mixture into the dish and top with 4 layers of phyllo dough, brushing each layer with melted butter or spraying with cooking spray. Drizzle the remaining butter over the top.

4. Bake in the preheated oven for 20 minutes. **Yield:** 9 servings.

Per serving: 539 calories, 19g protein, 32g carbohydrate, 38g fat, 2g fiber, 105mg cholesterol, 1138mg sodium

Cholay (Curried Chickpeas)

Submitted by: **Shammi Edwards**

"This is a very flavorful recipe from North India, usually eaten with fried bread like bhatura or puri. I like to serve it over rice for a very filling meal. You can also try it as a quick snack over toasted bread."

2	cups water	1	teaspoon ground coriander
1	tea bag	1	teaspoon cumin seeds
1	bay leaf	1	teaspoon grated fresh
2	(15 ounce) cans garbanzo		ginger root
	beans, drained and divided	1	teaspoon grated garlic
2	tablespoons vegetable oil,	1	teaspoon ground turmeric
	divided		(optional)
1	onion, sliced	1	onion, finely chopped
3	tomatoes, chopped and		Salt and cayenne pepper
	divided		to taste
¼	cup fresh cilantro leaves,		Pinch garam masala
	divided		(optional)

1. Place 2 cups water, tea bag, and bay leaf in a pot and bring water to a boil. Reserve about ½ cup garbanzo beans and set aside. Stir remaining beans into boiling water. When beans are heated through, discard tea bag and bay leaf. Remove from heat. Drain beans, reserving water, and set aside.

2. Heat 2 teaspoons oil in a skillet over medium heat; add sliced onion and sauté until tender. Remove from heat, cool, and mix in reserved ½ cup garbanzo beans, 1 chopped tomato, and half of cilantro. Set aside.

3. Heat remaining oil in a skillet over medium heat. Blend in coriander, cumin seeds, ginger, and garlic. Cook and stir for 15 to 20 seconds or until lightly browned. Mix in turmeric, if desired. Add chopped onion to the skillet and cook until tender. Mix in the remaining chopped tomato. Season with salt and cayenne pepper to taste; add garam masala, if desired. Bring the tomato liquid to a boil and cook about 5 minutes. Stir in the boiled garbanzo beans, sliced onion mixture, and enough of the reserved water to reach a thick, gravy-like consistency. Continue to cook and stir 5 minutes. Garnish with the remaining cilantro leaves to serve. **Yield:** 6 servings.

Note: If you are using dried garbanzo beans, soak them overnight (about 8 hours) and cook them in boiling water to cover along with tea bag and bay leaf until the beans are soft enough to mash between two fingers but still hold their shape. Remove tea bag and bay leaf once beans are cooked.

Per serving: 243 calories, 8g protein, 39g carbohydrate, 7g fat, 8g fiber, 0mg cholesterol, 436mg sodium

◄ AROUND-THE-WORLD CUISINE

Prep Time: 20 minutes

Cook Time: 25 minutes

Average Rating: ★★★★☆

What other cooks have done:

"This is a delicious and nutritious dinnertime favorite! It's not too complicated, and it has an excellent flavor. I served it with plain couscous, and it was even better the next day served with whole wheat pitas! It was a big hit with both my husband and me, and it will become a regular for us vegetarians."

Braised Tofu

Submitted by: **Melissa**

"This dish is good either over rice or by itself."

QUICK & EASY ▶

Prep Time: 10 minutes

Cook Time: 30 minutes

Average Rating: ★★★★☆

What other cooks have done:

"This was great! I used a bit of onion and a lot of broccoli instead of the veggies recommended, and everything still worked out brilliantly. Be sure to use a nonstick pan."

1	(14 ounce) package firm tofu	3	ounces fresh shiitake mushrooms, stems removed
3	teaspoons sesame oil, divided	1½	cups snow peas, trimmed
1	(8 ounce) can water chestnuts, drained	1	cup water
		½	teaspoon oyster sauce

1. Slice tofu lengthwise into 3 long sections. Wrap each section in paper towels and press to remove excess water.

2. Coat a large skillet with cooking spray and add 2 teaspoons sesame oil. Heat over medium-high heat; add tofu to the hot skillet. Fry for about 5 minutes on each side or until delicately browned.

3. Remove tofu from skillet and slice into cubes. Add remaining oil to skillet and stir-fry the water chestnuts, mushrooms, and snow peas. Return tofu to skillet.

4. In a small bowl, mix together water and oyster sauce; add to tofu. Cover and cook over low heat for about 10 minutes. **Yield:** 4 servings.

Per serving: 163 calories, 10g protein, 15g carbohydrate, 8g fat, 3g fiber, 0mg cholesterol, 237mg sodium

Fast and Easy Tofu Lo Mein (pictured on page 192)

Submitted by: **Dasibelle**

"Try different ramen noodle flavors to perk up this dish and make it your own."

5 INGREDIENTS OR LESS ▶

Prep Time: 10 minutes

Cook Time: 15 minutes

Average Rating: ★★★★☆

What other cooks have done:

"Very easy to make! Clean-up was a cinch, too. For a different texture, try freezing the tofu first; then defrost and fry. I also added some teriyaki sauce for extra zing!"

1	(14 ounce) package extra firm tofu	1	(16 ounce) package frozen stir-fry vegetables
2	tablespoons olive oil	1	tablespoon soy sauce (or to taste)
1½	cups water		
2	(3 ounce) packages Oriental-flavored ramen noodles		

1. Press tofu between paper towels to remove excess water; cut into cubes. Heat olive oil in a large skillet over medium-high heat. Add tofu and fry until golden brown, about 12 minutes, stirring occasionally.

2. Meanwhile, bring 1½ cups water to a boil in a medium saucepan. Add ramen noodles, reserving seasoning packets. Boil for about 2 minutes or until the noodles just break apart. Drain.

3. Add stir-fry vegetables to tofu and season with the ramen seasoning packets. Cook, stirring occasionally, until vegetables are tender but not mushy. Add noodles and stir to blend. Season with soy sauce to taste and serve. **Yield:** 4 servings.

Per serving: 388 calories, 18g protein, 39g carbohydrate, 20g fat, 4g fiber, 0mg cholesterol, 1341mg sodium

Soups & Stews

*What's the best cure for the rainy-day blues?
A steaming bowl of rich, hearty soup. Set your stove
with a pot of soup that's chock-full of your favorite
flavors. Garnish each bowlful with a touch of cheese
or sour cream for a hearty meal no family can resist.*

Cream of Fresh Asparagus Soup II

(pictured on page 226)

Submitted by: **Holly**

"There's nothing like fresh asparagus when it's in season—take advantage!"

RESTAURANT FARE ▶

Prep Time: 15 minutes

Cook Time: 25 minutes

Average Rating: ★★★★★

What other cooks have done:

"This is a great recipe. Tastes like a gourmet soup you would pay 15 dollars a bowl for at a fancy restaurant. I had some leftover French onion soup that I used in place of the onions and some of the liquid. It was very good."

1   pound fresh asparagus, trimmed and cut into 1 inch pieces
½   cup chopped onion
1   (14 ounce) can chicken broth, divided
2   tablespoons butter
2   tablespoons all-purpose flour
1   teaspoon salt
    Pinch ground black pepper
1   cup milk
1   teaspoon fresh lemon juice
    Sour cream

1. In a large saucepan, combine asparagus, chopped onion, and ½ cup chicken broth. Cover and bring to a boil over high heat. Reduce heat and simmer, uncovered, until asparagus is tender, about 12 minutes. Process the mixture in a blender to puree the vegetables. Set aside.

2. In the same saucepan, melt the butter over medium-low heat. Stir in the flour, salt, and pepper. Cook, stirring constantly, for 2 minutes. Whisk in the remaining chicken broth, and increase heat to medium. Cook, stirring constantly, until the mixture boils. Stir in asparagus puree and milk.

3. Add lemon juice to soup. Stir until heated through but don't allow it to boil. Serve immediately with sour cream. **Yield:** 4 servings.

Per serving: 205 calories, 7g protein, 15g carbohydrate, 14g fat, 3g fiber, 33mg cholesterol, 1127mg sodium

Cream of Fresh Tomato Soup

Submitted by: **Karen Gibson**

"This homemade soup is much better than store-bought soup. It's so creamy and flavorful."

QUICK & EASY ▶

Prep Time: 10 minutes

Cook Time: 35 minutes

Average Rating: ★★★★☆

What other cooks have done:

"Thank you for this quick and easy tomato soup recipe. I removed the tomatoes' skins first by placing them in boiling water."

2   large tomatoes, peeled, seeded, and chopped
½   cup chopped onion
½   teaspoon white sugar
    Salt and ground black pepper to taste
2   tablespoons butter
2   tablespoons all-purpose flour
2   cups milk

1. In a large covered pan, simmer tomato, onion, sugar, and salt and pepper to taste until onion is soft. Remove mixture from heat; puree.

2. In a saucepan, melt butter. Stir in flour. Whisk in milk and cook until slightly thickened. Slowly add tomato mixture and gently heat. Serve hot. **Yield:** 2 servings.

Per serving: 303 calories, 11g protein, 31g carbohydrate, 16g fat, 3g fiber, 20mg cholesterol, 264mg sodium

Cauliflower-Cheese Soup

Submitted by: **Jane Snider**

"A soothing, cheesy soup. Serve with a roll and a salad."

¾ cup water	¼ cup all-purpose flour
1 cup chopped cauliflower	3 cups milk
1 cup cubed potatoes	Salt and ground black
½ cup finely chopped celery	pepper to taste
½ cup diced carrots	1 cup shredded Cheddar
¼ cup chopped onion	cheese
¼ cup butter	

1. In a large saucepan, combine water, cauliflower, potatoes, celery, carrots, and onion. Boil for 5 to 10 minutes or until tender. Set aside.
2. Melt butter in separate saucepan over medium heat. Stir in flour, and cook for 2 minutes. Remove from heat and gradually stir in milk. Return to heat and cook until thickened. Stir in vegetables with cooking liquid; season with salt and pepper to taste. Add cheese; stir until melted. **Yield:** 4 servings.

Per serving: 386 calories, 16g protein, 26g carbohydrate, 25g fat, 3g fiber, 75mg cholesterol, 415mg sodium

◄ KID-FRIENDLY

Prep Time: 20 minutes

Cook Time: 25 minutes

Average Rating: ★★★★★

What other cooks have done:

"This soup is delicious! I added more cauliflower and some broccoli, and I used low-fat chicken broth instead of water. I also used more cheese and added some hot pepper sauce and crushed red pepper flakes."

My Favorite Soup

Submitted by: **Suzanne**

"This is absolutely wonderful and easy to make. It's a lovely cream cheese and potato soup with shrimp and green onions."

1 (8 ounce) package cream cheese	1 (15.25 ounce) can whole kernel corn
½ cup butter	½ cup milk
1 cup chopped green onions	1 pound cooked shrimp
2 (10.75 ounce) cans condensed cream of potato soup	

1. In a large Dutch oven, slowly melt cream cheese and butter over low heat. Add green onions and simmer 10 to 15 minutes. Stir in condensed soup and corn. Simmer 10 to 15 minutes.
2. Stir in milk; add more milk if needed to reach desired consistency (soup will be thick). Add shrimp and heat thoroughly. **Yield:** 5 servings.

Per serving: 582 calories, 27g protein, 33g carbohydrate, 40g fat, 3g fiber, 286mg cholesterol, 1632mg sodium

◄ QUICK & EASY

Prep Time: 10 minutes

Cook Time: 35 minutes

Average Rating: ★★★★★

What other cooks have done:

"I'm a soupaholic and will definitely be adding this to my collection of favorites. I doubled it and shared it with my mom and dad, and we all loved it."

Hungarian Mushroom Soup

Submitted by: **Cathy T**

"My family loves soup, and this is one of their favorites. It has lots of flavor and is fairly quick to make. It's primarily a mushroom soup, but it derives a lot of its flavor from other ingredients."

AROUND-THE-WORLD CUISINE ▶

Prep Time: 15 minutes

Cook Time: 45 minutes

Average Rating: ★★★★★

What other cooks have done:

"This soup is definitely gourmet fare, but it's easy to make. I used a white onion in mine, along with a combination of button and cremini mushrooms, plus one portobello. Instead of mixing in the sour cream, I served the soup with a dollop of it on top. The soup was very spicy. The sour cream complemented it well. No more canned mushroom soup for me!"

4	tablespoons unsalted butter	3	tablespoons all-purpose flour
2	cups chopped onion	1	teaspoon salt
2	(8 ounce) packages fresh mushrooms, sliced		Ground black pepper to taste
2	teaspoons dried dill weed	2	teaspoons lemon juice
1	tablespoon paprika	¼	cup chopped fresh parsley
1	tablespoon soy sauce	½	cup sour cream
2	cups chicken broth		
1	cup milk		

1. Melt butter in a large Dutch oven over medium heat. Sauté onion in butter for 5 minutes. Add mushrooms and sauté for 5 more minutes. Stir in dill weed, paprika, soy sauce, and broth. Reduce heat to low, cover, and simmer for 15 minutes.

2. In a small bowl, whisk together milk and flour. Add to soup and stir well to blend. Cover and simmer for 15 minutes, stirring occasionally.

3. Stir in salt, pepper, lemon juice, parsley, and sour cream. Mix together and heat through, about 3 to 5 minutes (do not boil). Serve immediately. **Yield:** 6 servings.

Per serving: 202 calories, 7g protein, 15g carbohydrate, 14g fat, 2g fiber, 32mg cholesterol, 833mg sodium

African Sweet Potato and Peanut Soup

Submitted by: **GREGMCE**

"This delicious soup combines the complementary tastes of sweet potatoes, peanuts, and tomatoes."

1	tablespoon vegetable oil		1	carrot, peeled and chopped
1	large onion, chopped		4½	cups water
2	cloves garlic, minced		1	teaspoon salt
2	teaspoons minced fresh ginger root		¼	cup chopped, unsalted dry-roasted peanuts
1½	teaspoons ground cumin			Pinch cayenne pepper
1½	teaspoons ground coriander		2	tablespoons creamy peanut butter
½	teaspoon ground cinnamon		1	bunch chopped fresh cilantro
	Pinch ground cloves			
3	medium tomatoes, chopped			
1½	pounds sweet potatoes, peeled and chopped			

1. Heat oil in a large saucepan over medium-high heat. Sauté onion in oil 10 minutes or until lightly browned. Mix in garlic, ginger, cumin, coriander, cinnamon, and cloves. Stir in tomato, sweet potatoes, and carrot and continue to cook and stir about 5 minutes.

2. Pour water into the saucepan and season the mixture with salt. Bring to a boil, reduce heat, and simmer 30 minutes.

3. Remove soup from heat. In a food processor or blender, blend soup and peanuts until almost smooth. Season with cayenne pepper. Return soup to saucepan. Whisk in peanut butter and heat through. Serve warm topped with fresh cilantro. **Yield:** 6 servings.

Per serving: 244 calories, 6g protein, 38g carbohydrate, 9g fat, 7g fiber, 0mg cholesterol, 450mg sodium

◄ OUT-OF-THE-ORDINARY

Prep Time: 20 minutes

Cook Time: 55 minutes

Average Rating: ★★★★☆

What other cooks have done:

"I love this recipe. I wouldn't change a thing. The soup doesn't need the cilantro if you don't want it. It has plenty of flavor on its own. Just make sure you spice it to your taste."

Beef Noodle Soup

Submitted by: **Brenda**

"This delicious soup was a favorite of mine while attending college. My family has been enjoying it ever since! Very easy and quick to make. It includes stew meat, mixed vegetables, and egg noodles in a beef broth base."

ONE-DISH MEAL ▶

Prep Time: 15 minutes

Cook Time: 35 minutes

Average Rating: ★★★★★

What other cooks have done:

"This is a keeper. When I use too many bouillon granules, I place some sliced potatoes in to soak up the salt, and then I discard them. Great comfort food!"

1	pound cubed beef stew meat	¼	teaspoon dried parsley
1	cup chopped onion		Pinch ground black pepper
1	cup chopped celery	1	cup chopped carrots
¼	cup beef bouillon granules	5¾	cups water
		2½	cups dried egg noodles

1. In a large saucepan over medium-high heat, sauté stew meat, onion, and celery for 5 minutes or until meat is browned on all sides.
2. Stir in bouillon granules, parsley, pepper, carrots, and water. Bring to a boil, reduce heat to low, and simmer for 20 minutes. Add egg noodles and simmer for 10 more minutes. **Yield:** 6 servings.

Per serving: 365 calories, 25g protein, 24g carbohydrate, 19g fat, 2g fiber, 89mg cholesterol, 214mg sodium

Reuben Soup

Submitted by: **Holly**

"Unique and delicious soup with sauerkraut, corned beef, and Swiss cheese."

COVERED-DISH FAVORITE ▶

Prep Time: 15 minutes

Cook Time: 45 minutes

Average Rating: ★★★★★

What other cooks have done:

"I made this for a potluck at church, and it disappeared in a hurry. I put it in a slow cooker and served toasted rye bread and shredded Swiss cheese on the side. Several people asked for the recipe. I added a little lemon pepper, which seemed to add an extra dimension of flavor. I will definitely make this again!"

½	cup chopped onion	1	cup sauerkraut, drained
¼	cup chopped celery	3	cups half-and-half
3	tablespoons butter	3	cups shredded Swiss cheese, divided
¼	cup all-purpose flour		
3	cups water	8	slices rye bread, toasted and cut into triangles
4	beef bouillon cubes		
8	ounces shredded corned beef		

1. In a large saucepan, cook onion and celery in butter until tender; stir in flour until smooth. Gradually stir in water and bouillon and bring to a boil. Reduce heat to low and simmer for 5 minutes.
2. Stir in corned beef, sauerkraut, half-and-half, and 1 cup cheese. Cook, stirring occasionally, for 30 minutes or until slightly thickened.
3. Preheat broiler.
4. Ladle soup into 8 ovenproof bowls. Top each bowl with a slice of bread and sprinkle ¼ cup cheese on top of each slice of bread. Broil in the preheated oven until the cheese melts and lightly browns. **Yield:** 8 servings.

Per serving: 463 calories, 25g protein, 23g carbohydrate, 30g fat, 2g fiber, 107mg cholesterol, 1168mg sodium

Cheeseburger Soup I

Submitted by: **Arlene**

"I use sharp Cheddar cheese because I like the taste, but any variety of Cheddar is good."

¼ cup butter, divided	3 cups chicken broth
½ pound lean ground beef	4 cups cubed potatoes
¾ cup chopped onion	¼ cup all-purpose flour
¾ cup shredded carrots	1½ cups milk
¾ cup chopped celery	2 cups cubed Cheddar cheese
1 teaspoon dried basil	¼ cup sour cream
1 teaspoon dried parsley	

1. In a large pot, melt 1 tablespoon butter over medium heat; cook beef, onion, carrots, and celery, stirring frequently, until beef is browned.

2. Stir in basil and parsley. Add broth and potatoes. Bring to a boil. Reduce heat and simmer until potatoes are tender, about 10 to 12 minutes.

3. In a small skillet, melt remaining butter and stir in flour. Add the milk, stirring until smooth.

4. Gradually add milk mixture to the soup, stirring constantly. Bring to a boil and reduce heat to simmer. Stir in cheese. When cheese is melted, add sour cream and heat through. **Yield:** 7 servings.

Per serving: 471 calories, 22g protein, 26g carbohydrate, 31g fat, 3g fiber, 93mg cholesterol, 703mg sodium

◄ KID-FRIENDLY

Prep Time: 20 minutes

Cook Time: 30 minutes

Average Rating: ★★★★★

What other cooks have done:

"Great soup! I made this with ground turkey, and we really enjoyed it. I'll cut the potatoes a little smaller next time."

Cajun-Style Corn Soup

Submitted by: **Maurice Tate, Jr.**

"This old Cajun-style recipe comes from Mamou, Louisiana, courtesy of my mom's notes. If you like spicy soup, double the amount of cayenne pepper."

HOT & SPICY ▶

Prep Time: 20 minutes

Cook Time: 1 hour

Average Rating: ★★★★☆

What other cooks have done:

"Love this recipe! This is a great success with all my friends. I add two cubes of bouillon to the water, which makes it a bit richer. I also use slightly less garlic, and I add some chili powder. Serve it with hot bread and butter."

4	cups water	1	green bell pepper, chopped
1⅓	(6 ounce) cans tomato paste	1	red bell pepper, chopped
1	teaspoon salt	2	cups fresh corn kernels
1	teaspoon ground black pepper	1	tablespoon vegetable oil
½	teaspoon ground cayenne pepper	½	onion, chopped
		4	cloves garlic, minced
		½	pound ground beef

1. In a large pot over high heat, combine the water, tomato paste, salt, ground black pepper, cayenne pepper, green bell pepper, red bell pepper, and corn. Bring to a boil, reduce heat to medium-low, and allow to simmer at a low boil for 35 minutes.

2. In a large saucepan over medium heat, combine the oil, onion, and garlic and sauté for 3 to 5 minutes. Add to the simmering soup. In the same saucepan over medium heat, sauté the ground beef for 10 minutes or until well browned; drain and add to the soup. Stir well and simmer for 10 more minutes. **Yield:** 4 servings.

Per serving: 347 calories, 15g protein, 32g carbohydrate, 20g fat, 6g fiber, 48mg cholesterol, 1089mg sodium

Hot Dog Soup

Submitted by: **Nancy Carole**

"My mother, Marea Mooney, made this soup for her six children. It's a warm and filling mixture of potatoes, green beans, and frankfurters. It's easy to make, and you can adjust the ingredients to taste. We all love it, and we hope you do, too! Serve with salad and warm rolls."

KID-FRIENDLY ▶

Prep Time: 15 minutes

Cook Time: 45 minutes

Average Rating: ★★★★☆

What other cooks have done:

"My husband thought this soup sounded weird. He said he wouldn't like it. We were surprised at how good this soup turned out to be, and my husband loved it. I highly recommend this recipe."

1	onion, chopped	1	(9 ounce) package frozen green beans
2	tablespoons butter		
3	potatoes, peeled and cubed	1	(16 ounce) package beef frankfurters, cut into bite-size pieces
1	(8 ounce) can tomato sauce		
1	(14 ounce) can chicken broth		

1. Place the onion and butter in a large saucepan over medium heat. Slowly cook and stir until the onion is soft. Mix in the potatoes and add enough water to cover. Bring to a boil. Reduce heat and mix in the tomato sauce, chicken broth, green beans, and frankfurters. Simmer 30 minutes or until potatoes are tender. **Yield:** 6 servings.

Per serving: 355 calories, 12g protein, 20g carbohydrate, 26g fat, 3g fiber, 46mg cholesterol, 1330mg sodium

Venison Italian Soup

Submitted by: **Joelene Craver**

"This is a hearty all-in-one meal that contains vegetables, meat, and pasta. Served with mozzarella-garlic bread, it makes a great meal on a cold winter day. This is a variation of a soup made with beef. I like venison because it is low in fat. Garnish with your favorite cheese."

1	pound ground venison	½	teaspoon ground black pepper
1	onion, chopped		
1	tablespoon minced garlic	1	(15 ounce) can pinto beans
1	(14.5 ounce) can stewed tomatoes	1	(15 ounce) can green beans
		1	carrot, chopped
2	(8 ounce) cans tomato sauce	1	zucchini, chopped
		½	(16 ounce) package fusilli (spiral) pasta
3	cups water		
2	teaspoons dried basil	1½	cups shredded mozzarella cheese
2	teaspoons dried oregano		
1	teaspoon salt		

1. Brown venison, onion, and garlic over medium heat until meat is no longer pink. Add tomatoes, tomato sauce, water, basil, oregano, salt, and pepper. Bring to a boil and simmer for about 30 minutes.
2. Stir in beans, carrot, and zucchini. Simmer soup for 1½ hours.
3. Add pasta and cook until tender. Top individual servings evenly with cheese. **Yield:** 8 servings.

Per serving: 324 calories, 26g protein, 42g carbohydrate, 6g fat, 7g fiber, 60mg cholesterol, 1137mg sodium

◄ **ONE-DISH MEAL**

Prep Time: 10 minutes

Cook Time: 2 hours 40 minutes

Average Rating: ★★★★★

What other cooks have done:

"I loved the way this made my kitchen smell. I've made it twice, and the second time, I omitted the pasta altogether and served it with crackers instead. My family loved it!"

Harira

Submitted by: **Usman**

"This is the soup that Moroccans traditionally use to break the fast every night of Ramadan. Season with salt, pepper, mint leaves, and cinnamon to taste."

AROUND-THE-WORLD CUISINE ▶

Prep Time: 15 minutes

Cook Time: 2 hours 35 minutes

Average Rating: ★★★★★

What other cooks have done:

"An instant family favorite! Sticks to the ribs but does not weigh too much on the stomach. Using a can or two of organic lentil soup will shorten the cooking time by half (adjust amount of water added accordingly). Add a little pinch of crushed bay leaves and some oregano for a slight French twist. Great alone or with a side dish of couscous."

1	pound cubed lamb meat	1	red onion, chopped
1	teaspoon ground turmeric	½	cup chopped fresh cilantro
1½	teaspoons ground black pepper	1	(29 ounce) can diced tomatoes
1	teaspoon ground cinnamon	7	cups water
¼	teaspoon ground ginger	¾	cup green lentils
¼	teaspoon ground cayenne pepper	1	(15 ounce) can garbanzo beans, drained
2	tablespoons butter	4	ounces vermicelli pasta
¾	cup chopped celery	2	eggs, beaten
1	white onion, chopped	1	lemon, juiced

1. Place the lamb, turmeric, black pepper, cinnamon, ginger, cayenne, butter, celery, white onion, red onion, and cilantro in a large Dutch oven over low heat. Stir frequently for 5 minutes. Drain tomatoes, reserving juice. Pour tomatoes into the mixture; let simmer for 15 minutes.

2. Pour tomato juice, 7 cups water, and the lentils into the pot. Bring the mixture to a boil; reduce heat and simmer, covered, for 2 hours.

3. About 10 minutes before serving, increase heat to medium-high. Add garbanzo beans and pasta to soup and cook about 10 minutes or until noodles are al dente. Stir in eggs and lemon juice and cook 1 minute. **Yield:** 6 servings.

Per serving: 493 calories, 31g protein, 55g carbohydrate, 17g fat, 15g fiber, 125mg cholesterol, 750mg sodium

Italian Sausage Soup with Tortellini *(pictured on page 225)*

Submitted by: **Mary P**

"This soup embodies all the wonders of Italian cooking—Italian sausage, garlic, tomatoes, and red wine. Serve with hot bread and a salad for a delicious meal. Garnish with Parmesan cheese."

1	pound sweet Italian sausage, casings removed	1	cup thinly sliced carrots	
1	cup chopped onion	½	teaspoon dried basil	
2	cloves garlic, minced	½	teaspoon dried oregano	
5	cups beef broth	1	(8 ounce) can tomato sauce	
½	cup water	1½	cups sliced zucchini	
½	cup red wine	3	tablespoons chopped fresh parsley	
4	large tomatoes, seeded and chopped	8	ounces fresh tortellini pasta Parmesan cheese (optional)	

1. In a 5 quart Dutch oven, brown sausage. Drain sausage, reserving 1 tablespoon drippings. Remove sausage and set aside.

2. Sauté onion and garlic in drippings. Stir in beef broth, water, wine, tomatoes, carrots, basil, oregano, tomato sauce, and sausage. Bring to a boil. Reduce heat; simmer, uncovered, for 30 minutes.

3. Skim fat from soup. Stir in zucchini and parsley. Simmer, covered, for 20 minutes. Add tortellini and simmer 10 more minutes. Garnish each serving with Parmesan cheese, if desired. **Yield:** 8 servings.

Per serving: 326 calories, 15g protein, 20g carbohydrate, 20g fat, 3g fiber, 50mg cholesterol, 1164mg sodium

◄ RESTAURANT FARE

Prep Time: 20 minutes

Cook Time: 1 hour 15 minutes

Average Rating: ★★★★★

What other cooks have done:

"Tastes like something from a restaurant! This has a unique flavor and is something fancy to serve to guests. This soup got my husband to eat zucchini, which I never thought would be possible."

Cajun-Style Red Bean and Rice Soup

Submitted by: **Holly**

"This is a very hearty, spicy soup. Makes for a filling first-course serving."

HOT & SPICY ▶

Soak Time: overnight

Prep Time: 15 minutes

Cook Time: 1 hour 21 minutes

Stand Time: 20 minutes

Average Rating: ★★★★★

What other cooks have done:

"Absolutely delicious. Just add corn-bread, and it's a full meal. We had a group of people over, and everyone loved it. It was easy to make."

1	tablespoon olive oil	2	cups dry kidney beans, soaked overnight
8	ounces bacon, cooked and crumbled	1	teaspoon Cajun seasoning
1½	cups chopped onion	1	teaspoon Worcestershire sauce
¼	cup chopped green bell pepper	8	cups chicken broth
1	tablespoon minced garlic	1	teaspoon salt
4	bay leaves	1½	cups cooked rice, divided
6	ounces andouille sausage, sliced	6	tablespoons thinly sliced green onions, divided
1	small smoked ham hock		

1. In a large pot over high heat, heat oil. Add bacon and sauté for 2 minutes. Add onion, bell pepper, garlic, bay leaves, sausage, and ham hock and sauté for 2 more minutes.

2. Add beans and sauté for 2 more minutes. Stir in Cajun seasoning, Worcestershire sauce, and broth. Bring to a boil, reduce heat to low, and simmer for 1 hour, stirring occasionally.

3. Add salt; cover pot and simmer for 15 more minutes. Remove from heat and allow the pot to sit, covered, for about 20 minutes. Discard ham hock and bay leaves.

4. Ladle soup into individual bowls. Top each serving with ¼ cup rice and 1 tablespoon green onions. **Yield:** 6 servings.

Per serving: 507 calories, 31g protein, 57g carbohydrate, 18g fat, 16g fiber, 43mg cholesterol, 2359mg sodium

Green Chile Stew with Pork

Submitted by: **Christine L.**

"Pueblo tradition calls for the addition of corn or potatoes to this dish. It makes a wonderful filling for enchiladas. Serve with a big green salad and a pile of wheat tortillas."

3	pounds boneless pork loin, cubed	4	cloves garlic, crushed
3	tablespoons peanut oil	4	cups chicken broth, divided
3	stalks celery, chopped		Salt to taste
2	tomatoes, chopped		Prepared green chile salsa (optional)
7	green chile peppers, chopped		

1. In a large skillet over medium-high heat, brown the pork, in batches, in oil.

2. Place the meat in a 3 to 4 quart casserole dish and add celery, tomato, chiles, and garlic.

3. Add about 1 cup chicken broth to skillet pork was cooked in, stirring over high heat to scrape up browned bits; bring to a boil. Add to pot with enough additional broth to just cover the ingredients. Cover and simmer until stew is thick and meat is very tender, about 1½ hours. Add salt to taste before serving. If stew is not spicy enough, add a bit of green chile salsa. **Yield:** 8 servings.

Per serving: 463 calories, 38g protein, 9g carbohydrate, 30g fat, 2g fiber, 102mg cholesterol, 605mg sodium

◀ HOT & SPICY

Prep Time: 25 minutes

Cook Time: 2 hours

Average Rating: ★★★★★

What other cooks have done:

"I made this stew for the first time for a Super Bowl party. It was a huge hit! Since then, I have made it several times for friends, family, and coworkers. People always ask me for the recipe. I have used both beef and pork, and both worked really well. I love that I can adjust the heat according to taste. The stew takes a little time to prepare, but if you throw everything into a slow cooker, you'll have a wonderful meal waiting for you when you get home."

Delicious Ham and Potato Soup

Submitted by: **ELLIE11**

"A friend gave me this is delicious recipe for ham and potato soup. It is very easy, and the great thing about it is that you can add additional ingredients, like more ham or potatoes, and it still turns out great."

QUICK & EASY ▶

Prep Time: 20 minutes

Cook Time: 25 minutes

Average Rating: ★★★★★

What other cooks have done:

"This was great and so easy to make. I have just started cooking, and this is the first soup I have ever made from scratch. I am so happy with how it turned out. I did add corn and some shredded cheese on top before serving. I will make this again and again."

3½ cups peeled and diced
    potatoes
⅓ cup diced celery
⅓ cup finely chopped onion
¾ cup diced cooked ham
3¼ cups water
2 tablespoons chicken
    bouillon granules
½ teaspoon salt (or to taste)
1 teaspoon ground white or
    black pepper (or to taste)
5 tablespoons butter
5 tablespoons all-purpose
    flour
2 cups milk

1. Combine potatoes, celery, onion, ham, and water in a stockpot. Bring to a boil; reduce heat to medium and cook until potatoes are tender, about 10 to 15 minutes. Stir in chicken bouillon, salt, and pepper.
2. In a separate saucepan, melt butter over medium–low heat. Whisk in flour with a fork and cook, stirring constantly, until thick, about 1 minute. Slowly stir in milk, whisking to prevent lumps from forming, until all of the milk has been added. Continue stirring over medium–low heat until thick, about 4 to 5 minutes.
3. Stir the milk mixture into the stockpot and cook soup until heated through. Serve immediately. **Yield:** 8 servings.

Per serving: 199 calories, 7g protein, 20g carbohydrate, 10g fat, 2g fiber, 34mg cholesterol, 292mg sodium

Turkey-Wild Rice Soup

Submitted by: **Jordanna Novak**

"You can use long-grain white rice for all or part of the wild rice, but reduce the simmering time to 20 to 30 minutes."

3	(10.5 ounce) cans condensed chicken broth	½	teaspoon salt
2	cups water	¼	teaspoon poultry seasoning
½	cup finely chopped green onions	⅛	teaspoon ground black pepper
½	cup uncooked wild rice	2	cups half-and-half
8	slices bacon	1½	cups diced cooked turkey meat
½	cup butter	2	tablespoons dry sherry
¾	cup all-purpose flour		

1. In a large pot over medium heat, combine chicken broth, water, green onions, and wild rice. Bring to a boil; reduce heat and simmer until rice is tender, about 35 to 40 minutes.
2. Meanwhile, cook the bacon in a large skillet over medium heat until crisp. Allow to cool; crumble. Set aside.
3. When rice is tender, melt butter in a medium saucepan over medium-low heat. Stir in flour, salt, poultry seasoning, and pepper. Cook, stirring constantly, until smooth and bubbly. Stir in half-and-half and cook until thickened, about 2 minutes. Stir half-and-half mixture into rice mixture. Stir in bacon, turkey, and sherry. Heat through and serve. **Yield:** 9 servings.

Per serving: 433 calories, 17g protein, 17g carbohydrate, 33g fat, 1g fiber, 55mg cholesterol, 1113mg sodium

◀ CROWD-PLEASER

Prep Time: 15 minutes

Cook Time: 1 hour

Average Rating: ★★★★★

What other cooks have done:

"I made this soup on the Friday after Thanksgiving. It was great! Even my picky 4-year-old liked it. I made it exactly as the recipe called for except for the sherry (my mom did not have any). This is a new family favorite!"

Peanut Butter-Vegetable Chicken Soup

Submitted by: **Annie Nordmark**

"The peanut butter adds something wonderful without really tasting like itself. This is the best soup I have ever had."

8 cups chicken broth	½ cup chopped onion
2 cups diced cooked chicken	½ cup chopped green bell pepper
1 cup peeled and cubed potatoes	2 cloves garlic, minced
1 cup diced carrots	½ cup peanut butter
1 cup diced zucchini	1 tablespoon chopped fresh parsley
1 cup broccoli florets	Salt and ground black pepper to taste
1 cup canned whole tomatoes, chopped	
½ cup chopped celery	

1. In a large stockpot, combine the broth, chicken, potatoes, and carrots. Bring the soup to a boil and reduce heat to medium. Cook for about 10 minutes or until potatoes and carrots are tender.

2. Add zucchini, broccoli, tomatoes, celery, onion, bell pepper, and garlic. Simmer for about 8 minutes.

3. Add peanut butter, parsley, and salt and black pepper to taste; stir until peanut butter is fully blended. Simmer for 3 more minutes.

Yield: 8 servings.

Per serving: 230 calories, 20g protein, 13g carbohydrate, 11g fat, 3g fiber, 26mg cholesterol, 929mg sodium

Italian Sausage Soup with Tortellini, page 219,
and Soft Garlic-Parmesan Breadsticks, page 279

Cream of Fresh Asparagus Soup II,
page 210

Kielbasa-Kale Stew, page 234

Gramma Brown's Corn Chowder, page 231

Lamb and Winter Vegetable Stew,
page 235

Vietnamese-Style Chicken Curry Soup

Submitted by: **Billy Tran**

"I use Vietnamese-style curry powder found at Asian food stores (usually called cari). If you can't find it, use Madras curry powder. I make my stew soupy, but you can make a thick stew by reducing the amount of chicken broth and water by half. Serve with rice or French bread or both."

2	tablespoons vegetable oil		2	carrots, sliced diagonally
1	(3 pound) whole chicken, skin removed, cut into pieces		1	quart chicken broth
			1	quart water
			2	tablespoons fish sauce
1	onion, cut into chunks		2	kaffir lime leaves
2	shallots, thinly sliced		1	bay leaf
2	cloves garlic, chopped		2	teaspoons red pepper flakes
⅛	cup thinly sliced fresh ginger root		8	small potatoes, quartered
1	stalk lemon grass, cut into 2 inch pieces		1	(14 ounce) can coconut milk
¼	cup curry powder		1	bunch fresh cilantro
1	green bell pepper, cut into 1 inch pieces			

1. Heat oil in a large Dutch oven over medium heat. Cook chicken and onion in oil until onion is soft and translucent; remove onion and chicken from pot and set aside.

2. Sauté shallots in pot for about 1 minute; stir in garlic, ginger, lemon grass, and curry powder. Continue to cook for about 5 minutes; stir in bell pepper and carrots. Return chicken and onion to pot and stir in chicken broth, water, and fish sauce. Season with lime leaves, bay leaf, and red pepper flakes.

3. Bring to a boil and add potatoes. Return to a boil and pour in coconut milk. Reduce heat and simmer 40 minutes to 1 hour or until potatoes and chicken are tender. Remove lime leaves and bay leaf before serving. Garnish each serving with a sprig of fresh cilantro.

Yield: 8 servings.

Per serving: 470 calories, 29g protein, 28g carbohydrate, 28g fat, 5g fiber, 75mg cholesterol, 869mg sodium

◀ AROUND-THE-WORLD CUISINE

Prep Time: 30 minutes

Cook Time: 1 hour 20 minutes

Average Rating: ★★★★★

What other cooks have done:

"This soup is excellent! The fresh ginger, lime leaves, and lemon grass really complement the curry. It's a lot of work to chop up everything, but if you don't, you'll never get to experience the pure wonder and joy of this soup. I went overboard and threw on a handful of fresh bean sprouts as a garnish. This recipe has become my new and final favorite."

Polish Chicken and Dumplings

Submitted by: **Linda Bilski Johnson**

"This is an old family recipe for dumplings, which were originally Polish egg noodles (kluski). Over the years, I have modified it to make homemade dumplings."

CROWD-PLEASER ▶

Prep Time: 30 minutes

Cook Time: 3 hours

Average Rating: ★★★★★

What other cooks have done:

"Excellent—just like my mom's dumplings. These are heavier than other dumplings, which is just the way I like them. My mom never uses a recipe, so I've struggled trying to replicate hers. Thank you so much."

1	(3 pound) whole chicken	1	teaspoon seasoning salt
1	onion, chopped	1	(10.75 ounce) can
1	stalk celery, with leaves		condensed cream of
1	tablespoon poultry		chicken soup (optional)
	seasoning	4	eggs
1	teaspoon whole allspice	2	tablespoons olive oil
1	teaspoon dried basil	1	tablespoon salt
½	teaspoon salt	2	cups water
2	teaspoons ground black	4	cups all-purpose flour
	pepper, divided		

1. Place chicken, onion, and celery in a large pot and fill pot with water. Season with poultry seasoning, whole allspice, basil, ½ teaspoon salt, 1 teaspoon pepper, and seasoning salt. Bring to a boil. Reduce heat and simmer for approximately 2 hours or until chicken is done.

2. Remove chicken from broth and set chicken aside. Strain broth and stir in cream of chicken soup, if desired; simmer.

3. In a medium bowl, stir together eggs, olive oil, 1 tablespoon salt, remaining 1 teaspoon pepper, and 2 cups water. Gradually add flour and stir until thick.

4. Using a large spoon, scoop a spoonful of the dough. Cut small pieces from the spoonful of dough with a knife and drop the pieces into the broth. Repeat until all of the dough has been used. Stir, cover, and simmer for about 15 minutes.

5. Meanwhile, skin and debone the chicken. Cut the meat into small pieces, add to the broth, and heat through. **Yield:** 8 servings.

Note: You can substitute cream of celery soup for the cream of chicken soup, or thicken the broth with a little flour, if desired.

Per serving: 706 calories, 43g protein, 53g carbohydrate, 35g fat, 2g fiber, 237mg cholesterol, 1591mg sodium

Gramma Brown's Corn Chowder

(pictured on page 227)

Submitted by: **Halle Hardin**

"This is my great-grandmother's recipe. This chowder is very good to eat on a cold day."

½ pound bacon	2 carrots, chopped
2 small onions, diced	6 small potatoes, cubed
2 stalks celery, chopped	2 tablespoons all-purpose
1 (14.75 ounce) can cream-style corn	flour
1 (15.25 ounce) can whole kernel corn	1 tablespoon water (or as needed)
2 tablespoons butter	2 cups milk
4 cups chicken broth	Salt and ground black pepper to taste

1. Fry bacon in a skillet over medium-high heat until almost done. Remove some bacon for garnish, if desired; crumble and set aside. Add onion and celery and sauté until lightly browned.

2. Transfer remaining bacon to a Dutch oven. Add cream-style corn, whole kernel corn, butter, and broth. Add carrots and potatoes. Cook for about 15 minutes.

3. Mix together flour and enough water to form a paste.

4. Add milk and flour paste to Dutch oven. You might want to add more flour paste, depending on how thick you like your chowder. Simmer for 30 minutes or until ready to serve. Add salt and pepper to taste. Garnish with crumbled bacon, if desired. **Yield:** 10 servings.

Per serving: 314 calories, 9g protein, 33g carbohydrate, 17g fat, 4g fiber, 19mg cholesterol, 746mg sodium

◄ CROWD-PLEASER

Prep Time: 15 minutes

Cook Time: 1 hour

Average Rating: ★★★★★

What other cooks have done:

"Excellent corn chowder. I suggest stir-frying the onion and celery in the butter while the bacon is cooking and then adding the vegetables, broth, and bacon to the onion mixture. I prefer to fry the bacon and then let it cool on a paper towel to get rid of as much fat as possible. This is a soup that I will be serving again."

Tim's Sausage Stew

Submitted by: **Tim**

"This firehouse favorite is very hearty, and it has a great flavor. Your family will love it."

QUICK & EASY ▶

Prep Time: 20 minutes

Cook Time: 30 minutes

Average Rating: ★★★★☆

What other cooks have done:

"My family loved this. My husband decided to make a pot of rice to pour this over in order to fully enjoy the sauce that it makes. I didn't follow the recipe to the letter. I felt the need to make it mine, so I added a few spices that were not listed. We were practically fighting over the left-overs. This is definitely a keeper."

1 tablespoon butter	1 teaspoon dried basil
2 pounds smoked sausage, sliced	1 tablespoon dried oregano
1 tablespoon all-purpose flour	3 zucchini, sliced
8 cups chicken broth	½ cup rice-shaped pasta
1 (28 ounce) can peeled and diced tomatoes, undrained	

1. Melt butter in a large pot and brown sausage slices in butter; drain. Stir in flour; mix in chicken broth, tomatoes, basil, and oregano. Bring to a boil. Lower heat and simmer about 20 minutes or until sausage is fully cooked. Add zucchini slices and pasta. Continue cooking until zucchini and pasta are done. **Yield:** 6 servings.

Per serving: 776 calories, 28g protein, 29g carbohydrate, 60g fat, 3g fiber, 113mg cholesterol, 3012mg sodium

Super Soup

Most soup recipes require the addition of broth, and most every time, the kind that comes from a can or bouillon cubes or granules works just fine. However, if you want to add a depth of flavor to your soups that commercial broth can't quite reach, try making your own. Most broth recipes make a large quantity that you can freeze and have on hand for use anytime a soup or stew craving strikes you.

Making your own broth is as simple as simmering meat, poultry, vegetables, herbs, or seafood in water. Vegetables and herbs add layers of flavor; carrots and onions deepen the color and add sweetness. If you want to be healthy, trim fat from meat before using it.

Put your broth ingredients in a large pot and bring to a boil. Reduce heat and let the mixture simmer gently. If the mixture is allowed to boil, the broth will be cloudy. As the broth simmers, remove any scum that collects on the surface. Strain cooked broth through several layers of cheesecloth to remove meat, vegetables, and herbs. Cool the broth completely so the fat can rise to the surface and solidify. Then just spoon hardened fat off the top of the broth with a large spoon.

Refrigerate your homemade broth for up to 3 days or freeze it up to 3 months. Use various containers to freeze your broth—pint or quart containers, freezer bags, or ice cube trays—and you'll have broth at the ready for any need or occasion.

For more information, visit **Allrecipes.com**

Oven Stew with Burgundy Wine

Submitted by: Kathy Smith

"This is an awesome beef stew that will warm up the whole family."

2　pounds cubed beef stew
　　meat
3　tablespoons all-purpose
　　flour
4　carrots, sliced
2　stalks celery, sliced
2　onions, sliced
1　teaspoon salt
1　teaspoon dried thyme

1　teaspoon ground
　　mustard
¼　teaspoon ground black
　　pepper
3　beef bouillon cubes,
　　crumbled
1　cup water
1　cup Burgundy wine

1. Preheat oven to 350°F (175°C).
2. Cook beef in a large ovenproof pot over medium heat until browned. Remove from heat and stir in flour until cubes are coated. Stir in carrots, celery, and onion. Season with salt, thyme, mustard, pepper, and bouillon. Pour in water and wine. Cover.
3. Bake in the preheated oven for 4 hours. Serve hot.

Yield: 8 servings.

Per serving: 386 calories, 32g protein, 9g carbohydrate, 21g fat, 2g fiber, 99mg cholesterol, 717mg sodium

◄ COMPANY IS COMING

Prep Time: 15 minutes

Cook Time: 4 hours 15 minutes

Average Rating: ★★★★

What other cooks have done:

"This is a very good stew with a different flavor because of the mustard and the wine. I found the beef to be melt-in-your-mouth tender after 3 hours. I added potatoes and mushrooms and doubled the liquid."

Kielbasa-Kale Stew

(pictured on page 226)

Submitted by: **Sara**

"Try this thick stew with a rich potato base, fresh kale, and chunks of savory kielbasa. This is a meal all by itself."

ONE-DISH MEAL ▶

Prep Time: 15 minutes

Cook Time: 50 minutes

Average Rating: ★★★★☆

What other cooks have done:

"Very good recipe. I added some chopped onion, substituted some evaporated milk for part of the water, and used turkey kielbasa. This was a big hit with kids and adults."

6	large potatoes, peeled and cubed	1½	pounds kale, rinsed, dried, and chopped
¼	cup butter	1	pound kielbasa sausage, sliced into ½ inch pieces
10	cups water		
1	teaspoon salt		
1	teaspoon ground black pepper		

1. Place the potatoes in a large pot over medium–high heat. Add butter and water and bring to a boil. Cook potatoes until tender, about 10 minutes. Reserve liquid and mash potatoes in the pot until smooth. Return the potato water to the pot and stir in salt and pepper. Simmer for 20 minutes.

2. Stir in the fresh kale and sausage and simmer for 20 more minutes. Serve hot. **Yield:** 8 servings.

Per serving: 360 calories, 12g protein, 32g carbohydrate, 22g fat, 4g fiber, 53mg cholesterol, 972mg sodium

Soup 101

One of soup's greatest characteristics is how easy it is to make. Most of the time, just a large Dutch oven or stockpot is all the equipment you need; just add your ingredients and cook. If you're a big soup fan, however, you may want to add a few more tools to your kitchen.

An 8 or 10 quart stockpot and a 3 or 4 quart heavy-bottomed pot should cover soups with large and small yields alike. An electric blender or food processor comes in handy for pureeing a soup's ingredients to a smooth texture. A large strainer and sieve are needed for broth and stock. For serving soup, a ladle is essential. And a set each of double-handled soup bowls and ovenproof bowls should cover your bases for serving soup, chowder, and chili.

Cheat Sheet

Once you've got the basic equipment ready, use the tips below to get a head start on mastering the art of making delicious soup:

• A few slices of bacon will add a meaty depth of flavor to any soup or stew.

• The next time you chop up a bunch of celery, make sure you save the leaves. They add great flavor to a simmering soup.

• If you've added too much salt to a soup, simply drop in a peeled, raw potato and cook a few minutes. Remove the potato before serving the soup.

For more information, visit **Allrecipes.com**

Lamb and Winter Vegetable Stew

(pictured on page 228)

Submitted by: **Brandy**

"This hearty stew made with winter vegetables is definitely worth the time. Beef tips can be substituted for lamb."

1 tablespoon vegetable oil	2 cups butternut squash, peeled, seeded, and sliced
1 pound lamb stew meat, cubed	1 cup peeled, sliced parsnips
2 (14 ounce) cans beef broth	1 cup peeled, chopped sweet potatoes
1 cup dry red wine	
2 cloves garlic, minced	1 cup sliced celery
1 tablespoon chopped fresh thyme	1 medium onion, thinly sliced
¼ teaspoon salt	½ cup sour cream
¼ teaspoon ground black pepper	2 tablespoons all-purpose flour
1 bay leaf	

◄ OUT-OF-THE-ORDINARY

Prep Time: 30 minutes

Cook Time: 1 hour

Average Rating: ★★★★★

What other cooks have done:

"I used this recipe several times last year. It is easy to substitute ingredients if you'd like, and it makes a hearty evening meal when served with a fresh green salad and crusty bread."

1. Heat oil in a large Dutch oven and brown lamb meat on all sides. Stir in the beef broth and wine. Season with garlic, thyme, salt, pepper, and bay leaf. Bring the mixture to a boil. Reduce heat, cover, and simmer 20 minutes.

2. Mix in the squash, parsnips, sweet potatoes, celery, and onion. Bring to a boil; reduce heat and simmer 30 minutes or until vegetables are tender.

3. In a medium bowl, blend the sour cream and flour. Gradually stir ½ cup hot stew mixture into sour cream mixture.

4. Stir the sour cream mixture into the saucepan. Remove the bay leaf and continue to cook and stir until thickened. **Yield:** 8 servings.

Per serving: 213 calories, 14g protein, 16g carbohydrate, 10g fat, 3g fiber, 41mg cholesterol, 465mg sodium

Get-a-Husband Brunswick Stew

Submitted by: **RAKESTRAW**

"The thickest, most wonderful Brunswick stew you've ever had. Those of you who've never had Brunswick stew will just die. If you've had it before, you won't believe it. This is an old family recipe that makes the best stew around!"

1 tablespoon olive oil	1 cup ketchup
1 cup chopped onions	½ cup hickory-flavored barbecue sauce
2 stalks celery, chopped	Salt and ground black pepper to taste
1½ pounds ground pork	Hot pepper sauce to taste (optional)
1½ pounds ground beef	1 green bell pepper, halved and seeded
1 (3 pound) whole cooked chicken, deboned and shredded	3 (14.75 ounce) cans cream-style corn
3 (14.5 ounce) cans whole peeled tomatoes, undrained and chopped	

1. Heat olive oil in a large skillet and sauté onion and celery until soft. Mix in pork and beef and cook until evenly browned (do not drain).

2. Transfer the pork and beef mixture to a large stockpot over low heat. Stir in the shredded chicken, undrained tomatoes, ketchup, and barbecue sauce. Season with salt and black pepper to taste and, if desired, hot pepper sauce. Place green bell pepper into the mixture. Cook, stirring occasionally, 2 hours or until thickened.

3. Stir the cream-style corn into the stew mixture. Continue cooking 1 hour or to desired consistency. Remove green bell pepper; chop and return to the stew or discard. **Yield:** 16 servings.

Per serving: 383 calories, 29g protein, 26g carbohydrate, 19g fat, 2g fiber, 90mg cholesterol, 851mg sodium

Southwestern Black Bean Stew

Submitted by: **Lanay Bien**

"This mild stew from the Southwest has a wonderful flair."

1   pound ground beef
1   (1.25 ounce) package taco
    seasoning mix
1   (15 ounce) can whole
    kernel corn, drained
1   (15 ounce) can black beans,
    undrained
1   (6 ounce) can tomato paste
1½ cups water
½   cup sour cream
1   (8 ounce) package
    shredded Cheddar cheese

1. In a large skillet over medium-high heat, sauté ground beef until browned; drain. Add taco seasoning and stir. Reduce heat to low, cover, and simmer for 10 minutes.

2. In a large, heavy saucepan, combine the corn, beans, tomato paste, and water. Mix well. Add the seasoned meat and the sour cream. Cook over medium heat for 20 minutes. Pour into individual bowls and garnish with shredded Cheddar cheese. **Yield:** 6 servings.

Per serving: 483 calories, 32g protein, 28g carbohydrate, 26g fat, 7g fiber, 104mg cholesterol, 1087mg sodium

◀ FREEZER FRESH

Prep Time: 15 minutes

Cook Time: 40 minutes

Average Rating: ★★★★

What other cooks have done:

"I love this! I make it with ground turkey to lower the fat. A friend drains the beans, leaves out the water, and makes this into a dip. Either way, it's always a hit. This also freezes really well!"

Fusion Chili

Submitted by: **Lon F. Binder**

"A true fusion of 'Tex-' and 'Mex-' style chili. I've made this recipe dozens of times, and it is great. Each bite slowly delivers a sweet flavor followed by dry heat. It takes a while to prepare, but it's well worth it. You can use any type of beans you like. Try different dried chile varieties, too."

10	dried ancho chiles, stemmed, seeded, and chopped
½	cup water
¼	cup white wine vinegar
3	pounds hot Italian sausage, casings removed
3	pounds ground beef
1	white onion, diced
1	red onion, diced
1	sweet onion, diced
1	cup diced celery
1	cup diced carrots
10	cloves garlic, sliced
1	teaspoon salt
1	teaspoon ground black pepper
1	(6 ounce) can tomato paste
1	cup dry red wine
4	(14.5 ounce) cans diced tomatoes, undrained
¼	cup Worcestershire sauce
¼	cup hot pepper sauce
1	tablespoon chili powder
2	teaspoons ground cumin
1	tablespoon chopped fresh parsley
½	cup honey
1	(16 ounce) can kidney beans, drained
1	(16 ounce) can pinto beans, drained

1. In a small bowl, soak chiles in water and vinegar for 30 minutes. After soaking, puree in a blender or food processor until very smooth; set aside.

2. Cook sausage and ground beef in a large pot over medium–high heat until evenly browned. Drain meat, reserving 3 to 4 tablespoons drippings in pot.

3. Sauté white onion, red onion, sweet onion, celery, carrots, and garlic in drippings until onions are soft and translucent. Season with salt and black pepper. Stir in tomato paste and allow to caramelize. Pour in wine, scraping up any browned bits stuck to the bottom.

4. Stir in cooked meat, tomatoes, Worcestershire sauce, and hot pepper sauce. Season with chili powder, cumin, and parsley. Bring to a boil; stir in blended chile mixture and honey. Cover and simmer for 2 hours, stirring and scraping the bottom every hour or so. Carefully mix in kidney beans and pinto beans without breaking them. Cover and simmer 1 more hour, stirring occasionally. **Yield:** 16 servings.

Per serving: 649 calories, 29g protein, 30g carbohydrate, 45g fat, 7g fiber, 122mg cholesterol, 1186mg sodium

Sides & Salads

No home-cooked meal is complete without a heaping helping of mashed taters or vegetable casserole. Or if you're in a hurry, turn to an easy-to-assemble salad to keep meals fresh. No matter what's cooking, the perfect complement to your meal is right here.

Smushed Apples and Sweet Potatoes

Submitted by: **Elfindancer**

"This is a simple recipe for a sweet, easy side dish. This tastes a lot like apple pie, but is a bit healthier. As a variation, you can mix in cloves or nutmeg. This is also delicious topped with brown sugar and pecans."

COMPANY IS COMING ▶

Prep Time: 10 minutes

Cook Time: 30 minutes

Average Rating: ★★★★★

What other cooks have done:

"This is a wonderful side dish! I used brown sugar instead of white, and I cooked the apples for 20 minutes. My fiancée loves this so much that she asks for it all the time."

2	large sweet potatoes, peeled and diced	½	teaspoon ground allspice
2	tablespoons butter	1	Granny Smith apple, peeled, cored, and sliced
¼	cup white sugar	⅛	cup milk
1	teaspoon ground cinnamon		

1. Place potatoes in a medium saucepan and fill with water to cover. Bring to a boil; reduce heat to medium and simmer for about 20 minutes or until tender. Drain potatoes and set aside.

2. Melt butter over low heat in a small saucepan. Mix in the sugar, cinnamon, and allspice. Add the apple slices; cover and simmer for 5 minutes or until the apples are tender. Mix the apple mixture into the drained sweet potatoes; add milk. Using an electric mixer or fork, mix well until potatoes are mashed. **Yield:** 6 servings.

Per serving: 126 calories, 1g protein, 22g carbohydrate, 4g fat, 2g fiber, 11mg cholesterol, 48mg sodium

Prosciutto-Wrapped Asparagus

Submitted by: **Trish**

"My husband taught me to make this elegant, yet easy, side dish that dresses up everyday chicken. It's always a hit at the holidays."

PARTY FOOD ▶

Prep Time: 15 minutes

Cook Time: 15 minutes

Average Rating: ★★★★★

What other cooks have done:

"What a recipe! Talk about ease and presentation—this has it all. I blanched the asparagus spears for 1 minute in boiling water and then immediately plunged them into ice water. This really brought out the green color and ensured that the spears were crunchy, yet cooked, after baking."

½	pound prosciutto, sliced	12	spears fresh asparagus, trimmed
½	(8 ounce) package Neufchâtel cheese, softened		

1. Preheat oven to 450°F (230°C).

2. Spread prosciutto slices with Neufchâtel cheese. Wrap each slice around 3 asparagus spears. Arrange wrapped spears in a single layer on a medium baking sheet.

3. Bake in the preheated oven for 15 minutes or until asparagus is tender. **Yield:** 4 servings.

Per serving: 293 calories, 15g protein, 3g carbohydrate, 25g fat, 1g fiber, 71mg cholesterol, 1210mg sodium

Mom's Baked Beans I

Submitted by: **Bob Musser**

"This is a version of a recipe my mom used to make. I converted it to a lower-fat recipe, but it's still so good!"

2 (28 ounce) cans baked beans	½ cup barbecue sauce
2 onions, cut into wedges	1 tablespoon liquid smoke flavoring
¼ cup molasses	

1. Preheat oven to 325°F (165°C). Lightly grease a 3 quart casserole dish.
2. In prepared dish, combine beans, onion, molasses, barbecue sauce, and liquid smoke flavoring.
3. Bake in the preheated oven for 2 to 2½ hours, stirring every 20 minutes. **Yield:** 11 servings.

Per serving: 181 calories, 7g protein, 38g carbohydrate, 2g fat, 8g fiber, 0mg cholesterol, 662mg sodium

◄ CROWD-PLEASER

Prep Time: 15 minutes

Cook Time: 2 hours 30 minutes

Average Rating: ★★★★★

What other cooks have done:

"My aunt used to make the best baked beans in the world. Since losing her, I have been on the prowl for a recipe like hers. This is pretty close, except she added brown sugar and bacon. I'm going to play with it to get it more like hers."

Lemon Green Beans with Walnuts

Submitted by: **Karen David**

"Toss steamed green beans with butter, lemon zest, lemon juice, and toasted walnuts for a simple side that goes well with fish. This is excellent with asparagus, also. Substitute pecans for walnuts if you'd like."

½ cup chopped walnuts	1 lemon, juiced and zested
1 pound green beans, trimmed and cut into 2 inch pieces	Salt and ground black pepper to taste
2½ tablespoons unsalted butter, melted	

1. Preheat oven to 375°F (190°C). Arrange nuts in a single layer on a baking sheet.
2. Toast nuts in the preheated oven until lightly browned, about 5 to 10 minutes. Set aside.
3. Place green beans in a steamer basket over 1 inch of boiling water and cover. Steam for 8 to 10 minutes or until beans are tender but still bright green.
4. In a large bowl, combine butter, lemon juice, and lemon zest. Add cooked beans and toss to coat. Season with salt and pepper to taste. Transfer beans to a serving dish and sprinkle with toasted walnuts. Serve immediately. **Yield:** 4 servings.

Per serving: 202 calories, 5g protein, 13g carbohydrate, 17g fat, 6g fiber, 19mg cholesterol, 9mg sodium

◄ QUICK & EASY

Prep Time: 15 minutes

Cook Time: 20 minutes

Average Rating: ★★★★☆

What other cooks have done:

"This was an easy side dish. I loved the lemon flavor with the green beans. Before toasting the walnuts, I quickly dipped them into some melted honey."

Carrots Au Gratin

Submitted by: **Sharon**

"This rich and creamy carrot and cheese casserole with a buttery, crunchy topping makes an excellent complement to honey-glazed ham."

Prep Time: 20 minutes

Cook Time: 30 minutes

Average Rating: ★★★★★

What other cooks have done:

"I don't like carrots, but this recipe was quite good—kind of like baked macaroni and cheese but with carrots instead of pasta. I'll try this with broccoli or cauliflower, too. I didn't add the onions, and I used crushed croutons instead of crackers. Also, I used seasoning salt instead of regular salt and light Cheddar instead of processed cheese."

4½ cups sliced carrots	½ teaspoon salt
⅔ cup crushed buttery round crackers	¼ teaspoon ground black pepper
3 tablespoons butter, melted and divided	1½ cups milk
½ cup chopped onion	⅔ cup shredded processed cheese
3 tablespoons all-purpose flour	

1. Preheat oven to 350°F (175°C). Lightly grease a 9x13 inch baking dish.

2. Place carrots in a steamer basket over 1 inch of boiling water and cover. Steam until tender but still firm, about 6 to 10 minutes. Drain and set aside.

3. Meanwhile, in a small bowl, combine crushed crackers with 1 tablespoon melted butter. Mix well and set aside.

4. In a medium skillet over low heat, melt the remaining 2 tablespoons butter. Sauté onion in butter until tender. Stir in flour, salt, and pepper. Cook for 3 minutes, stirring to prevent browning. Gradually pour in milk, stirring constantly. Increase heat to medium and cook until bubbly and thickened. Add cheese and stir until smooth. Fold in carrots. Pour mixture into prepared dish and sprinkle with the cracker mixture.

5. Bake in the preheated oven for 20 minutes or until bubbly and golden brown. **Yield:** 8 servings.

Per serving: 177 calories, 6g protein, 16g carbohydrate, 10g fat, 2g fiber, 13mg cholesterol, 460mg sodium

Carroty Rice *(pictured on page 263)*

Submitted by: **Melissa Poor**

"I came up with this recipe because my family loves cheese and will not eat carrots. This dish passed for cheesy rice, and my family loved it. I have served it ever since."

2	cups water	1	carrot, shredded
1	chicken bouillon cube	2	tablespoons chopped fresh parsley
1	cup uncooked long-grain rice		

1. Bring water to a boil in a medium saucepan over medium-high heat. Add bouillon cube and let dissolve. Stir in rice and return to a boil.
2. Reduce heat to low. Cover and simmer for 20 minutes.
3. Remove from heat and let stand, covered, for 5 minutes. Stir in carrot and parsley. **Yield:** 6 servings.

Per serving: 126 calories, 3g protein, 27g carbohydrate, 0g fat, 1g fiber, 0mg cholesterol, 202mg sodium

◀ **5 INGREDIENTS OR LESS**
Prep Time: 10 minutes
Cook Time: 25 minutes
Stand Time: 5 minutes
Average Rating: ★★★★★
What other cooks have done:
"I added some raw shredded zucchini along with the carrot. My little one loves rice, and this is a great way for me to sneak in some veggies as well. It's a nice change from normal rice and really does look pretty."

Baked Spaghetti Corn

Submitted by: **Molly**

"I am 13 years old, and I love this recipe, which my mom makes every once in a while. This makes a good side dish. It is also very easy to make! Please have fun with this recipe."

½	(6 ounce) package uncooked spaghetti, broken	1	cup shredded Cheddar cheese
1	(15.25 ounce) can whole kernel corn	1	(15 ounce) can cream-style corn
		½	cup butter, melted

1. Preheat oven to 350°F (175°C). Lightly grease a 1½ quart casserole dish.
2. In prepared dish, combine broken spaghetti, whole kernel corn, cheese, cream-style corn, and butter.
3. Bake in the preheated oven for 20 to 25 minutes or until spaghetti is cooked. **Yield:** 6 servings.

Per serving: 377 calories, 10g protein, 39g carbohydrate, 23g fat, 3g fiber, 20mg cholesterol, 674mg sodium

◀ **FROM THE PANTRY**
Prep Time: 10 minutes
Cook Time: 25 minutes
Average Rating: ★★★★★
What other cooks have done:
"This was so good! I decreased the butter to ¼ cup and added ½ cup milk, half an onion, and some leftover mushrooms. It baked, covered, for 55 minutes. For my next attempt, I will try this in the slow cooker."

Easy Corn Pudding

Submitted by: **Elizabeth**

"My father-in-law was always a picky eater. However, the first Thanksgiving I made him this recipe, he went crazy! It soon became a tradition. He's gone now, but we fondly remember this dish as one of his favorites."

5 INGREDIENTS OR LESS ▶

Prep Time: 10 minutes

Cook Time: 30 minutes

Average Rating: ★★★★★

What other cooks have done:

"I host Thanksgiving at my home every year, and I triple this recipe for the occasion. It's the first request out of the mouths of invited guests! It gets the biggest payoff for the least work."

½ cup butter, softened
1 (15 ounce) can cream-style corn
1 (15.25 ounce) can whole kernel corn
1 (8.5 ounce) package cornbread mix
1 (8 ounce) container sour cream (optional)

1. Preheat oven to 350°F (175°C).
2. Put butter in a 2 quart casserole dish; place in oven until butter melts. Remove from oven.
3. Add cream-style corn, whole kernel corn, cornbread mix, and, if desired, sour cream to dish with butter. Mix well.
4. Bake in the preheated oven for about 30 minutes. **Yield:** 6 servings.

Per serving: 486 calories, 8g protein, 56g carbohydrate, 28g fat, 3g fiber, 59mg cholesterol, 1197mg sodium

Momma's Mashed Potatoes

Submitted by: **MINNESOTAMOM**

"This is my grandma's recipe for plain potatoes. They always come out fluffy and tasty. This is one of those old classics at our house—one of the 'nobody makes these like Momma' dishes."

COVERED-DISH FAVORITE ▶

Prep Time: 15 minutes

Cook Time: 20 minutes

Average Rating: ★★★★☆

What other cooks have done:

"Thanks to this recipe, I can finally make mashed potatoes—I've had disasters before! I used a masher on the potatoes, added the other ingredients, and then whipped the potatoes because I like them creamy. I used a little more than ¼ cup evaporated milk in place of the half-and-half, and I added about 2 teaspoons butter extract so they would have more butter flavor without the added fat and calories."

2½ pounds russet potatoes, peeled and cubed
¼ teaspoon lemon juice (optional)
1 egg white
½ cup half-and-half
¼ cup butter
Salt and ground black pepper to taste

1. Place potatoes and, if desired, lemon juice in a large saucepan and add water to cover. Bring to a boil over medium-high heat and cook until tender, about 15 minutes.
2. Meanwhile, stir together egg white and half-and-half in a small saucepan over medium heat until mixture reaches 160°F (70°C).
3. Drain water from potatoes; use a potato masher to mash potatoes. Stir in egg white mixture and butter. Add more half-and-half if necessary to reach desired consistency. Season with salt and pepper to taste. **Yield:** 6 servings.

Per serving: 246 calories, 5g protein, 35g carbohydrate, 10g fat, 5g fiber, 28mg cholesterol, 109mg sodium

Garden-Stuffed Baked Potatoes

Submitted by: **Hallie Guilfoyle**

"This is an excellent side dish that goes with any dinner. You can also serve it as a meal by itself. If you like potatoes, you will love this recipe."

4	large potatoes	1	tablespoon vegetable oil
2	tablespoons butter	2	teaspoons dried parsley
1	small onion, chopped		Salt and ground black
1	(10 ounce) package frozen chopped broccoli, thawed		pepper to taste
½	cup Ranch-style salad dressing		

1. Preheat oven to 425°F (220°C).

2. Pierce the skin of the potatoes with a fork. Microwave potatoes on High for 12 minutes.

3. Place potatoes in the preheated oven and bake for 15 minutes.

4. Slice off potato tops. Scoop out the bulk of the interior of the potatoes, being careful to leave the potato skins intact. In a medium bowl, mash the removed potato interior.

5. Heat butter in a small skillet over medium heat. Add onion and sauté until tender, about 5 minutes. Add onion to mashed potato; stir in broccoli and Ranch-style salad dressing. Brush the outside of the potato skins with oil. Spoon potato mixture into the skins. Arrange stuffed potatoes on a baking sheet.

6. Bake potatoes for 15 more minutes or until heated through. Season with parsley and salt and pepper to taste. **Yield:** 4 servings.

Per serving: 400 calories, 6g protein, 40g carbohydrate, 25g fat, 7g fiber, 24mg cholesterol, 377mg sodium

◄ FROM THE PANTRY

Prep Time: 20 minutes

Cook Time: 47 minutes

Average Rating: ★★★★☆

What other cooks have done:

"This recipe adds great variety to your baked potatoes! Since I was baking some pork chops, I baked these in the oven instead of using the microwave. I coated the skins lightly in olive oil. Also, I added some grated Parmesan cheese at the end."

Onion Meat Relish *(pictured on page 188)*

Submitted by: **Ariana**

"Spread this savory onion relish over your favorite meats and fish."

¾	pound onion, cut into wedges and separated	¼	tablespoon salt
2	tablespoons butter	¼	teaspoon ground black pepper
2	tablespoons red wine vinegar	2	teaspoons white sugar

1. In a large skillet over medium heat, slowly cook the onions and butter, stirring constantly, until onions are tender, about 10 minutes.

2. Stir vinegar, salt, pepper, and sugar into the skillet. Cook, stirring constantly, until mixture thickens to a chunky, spreadable consistency, about 10 minutes. Refrigerate until serving. **Yield:** 8 servings.

Per serving: 47 calories, 1g protein, 5g carbohydrate, 3g fat, 1g fiber, 8mg cholesterol, 249mg sodium

◄ QUICK & EASY

Prep Time: 15 minutes

Cook Time: 20 minutes

Average Rating: ★★★★★

What other cooks have done:

"This is a must for onion lovers! It's simple to make and tastes great with burgers, hot dogs, sandwiches, and so on. Make a batch, put it in a jar, and watch it disappear."

Parmesan Potatoes

Submitted by: **Marci Rogers**

"This is our family's favorite potato dish."

½ cup grated Parmesan cheese
½ cup all-purpose flour
   Salt and ground black
      pepper to taste
10 potatoes, peeled and cubed
½ cup butter, melted

1. Preheat oven to 350°F (175°C).
2. Combine Parmesan cheese, flour, and salt and pepper to taste in a large heavy-duty, zip-top plastic bag; mix well. Place potatoes in bag; seal and shake to coat.
3. Pour butter into a 9x13 inch baking dish. Stir in potatoes.
4. Bake in the preheated oven for 1½ hours, stirring occasionally.
Yield: 9 servings.

Per serving: 223 calories, 5g protein, 25g carbohydrate, 12g fat, 2g fiber, 32mg cholesterol, 420mg sodium

Fairy Godmother Rice

Submitted by: **Ryan Schwartz**

"My grandfather's second wife served this to us when we first met her. We've loved her ever since! This is a tasty side dish that's perfect with any dinner."

½ cup butter
5 ounces uncooked thin egg
      noodles
2 cups uncooked instant rice
2 (1 ounce) packages dry
      onion soup mix
4 cups vegetable broth
1 (5 ounce) can water
      chestnuts, drained and
      sliced
   Soy sauce to taste

1. Preheat oven to 350°F (175°C). Grease a 2 quart casserole dish.
2. Melt butter in a large skillet over medium heat. Brown noodles in butter.
3. In a large bowl, combine browned noodles, rice, soup mix, broth, water chestnuts, and soy sauce to taste. Mix well and transfer to prepared casserole dish.
4. Bake in the preheated oven for 45 minutes or until liquid has been absorbed and casserole is browned and crisp on top. **Yield:** 6 servings.

Per serving: 378 calories, 7g protein, 50g carbohydrate, 17g fat, 3g fiber, 61mg cholesterol, 1297mg sodium

Cream Cheese-Basil Summer Squash

Submitted by: **Laurel Pogue**

"Young, tender summer squash—yellow crookneck or yellow pattypan—are microwaved in this quick, absolutely delicious recipe. Even veggie-haters will love it."

3 yellow squash, cubed	1 (8 ounce) package cream
1 clove garlic, minced	cheese, cubed
Salt to taste	1 tablespoon dried basil

1. In a glass dish, combine squash and garlic. Season with salt to taste. Cover with plastic wrap and microwave on High for 5 to 8 minutes or until tender, stirring every 3 to 4 minutes.
2. Sprinkle cream cheese over squash and return to the microwave. Cook, uncovered, on High for about 1 minute or until cheese is melted. Stir until cheese is smooth and blended into the squash. Stir in basil. Let stand 1 to 2 minutes before serving. **Yield:** 4 servings.

Per serving: 227 calories, 6g protein, 8g carbohydrate, 20g fat, 3g fiber, 62mg cholesterol, 169mg sodium

◀ **5 INGREDIENTS OR LESS**

Prep Time: 10 minutes

Cook Time: 9 minutes

Stand Time: 2 minutes

Average Rating: ★★★★☆

What other cooks have done:

"Awesome recipe! I couldn't stop eating this! I pan-fried the squash, and there was no liquid to drain off. I used fresh basil instead of dried, and I only used half a package of cream cheese. This is the way I'll cook my summer squash from now on."

Cheesy Acorn Squash

Submitted by: **Linda**

"Very tasty squash! This dish is best with beef or ham."

1 acorn squash, halved and seeded	⅛ teaspoon salt
3 tablespoons butter	Pinch ground black pepper
1 cup diced celery	1 teaspoon chopped parsley
1 cup finely chopped onion	½ cup shredded Cheddar cheese
1 cup fresh mushrooms, sliced	

1. Preheat oven to 350°F (175°C).
2. Place squash, cut side down, in a glass dish. Microwave on High for 20 minutes or until almost tender.
3. Melt butter in a saucepan over medium heat and add celery and onion; sauté until transparent. Stir in mushrooms; cook 2 to 3 more minutes. Sprinkle with salt, pepper, and parsley. Spoon mixture evenly into squash halves; cover.
4. Bake in the preheated oven for 15 minutes. Uncover, sprinkle with cheese, and cook until cheese bubbles. **Yield:** 2 servings.

Per serving: 413 calories, 12g protein, 36g carbohydrate, 27g fat, 11g fiber, 76mg cholesterol, 560mg sodium

◀ **COMPANY IS COMING**

Prep Time: 15 minutes

Cook Time: 40 minutes

Average Rating: ★★★★★

What other cooks have done:

"I thought this recipe was amazing! The first time I made this, I added bread-crumbs to the filling. The next time I made it, I added some leftover wild rice, and it was even tastier."

Spinach and Mushroom Casserole

Submitted by: **Cathy Martin**

"This dish is a simple layered combination of spinach and mushrooms that goes wonderfully with roast beef or chicken."

2 tablespoons butter	1 teaspoon salt
1 pound fresh mushrooms, sliced	¼ cup butter, melted
2 (10 ounce) packages fresh spinach, rinsed and stems removed	¼ cup finely chopped onion
	1½ cups shredded Cheddar cheese, divided

1. Preheat oven to 350°F (175°C). Grease a 2 quart casserole dish.
2. Melt 2 tablespoons butter in a large skillet over medium heat. Sauté mushrooms in butter until tender, about 8 to 10 minutes.
3. Meanwhile, heat spinach in a large pot over medium heat until wilted; drain, squeezing out excess water. Place in prepared baking dish and top with salt, ¼ cup melted butter, onion, and half of the cheese. Layer mushrooms on top and sprinkle with remaining cheese.
4. Bake in the preheated oven for 20 minutes. **Yield:** 6 servings.

Per serving: 256 calories, 11g protein, 7g carbohydrate, 22g fat, 4g fiber, 61mg cholesterol, 757mg sodium

Baked Stuffed Tomatoes *(pictured on page 262)*

Submitted by: **Anita Rhodes**

"This is an easy and quick tomato side dish."

6 slices bacon	¾ cup croutons
4 medium tomatoes	Salt and ground black pepper to taste
½ cup chopped green bell pepper	Parsley sprigs
½ cup grated Parmesan cheese	

1. Preheat oven to 350°F (175°C). Grease a 7x11 inch baking dish.
2. Place bacon in a large, deep skillet. Cook over medium-high heat until evenly browned. Drain, crumble, and set aside.
3. Meanwhile, wash tomatoes and slice off stem ends. Gently scoop out pulp, leaving a ½ inch wall. Finely chop pulp and reserve ⅓ cup chopped pulp. Discard remaining pulp.
4. Stir crumbled bacon, bell pepper, cheese, croutons, and salt and black pepper to taste into reserved tomato pulp. Spoon evenly into tomatoes. Place tomatoes in prepared dish.
5. Bake in the preheated oven for 10 to 15 minutes or until heated through. Garnish with parsley sprigs. **Yield:** 4 servings.

Per serving: 105 calories, 6g protein, 8g carbohydrate, 6g fat, 1g fiber, 13mg cholesterol, 418mg sodium

Vicki's Hush Puppies

Submitted by: **Vicki Conley**

"Hush puppies are a good side for seafood. Cook these in small batches so that the oil will stay hot."

2	eggs, lightly beaten	1	cup self-rising flour
½	cup white sugar	1	cup self-rising cornmeal
1	large onion, diced		Oil for frying

1. In a medium bowl, mix together eggs, sugar, and onion. Blend in flour and cornmeal.

2. Pour oil to a depth of 2 inches into a large, heavy pan. Heat oil to 365°F (185°C). Drop batter by rounded teaspoonfuls into hot oil and fry until golden brown. Drain briefly on paper towels. Serve hot. **Yield:** 8 servings.

Per serving: 278 calories, 5g protein, 37g carbohydrate, 13g fat, 2g fiber, 53mg cholesterol, 405mg sodium

◀ QUICK & EASY

Prep Time: 10 minutes

Cook Time: 30 minutes

Average Rating: ★★★★★

What other cooks have done:

"These were fabulous. I added a teaspoon of salt and a can of corn. I had to add a little more flour and cornmeal because of the added moisture from the corn. I just slipped them into my deep fryer for 3 minutes per batch. They were perfect!"

Deep-Dish Layered Salad

Submitted by: **Nancy**

"It's the dressing that makes this salad so delicious. This salad can be made the night before, and you can substitute Cheddar cheese for the Parmesan."

2	eggs	2	cups mayonnaise
1½	heads iceberg lettuce, rinsed, dried, and shredded	2	tablespoons brown sugar
1	cup chopped celery	½	teaspoon garlic powder
1	cup chopped green bell pepper	½	teaspoon curry powder
1	cup chopped green onions	2	tablespoons bacon bits
2	cups sliced fresh mushrooms	2	tablespoons grated Parmesan cheese
2	cups frozen green peas, thawed		

1. Place eggs in a saucepan and cover with cold water. Bring water to a boil; cover, remove from heat, and let stand for 10 to 12 minutes. Remove eggs; cool, peel, and chop.

2. Layer half of the lettuce in the bottom of a large bowl. Follow with a layer each of celery, bell pepper, green onions, mushrooms, peas, and chopped egg. Top with remaining lettuce.

3. Prepare the dressing by whisking together the mayonnaise, brown sugar, garlic powder, and curry powder. Spread evenly over top of salad. Sprinkle with bacon bits and Parmesan cheese. Refrigerate until ready to serve. **Yield:** 10 servings.

Per serving: 396 calories, 6g protein, 13g carbohydrate, 37g fat, 4g fiber, 70mg cholesterol, 381mg sodium

◀ MAKE-AHEAD

Prep Time: 20 minutes

Cook Time: 2 minutes

Stand Time: 12 minutes

Average Rating: ★★★★★

What other cooks have done:

"This was an interesting salad, and the dressing made it sweet and spicy. I used only half of the dressing and put the other half on the table for those who wanted it. I had leftovers, and the salad was just as crisp and fresh as the night before. The dressing would be a nice change as a dip with your veggie tray."

Fresh Broccoli Salad

Submitted by: **Nora**

"This is a yummy summer salad that uses an interesting combination of fruit, vegetables, and meat. Before you decide you won't like it, try it. You'll be pleasantly surprised. You can add an extra head of broccoli, if you'd like."

CROWD-PLEASER ▶

Prep Time: 15 minutes

Cook Time: 10 minutes

Average Rating: ★★★★★

What other cooks have done:

"We loved this salad! I tweaked it a little and used sweetened dried cranberries instead of raisins and sunflower seeds instead of almonds. We had this with burgers from the grill. This is great for a potluck or a picnic."

½	pound bacon	1	cup mayonnaise
2	heads broccoli	½	cup white sugar
1	red onion	2	tablespoons white wine
¾	cup raisins		vinegar
¾	cup sliced almonds		

1. Place bacon in a large, deep skillet. Cook over medium-high heat until evenly browned; drain. Cool and crumble.

2. Cut the broccoli and onion into bite-size pieces. Combine with the bacon, raisins, and almonds; mix well.

3. To prepare the dressing, mix the mayonnaise, sugar, and vinegar together until smooth. Stir into the salad. Chill before serving.

Yield: 9 servings.

Per serving: 465 calories, 7g protein, 27g carbohydrate, 38g fat, 4g fiber, 31mg cholesterol, 343mg sodium

Greek Salad I

Submitted by: **Michelle**

"This is an incredibly good Greek salad recipe—nice and tangy and even better in the summer when you use fresh vegetables!"

QUICK & EASY ▶

Prep Time: 20 minutes

Average Rating: ★★★★☆

What other cooks have done:

"I added 3 tablespoons sugar, 3 tablespoons red wine vinegar, and garlic powder to the dressing. It made all the difference in the world. The dressing was so good that you could have lapped up what was left in the bottom of the bowl with some French or Italian bread and made a meal on that alone!"

1	head romaine lettuce, rinsed, dried, and chopped	2	large tomatoes, chopped
		1	cucumber, sliced
1	red onion, thinly sliced	1	cup crumbled feta cheese
1	(6 ounce) can pitted black olives	6	tablespoons olive oil
		1	teaspoon dried oregano
1	red bell pepper, chopped	1	lemon, juiced
1	green bell pepper, chopped		Ground black pepper to taste

1. In a large salad bowl, combine the lettuce, onion, olives, red and green bell peppers, tomato, cucumber, and feta cheese.

2. Whisk together the olive oil, oregano, lemon juice, and black pepper to taste. Pour dressing over salad, toss, and serve.

Yield: 6 servings.

Per serving: 265 calories, 6g protein, 14g carbohydrate, 22g fat, 5g fiber, 22mg cholesterol, 539mg sodium

Angie's Dad's Best Cabbage Coleslaw

Submitted by: **Dot**
"This absolutely delicious coleslaw is more tart and tangy than the creamy kind. Make it up to 2 weeks ahead of serving—it only gets better."

1	medium head cabbage, shredded	¾	cup vegetable oil
1	large red onion, diced	1	tablespoon salt
1	cup grated carrots	1	tablespoon ground mustard
2	stalks celery, chopped		Ground black pepper to taste
1	cup white sugar		
1	cup white vinegar		

1. In a large bowl, combine cabbage, onion, carrots, and celery. Sprinkle with sugar and mix well. In a small saucepan, combine vinegar, oil, salt, ground mustard, and pepper to taste. Bring to a boil. Pour hot dressing over cabbage mixture and mix well. **Yield:** 20 servings.

Per serving: 131 calories, 1g protein, 14g carbohydrate, 9g fat, 1g fiber, 0mg cholesterol, 363mg sodium

◀ CROWD-PLEASER

Prep Time: 30 minutes

Average Rating: ★★★★★

What other cooks have done:

"I suggest using two 1 pound bags of coleslaw mix for half of the recipe. The cabbage wilts a great deal when the hot dressing is poured over it. (It remained crunchy and delicious but was greatly reduced in volume.) The second time I made this recipe, I added purple cabbage for color. That was a big mistake—it colored all the cabbage purple."

Tropical Salad with Pineapple Vinaigrette

Submitted by: **Marianne**
"A bag of salad greens makes this salad easy to prepare. Use fresh pineapple if you can, and substitute toasted almonds for the macadamia nuts, if desired."

6	slices bacon	1	(10 ounce) package chopped romaine lettuce
¼	cup pineapple juice	1	cup diced fresh pineapple
3	tablespoons red wine vinegar	½	cup chopped macadamia nuts, toasted
¼	cup olive oil	3	green onions, chopped
	Salt and ground black pepper to taste	¼	cup flaked coconut, toasted

1. Place bacon in a large, deep skillet. Cook over medium-high heat until evenly browned. Drain, crumble, and set aside.
2. In a jar with a lid, combine pineapple juice, red wine vinegar, oil, and salt and pepper to taste. Cover and shake well.
3. In a large bowl, toss together the lettuce, diced pineapple, macadamia nuts, green onions, and bacon. Pour dressing over salad and toss to coat. Garnish with toasted coconut. **Yield:** 6 servings.

Per serving: 257 calories, 5g protein, 10g carbohydrate, 23g fat, 2g fiber, 8mg cholesterol, 258mg sodium

◀ QUICK & EASY

Prep Time: 20 minutes

Cook Time: 10 minutes

Average Rating: ★★★★★

What other cooks have done:

"I made this recipe for my gourmet group when I cooked for a luau theme. For presentation, I added some star fruit to each plate. Also, I used just two green onions, and I increased the coconut to ½ cup. I really wanted to bring out the tropical flavors of this salad."

Green Grape Salad

Submitted by: **Noreen**

"This is a wonderful dessert salad that never fails to be a hit. Make it the day before, and the brown sugar will make the sauce taste like caramel."

COVERED-DISH FAVORITE ▶

Prep Time: 15 minutes

Average Rating: ★★★★★

What other cooks have done:

"This recipe is so different and fabulous. It could be breakfast, lunch, a side dish, or even dessert! I used both green and red grapes. I sprinkled the brown sugar and nuts on top and melted the sugar under the broiler for 30 to 60 seconds for a crispy topping. I brought it to a potluck, and everyone begged for the recipe."

4 pounds seedless green grapes	½ cup white sugar
1 (8 ounce) package cream cheese	1 teaspoon vanilla extract
1 (8 ounce) container sour cream	2 tablespoons brown sugar
	1 cup chopped pecans

1. Wash and dry grapes. In a large bowl, mix together the cream cheese, sour cream, white sugar, and vanilla. Add grapes and mix until evenly incorporated. Sprinkle with brown sugar and pecans. Stir and refrigerate until ready to serve. **Yield:** 8 servings.

Per serving: 479 calories, 6g protein, 60g carbohydrate, 27g fat, 4g fiber, 43mg cholesterol, 104mg sodium

Insalata Caprese II

Submitted by: **Marina**

"Because this salad is so simple, fresh, top-quality ingredients are important to achieve the best flavor."

COMPANY IS COMING ▶

Prep Time: 15 minutes

Average Rating: ★★★★★

What other cooks have done:

"I used mozzarella cheese that was rolled in red pepper and sun-dried tomatoes. I also used fresh basil, and I sprinkled a dash or so of balsamic vinegar over the salad along with the olive oil. After adding salt and pepper to the layers, I let the salad marinate and soak up the flavors. My husband loved this recipe, and it was so easy."

4 large ripe tomatoes, sliced ¼ inch thick	3 tablespoons extra virgin olive oil
1 pound fresh mozzarella cheese, sliced ¼ inch thick	Fine sea salt to taste
⅓ cup fresh basil leaves	Ground black pepper to taste

1. On a large platter, alternate tomato slices, mozzarella cheese slices, and basil leaves in overlapping layers. Drizzle with olive oil. Season with sea salt and pepper to taste. **Yield:** 6 servings.

Per serving: 302 calories, 16g protein, 8g carbohydrate, 24g fat, 2g fiber, 59mg cholesterol, 499mg sodium

Spinach and Goat Cheese Salad with Beetroot Vinaigrette

Submitted by: **Nikki Miller**

"I tried this salad in a restaurant and vowed to duplicate it. The crunchy sugared walnuts and creamy goat cheese are addictive, and the vinaigrette is to die for. I don't care for beets, but I love them in this salad."

1 cup walnuts, coarsely chopped	1 teaspoon white sugar
2 tablespoons white sugar	½ teaspoon salt
⅓ (15 ounce) can pickled beets	½ teaspoon ground black pepper
¼ cup cider vinegar	¼ cup vegetable oil
1 teaspoon chicken bouillon granules	½ pound baby spinach, rinsed and dried
½ teaspoon garlic powder	4 ounces goat cheese, crumbled

1. In a small saucepan over medium heat, stir together the walnuts with 2 tablespoons sugar. Cook until walnuts are lightly browned and sugar is caramelized, stirring constantly to thoroughly coat the walnuts with the sugar.

2. In a blender or food processor, combine beets, cider vinegar, bouillon granules, garlic powder, 1 teaspoon sugar, salt, and pepper. Blend well. Gradually blend in the oil.

3. In a large bowl, toss together the sugar–coated walnuts and spinach. Before serving, drizzle with the blended beet mixture; toss. Sprinkle with goat cheese. **Yield:** 12 servings.

Per serving: 163 calories, 4g protein, 7g carbohydrate, 14g fat, 2g fiber, 7mg cholesterol, 223mg sodium

◄ CROWD-PLEASER

Prep Time: 25 minutes

Cook Time: 5 minutes

Average Rating: ★★★★★

What other cooks have done:

"This salad was fantastic! I didn't have bouillon granules, so I omitted them. I substituted some toasted pine nuts and sunflower seeds for the walnuts, and for sweetness, I added a bit of chopped mango."

Absolutely the Best Rich and Creamy Blue Cheese Dressing Ever!

Submitted by: **LUCKYME9**

"Top your favorite salad with my creamy and chunky blue cheese dressing. It has a nice sweetness with a great balance of textures."

MAKE-AHEAD ▶

Prep Time: 10 minutes

Average Rating: ★★★★★

What other cooks have done:

"I served this dressing on a chilled ice-berg wedge. I added extra blue cheese crumbles. Everyone simply raved! It took only a matter of minutes to make. So easy and so delicious!"

2½	ounces blue cheese	¼	teaspoon white sugar
3	tablespoons buttermilk	⅛	teaspoon garlic powder
3	tablespoons sour cream		Salt and ground black
2	tablespoons mayonnaise		pepper to taste
2	teaspoons white wine vinegar		

1. In a small bowl, mash blue cheese and buttermilk together with a fork until mixture resembles large-curd cottage cheese. Stir in sour cream, mayonnaise, vinegar, sugar, and garlic powder until well blended. Season with salt and pepper to taste. **Yield:** 6 servings.

Note: Whole milk may be used in place of buttermilk for a milder flavor. Dressing may be refrigerated in an airtight container for up to 2 weeks.

Per serving: 94 calories, 3g protein, 1g carbohydrate, 9g fat, 0g fiber, 15mg cholesterol, 251mg sodium

Tangy Ginger-Lime Salad Dressing

Submitted by: **Sara**

"This tangy, nutty dressing is enlivened by sesame oil, chili oil, fresh ginger, and lime juice."

FROM THE PANTRY ▶

Prep Time: 5 minutes

Average Rating: ★★★★★

What other cooks have done:

"This has very strong flavors. I've used it to marinate chicken and beef with delicious results. I added a little more garlic. I loved the extra zing of the ginger. I'll definitely use this again."

1	cup reduced-sodium soy sauce	2	teaspoons sesame oil
2	tablespoons minced garlic	1	teaspoon chili oil
2	tablespoons grated fresh ginger root	⅓	cup fresh lime juice
		¼	cup rice vinegar
		¼	teaspoon onion powder

1. Combine soy sauce, garlic, ginger, sesame oil, chili oil, lime juice, vinegar, and onion powder in a blender. Process until evenly combined. Chill until ready to serve. **Yield:** 12 servings.

Per serving: 26 calories, 1g protein, 3g carbohydrate, 1g fat, 0g fiber, 0mg cholesterol, 709mg sodium

Strawberry and Feta Salad

Submitted by: **MSCHEF**

"This unusual combination of strawberries, feta cheese, toasted almonds, and romaine lettuce in a sweet and tangy dressing is sure to please your guests. This is guaranteed to be a winner at any potluck or barbecue."

1 cup slivered almonds	2 tablespoons brown sugar
2 cloves garlic, minced	1 cup vegetable oil
1 teaspoon honey	1 head romaine lettuce, torn
1 teaspoon prepared Dijon-style mustard	1 pint fresh strawberries, sliced
¼ cup raspberry vinegar	1 cup crumbled feta cheese
2 tablespoons balsamic vinegar	

1. In a skillet over medium-high heat, cook the almonds, stirring frequently, until lightly toasted. Remove from heat and set aside.
2. In a small bowl, whisk together the garlic, honey, Dijon mustard, raspberry vinegar, balsamic vinegar, brown sugar, and vegetable oil.
3. In a separate large bowl, toss together the toasted almonds, romaine lettuce, strawberries, and feta cheese. Add the dressing mixture and toss to coat. **Yield:** 10 servings.

Per serving: 376 calories, 7g protein, 12g carbohydrate, 34g fat, 3g fiber, 22mg cholesterol, 302mg sodium

◄ PARTY FOOD

Prep Time: 15 minutes

Cook Time: 5 minutes

Average Rating: ★★★★★

What other cooks have done:

"What a pretty and delicious salad! Instead of almonds, I used coarsely chopped pecans. I didn't add all the dressing to the salad at once, since it makes a generous amount, even for two bags of lettuce. I tossed some with the salad and then put the rest on the side for people to add."

Artichoke Salad II

Submitted by: **Amy B.**

"This is a great year-round salad. You can use whatever veggies are in season."

1 cup low-fat sour cream	1 cup chopped broccoli
1 (0.7 ounce) package dry Italian-style salad dressing mix	1 cup sliced fresh mushrooms
	¼ cup diced onion
4 cups chopped romaine lettuce	1 (14 ounce) can artichoke hearts, drained and chopped
1 cup chopped red bell pepper	

1. In a small bowl, whisk together the sour cream and Italian salad dressing mix.
2. In a large bowl, toss together the lettuce, bell pepper, broccoli, mushrooms, onion, and artichoke hearts. Top with dressing and toss until evenly coated. Refrigerate until ready to serve. **Yield:** 6 servings.

Per serving: 119 calories, 5g protein, 15g carbohydrate, 5g fat, 4g fiber, 16mg cholesterol, 846mg sodium

◄ MAKE-AHEAD

Prep Time: 10 minutes

Average Rating: ★★★★☆

What other cooks have done:

"This was great. I didn't have any red bell peppers, so I omitted them. Using bagged veggies made this so easy, I couldn't believe how quickly it came together—or how good it tasted! I will make this many more times."

Sunday-Best Fruit Salad

Submitted by: **Pattie Price**
"This is a wonderful and easy fruit salad that is also pretty for special occasions or holidays."

2 apples, peeled, cored, and chopped	2 bananas, peeled and diced
1 (20 ounce) can pineapple chunks, juice reserved	3 kiwis
1 (21 ounce) can peach pie filling	1 pint strawberries, divided

1. In a small bowl, toss the chopped apples in reserved pineapple juice. Allow to sit for 5 to 10 minutes.
2. In a large salad bowl, combine the peach pie filling and pineapple chunks. Remove apples from pineapple juice and add to pie filling mixture. Add diced bananas to reserved pineapple juice and let sit for 5 to 10 minutes.
3. Peel kiwis; slice kiwis and half of the strawberries. Chop the other half of the strawberries and set aside.
4. Remove bananas from pineapple juice and add to pie filling mixture. Add chopped strawberries to pie filling mixture; toss together. Garnish with kiwi and strawberry slices. Chill and serve.
Yield: 8 servings.

Per serving: 186 calories, 2g protein, 46g carbohydrate, 1g fat, 5g fiber, 0mg cholesterol, 15mg sodium

Summer Potato Salad

Submitted by: **jen**
"This is a lemony potato salad; it tastes lighter than a traditional potato salad."

5 cups peeled and cubed potatoes	1 teaspoon ground mustard
3 eggs	¼ teaspoon ground black pepper
⅓ cup lemon juice	½ cup mayonnaise
¼ cup vegetable oil	¼ cup chopped green onions
2 teaspoons white sugar	⅓ cup chopped celery
1½ teaspoons seasoning salt	3 tablespoons chopped fresh parsley
1½ teaspoons Worcestershire sauce	

1. Bring a large pot of salted water to a boil. Add potatoes; cook until tender but still firm, about 15 minutes. Drain; transfer to a large bowl.
2. Place eggs in a saucepan and cover completely with cold water. Bring water to a boil. Cover, remove from heat, and let stand for 10 to 12 minutes. Remove eggs and cool; peel and chop. Add eggs to potatoes.

3. In a small bowl, combine lemon juice, oil, sugar, seasoning salt, Worcestershire sauce, mustard, and black pepper; mix well. Blend in mayonnaise. Pour lemon dressing over potatoes and stir to coat.
4. Mix in green onions, celery, and parsley. Refrigerate for at least 2 hours before serving. **Yield:** 7 servings.

Per serving: 316 calories, 5g protein, 24g carbohydrate, 23g fat, 3g fiber, 100mg cholesterol, 339mg sodium

Southwestern Pasta Salad

Submitted by: **Lisa P**
"Make a double batch because this very easy and very delicious salad is really popular at potlucks."

1	(8 ounce) package rotini pasta	1½	cups whole kernel corn
⅓	cup vegetable oil	1	(15 ounce) can black beans, drained and rinsed
¼	cup fresh lime juice	½	cup diced green bell pepper
2	tablespoons chili powder (or to taste)	½	cup diced red bell pepper
2	teaspoons ground cumin	½	cup fresh cilantro leaves, divided
½	teaspoon salt	1	cup chopped roma (plum) tomatoes
2	cloves garlic, crushed		

1. Bring a large pot of lightly salted water to a boil. Add pasta and cook for 8 to 10 minutes or until al dente; drain.
2. In a large bowl, combine oil, lime juice, chili powder, cumin, salt, and garlic. Stir in pasta and cool to room temperature, stirring occasionally.
3. Stir in corn, beans, green bell pepper, red bell pepper, and half of the cilantro leaves. Spoon onto a platter and garnish with tomato and remaining cilantro. Serve chilled or at room temperature.
Yield: 8 servings.

Per serving: 217 calories, 6g protein, 28g carbohydrate, 10g fat, 6g fiber, 0mg cholesterol, 441mg sodium

◄ **COVERED-DISH FAVORITE**
Prep Time: 20 minutes

Cook Time: 12 minutes

Average Rating: ★★★★☆

What other cooks have done:
"The first time I made this recipe, I used canned tomatoes and dried parsley because that's all I had, and it was very good. The next time, I used fresh ingredients, and it was even better. To make this a main dish, I served it in corn tortilla 'bowls' on a bed of shredded lettuce. I topped it with grated Cheddar cheese and a dollop of sour cream."

Red Bean Salad with Feta and Peppers

Submitted by: **Daylene**

"This tasty, nutrient-packed salad that can be eaten by itself or as a side dish makes a great lunch the next day, too! Add more lemon juice and olive oil if you like your salad to have a lot of dressing. You can substitute garbanzo beans for the kidney beans."

MAKE-AHEAD ▶

Prep Time: 20 minutes

Average Rating: ★★★★★

What other cooks have done:

"I don't normally get so excited about a salad, but this was just amazing! I added 2 teaspoons minced garlic and 3 tablespoons each of lemon juice and olive oil. I also used garlic-and-herb feta. This is a flavor sensation!"

1	(15 ounce) can kidney beans, rinsed and drained	1	cup crumbled feta cheese
1	red bell pepper, chopped	⅓	cup chopped fresh parsley
2	cups chopped cabbage	1	clove garlic, minced
2	green onions, chopped	2	tablespoons lemon juice
		1	tablespoon olive oil

1. In a large salad bowl, combine all ingredients. Cover and refrigerate for up to 3 days. **Yield:** 4 servings.

Per serving: 244 calories, 12g protein, 24g carbohydrate, 12g fat, 9g fiber, 33mg cholesterol, 789mg sodium

Sesame-Pasta-Chicken Salad *(pictured on page 262)*

Submitted by: **Olivia Hines**

"This is a refreshing pasta salad with a delicious Asian flair that's great for a summer cookout or picnic. It tastes best if allowed to marinate for a while."

COVERED-DISH FAVORITE ▶

Prep Time: 20 minutes

Cook Time: 12 minutes

Average Rating: ★★★★★

What other cooks have done:

"This is to die for! I reduced the vegetable oil to ⅓ cup to make it lower in fat, and I added a cup of frozen cooked peas and two chopped roma tomatoes. Since I love cilantro so much, I increased it to ½ cup. The dressing was just amazing!"

1	(16 ounce) package bow tie pasta	½	teaspoon ground ginger
¼	cup sesame seeds	¼	teaspoon ground black pepper
½	cup vegetable oil	3	cups shredded cooked chicken
⅓	cup lite soy sauce		
⅓	cup rice vinegar	⅓	cup chopped fresh cilantro
1	teaspoon sesame oil	⅓	cup chopped green onions
3	tablespoons white sugar		

1. Bring a large pot of lightly salted water to a boil. Add pasta and cook for 8 to 10 minutes or until al dente. Drain pasta and rinse under cold water until cool. Transfer to a large bowl.
2. Meanwhile, heat a skillet over medium–high heat. Add sesame seeds; cook, stirring frequently, until toasted. Remove from heat; set aside.
3. In a jar with a tight-fitting lid, combine vegetable oil, soy sauce, vinegar, sesame oil, sugar, sesame seeds, ginger, and pepper. Shake well.
4. Pour sesame dressing over pasta and toss to coat evenly. Gently mix in chicken, cilantro, and green onions. **Yield:** 10 servings.

Per serving: 349 calories, 16g protein, 38g carbohydrate, 15g fat, 2g fiber, 24mg cholesterol, 308mg sodium

Black Bean and Couscous Salad

Submitted by: **Paula**

"This is great for a buffet, with interesting textures and Southwestern flavors combined in one delicious salad. Leftovers keep well in the refrigerator."

1¼	cups chicken broth
1	cup uncooked couscous
3	tablespoons extra virgin olive oil
2	tablespoons fresh lime juice
1	teaspoon red wine vinegar
½	teaspoon ground cumin
8	green onions, chopped
1	red bell pepper, seeded and chopped
¼	cup chopped fresh cilantro
1	cup frozen corn kernels, thawed
2	(15 ounce) cans black beans, drained
	Salt and ground black pepper to taste

1. Bring chicken broth to a boil in a 2 quart or larger saucepan and stir in the couscous. Cover the pot and remove from heat. Let stand for 5 minutes.

2. Meanwhile, in a large bowl, whisk together the olive oil, lime juice, vinegar, and cumin. Add green onions, bell pepper, cilantro, corn, and beans; toss to coat.

3. Fluff the couscous well, breaking up any chunks. Add to the bowl with the vegetables and mix well. Season with salt and black pepper to taste and serve at once or refrigerate until ready to serve.

Yield: 8 servings.

Per serving: 258 calories, 11g protein, 41g carbohydrate, 6g fat, 10g fiber, 0mg cholesterol, 566mg sodium

◀ MAKE-AHEAD

Prep Time: 30 minutes

Cook Time: 2 minutes

Stand Time: 5 minutes

Average Rating: ★★★★★

What other cooks have done:

"This is easy and healthy. You can make so many substitutions—basically, you can put in any legume you like. I like using a can of lima beans and a can of black beans. To get more dressing, I always double everything in the dressing mixture except for the olive oil."

Vegan Moroccan Couscous *(pictured on facing page)*

Submitted by: **Cigall Daboosh**

"To make this dish cook faster, julienne all of the vegetables."

1   tablespoon olive oil
1   onion, diced
3   cups vegetable broth
2   carrots, peeled and sliced
2   turnips, peeled and diced
1   sweet potato, diced
1   zucchini, diced
1   red bell pepper, diced
1   (15 ounce) can garbanzo
     beans, drained

1   (15 ounce) can tomato
     sauce
½   teaspoon salt
¼   teaspoon ground cinnamon
½   teaspoon ground turmeric
     Pinch saffron
     Pinch curry powder
1   (10 ounce) box couscous

1. Heat oil in a large pot over medium–high heat; sauté onion until golden. Add vegetable broth; bring to a boil. Stir in carrots, turnips, and sweet potato. Reduce heat to medium and simmer 10 minutes.
2. Add zucchini, bell pepper, garbanzo beans, tomato sauce, salt, cinnamon, turmeric, saffron, and curry powder. Simmer 8 minutes or until heated through.
3. Meanwhile, prepare couscous according to package directions. Fluff with a fork and serve with vegetables on top. **Yield:** 8 servings.

Per serving: 313 calories, 10g protein, 62g carbohydrate, 3g fat, 8g fiber, 0mg cholesterol, 741mg sodium

Vegan Moroccan Couscous

Baked Stuffed Tomatoes,
page 248

Sesame-Pasta-Chicken Salad,
page 258

Carroty Rice,
page 243

English Muffins,
page 282

Pumpkin Gingerbread,
page 285

Breads

Nothing says "home cooked" quite like bread that's warm from the oven. Fresh muffins, scones, cornbread, and fruit and nut loaves evoke hearth and home like few other foods.

Syrian Bread

Submitted by: **Sue Litster**

"Mix this dough in your bread machine and bake it in the oven. Serve this versatile Middle Eastern–style flat bread with lunch or dinner."

FROM THE PANTRY ▶

Prep Time: 20 minutes

Cook Time: 20 minutes

Stand Time: 3 hours

Average Rating: ★★★★★

What other cooks have done:

"When I was a child, my grandmother and I made Syrian bread the old-fashioned way. Now I can make it in less than half the time, and I can keep the tradition going. I took some to my grandmother, and she couldn't tell the difference."

1⅛	cups water	½	teaspoon white sugar
2	tablespoons vegetable oil	3	cups all-purpose flour
1½	teaspoons salt	1½	teaspoons active dry yeast

1. Place all ingredients into the bread machine pan in the order suggested by the manufacturer. Select Dough setting; press Start.
2. Preheat oven to 475°F (245°C). Preheat baking sheets or a baking stone.
3. Once the dough has risen, turn it out onto a lightly floured surface. Divide the dough into 8 equal pieces and form into rounds. Cover the rounds with a damp cloth and let rest. Roll each round into a thin, flat circle, about 8 inches in diameter.
4. Bake circles, 2 at a time, on the preheated baking sheets or baking stone in the preheated oven for about 5 minutes or until puffed up and golden brown. **Yield:** 8 servings.

Per serving: 204 calories, 5g protein, 36g carbohydrate, 4g fat, 1g fiber, 0mg cholesterol, 438mg sodium

Turkey-Dressing Bread

Submitted by: **Sue**

"Tired of plain turkey sandwiches in your lunch? Try packing a sandwich made with this bread! Spread a little cranberry sauce on your sandwich, and it tastes just like Thanksgiving dinner!"

CROWD-PLEASER ▶

Prep Time: 10 minutes

Cook Time: 2 hours 40 minutes

Average Rating: ★★★★☆

What other cooks have done:

"This recipe is the only bread-machine recipe I have that turns out foolproof every single time I make it! I use this recipe to make stuffing. I've also made turkey sandwiches with cranberry sauce as suggested, and I often get requests to make those."

1	cup milk, at room temperature	4½	teaspoons dried minced onion flakes
1	egg	1½	teaspoons celery seed
2	tablespoons brown sugar	¾	teaspoon poultry seasoning
1	tablespoon butter, softened	½	teaspoon rubbed sage
1½	teaspoons salt	½	teaspoon ground black pepper
⅓	cup yellow cornmeal		
3	cups bread flour	2¼	teaspoons active dry yeast

1. Place all ingredients into the bread machine pan in the order suggested by the manufacturer. Select Basic Bread setting; press Start.
2. Check dough after 5 minutes of mixing and add 1 to 2 tablespoons of water or flour if needed to allow dough to come together. Let machine resume cycle. **Yield:** 1 (1½ pound) loaf (12 servings).

Per serving: 176 calories, 6g protein, 32g carbohydrate, 3g fat, 1g fiber, 22mg cholesterol, 319mg sodium

Argentine Chimichurri Bread

Submitted by: **Tom Pampas**

"This spicy bread made with lots of herbs has tons of flavor. It's great for meat sandwiches."

1	cup water	3	tablespoons chopped onion
1½	tablespoons white wine vinegar	3	tablespoons fresh parsley
3	tablespoons olive oil	3	tablespoons wheat bran
¾	teaspoon dried oregano	1	tablespoon white sugar
⅛	teaspoon cayenne pepper	1½	teaspoons salt
2	cloves garlic, minced	3	cups bread flour
		2	teaspoons active dry yeast

1. Place all ingredients into the bread machine pan in the order suggested by the manufacturer. Select Basic or White Bread setting; press Start. **Yield:** 1 (1½ pound) loaf (15 servings).

Per serving: 131 calories, 4g protein, 22g carbohydrate, 3g fat, 1g fiber, 0mg cholesterol, 234mg sodium

◀ HOT & SPICY

Prep Time: 5 minutes

Cook Time: 30 minutes

Average Rating: ★★★★☆

What other cooks have done:

"I used my bread machine to mix the dough, and then I baked the loaf in a 5x9 pan at 400°F (200°C) for 30 minutes. After cooling for 10 minutes, it was soft and very easy to slice. This bread complemented our pork and sauerkraut dinner wonderfully."

Buttermilk-Honey Wheat Bread

Submitted by: **Tom Denney**

"A very nice whole wheat bread with a taste of honey. Great right out of the oven."

2½	teaspoons active dry yeast	3	tablespoons honey
1	cup whole wheat flour	1½	tablespoons vegetable oil
2	cups all-purpose flour	1½	cups buttermilk, at room temperature
½	teaspoon baking soda		
1	teaspoon salt		

1. Place all ingredients into the bread machine pan in the order suggested by the manufacturer. Select Dough setting; press Start.
2. Preheat oven to 350°F (175°C). Grease a 5x9 inch loaf pan.
3. Remove dough from bread machine and place in prepared pan. Let rise until doubled in bulk.
4. Bake in the preheated oven for 25 minutes or until loaf sounds hollow when tapped. **Yield:** 1 loaf (12 servings).

Per serving: 156 calories, 5g protein, 29g carbohydrate, 2g fat, 2g fiber, 1mg cholesterol, 280mg sodium

◀ FROM THE PANTRY

Prep Time: 5 minutes

Stand Time: 3 hours

Cook Time: 25 minutes

Average Rating: ★★★★★

What other cooks have done:

"I never have buttermilk on hand, so for bread recipes, I always substitute regular milk plus 1 tablespoon apple cider vinegar. It works really well. Even my picky kids love this recipe!"

Kolaches from the Bread Machine

Submitted by: **Amy**

"This is a family favorite made easy. Preparing the dough in a bread machine saves time, since you don't knead the dough by hand. My grandmother used to make these when we visited her. Now I can make them for her."

AROUND-THE-WORLD CUISINE ▶

Prep Time: 30 minutes

Stand Time: 1 hour 30 minutes

Cook Time: 15 minutes

Average Rating: ★★★★★

What other cooks have done:

"I will start using this recipe for kolaches instead of my old one. To prevent the filling from running, make deep indentations and do not fill them completely full. I used apricot preserves as the filling and made a streusel topping to sprinkle over the kolaches."

1¼	cups warm water (110°F/45°C)	1	teaspoon salt
½	cup butter, softened	3⅞	cups bread flour
1	egg	2	teaspoons active dry yeast
1	egg yolk	1	(12 ounce) can cherry pie filling
⅓	cup milk powder	1	(12 ounce) can poppy seed filling
¼	cup instant mashed potato flakes	¼	cup butter, melted
¼	cup white sugar		

1. Place water, softened butter, egg, egg yolk, milk powder, potato flakes, sugar, salt, flour, and yeast into the bread machine pan in the order suggested by the manufacturer. Select Dough setting; press Start. Check dough after 5 minutes of mixing, adding 1 to 2 tablespoons of water if necessary.

2. When the cycle is complete, spoon out dough and roll into walnut-size balls. Place 2 inches apart on a lightly greased baking sheet. Cover and let rise until doubled in bulk, about 1 hour.

3. Combine cherry pie filling and poppy seed filling. Flatten balls slightly with the palm of your hand and make a depression in center with your thumb. Fill with 1 tablespoon of filling mixture. Cover and let rise in a warm place free from drafts for about 30 minutes. Meanwhile, preheat oven to 375°F (190°C).

4. Bake in the preheated oven for 13 to 15 minutes or until lightly browned. Remove from oven and brush with melted butter. Cool on a wire rack. **Yield:** 2 dozen kolaches.

Per kolache: 216 calories, 5g protein, 32g carbohydrate, 8g fat, 1g fiber, 34mg cholesterol, 182mg sodium

Russian Black Bread

Submitted by: **Mary**

"I have been looking for a good Russian black bread recipe. This one is the best I have found. The vinegar adds a bit of a bite, and with cheese, it is marvelous."

1½   cups water
2   tablespoons cider vinegar
2½   cups bread flour
1   cup rye flour
1   teaspoon salt
2   tablespoons butter
2   tablespoons dark corn syrup
1   tablespoon brown sugar

3   tablespoons unsweetened cocoa powder
1   teaspoon instant coffee granules
1   tablespoon caraway seeds
¼   teaspoon fennel seeds (optional)
2   teaspoons active dry yeast

1. Place all ingredients into the bread machine pan in the order suggested by the manufacturer. Select the Whole Wheat and Regular Crust settings; press Start.
2. After the baking cycle ends, remove bread from pan, place on a wire rack, and allow to cool for 1 hour before slicing.
Yield: 1 (1½ pound) loaf (12 servings).

Per serving: 171 calories, 5g protein, 33g carbohydrate, 3g fat, 3g fiber, 0mg cholesterol, 223mg sodium

◀ AROUND-THE-WORLD CUISINE

Prep Time: 5 minutes

Cook Time: 3 hours

Cool Time: 1 hour

Average Rating: ★★★★

What other cooks have done:

"This is an excellent and easy recipe. The bread is light and moist, and it seems to stay fresher for much longer than many other breads I have made in my bread machine. I use the ends (crusts) to make some truly delicious croutons for soups and salads. I make the recipe exactly as stated and am very happy with the results. I will definitely keep using this one."

Jo's Rosemary Bread

Submitted by: **Jo Lager**

"This bread has a great flavor. It's moist and light and has a crispy crust."

COMPANY IS COMING ▶

Prep Time: 5 minutes

Cook Time: 40 minutes

Average Rating: ★★★★★

What other cooks have done:

"This is an awesome bread! I used fresh rosemary, and it came out divine—perfect for ripping up and dipping in balsamic vinegar and olive oil."

1	cup water	¼	teaspoon ground black
3	tablespoons olive oil		pepper
1½	teaspoons white sugar	1	tablespoon dried rosemary
1½	teaspoons salt	2½	cups bread flour
¼	teaspoon Italian seasoning	1½	teaspoons active dry yeast

1. Place all ingredients into the bread machine pan in the order suggested by the manufacturer. Select White Bread setting; press Start.
Yield: 1 (1½ pound) loaf (12 servings).

Per serving: 137 calories, 4g protein, 22g carbohydrate, 4g fat, 1g fiber, 0mg cholesterol, 292mg sodium

Batter White Bread

Submitted by: **Ed**

"This is a no-knead yeast bread. All yeast breads rise best at about 85°F (30°C). Put this in oven the on the center rack with a bowl of hot water on the bottom rack."

KID-FRIENDLY ▶

Prep Time: 25 minutes

Stand Time: 1 hour 30 minutes

Cook Time: 45 minutes

Average Rating: ★★★★☆

What other cooks have done:

"This bread was really great. It was a snap to make! I used olive oil and honey in place of the shortening and sugar. For the second rising, I put it on top of the stove to rise in the pan while the oven heated. It rose very well. It was flatter on top than kneaded bread, but all yeast batter breads are like that. It sliced very nicely. Next time, I will try making it with a little whole wheat flour."

2	tablespoons shortening	3	cups sifted all-purpose
2	tablespoons white sugar		flour, divided
2	teaspoons salt	1¼	cups warm water
1	(0.25 ounce) package active		(110°F/45°C)
	dry yeast	1	tablespoon butter, melted

1. Mix together shortening, sugar, salt, yeast, and 1 cup plus 3 tablespoons flour. Add warm water and beat by hand about 300 strokes or beat 3 minutes with an electric mixer. Add remaining flour, scraping bowl often, and mix until smooth. Cover with a clean cloth and let rise until doubled in bulk.
2. Stir dough down gently and spoon into a lightly greased 5x9 inch loaf pan (the batter should be sticky). Pat down with floured hands to help shape. Cover again and let rise for about 30 minutes.
3. Preheat oven to 375°F (190°C).
4. Bake in the preheated oven for about 45 minutes. Place on a wire rack and brush the top with melted butter.
Yield: 1 (5x9 inch) loaf (12 servings).

Per serving: 151 calories, 4g protein, 26g carbohydrate, 3g fat, 1g fiber, 3mg cholesterol, 399mg sodium

Grandma Cornish's Whole Wheat Potato Bread

Submitted by: **Sandra J. Cornish**

"This is the recipe that my husband's grandmother made for her family and my mother-in-law made for hers. I have inherited the making of this bread for mine. We particularly like this fresh out of the oven, and we eat it daily for breakfast."

3	(0.25 ounce) packages active dry yeast	1	medium potato, peeled
1	teaspoon white sugar	⅓	cup white sugar
½	cup warm water (110°F/45°C)	⅓	cup shortening
2	cups water	1	tablespoon salt
1	teaspoon salt	6	cups warm milk
		15	cups whole wheat flour

1. Dissolve yeast and 1 teaspoon sugar in ½ cup warm water.

2. Bring 2 cups water to a boil. Add 1 teaspoon salt and potato. Cook until potato is done. Reserve potato water. In a medium bowl, mash the potato. Combine the mashed potato, potato water, ⅓ cup sugar, shortening, 1 tablespoon salt, and milk in a large bowl. Add yeast mixture. Stir in 15 cups whole wheat flour.

3. Turn dough out onto a lightly floured surface. Knead for about 10 minutes. Place in greased bowl, turning to coat dough. Cover with a damp cloth and allow to rise until doubled in bulk, about 1½ hours. Punch down dough and knead again for 3 minutes. Place back in bowl and allow to rise again until doubled in bulk, about 1 hour. Punch down dough. Form dough into 4 loaves; place each loaf into a greased 5x9 inch loaf pan. Let dough rise again for 30 minutes to 1 hour.

4. Preheat oven to 325°F (165°C).

5. Bake in the preheated oven for 1 hour.

Yield: 4 (5x9 inch) loaves (48 servings).

Per serving: 164 calories, 6g protein, 31g carbohydrate, 3g fat, 5g fiber, 2mg cholesterol, 212mg sodium

◄ MAKE-AHEAD

Prep Time: 25 minutes

Stand Time: 3 hours 30 minutes

Cook Time: 1 hour

Average Rating: ★★★★☆

What other cooks have done:

"I use ⅓ cup honey and ⅓ cup oil instead of the sugar and shortening. Sometimes I don't add the potato. Instead, I use water that I have drained off potatoes that I have cooked the night before for dinner."

A Number One Egg Bread

Submitted by: **Kevin Ryan**

"This makes the best bread pudding and French toast imaginable. Try cutting it into chunks and dipping it in fondue—wow!"

HOLIDAY GIFT GIVING ▶

Prep Time: 20 minutes

Stand Time: 2 hours 15 minutes

Cook Time: 40 minutes

Average Rating: ★★★★★

What other cooks have done:

"This makes one gigantic loaf of bread, and it is delicious. I baked it for 45 minutes, but I covered it with foil during the first 30 minutes. You could easily get two loaves out of this."

2	(0.25 ounce) packages active dry yeast	¼	cup white sugar
⅔	cup warm water (110°F/45°C)	1	teaspoon salt
6	egg yolks	4½	cups all-purpose flour, divided
3	eggs, at room temperature	1	egg
½	cup vegetable oil		Pinch salt

1. In a large bowl, dissolve yeast in water. Stir in the yolks, 3 eggs, oil, sugar, and salt. Add about 3½ cups of flour to make a sticky dough.

2. Turn dough out onto a lightly floured surface. Knead with remaining flour until smooth and elastic, about 7 minutes. Place in a well-greased bowl, turning to coat the entire surface of the dough. Cover with a damp cloth. Place in a warm place and let rise until doubled in bulk, about 1½ hours.

3. Punch down dough and divide into 3 pieces. Roll each piece into a rope about 12 inches long. Braid the 3 strands together and seal the ends. Place the bread on a greased baking sheet. Beat the remaining egg with a pinch of salt; brush onto bread. Let the bread rise until doubled in bulk, about 45 minutes.

4. Preheat oven to 375°F (190°C). Brush the bread with the egg wash again.

5. Bake in the preheated oven for 40 minutes or until golden. Cool on a wire rack. **Yield:** 1 braided loaf (18 servings).

Per serving: 217 calories, 6g protein, 27g carbohydrate, 9g fat, 1g fiber, 118mg cholesterol, 168mg sodium

Grandma VanDoren's White Bread

Submitted by: **Marilyn VanDoren Sim**

"This is what Grandma used to make! Our family's favorite. The recipe was never written down (that I know of) until she shared it with me when she was in her 90s."

3 cups warm water (110°F/45°C)	4 tablespoons vegetable oil
3 tablespoons active dry yeast	½ cup white sugar
3 teaspoons salt	8 cups bread flour, divided

1. In a large bowl, combine warm water, yeast, salt, oil, sugar, and 4 cups flour. Mix thoroughly and let rise until doubled in bulk.
2. Gradually add remaining flour, kneading until smooth. Place dough in a greased bowl, turning several times to coat. Cover with a damp cloth. Allow to rise until doubled in bulk.
3. Punch down dough and let rest. Divide dough into 3 equal parts. Shape into loaves and place each loaf in a 4½x8½ inch greased loaf pan. Let rise until almost doubled in bulk.
4. Preheat oven to 350°F (175°C).
5. Bake in the preheated oven for 35 to 45 minutes. The loaves may need to be covered with aluminum foil during the last few minutes to prevent excessive browning.

Yield: 3 (1½ pound) loaves (36 servings).

Per serving: 137 calories, 4g protein, 25g carbohydrate, 2g fat, 1g fiber, 0mg cholesterol, 196mg sodium

◀ RESTAURANT FARE

Prep Time: 15 minutes

Stand Time: 4 hours

Cook Time: 45 minutes

Average Rating: ★★★★★

What other cooks have done:

"When eaten right out of the oven, the crust is nice and crunchy. The inside is very fluffy, moist, and slightly sweet. I prepared the dough and let it rise until doubled in bulk. Then I placed it in the fridge overnight so I could bake it this morning. I let it rise in the prepared pans near my stove when I was making breakfast, and it rose fairly quickly. This is the best recipe for white bread I have come across."

Cinnamon-Raisin Bread I

Submitted by: **Faye Salisbury**

"This is my dad's recipe for a yummy, moist bread loaded with raisins and cinnamon. It's the best cinnamon-raisin bread I've ever had. Try it plain, toasted, or with a light glaze of buttercream frosting."

HOLIDAY GIFT GIVING ▶

Prep Time: 30 minutes

Stand Time: 3 hours

Cook Time: 45 minutes

Average Rating: ★★★★★

What other cooks have done:

"This is the perfect loaf of cinnamon-raisin bread! I doubled the raisins to 2 cups, and it was great. If you have a super-mondo mixer, you'll probably be able to knead this in it. It was too much for my 5-quart mixer!"

1½	cups milk	1	teaspoon salt
2	(0.25 ounce) packages active dry yeast	1	cup raisins
		8	cups all-purpose flour
1	cup warm water (110°F/45°C)	2	tablespoons milk
		¾	cup white sugar
3	eggs	2	tablespoons ground cinnamon
½	cup white sugar		
½	cup butter, softened	2	tablespoons butter, melted

1. Warm 1½ cups milk in a small saucepan until it bubbles; remove from heat. Let cool until lukewarm.

2. Dissolve yeast in warm water and set aside until yeast is frothy. Mix in eggs, ½ cup sugar, butter, salt, and raisins. Stir in lukewarm milk. Add the flour gradually to make a stiff dough.

3. Turn dough out onto a lightly floured surface and knead for a few minutes. Place in a large, greased mixing bowl and turn to coat. Cover with a damp cloth. Allow to rise until doubled in bulk.

4. Roll out on a lightly floured surface into a large ½ inch thick rectangle. Moisten dough with 2 tablespoons milk. Mix together ¾ cup sugar and 2 tablespoons cinnamon; sprinkle mixture on top of the moistened dough. Roll tightly into a cylinder about 3 inches in diameter. Cut into thirds and tuck ends under. Place each into a well-greased 5x9 inch loaf pan. Lightly grease tops of loaves. Let rise for 1 hour.

5. Preheat oven to 350°F (175°C).

6. Bake in the preheated oven for 45 minutes or until loaves are lightly browned and sound hollow when tapped. Remove loaves from pans and brush with melted butter. Cool before slicing.

Yield: 3 (5x9 inch) loaves (36 servings).

Per serving: 182 calories, 4g protein, 32g carbohydrate, 4g fat, 1g fiber, 20mg cholesterol, 117mg sodium

Garden Herb Loaf

Submitted by: **Theresa Malone**

"This bread draws raves whenever I make it."

4¼	cups all-purpose flour, divided	1	teaspoon dried thyme	
3	tablespoons white sugar	1	teaspoon dried rosemary	
2	(0.25 ounce) packages instant yeast	¾	cup milk	
		½	cup water	
1½	teaspoons salt	¼	cup butter, cut into pieces	
1	teaspoon dried marjoram	1	egg	
		1	tablespoon butter, melted	

1. In large bowl, combine 1½ cups flour, sugar, yeast, salt, marjoram, thyme, and rosemary.

2. Combine milk, water, and ¼ cup butter in a medium saucepan and heat over low heat just until very warm (120° to 130°F/50° to 55°C); do not let simmer. Stir into dry ingredients. Stir in egg and enough remaining flour to make a soft dough.

3. Knead on a lightly floured surface until smooth and elastic, about 4 to 6 minutes. Cover; let rest for 10 minutes.

4. Divide dough into 3 equal pieces. Roll each piece into a 30 inch rope. Braid ropes; pinch ends to seal. Tie knot in center of braid; wrap ends around knot, in opposite directions, and tuck under to make a round loaf. Place on a greased baking sheet. Cover; let rise in a warm, draft-free place until doubled in bulk, about 20 to 40 minutes.

5. Preheat oven to 375°F (190°C).

6. Bake in the preheated oven for about 30 to 35 minutes or until done, covering with aluminum foil during last 10 minutes of baking to prevent excessive browning. Brush 1 tablespoon butter over loaf. Let cool on a wire rack. **Yield:** 1 large round loaf (20 servings).

Per serving: 140 calories, 4g protein, 23g carbohydrate, 4g fat, 1g fiber, 19mg cholesterol, 213mg sodium

◄ COMPANY IS COMING

Prep Time: 25 minutes

Stand Time: 50 minutes

Cook Time: 35 minutes

Average Rating: ★★★★★

What other cooks have done:

"Great recipe. Came out nice and soft on the inside and not too dense. This was perfect with pasta. I didn't have all of the herbs on hand, so I used rosemary, oregano, and basil."

Orange Pull-Aparts

Submitted by: **Cathleen Sinclair**
"A nice coffee bread. It's been approved by Grandpa!"

¼	cup milk	2	tablespoons butter
1	egg	½	teaspoon ground cinnamon
1	tablespoon orange zest	¼	cup butter, melted
1	large orange, juiced	3	tablespoons white sugar
	About ½ cup water	1	cup confectioners' sugar
2¼	cups all-purpose flour		(optional)
3	tablespoons white sugar	1½	tablespoons orange juice
2¼	teaspoons active dry yeast		(optional)
1	teaspoon salt		

1. In a 1 cup measure, combine milk, egg, orange zest, juice from orange, and enough water to equal 1 cup. Place into the bread machine pan. Add flour, 3 tablespoons white sugar, yeast, salt, 2 tablespoons butter, and cinnamon to the bread machine pan in the order suggested by the manufacturer. Select Dough setting; press Start.

2. When the cycle is complete, divide the dough into 20 equal portions and roll into balls. Dip balls into melted butter and then into 3 tablespoons white sugar. Place in a large greased Bundt pan. Let rise for 35 to 45 minutes.

3. Preheat oven to 375°F (190°C).

4. Bake in the preheated oven for 25 to 30 minutes. Let cool for 5 minutes; remove from pan.

5. If desired, combine confectioners' sugar and 1½ tablespoons orange juice and stir well to form a glaze. Drizzle over bread and serve.

Yield: 1 ring (20 servings).

Per serving: 132 calories, 2g protein, 22g carbohydrate, 4g fat, 1g fiber, 17mg cholesterol, 158mg sodium

French Bread Rolls to Die For

Submitted by: **Jo Catlin**

"These French bread rolls are easy to make. The dough can be made in a mixer, a bread machine, or by hand. Before baking, brush rolls with a mixture of 1 beaten egg white mixed with 1 tablespoon water, if desired."

1½	cups warm water (110°F/45°C)	2	tablespoons vegetable oil	
1	tablespoon active dry yeast	1	teaspoon salt	
2	tablespoons white sugar	4	cups bread flour, divided	

1. In a large bowl, stir together warm water, yeast, and sugar. Let stand until creamy, about 10 minutes.

2. Add the oil, salt, and 2 cups flour to the yeast mixture. Stir in the remaining flour, ½ cup at a time, until the dough pulls away from the sides of the bowl. Turn out onto a lightly floured surface and knead until smooth and elastic, about 8 minutes. Place dough in a large, lightly greased bowl and turn to coat. Cover with a damp cloth and let rise in a warm place until doubled in bulk, about 1 hour.

3. Punch down dough and turn it out onto a lightly floured surface. Divide the dough into 16 equal pieces and form into round balls. Place on lightly greased baking sheets at least 2 inches apart. Cover the rolls with a damp cloth and let rise until doubled in bulk, about 40 minutes.

4. Preheat oven to 400°F (200°C).

5. Bake in the preheated oven for 18 to 20 minutes or until golden brown. **Yield:** 16 rolls.

Per roll: 147 calories, 4g protein, 27g carbohydrate, 2g fat, 1g fiber, 0mg cholesterol, 147mg sodium

◀ RESTAURANT FARE

Prep Time: 20 minutes

Stand Time: 1 hour 50 minutes

Cook Time: 20 minutes

Average Rating: ★★★★★

What other cooks have done:

"Best roll recipe I have ever tried. I have been through dozens of recipes, including one handed down by my grandmother, but this recipe beats them all. Easy to prepare and absolutely delicious. I tried spreading butter on the tops 5 minutes after taking them out of the oven, and the butter produced a softer roll, not a crunchy top. Either way, they are incredible."

Ooey-Gooey Cinnamon Buns

Submitted by: **Jen**

"These buns are so good hot from the oven when they're gooey and warm."

HOLIDAY GIFT GIVING ▶

Prep Time: 20 minutes

Stand Time: 2 hours 13 minutes

Cook Time: 30 minutes

Average Rating: ★★★★★

What other cooks have done:

"This is a good cinnamon roll recipe. Here's a trick for cutting the rolls without mashing the dough: Slide a piece of thread under the roll, cross the thread over the top of the roll, and pull quickly. It works like magic, and you don't have a sticky knife to clean up!"

1	teaspoon white sugar	4	cups all-purpose flour, divided
1	(0.25 ounce) package active dry yeast	¾	cup butter
½	cup warm water (110°F/45°C)	1½	cups packed brown sugar, divided
½	cup milk	1	cup chopped pecans, divided
¼	cup white sugar	1	tablespoon ground cinnamon
¼	cup butter	¼	cup melted butter, divided
1	teaspoon salt		
2	eggs, lightly beaten		

1. In a small bowl, dissolve 1 teaspoon white sugar and yeast in warm water. Let stand until creamy, about 10 minutes. Warm the milk in a small saucepan until it bubbles and remove from heat. Mix in ¼ cup white sugar, ¼ cup butter, and salt; stir until butter is melted. Let cool until lukewarm.

2. In a large bowl, combine the yeast mixture, milk mixture, eggs, and 1½ cups flour; stir well to combine. Stir in the remaining flour, ½ cup at a time, beating well after each addition. When the dough has pulled together, turn it out onto a lightly floured surface and knead until smooth and elastic, about 8 minutes.

3. Place the dough in a large, lightly greased bowl and turn to coat. Cover with a damp cloth and let rise in a warm place until doubled in bulk, about 1 hour.

4. While dough is rising, melt ¾ cup butter in a small saucepan over medium heat. Stir in ¾ cup brown sugar, whisking until smooth. Pour into a greased 9x13 inch pan. Sprinkle bottom of pan with ½ cup pecans; set aside. Combine remaining ¾ cup brown sugar, remaining ½ cup pecans, and cinnamon; set aside.

5. Turn dough out onto a lightly floured surface and roll into a 14x18 inch rectangle. Brush with 2 tablespoons melted butter, leaving a ½ inch border; sprinkle with cinnamon mixture. Starting at long side, tightly roll up, pinching seam to seal. Brush with remaining 2 tablespoons butter. With a serrated knife, cut into 15 pieces; place pieces, cut side down, in prepared pan. Cover and let rise for 1 hour or until doubled in bulk.

6. Preheat oven to 375°F (190°C).

7. Bake in the preheated oven for 25 to 30 minutes or until golden brown. Let cool in pan for 3 minutes and invert onto a serving platter. Scrape remaining filling from the pan onto the rolls.

Yield: 15 rolls.

Per roll: 397 calories, 6g protein, 45g carbohydrate, 22g fat, 2g fiber, 70mg cholesterol, 331mg sodium

Soft Garlic-Parmesan Breadsticks

(pictured on page 225)

Submitted by: **Andi Flanagan**
"These breadsticks are better than the ones served at pizza parlors! I usually have to make two batches because they go so fast! I use my food processor to do the mixing."

2½	cups bread flour	¼	cup warm water
1	tablespoon instant yeast		(110°F/45°C)
1	tablespoon white sugar	½	cup milk
½	teaspoon salt	1	egg
¾	teaspoon Italian seasoning	¼	cup butter, melted and
1	tablespoon minced garlic		divided
¼	cup grated Parmesan cheese	½	cup grated Parmesan
1	tablespoon butter, softened		cheese, divided

1. Fit your food processor with a steel blade. Place the bread flour, yeast, sugar, salt, Italian seasoning, garlic, ¼ cup grated Parmesan cheese, and 1 tablespoon butter in the processor; pulse to blend. Stir together warm water, milk, and egg. Start the processor and slowly pour the milk mixture into the feed tube until a ball forms around the blade. Process for 30 seconds to knead. Remove dough from processor and knead briefly by hand. Place the dough in a large, lightly greased bowl and turn to coat. Cover with a damp cloth and let rise in a warm place until doubled in bulk, about 1 hour.
2. Punch down dough and turn it out onto a lightly floured surface. Roll the dough into a 10x12 inch rectangle. Use a knife or pizza cutter to slice the dough lengthwise into 10 strips; cut the strips in half. Brush tops of strips with 2 tablespoons melted butter and sprinkle with ¼ cup Parmesan cheese. Cover and let rise until nearly doubled, about 30 minutes.
3. Preheat oven to 375°F (190°C).
4. Bake in the preheated oven for 18 to 23 minutes or until golden brown. Turn broiler on and brush breadsticks with remaining melted butter and Parmesan cheese. Broil just until the cheese starts to turn light brown, about 2 to 3 minutes. Serve warm. **Yield:** 20 breadsticks.

Per breadstick: 116 calories, 4g protein, 14g carbohydrate, 5g fat, 1g fiber, 22mg cholesterol, 165mg sodium

◄ RESTAURANT FARE

Prep Time: 30 minutes

Stand Time: 1 hour 30 minutes

Cook Time: 26 minutes

Average Rating: ★★★★☆

What other cooks have done:

"I let my bread machine do the work with this dough, and the breadsticks were wonderful. Watch them carefully when they're under the broiler—they brown really quickly."

Light Wheat Rolls

Submitted by: **Susan Harshbarger**

"This is a yummy recipe for a light wheat roll. I keep this in my special book of favorite recipes. It is not complicated at all to make."

2 (0.25 ounce) packages active dry yeast
1¾ cups warm water (110°F/45°C)
½ cup white sugar
1 teaspoon salt
¼ cup butter, melted and at room temperature
1 egg, lightly beaten
2¼ cups whole wheat flour
2½ cups all-purpose flour, divided
¼ cup butter, melted

1. In a large bowl, dissolve yeast in warm water. Let stand until creamy, about 10 minutes.
2. Mix sugar, salt, ¼ cup room-temperature butter, egg, and whole wheat flour into yeast mixture. Stir in all-purpose flour, ½ cup at a time, until dough pulls away from the sides of the bowl. Turn dough out onto a well-floured surface and knead until smooth and elastic, about 8 minutes. Place dough in a large, lightly greased bowl and turn to coat. Cover with a damp cloth and let rise in a warm place until doubled in bulk, about 1 hour.
3. Punch down dough, cover, and let rise in warm place until doubled in bulk again, about 30 minutes.
4. Grease 2 muffin pans. Punch down dough and divide into 2 equal portions. Roll each portion into a 6x14 inch rectangle and cut each rectangle into 12 (1x7 inch) strips. Roll strips up into spirals and place into prepared muffin cups. Brush tops with ¼ cup butter. Let rise, uncovered, in a warm place 40 minutes or until doubled in bulk.
5. Preheat oven to 400°F (200°C).
6. Bake in the preheated oven for 12 to 15 minutes or until golden brown. Remove from oven and brush again with melted butter.
Yield: 2 dozen rolls.

Note: If you would like to freeze the rolls, bake for 8 minutes, remove from the oven, and allow to cool. Bag rolls and freeze. When ready to use, thaw and bake until golden brown.

Per roll: 140 calories, 3g protein, 23g carbohydrate, 4g fat, 2g fiber, 19mg cholesterol, 140mg sodium

Butter Crescents

Submitted by: **Rita Fay**

"This recipe for melt-in-your-mouth crescent rolls takes a little time, but the results are worth the wait."

½	cup milk	½	cup warm water
½	cup butter, softened		(110°F/45°C)
⅓	cup white sugar	1	egg
½	teaspoon salt	3½	cups all-purpose flour,
1	(0.25 ounce) package active		divided
	dry yeast	1	egg, lightly beaten

1. Warm the milk in a small saucepan until bubbles form at the edges; remove from heat. Mix in the butter, sugar, and salt. Stir until butter melts. Let cool until lukewarm. In a small bowl, dissolve yeast in warm water. Let stand until creamy, about 10 minutes.

2. In a large bowl, combine milk mixture and yeast mixture. Stir in 1 egg. Beat in flour, 1 cup at a time, until dough pulls together. Turn out onto a lightly floured surface and knead until smooth and elastic, about 8 minutes. Place the dough in a large, lightly greased bowl and turn to coat. Cover with a damp cloth and let rise in a warm place until doubled in bulk, about 1 hour.

3. Punch down dough and turn it out onto a lightly floured surface. Divide the dough into 2 equal pieces and form into rounds. Cover and let rest 10 minutes.

4. Using a floured rolling pin, roll each round into a 12 inch circle. Cut each circle into 6 wedges. Roll each wedge up, starting at the wide end. Bend inward to form crescents and place, point side down, on lightly greased baking sheets. Cover and let rise until doubled in bulk, about 30 minutes.

5. Preheat oven to 400°F (200°C).

6. Brush rolls with beaten egg and bake in the preheated oven for 12 to 15 minutes or until golden brown. **Yield:** 1 dozen rolls.

Per roll: 241 calories, 5g protein, 34g carbohydrate, 9g fat, 1g fiber, 57mg cholesterol, 192mg sodium

◀ RESTAURANT FARE

Prep Time: 30 minutes

Stand Time: 1 hour 50 minutes

Cook Time: 15 minutes

Average Rating: ★★★★★

What other cooks have done:

"Easy directions and good-looking rolls. You can make a softer finish by brushing them with melted butter instead of egg. This dough is ample enough to produce more rolls. By rolling out the dough into larger circles, you can get 12 to 14 more rolls per circle."

English Muffins *(pictured on page 263)*

Submitted by: **Linda Letellier**

"I've used this delicious recipe for about 29 years. These are very good—much better than any store-bought English muffins I've ever had. These are great with orange butter; try them with cream cheese and jam, too."

RESTAURANT FARE ▶

Prep Time: 25 minutes

Stand Time: 1 hour 30 minutes

Cook Time: 20 minutes per batch

Average Rating: ★★★★★

What other cooks have done:

"Very good. Lacked the 'nooks and crannies' that I'm used to, but these were yummy. I'll use this recipe instead of buying them at the store."

1	cup milk	¼	cup melted shortening
2	tablespoons white sugar	6	cups all-purpose flour, divided
1	(0.25 ounce) package active dry yeast	1	teaspoon salt
1	cup warm water (110°F/45°C)		Cornmeal

1. Warm the milk in a small saucepan until it bubbles and remove from heat. Mix in the sugar, stirring until dissolved. Let cool until lukewarm. In a small bowl, dissolve yeast in warm water. Let stand until creamy, about 10 minutes.

2. In a large bowl, combine milk mixture, yeast mixture, shortening, and 3 cups flour. Beat until smooth. Add salt and enough remaining flour to make a soft dough. Knead until smooth and elastic. Place in a greased bowl, turning to coat. Cover and let rise until doubled in bulk.

3. Punch down dough. Roll out to about ½ inch thick. Cut rounds with a biscuit cutter, drinking glass, or empty tuna can. Sprinkle wax paper with cornmeal. Set rounds on prepared wax paper. Dust tops of rounds with cornmeal. Cover and let rise 30 minutes.

4. Heat a greased griddle. Cook muffins on griddle about 10 minutes on each side over medium heat. Keep cooked muffins in a warm oven until all have been cooked. Allow to cool and place in plastic bags for storage. To use, split and toast. **Yield:** about 18 muffins.

Per muffin: 190 calories, 5g protein, 34g carbohydrate, 4g fat, 1g fiber, 1mg cholesterol, 137mg sodium

Darbey Bread

Submitted by: **Gina Paradise**

"This bread uses two loaves of frozen bread dough, cheese, onions, olive oil, and Italian spices. Crumbled crisp bacon can be added before baking, if desired."

2	(1 pound) loaves frozen bread dough, thawed	1	onion, finely diced
1½	cups shredded sharp Cheddar cheese	¼	cup olive oil
		1	tablespoon Italian seasoning

1. Cut bread dough into 1 inch cubes.

2. Toss bread cubes with the shredded sharp Cheddar cheese, diced onion, olive oil, and Italian seasoning. Place in a 9x9 inch pan. Let rise in a warm place until bread has doubled in bulk.

3. Preheat oven to 350°F (175°C).

4. Bake in the preheated oven for about 20 minutes or until golden brown and cheese has melted. **Yield:** 12 squares.

Per square: 323 calories, 12g protein, 40g carbohydrate, 14g fat, 3g fiber, 18mg cholesterol, 529mg sodium

◀ 5 INGREDIENTS OR LESS

Prep Time: 15 minutes

Stand Time: 1 hour

Cook Time: 20 minutes

Average Rating: ★★★★☆

What other cooks have done:

"This is a great bread. I served it with a large pot of chili, and my family loved it. I used herbes de Provence instead of Italian seasoning."

Grandpa McAndrew's Irish Soda Bread

Submitted by: **Nancy**

"My mom bugged Grandpa for this recipe, but he told her he didn't have one. So when he made the bread one day, she captured each ingredient in a bowl, measured it, and wrote down the amount before putting it in his mixing bowl."

3	cups all-purpose flour	1	egg, lightly beaten
½	teaspoon baking soda	1	cup buttermilk
2	tablespoons white sugar	2	tablespoons butter, melted
½	cup raisins		

1. Preheat oven to 350°F (175°C). Grease a large cast-iron skillet.

2. In a medium bowl, mix together the flour, baking soda, and sugar. Toss the raisins with the flour mixture until coated. Make a well in the center and add the egg, buttermilk, and melted butter. Stir until all of the dry ingredients are absorbed. Turn the dough out onto a floured surface and knead a few times just to even out the dough, handling the dough as little as possible. Pat into a flat circle and place in the prepared skillet.

3. Bake in the preheated oven for 40 to 45 minutes or until the edges are golden. **Yield:** 1 loaf (8 servings).

Per serving: 255 calories, 7g protein, 48g carbohydrate, 4g fat, 2g fiber, 28mg cholesterol, 152mg sodium

◀ MAKE-AHEAD

Prep Time: 10 minutes

Cook Time: 45 minutes

Average Rating: ★★★★☆

What other cooks have done:

"I made this with 3 tablespoons butter and ½ teaspoon salt. Next time, I'll brush the top with an egg white/water mixture before baking. This bread was very heavy and slightly sweet. I served it with whipped cream cheese."

Lauri's Yummy Nut Bread

Submitted by: **Lauri**

"This recipe for nut bread has been handed down from my grandmother. It's easy to make, and everyone who tries it always asks for the recipe. For the best results, mix with a wooden spoon, not with an electric mixer. Otherwise, you will overmix the batter, and the bread will be tough."

HOLIDAY GIFT GIVING ▶

Prep Time: 10 minutes

Cook Time: 55 minutes

Cool Time: 10 minutes

Average Rating: ★★★★☆

What other cooks have done:

"Yummy! I made sure I kept the stirring to a minimum, and the loaves turned out wonderfully and with a perfect texture. I'm so glad it made two loaves so I could share!"

2	cups white sugar	2	teaspoons baking soda
2	eggs	1	teaspoon salt
2	tablespoons vegetable oil	1	teaspoon ground cinnamon
1	teaspoon vanilla extract	2	cups buttermilk
4	cups all-purpose flour	1	cup chopped walnuts

1. Preheat oven to 350°F (175°C). Grease 2 (5x9 inch) loaf pans.
2. In a large bowl, stir together sugar, eggs, vegetable oil, and vanilla until smooth. In a separate bowl, combine flour, baking soda, salt, and cinnamon; stir into the sugar mixture alternately with the buttermilk just until mixed. Stir in the walnuts. Divide the batter evenly between the 2 prepared pans.
3. Bake in the preheated oven for 55 minutes or until a toothpick inserted into the center of a loaf comes out clean. Allow the bread to cool for about 10 minutes before removing from the pans. Wrap in aluminum foil to store. **Yield:** 2 (5x9 inch) loaves (24 servings).

Per serving: 198 calories, 4g protein, 34g carbohydrate, 5g fat, 1g fiber, 19mg cholesterol, 229mg sodium

Banana-Sour Cream Bread

Submitted by: **Esther Nelson**

"I know that you're probably thinking, 'Oh no! Another banana bread recipe!' But this one is a little different—the sour cream makes this one so moist that it melts in your mouth. The flavor is just wonderful! This one is great for gift giving and holidays. The loaves freeze well."

FREEZER FRESH ▶

Prep Time: 10 minutes

Cook Time: 1 hour

Average Rating: ★★★★★

What other cooks have done:

"One of the best banana bread recipes I've made! This is moist and addictive. What a great way to use overripe bananas! I topped these with chopped walnuts, cinnamon sugar, and some coconut—delicious!"

¼	cup white sugar	2	teaspoons vanilla extract
1	teaspoon ground cinnamon	2	teaspoons ground cinnamon
¾	cup butter, softened		
3	cups white sugar	½	teaspoon salt
3	eggs	1	tablespoon baking soda
6	very ripe bananas, mashed	4½	cups all-purpose flour
1	(16 ounce) container sour cream	1	cup chopped walnuts (optional)

1. Preheat oven to 300°F (150°C). Grease 4 (3x7 inch) loaf pans. In a small bowl, stir together ¼ cup white sugar and 1 teaspoon cinnamon. Dust pans lightly with cinnamon and sugar mixture.
2. In a large bowl, cream together butter and 3 cups sugar. Mix in eggs, mashed bananas, sour cream, vanilla, and 2 teaspoons cinnamon.

Mix in salt, baking soda, and flour. Stir in nuts, if desired. Divide between prepared pans.

3. Bake in the preheated oven for 1 hour or until a toothpick inserted into the center of a loaf comes out clean.

Yield: 4 (3x7 inch) loaves (32 servings).

Per serving: 264 calories, 4g protein, 40g carbohydrate, 11g fat, 1g fiber, 38mg cholesterol, 213mg sodium

Pumpkin Gingerbread *(pictured on page 264)*

Submitted by: **Terri**

"Bake this wonderfully flavorful and fragrant bread for the holidays or for special occasions."

3	cups white sugar	1	teaspoon ground allspice
1	cup vegetable oil	1	teaspoon ground cinnamon
4	eggs	1	teaspoon ground cloves
⅔	cup water	3½	cups all-purpose flour
1	(15 ounce) can pumpkin puree	2	teaspoons baking soda
		1½	teaspoons salt
2	teaspoons ground ginger	½	teaspoon baking powder

1. Preheat oven to 350°F (175°C). Grease 2 (5x9 inch) loaf pans.
2. In a large mixing bowl, combine sugar, oil, and eggs; beat until smooth. Add water and beat until well blended. Stir in pumpkin, ginger, allspice, cinnamon, and cloves.
3. In a separate medium bowl, combine flour, baking soda, salt, and baking powder. Add dry ingredients to pumpkin mixture and blend just until all ingredients are mixed. Divide batter between prepared loaf pans.
4. Bake in the preheated oven for about 1 hour or until a toothpick inserted into the center of a loaf comes out clean. Cool in pans for 5 minutes before removing to a wire rack to cool completely.

Yield: 2 (5x9 inch) loaves (24 servings).

Per serving: 263 calories, 3g protein, 41g carbohydrate, 10g fat, 1g fiber, 35mg cholesterol, 310mg sodium

◀ COMPANY IS COMING

Prep Time: 10 minutes

Cook Time: 1 hour

Average Rating: ★★★★★

What other cooks have done:

"We call this 'sell-your-home bread' because when we recently had our house up for sale, each time we showed it, I had one of these loaves baking in the oven. This is so good, and it makes your home smell great. I used half white and half brown sugar, and I added some pumpkin pie spice. The bread froze well, and everyone loved it."

Mom's Zucchini Bread

Submitted by: **v monte**

"My kids eat this bread as quickly as I can make it. It freezes well, and you can keep it in the refrigerator for weeks."

MAKE-AHEAD ▶

Prep Time: 20 minutes

Cook Time: 1 hour

Cool Time: 20 minutes

Average Rating: ★★★★★

What other cooks have done:

"This is a very tasty bread. Instead of using cinnamon, I used 1 tablespoon pumpkin pie spice. I added 1 cup raisins and ¾ cup shredded coconut for a little something extra."

3	cups all-purpose flour	3	eggs
1	teaspoon salt	1	cup vegetable oil
1	teaspoon baking powder	2¼	cups white sugar
1	teaspoon baking soda	1	tablespoon vanilla extract
1	tablespoon ground cinnamon	2	cups grated zucchini
		1	cup chopped walnuts

1. Preheat oven to 325°F (165°C). Grease and flour 2 (4x8 inch) pans.
2. Sift together flour, salt, baking powder, baking soda, and cinnamon in a bowl.
3. Beat together eggs, oil, sugar, and vanilla in a large bowl. Add sifted ingredients to the egg mixture and beat well. Stir in zucchini and nuts until well combined. Pour batter into prepared pans.
4. Bake in the preheated oven for 40 minutes to 1 hour or until a toothpick inserted in the center of a loaf comes out clean. Cool in pans on wire racks for 20 minutes. Remove bread from pans to cool completely. **Yield:** 2 (4x8 inch) loaves (24 servings).

Per serving: 256 calories, 3g protein, 32g carbohydrate, 13g fat, 1g fiber, 27mg cholesterol, 179mg sodium

Coconut Bread II

Submitted by: **Susan Rolapp**

"I got this recipe from my mother-in-law. Even people who don't like coconut love this sweet, yummy bread."

COMPANY IS COMING ▶

Prep Time: 10 minutes

Cook Time: 45 minutes

Average Rating: ★★★★☆

What other cooks have done:

"This is just like my grandma's recipe that she got from some folks who visited Hawaii about 50 years ago. She makes it as dessert loaves in 3x6 inch loaf pans. It will make 3½ of these. Use the same oven temperature and cook for 10 to 14 minutes."

2	cups white sugar	½	teaspoon salt
1	cup vegetable oil	½	teaspoon baking powder
4	eggs	½	teaspoon baking soda
2	teaspoons coconut extract	1	cup buttermilk
3	cups all-purpose flour	1	cup shredded coconut

1. Preheat oven to 375°F (190°C). Lightly grease a 5x9 inch loaf pan.
2. In a large bowl, beat together sugar and vegetable oil. Beat in eggs and coconut extract. In a separate bowl, sift together flour, salt, baking powder, and baking soda. Stir flour mixture into egg mixture alternately with buttermilk. Stir in coconut.
3. Bake in the preheated oven for 45 minutes or until a toothpick inserted into the center of the loaf comes out clean.
Yield: 1 (5x9 inch) loaf (12 servings).

Per serving: 489 calories, 7g protein, 60g carbohydrate, 25g fat, 2g fiber, 72mg cholesterol, 206mg sodium

Pear Bread II

Submitted by: **Anna**

"The delicate flavor of fresh pears is complemented by pecans in this lovely summer loaf. This freezes well if it's double wrapped. Delicious and easy."

1	cup vegetable oil	3	cups all-purpose flour
2	cups white sugar	1	teaspoon baking soda
3	eggs	1	teaspoon baking powder
2½	cups peeled, cored, and chopped pears	1	teaspoon salt
1	cup chopped pecans	1	teaspoon ground cinnamon
2	teaspoons vanilla extract	½	teaspoon ground nutmeg

1. Preheat oven to 350°F (175°C). Lightly grease 2 (4x8 inch) loaf pans.

2. In a large mixing bowl, combine oil, sugar, and eggs; beat well. Stir in pears, pecans, and vanilla. In a separate bowl, combine flour, baking soda, baking powder, salt, cinnamon, and nutmeg. Stir dry ingredients into the pear mixture; mix well. Pour batter into prepared loaf pans.

3. Bake in the preheated oven for 1 hour or until a toothpick inserted into the center of a loaf comes out clean. Allow loaves to cool in pans for 10 minutes before moving to a wire rack to cool completely.

Yield: 2 (4x8 inch) loaves (20 servings).

Per serving: 309 calories, 4g protein, 39g carbohydrate, 16g fat, 2g fiber, 32mg cholesterol, 202mg sodium

◀ FREEZER FRESH

Prep Time: 10 minutes

Cook Time: 1 hour

Cool Time: 10 minutes

Average Rating: ★★★★★

What other cooks have done:

"I was feeling lazy, so I just threw the pears into the food processor and shredded them. The bread was excellent! I did have to bake it for an extra 10 minutes due to the extra juice the processor created."

Navajo Fry Bread II

Submitted by: **Saundra**

"As far as I know, this is the original recipe for Navajo bread. It's great served with honey and butter. We also put chiles, cheese, onion, lettuce, and beans on this bread to make Navajo tacos."

	Vegetable oil for frying	2	teaspoons salt
4	cups all-purpose flour	2½	cups warm milk
3	tablespoons baking powder		

1. In a large, heavy skillet, heat 1 inch of vegetable oil to 365°F (185°C).

2. In a large mixing bowl, combine flour, baking powder, salt, and milk; mix well. When the dough pulls together, form it into 18 small balls. Pat the balls flat into rounds.

3. Place 3 or 4 rounds at a time into the hot oil. When the rounds begin to bubble, flip them over and cook until golden. Drain on paper towels and serve hot. **Yield:** 18 rounds.

Per round: 163 calories, 4g protein, 23g carbohydrate, 6g fat, 1g fiber, 3mg cholesterol, 521mg sodium

◀ AROUND-THE-WORLD CUISINE

Prep Time: 15 minutes

Cook Time: 25 minutes

Average Rating: ★★★★☆

What other cooks have done:

"I made vegetarian Navajo tacos with this recipe using chili beans, black beans, and assorted sides, such as lettuce, tomato, avocado, and onion. They were great! The bread is also really good dusted with cinnamon and sugar for a light dessert."

Basil, Roasted Peppers, and Monterey Jack Cornbread

Submitted by: **Stephanie**

"I just started adding my favorite things to basic cornbread, and I came up with something great!"

COMPANY IS COMING ▶

Prep Time: 25 minutes

Cook Time: 55 minutes

Cool Time: 20 minutes

Average Rating: ★★★★☆

What other cooks have done:

"Very good and moist. This has lots of different flavors complementing each other, and we enjoy it with spicy bean soup on a rainy night."

½	cup unsalted butter, chilled, cubed, and divided
1	cup chopped onion
1¾	cups cornmeal
1¼	cups all-purpose flour
¼	cup white sugar
1	tablespoon baking powder
1½	teaspoons salt
½	teaspoon baking soda
1½	cups buttermilk
3	eggs
1½	cups shredded pepper Jack cheese
1⅓	cups frozen corn kernels, thawed and drained
2	ounces roasted marinated red bell peppers, drained and chopped
½	cup chopped fresh basil

1. Preheat oven to 400°F (200°C). Butter a 9x9 inch pan.

2. Melt 1 tablespoon butter in a medium nonstick skillet over medium-low heat. Add onion and sauté until tender, about 10 minutes. Set aside to cool.

3. Mix together cornmeal, flour, sugar, baking powder, salt, and baking soda in a large bowl. Add remaining butter and mix with fingertips until mixture resembles coarse meal.

4. Whisk together buttermilk and eggs in a medium bowl. Add buttermilk mixture to dry ingredients and stir until blended. Mix in cheese, corn, red bell peppers, basil, and cooled onion. Transfer to prepared pan.

5. Bake in the preheated oven until golden and a toothpick inserted in the center of bread comes out clean, about 45 minutes. Cool 20 minutes in pan before cutting. **Yield:** 12 servings.

Per serving: 314 calories, 10g protein, 36g carbohydrate, 15g fat, 3g fiber, 93mg cholesterol, 632mg sodium

Walnut-Raisin Scones

Submitted by: **Eleanor Johnson**

"These are a good choice for breakfast, brunch, or tea. Their sweetness comes from the raisins. Walnuts and lemon zest provide crunchiness and tang. Serve warm and spread with butter and honey or jam."

2	cups all-purpose flour	¾	cup chopped walnuts
2	tablespoons white sugar	½	cup raisins
2	teaspoons baking powder	¾	cup buttermilk
½	teaspoon baking soda	1	tablespoon buttermilk
½	teaspoon salt	2	tablespoons white sugar
1	tablespoon grated lemon zest	2	tablespoons chopped walnuts
½	cup butter, cubed		

1. In a large bowl, combine flour, 2 tablespoons sugar, baking powder, baking soda, salt, and lemon zest.

2. With a pastry blender or 2 knives, cut in butter until mixture resembles coarse meal. Mix in ¾ cup walnuts and raisins. Mix in ¾ cup buttermilk with a fork.

3. Preheat oven to 425°F (220°C). Grease a baking sheet.

4. Gather the dough into a ball and knead for about 2 minutes on a lightly floured surface. Roll or pat out into a ¾ inch thick circle. With a chef's knife, cut into 14 (3 inch) triangles. Place triangles, 1 inch apart, on prepared baking sheet. Brush tops with 1 tablespoon buttermilk; sprinkle with 2 tablespoons sugar and 2 tablespoons walnuts.

5. Bake in the preheated oven on center rack for about 15 minutes or until nicely browned. Serve warm. **Yield:** 14 scones.

Per scone: 208 calories, 4g protein, 23g carbohydrate, 12g fat, 1g fiber, 18mg cholesterol, 282mg sodium

◀ QUICK & EASY

Prep Time: 15 minutes

Cook Time: 15 minutes

Average Rating: ★★★★

What other cooks have done:

"Definitely a good recipe. I made these for Mother's Day, and everyone wanted seconds, including my father, who never eats scones. These were easy to make, and they tasted delicious. Definitely don't skip the lemon zest!"

Spicy Scones

Submitted by: **Carol**
"Amaze your guests with the aroma of scones fresh from the oven. Maple butter goes very well with these."

COMPANY IS COMING ▶

Prep Time: 15 minutes

Cook Time: 15 minutes

Average Rating: ★★★★★

What other cooks have done:

"I love these scones. They are delicious fresh from the oven, and they have a great flavor the next day, too. I always add more spices and currants."

1	cup all-purpose flour	½	teaspoon salt
1	cup whole wheat flour	⅓	cup butter, chilled
¼	cup white sugar	½	cup currants
4	teaspoons baking powder	1	egg
1½	teaspoons ground cinnamon	⅔	cup milk
½	teaspoon ground nutmeg	2	tablespoons milk
		2	tablespoons white sugar

1. Preheat oven to 425°F (220°C). Grease a baking sheet.
2. Combine all-purpose flour, whole wheat flour, ¼ cup sugar, baking powder, cinnamon, nutmeg, and salt in a bowl. Cut in the butter until crumbly; stir in the currants. Make a well in the center.
3. In a small bowl, beat the egg until frothy. Mix in ⅔ cup milk and pour into the dry ingredients. Stir to make a soft dough.
4. Turn dough out onto a lightly floured surface. Knead gently 8 to 10 times. Pat dough into 2 (6 inch) circles and transfer to the prepared baking sheet. Brush tops with 2 tablespoons milk and sprinkle with 2 tablespoons sugar. Score each circle into 6 pie-shaped wedges.
5. Bake in the preheated oven for 15 minutes or until well risen and browned. Serve hot. **Yield:** 1 dozen scones.

Per scone: 174 calories, 4g protein, 28g carbohydrate, 6g fat, 2g fiber, 19mg cholesterol, 332mg sodium

Mom's Baking Powder Biscuits

Submitted by: **Jodeen Brown**
"This is the recipe my mom always made. I like to use butter-flavored shortening, but you can use regular."

KID-FRIENDLY ▶

Prep Time: 15 minutes

Cook Time: 15 minutes

Average Rating: ★★★★☆

What other cooks have done:

"This is an easy and very good recipe, and I have used it several times. I use butter instead of shortening, and it works well. Double or triple the recipe and cut thick biscuits to make them soft and large enough to be split and buttered."

2	cups all-purpose flour	5	tablespoons shortening
2½	teaspoons baking powder	¾	cup milk
¾	teaspoon salt		Melted shortening

1. Preheat oven to 450°F (230°C).
2. In a bowl, mix flour, baking powder, and salt. Add shortening; mix until in little pieces. Add milk slowly and stir until dough forms a ball.
3. Turn dough out onto a floured surface; roll dough to ¼ inch to ½ inch thickness. Cut out in desired size and dip in melted shortening. Place biscuits on an ungreased baking sheet.
4. Bake in the preheated oven for 12 to 15 minutes.
Yield: 2 dozen biscuits.

Per biscuit: 66 calories, 1g protein, 8g carbohydrate, 3g fat, 0g fiber, 0mg cholesterol, 127mg sodium

Classic Bran Muffins

Submitted by: **Janet Kalman Villada**

"A delicious source of fiber! My family has these almost every morning. You may substitute dates for the raisins, if you wish."

1½	cups wheat bran	1	cup all-purpose flour
1	cup buttermilk	1	teaspoon baking soda
⅓	cup vegetable oil	1	teaspoon baking powder
1	egg	½	teaspoon salt
⅔	cup packed brown sugar	½	cup raisins
½	teaspoon vanilla extract		

1. Preheat oven to 375°F (190°C). Grease a muffin pan or line with paper liners.
2. Mix together wheat bran and buttermilk; let stand for 10 minutes.
3. Beat together oil, egg, sugar, and vanilla and add to buttermilk mixture. In a separate bowl, sift together flour, baking soda, baking powder, and salt. Stir flour mixture into buttermilk mixture just until blended. Fold in raisins and spoon batter into prepared muffin cups.
4. Bake in the preheated oven for 15 to 20 minutes or until a toothpick inserted into the center of a muffin comes out clean.
Yield: 1 dozen muffins.

Per muffin: 168 calories, 4g protein, 26g carbohydrate, 7g fat, 4g fiber, 19mg cholesterol, 253mg sodium

◀ QUICK & EASY

Prep Time: 15 minutes

Stand Time: 10 minutes

Cook Time: 20 minutes

Average Rating: ★★★★

What other cooks have done:

"I make these all the time and have used bran flakes cereal for all or part of the wheat bran. You can add nuts and dates, and for those who want their muffins a bit more moist, try adding some drained crushed pineapple. These are great little muffins."

Easy Oatmeal Muffins

Submitted by: **Tony**

"A simple but delicious recipe for oatmeal muffins."

1	cup milk	1	cup all-purpose flour
1	cup quick cooking oats	¼	cup white sugar
1	egg	2	teaspoons baking powder
¼	cup vegetable oil	½	teaspoon salt

1. Preheat oven to 425°F (220°C). Grease a muffin pan or line with paper liners.
2. In a small bowl, combine milk and oats; let soak for 15 minutes.
3. In a separate bowl, beat together egg and oil; stir in oatmeal mixture. In a third bowl, sift together flour, sugar, baking powder, and salt. Stir flour mixture into wet ingredients just until combined. Fill prepared muffin cups two-thirds full with batter.
4. Bake in the preheated oven for 20 to 25 minutes or until a toothpick inserted into the center of a muffin comes out clean.
Yield: 1 dozen muffins.

Per muffin: 137 calories, 3g protein, 18g carbohydrate, 6g fat, 1g fiber, 19mg cholesterol, 154mg sodium

◀ FROM THE PANTRY

Prep Time: 15 minutes

Stand Time: 15 minutes

Cook Time: 25 minutes

Average Rating: ★★★★★

What other cooks have done:

"I threw in a cup of chocolate chips before mixing the wet ingredients with the dry ingredients. Also, instead of making a dozen muffins, I made seven large muffins. They baked in a 375°F (190°C) oven for 20 minutes. These also would be great made with peanut butter and banana or coconut and pineapple."

French Breakfast Muffins

Submitted by: **Kelly**

"This is my 10-year-old brother's favorite recipe."

1½	cups all-purpose flour	½	cup milk
½	cup white sugar	⅓	cup butter, melted
1½	teaspoons baking powder	¼	cup white sugar
¼	teaspoon ground nutmeg	½	teaspoon ground cinnamon
⅛	teaspoon salt	⅓	cup butter, melted
1	egg, lightly beaten		

1. Preheat oven to 350°F (175°C). Grease a muffin pan.

2. In a medium bowl, stir together flour, ½ cup sugar, baking powder, nutmeg, and salt. Make a well in center of mixture. In a separate bowl, stir together egg, milk, and ⅓ cup butter. Add egg mixture to flour mixture; stir until just moistened. Spoon batter into prepared pan.

3. Bake in the preheated oven for 20 to 25 minutes. Meanwhile, combine ¼ cup sugar and cinnamon. Dip tops of cooked muffins in ⅓ cup butter and then in sugar mixture. Serve warm. **Yield:** 1 dozen muffins.

Per muffin: 208 calories, 3g protein, 25g carbohydrate, 11g fat, 1g fiber, 46mg cholesterol, 170mg sodium

Fudgy Chocolate Chip Muffins

Submitted by: **Sue Litster**

"These easy muffins are a chocolaty treat!"

¼	cup butter, softened	½	teaspoon baking soda
½	cup white sugar	¼	teaspoon ground cinnamon (optional)
½	cup packed brown sugar		
1	egg	1	cup semisweet chocolate chips
½	teaspoon vanilla extract		
½	cup applesauce	2	tablespoons confectioners' sugar (optional)
1	cup all-purpose flour		
¼	cup unsweetened cocoa powder		

1. Preheat oven to 350°F (175°C). Line muffin cups with paper liners.

2. In large bowl, beat together butter, white sugar, brown sugar, egg, and vanilla until well blended. Add applesauce; blend well.

3. In a separate bowl, stir together flour, cocoa powder, baking soda, and cinnamon, if desired. Add to butter mixture, blending well. Stir in chocolate chips. Fill muffin cups three-quarters full with batter.

4. Bake in the preheated oven for 22 minutes or until toothpick inserted in a muffin comes out almost clean. Cool in pan. Sprinkle with confectioners' sugar, if desired. Serve warm. **Yield:** 1 dozen muffins.

Per muffin: 233 calories, 3g protein, 39g carbohydrate, 9g fat, 2g fiber, 18mg cholesterol, 116mg sodium

Desserts

No meal is complete without a little something sweet. Whether you crave velvety chocolate treats, slices of pie, or overflowing cookie jars, the ultimate decadent dessert is here.

Banana-Nut-Coconut Cake *(pictured on page 298)*

Submitted by: **Rosemary Stoker**

"The combination of banana, coconut, and pecans gives this cake a unique flavor. This is best if made a day before serving."

COMPANY IS COMING ▶

Prep Time: 35 minutes

Cook Time: 50 minutes

Average Rating: ★★★★★

What other cooks have done:

"Yum. I didn't have time to cool and frost the cake, so I put a boiled coconut icing on it and served it warm."

1½	cups white sugar	2	teaspoons vanilla extract, divided
1	cup butter, softened and divided	2	cups chopped pecans, divided
2	eggs	2	cups sweetened flaked coconut, divided
3	ripe bananas, mashed		
2	cups all-purpose flour	3	cups confectioners' sugar
1	teaspoon baking soda	1	ripe banana, mashed
¼	cup buttermilk		

1. Preheat oven to 350°F (175°C). Grease and flour 2 (9 inch) round cake pans or a 9x13 inch pan.

2. Cream together white sugar and ½ cup butter. Add the eggs and 3 mashed bananas; mix well.

3. In a separate bowl, sift together flour and baking soda; add to the creamed mixture alternately with buttermilk, mixing well after each addition. Blend in 1 teaspoon vanilla. Fold in 1 cup pecans and 1 cup coconut. Pour batter into prepared pans.

4. Bake in the preheated oven for 45 to 50 minutes. Cool in pans on wire racks 10 minutes. Invert onto wire racks to cool completely before frosting.

5. To make frosting, cream together remaining ½ cup butter and 3 cups confectioners' sugar until light and fluffy. Stir in 1 mashed banana, remaining 1 cup pecans, remaining 1 cup coconut, and remaining 1 teaspoon vanilla; mix well. Spread frosting between layers and over top of cake. **Yield:** 24 servings.

Per serving: 351 calories, 3g protein, 48g carbohydrate, 17g fat, 2g fiber, 39mg cholesterol, 155mg sodium

Double-Chocolate Brownie
Cake *(pictured on cover)*

Submitted by: **Tomi Rotchford**

"Chocolate lovers, beware! This easy Bundt cake made with cake mix, instant pudding, sour cream, and chocolate chips has your number. Drizzle with melted semisweet chocolate chips and white chocolate chips for a pretty presentation."

1 (18.25 ounce) package devil's food cake mix	2 cups semisweet chocolate chips
1 (3.9 ounce) package instant chocolate pudding mix	Semisweet chocolate drizzle (optional)
4 eggs	White chocolate drizzle (optional)
1 cup sour cream	Fresh raspberries (optional)
½ cup vegetable oil	
½ cup water	

1. Preheat oven to 350°F (175°C). Grease and flour a 10 inch Bundt pan. Bring all ingredients to room temperature.

2. In a large bowl, stir together cake mix and pudding mix. Make a well in the center and pour in eggs, sour cream, oil, and water. Beat at low speed with an electric mixer until blended. Scrape bowl and beat at medium speed for 4 minutes. Stir in chocolate chips. Pour batter into prepared pan.

3. Bake in the preheated oven for 50 minutes to 1 hour or until a toothpick inserted into the center of cake comes out clean. Cool in pan on wire rack 15 minutes. Invert onto wire rack to cool completely. Drizzle with melted chocolate, if desired. Garnish with fresh raspberries, if desired. **Yield:** 12 servings.

Per serving: 500 calories, 8g protein, 57g carbohydrate, 29g fat, 2g fiber, 88mg cholesterol, 481mg sodium

◀ COMPANY IS COMING

Prep Time: 10 minutes

Cook Time: 1 hour

Average Rating: ★★★★★

What other cooks have done:

"Look no further for an amazing, easy cake recipe. This was by far the most delicious, rich cake I have ever made. I've made it twice, and it received rave reviews both times. For an easy chocolate glaze, mix together 2 tablespoons butter, melted; ⅔ cup chocolate chips, melted; and 2 tablespoons corn syrup. Drizzle over the cake. I've also dusted confectioners' sugar on the cake and dotted it with chocolate mini-chips. You've got to try this cake to believe it."

Buttermilk Pound Cake II *(pictured on facing page)*

Submitted by: **Cathy**

"Enjoy this tangy, moist, and flavorful pound cake plain or use it as a base for numerous dessert ideas."

1	cup butter	3	cups all-purpose flour
3	cups white sugar	½	teaspoon salt
6	eggs	¼	teaspoon baking soda
1	teaspoon lemon extract	1	cup buttermilk
1	teaspoon vanilla extract		

1. Preheat oven to 325°F (165°C). Grease a 9 or 10 inch tube pan.
2. Blend together butter and sugar. Add the eggs, 1 at time, beating well after each addition. Stir in the lemon extract and the vanilla.
3. In a separate bowl, mix together flour, salt, and baking soda. Add flour mixture alternately with buttermilk to the egg mixture. Pour batter into prepared pan.
4. Bake in the preheated oven for 1½ hours or until a toothpick inserted in center of cake come sout clean. Cool in pan on wire rack 15 minutes. Invert onto wire rack to cool completely.
Yield: 14 servings.

Per serving: 419 calories, 6g protein, 64g carbohydrate, 16g fat, 1g fiber, 127mg cholesterol, 286mg sodium

Barbadian Plain Cake

Submitted by: **Bernadette Beekman**

"My grandmother came here from Barbados around 1906. She read this recipe to me over the phone when I was in law school in 1978. It's a great, simple pound cake that's good with tea."

2	cups butter	4½	teaspoons baking powder
1½	cups white sugar	2	cups milk, divided
4	eggs	1	tablespoon vanilla extract
3	cups all-purpose flour	1	teaspoon almond extract

1. Preheat oven to 350°F (175°C). Lightly grease and flour a 9 or 10 inch Bundt pan.
2. Cream together butter and sugar until light and fluffy. Add eggs all at once and beat well.
3. In a separate bowl, sift together the flour and baking powder. Add to butter mixture along with 1 cup milk. Continue to beat well with a spatula (batter will be doughy). Add the remaining 1 cup milk, vanilla, and almond extract. Pour batter into prepared pan.
4. Bake in the preheated oven for 1 hour. Cool in pan on wire rack 15 minutes. Invert onto wire rack to cool completely. **Yield:** 12 servings.

Per serving: 537 calories, 7g protein, 52g carbohydrate, 33g fat, 1g fiber, 157mg cholesterol, 539mg sodium

Buttermilk Pound Cake II

Easy Baklava, page 317

Banana-Nut-Coconut Cake,
page 294

Apple Butter-Pumpkin Pie,
page 312

Blackberry and Blueberry Pie, page 311

Cinnamon Ice Cream, page 321

Butterscotch Bread Pudding,
page 320

Chocolate-Cappuccino Cheesecake, page 306

Pumpkin Pie Squares, page 322

Raspberry Trifle

Submitted by: **Bonnie**

"Here's a layered dessert that's not a typical cake—it's much better than that! And it really does feed a lot of people!"

1½	cups whipping cream	1		(10.75 ounce) package prepared pound cake
¼	cup white sugar			
2	(8 ounce) packages cream cheese, softened	2		(10 ounce) packages frozen raspberries, thawed and divided
2	teaspoons lemon juice			
1½	teaspoons vanilla extract	2		tablespoons unsweetened cocoa powder, divided
½	cup white sugar			

1. In a medium bowl, beat together whipping cream and ¼ cup sugar until stiff peaks form. In a separate bowl, cream together cream cheese, lemon juice, vanilla, and ½ cup sugar. Fold 2 cups of whipped cream mixture into cream cheese mixture. Reserve remaining whipped cream mixture.

2. Slice pound cake into 18 (½ inch) slices. Drain raspberries, reserving juice. Line the bottom of a 3 quart glass bowl or trifle bowl with one-third of the cake slices. Drizzle with some reserved raspberry juice. Spread one-fourth of the cream cheese mixture over cake. Sift one-fourth of the cocoa on top. Sprinkle with one-third of the raspberries. Repeat layers twice. Top with remaining cream cheese mixture, whipped cream, and cocoa. Cover and refrigerate 4 hours before serving. **Yield:** 18 servings.

Per serving: 287 calories, 4g protein, 26g carbohydrate, 20g fat, 2g fiber, 92mg cholesterol, 148mg sodium

◀ CROWD-PLEASER

Prep Time: 20 minutes

Chill Time: 4 hours

Average Rating: ★★★★★

What other cooks have done:

"Instead of the cream cheese mixture, I used a large box of instant vanilla pudding to cream with the whipped cream mixture. I dribbled a little liqueur on the cake. The pudding made it really easy, and everyone at my Mother's Day party was in awe. This was very yummy and fast to make."

Chocolate-Cappuccino Cheesecake *(pictured on page 303)*

Submitted by: **Cigdem Buke Ugur**

"This recipe becomes a favorite at the first bite. It was once referred to as 'sinfully rich and velvety smooth.' It's best if made a day before serving."

COMPANY IS COMING ▶

Prep Time: 30 minutes

Cook Time: 1 hour

Stand Time: 45 minutes

Chill Time: 12 hours

Average Rating: ★★★★★

What other cooks have done:

"This recipe turned out exactly as promised—creamy, rich, and delicious. I normally don't like chocolate cheesecake, but this one was to die for! My guests all raved. I used espresso in place of both the coffee and liqueur in the base. I used rum extract instead of liqueur in the whipped cream topping. I will definitely make this again."

1¾	cups chocolate sandwich cookie crumbs
2	tablespoons white sugar
2	tablespoons butter, softened
¼	teaspoon ground cinnamon
3	(8 ounce) packages cream cheese, softened
1	cup white sugar
3	eggs
8	(1 ounce) squares semisweet chocolate
¼	cup whipping cream
1	cup sour cream
¼	teaspoon salt

2	teaspoons instant coffee granules, dissolved in ¼ cup hot water
¼	cup coffee-flavored liqueur
2	teaspoons vanilla extract
1	(1 ounce) square semisweet chocolate
1	cup whipping cream
2	tablespoons confectioners' sugar
2	tablespoons coffee-flavored liqueur

1. Preheat oven to 325°F (165°C). Butter a 9 or 10 inch spring-form pan.

2. Combine the chocolate cookie crumbs, 2 tablespoons white sugar, softened butter, and cinnamon. Mix well and press mixture into prepared pan; set aside.

3. In a medium bowl, beat cream cheese until smooth. Gradually add 1 cup white sugar, mixing until well blended. Add eggs, 1 at a time. Beat at low speed until very smooth.

4. Melt 8 squares semisweet chocolate with ¼ cup whipping cream in a pan or bowl set over boiling water; stir until smooth.

5. Add chocolate mixture to cream cheese mixture and blend well. Stir in sour cream, salt, coffee, ¼ cup coffee-flavored liqueur, and vanilla; beat until smooth. Pour mixture into prepared pan.

6. Bake in the preheated oven for 45 minutes (do not overbake). Center will be soft but will firm up when chilled. Leave cake in oven with the heat turned off and the oven door open for 45 minutes. Remove cake from oven and chill for at least 12 hours.

7. Melt 1 ounce semisweet chocolate in a pan or bowl set over boiling water; stir until smooth. Brush food-safe leaves (such as orange leaves) on 1 side with melted chocolate. Freeze until firm; peel off leaves. Freeze chocolate leaves until ready to serve.

8. Beat 1 cup whipping cream until soft peaks form. Beat in confectioners' sugar and 2 tablespoons coffee-flavored liqueur. Top cake with flavored whipped cream and chocolate leaves. **Yield:** 12 servings.

Per serving: 619 calories, 9g protein, 45g carbohydrate, 45g fat, 2g fiber, 164mg cholesterol, 343mg sodium

Carrot Cheesecake with Crumb Crust

Submitted by: **Suzanne Stull**

"Serve slices of this very elegant cheesecake to impress dinner guests."

4	cups water	1	tablespoon lemon juice
¾	pound carrots, cut into 2 inch pieces	1	teaspoon orange zest
⅔	cup finely ground graham cracker crumbs	1	teaspoon minced fresh ginger root
⅔	cup gingersnap cookie crumbs	¼	teaspoon ground cinnamon
⅔	cup ground pecans	¼	teaspoon ground mace
⅓	cup white sugar	¼	teaspoon ground allspice
¼	cup unsalted butter, softened	2	(8 ounce) packages cream cheese, diced and softened
½	cup packed brown sugar	4	eggs
		¼	cup chopped pecans

1. Bring 4 cups water to a boil. Add carrots and cook until very tender, about 45 minutes. Drain cooked carrots. Return to heat for 1 minute or so to cook off excess moisture.
2. Preheat oven to 400°F (200°C). Grease a 9 inch springform pan.
3. In a medium bowl, combine graham cracker crumbs, gingersnap crumbs, ground pecans, and white sugar; toss well. Work in butter until mixture is crumbly. Pat in bottom and up sides of prepared pan.
4. Bake in the preheated oven for 7 minutes. Remove from oven and reduce oven temperature to 350°F (175°C).
5. Transfer carrots to a food processor and puree for 30 seconds. Scrape down sides and puree again until absolutely smooth. Add brown sugar, lemon juice, orange zest, ginger, cinnamon, mace, and allspice to processor; puree for 30 seconds. Scrape down sides and repeat. Let mixture stand until cool. Add cream cheese to cooled carrot mixture and puree for 1 minute, scraping down sides every 20 seconds. Beat in eggs, 1 at a time. Pour batter into crust and sprinkle with ¼ cup chopped nuts.
6. Bake in the preheated oven for about 50 minutes or until a knife inserted near the center of cake comes out clean. Let cool. Cover loosely and refrigerate at least 4 hours before serving.

Yield: 12 servings.

Per serving: 350 calories, 6g protein, 27g carbohydrate, 25g fat, 2g fiber, 122mg cholesterol, 193mg sodium

◀ MAKE-AHEAD

Prep Time: 30 minutes

Cook Time: 1 hour 45 minutes

Chill Time: 4 hours

Average Rating: ★★★★★

What other cooks have done:

"I've used this recipe many times. It's pretty easy to make once you get the hang of it. But what's even more important to me is that it is very delicious. Have a slice with a cup of coffee, tea, or cappuccino; they all complement this dessert well."

French Coconut Pies

Submitted by: **Shirley Allen**

"This very rich, custardlike pie made with coconut and pecans is sure to please. If using a single 9 inch deep-dish pie plate instead of 2 (8 inch) pie plates, bake for 1 hour."

2¼	cups white sugar	1	cup flaked coconut
2	tablespoons all-purpose flour	1	cup chopped pecans
6	eggs		Pastry for 2 (8 inch) single-crust pies
1	cup buttermilk		
½	cup butter, melted		

1. Preheat oven to 350°F (175°C).
2. In a small bowl, mix together the sugar and flour. In a large bowl, beat eggs with a wire whisk. Whisk flour mixture into eggs, stirring until smooth. Stir in buttermilk, butter, coconut, and pecans. Line each of 2 (8 inch) pie plates with a crust. Pour filling into crusts.
3. Bake in the preheated oven for 45 minutes. **Yield:** 12 servings.

Per serving: 446 calories, 6g protein, 53g carbohydrate, 25g fat, 1g fiber, 107mg cholesterol, 226mg sodium

Coconut Craze

You can find coconut in several forms at your grocery store—canned, frozen, shredded, flaked, grated, sweetened, and unsweetened—but if you have time (and a hammer), you should give fresh coconut a try.

Fresh coconuts are at their peak from October through December. Coconuts have a hard outer shell that's hairy with three soft spots, sometimes referred to as eyes, on one end. Once the outer shell is broken open, the nut inside has a dark brown skin covering the white, firm-textured coconut meat.

So how do you get past the outer shell? Start by piercing the three eyes of the shell with a long nail, screwdriver, or ice pick and draining the milky liquid; this can be used as a beverage, but it should not be confused with coconut milk, which is actually derived from the coconut meat. Next, place the shell on a hard surface and gently but firmly tap it all around with a hammer until it cracks and splits. Break the shell apart with your hands and carefully cut the white meat from the shell; peel the brown skin from the coconut meat. The meat can be grated or chopped using a grater, food processor, or knife. About 1½ tablespoons grated fresh coconut equal 1 tablespoon flaked coconut from the grocery store. You can also use a vegetable peeler to quickly shave pretty garnishes of fresh coconut.

For more information, visit **Allrecipes.com**

Glazed Apple Cream Pie

Submitted by: **Kathy**

"A friend who used to never bake gave me this recipe recently. I think she's made this pie once a week for the past 6 weeks!"

½	cup white sugar	1	tablespoon all-purpose flour
½	cup milk	¼	teaspoon ground cinnamon
½	cup whipping cream	1	(15 ounce) package refrigerated pie crusts
¼	cup butter	½	cup confectioners' sugar
2	tablespoons cornstarch	1	tablespoon milk
2	tablespoons milk	¼	teaspoon vanilla extract
1	teaspoon vanilla extract	1	tablespoon butter, softened
2	tart apples, peeled, cored, and sliced		

1. In a medium saucepan over medium heat, combine ½ cup white sugar, ½ cup milk, ½ cup cream, and ¼ cup butter. Heat until butter is melted, stirring occasionally. In a small bowl, whisk together the cornstarch, 2 tablespoons milk, and 1 teaspoon vanilla; stir into saucepan. Cook until thickened, stirring constantly. Remove from heat and set aside to cool slightly.

2. Preheat oven to 400°F (200°C). In a medium bowl, combine the apples, flour, and cinnamon. Mix well.

3. Line a 9 inch pie plate with 1 pie crust. Pour thickened filling mixture into crust. Arrange apple mixture evenly over filling. Top with second crust; seal and flute the edges. Cut slits in top crust.

4. Bake in the preheated oven for 30 to 40 minutes or until crust is golden brown and apples are tender. Cool for at least 30 minutes.

5. In a small bowl, combine confectioners' sugar, 1 tablespoon milk, ¼ teaspoon vanilla, and 1 tablespoon butter. Blend until smooth; pour evenly over pie. Refrigerate for at least 1½ hours before serving.

Yield: 8 servings.

Per serving: 483 calories, 4g protein, 52g carbohydrate, 29g fat, 3g fiber, 41mg cholesterol, 343mg sodium

◀ MAKE-AHEAD

Prep Time: 15 minutes

Cook Time: 45 minutes

Cool Time: 30 minutes

Chill Time: 1 hour 30 minutes

Average Rating: ★★★★

What other cooks have done:

"I'm not a baker, but I've made this pie many times, and it's never failed to get rave reviews. People have fought over seconds. Thinly slice the apples or precook them if you like thick chunks of apple. Try adding pear or peach slices for great-tasting variations. Shield the crust with aluminum foil at the end of baking to keep it from getting too brown."

Chocolate-Banana Cream Pie

Submitted by: **Holly**

"This pie has layers of chocolate, bananas, and vanilla pudding with coconut."

QUICK & EASY ▶

Prep Time: 15 minutes

Cook Time: 2 minutes

Chill Time: 4 hours

Average Rating: ★★★★★

What other cooks have done:

"This was a great mix of flavors—all of my favorite pies in one. The chocolate flavor is subtle. Next time, I'll try doubling the ingredients for the chocolate layer and using a graham cracker crust."

2	(1 ounce) squares semisweet chocolate	1	(3.4 ounce) package instant vanilla pudding mix
1	tablespoon milk	1½	cups shredded coconut
1	tablespoon butter	1½	cups frozen whipped topping, thawed
1	(9 inch) deep-dish pie crust, baked and cooled	2	tablespoons flaked coconut, toasted
2	bananas, sliced		
1½	cups cold milk		

1. Combine chocolate, 1 tablespoon milk, and butter in a medium microwave-safe bowl. Microwave on High for 1 to 2 minutes, stirring every 30 seconds, or until chocolate is melted. Spread in pie crust.
2. Arrange banana slices over chocolate.
3. Whisk together 1½ cups milk and pudding mix for 2 minutes. Stir in 1½ cups coconut. Spoon over banana slices in crust.
4. Spread whipped topping over pie. Sprinkle with 2 tablespoons toasted coconut. Refrigerate 4 hours or until set. Store leftovers in refrigerator. **Yield:** 8 servings.

Per serving: 377 calories, 4g protein, 46g carbohydrate, 21g fat, 2g fiber, 8mg cholesterol, 405mg sodium

Fresh Pear Pie

Submitted by: **Carol**

"This is quite a refreshing dessert. Serve plain or with whipped cream."

MAKE-AHEAD ▶

Prep Time: 15 minutes

Cook Time: 50 minutes

Average Rating: ★★★★★

What other cooks have done:

"This pie was a great hit with my family. I added ½ cup of sweetened dried cranberries and one sliced green apple to the pie."

	Pastry for a 9 inch double-crust pie	1	teaspoon ground cinnamon
½	cup white sugar	1	teaspoon lemon zest
3	tablespoons all-purpose flour	5	cups peeled and sliced pears
¼	teaspoon salt	1	tablespoon butter
		1	tablespoon lemon juice

1. Preheat oven to 450°F (230°C).
2. Line a 9 inch pie plate with 1 pie crust.
3. Combine sugar, flour, salt, cinnamon, and lemon zest in a mixing bowl. Arrange pears in layers in pie crust, sprinkling sugar mixture over each layer. Dot with butter. Sprinkle with lemon juice. Moisten rim of bottom crust. Place top crust over filling. Fold edge under bottom crust, pressing to seal; flute. Cut slits in top to vent steam.
4. Bake in the preheated oven for 10 minutes. Reduce temperature to 350°F (175°C); bake for 35 to 40 more minutes. **Yield:** 8 servings.

Per serving: 361 calories, 4g protein, 51g carbohydrate, 17g fat, 4g fiber, 4mg cholesterol, 321mg sodium

Blackberry and Blueberry Pie

(pictured on page 300)

Submitted by: **Debbie Sanchez**

"This is a delicious berry pie that combines both blueberries and blackberries."

2	cups all-purpose flour	½	teaspoon ground cinnamon
1	teaspoon salt	4	cups fresh blueberries
⅔	cup shortening	1½	cups fresh blackberries
5	tablespoons cold water	1	tablespoon lemon juice
¾	cup white sugar	2	tablespoons butter, melted
⅓	cup all-purpose flour		

1. Preheat oven to 425°F (220°C).
2. Combine 2 cups flour and salt. Cut in shortening with a pastry blender or 2 knives until particles are the size of small peas. Sprinkle water into flour mixture, 1 tablespoon at a time, until flour is moistened. Gather into a ball and roll out onto a lightly floured surface. Make 2 rounds. Place 1 crust in a 9 inch pie plate.
3. Mix together sugar, ⅓ cup flour, and cinnamon. Stir in berries to coat. Pour filling into pie crust. Sprinkle with lemon juice and drizzle with butter. Cover with top crust and cut slits in the top or cut the top into strips and weave into a lattice pattern over the pie.
4. Bake in the preheated oven for 40 minutes, shielding the edges with aluminum foil after 35 minutes. **Yield:** 8 servings.

Per serving: 437 calories, 5g protein, 61g carbohydrate, 21g fat, 5g fiber, 8mg cholesterol, 326mg sodium

◄ OUT-OF-THE-ORDINARY

Prep Time: 25 minutes

Cook Time: 40 minutes

Average Rating: ★★★★★

What other cooks have done:

"I have a variation of this recipe: Cover pie with the top crust, cut an 'X' in the middle, and peel back the flaps; bake. When the pie is right out of the oven, pour a little whipping cream into the middle. Yum!"

Baked Fresh Cherry Pie

Submitted by: **Cali**

"If you've never eaten a fresh cherry pie, you're in for a treat."

	Pastry for a 9 inch double-crust pie	4	cups pitted cherries
¼	cup quick cooking tapioca	¼	teaspoon almond extract
⅛	teaspoon salt	½	teaspoon vanilla extract
1	cup white sugar	1½	tablespoons butter

1. Preheat oven to 400°F (200°C). Line a 9 inch pie plate with 1 pie crust.
2. In a large bowl, combine tapioca, salt, sugar, cherries, almond extract, and vanilla. Let stand 15 minutes. Pour into pie crust and dot with butter. Cover with top crust; seal and flute edges. Cut slits in top crust to vent. Place pie on a foil-lined baking sheet (in case of drips).
3. Bake in the preheated oven for 50 minutes or until golden brown. **Yield:** 8 servings.

Per serving: 411 calories, 4g protein, 61g carbohydrate, 18g fat, 3g fiber, 6mg cholesterol, 293mg sodium

◄ COMPANY IS COMING

Prep Time: 25 minutes

Stand Time: 15 minutes

Cook Time: 50 minutes

Average Rating: ★★★★☆

What other cooks have done:

"I had tart cherries fresh from the farmers' market and was determined to create something special with them. This recipe did the trick. The only addition I made was to add about 2 teaspoons of cognac to the filling. It added an elegant dimension to the dessert."

Apple Butter-Pumpkin Pie *(pictured on page 299)*

Submitted by: **Joyce Lowe**

"This lightly spiced pie combines two autumn standards—apple and pumpkin—with a streusel topping."

COMPANY IS COMING ▶

Prep Time: 30 minutes

Cook Time: 1 hour 15 minutes

Average Rating: ★★★★☆

What other cooks have done:

"These two flavors complement each other very well! I added a little ground cloves, used my cookie pie crust recipe, and served the pie with homemade whipped cream. I added a little too much butter to the streusel topping, but it was still great. Do not skip the streusel; it really pairs well with this pie."

Pastry for a 9 inch deep-dish single-crust pie		¼	teaspoon salt
		3	eggs, lightly beaten
1	cup canned pumpkin puree	1	cup evaporated milk
1	cup apple butter	½	cup all-purpose flour
¼	cup dark brown sugar	3	tablespoons butter
½	teaspoon ground cinnamon	⅓	cup dark brown sugar
½	teaspoon ground nutmeg	½	cup chopped pecans

1. Preheat oven to 350°F (175°C).
2. Line a 9 inch deep-dish pie plate with crust.
3. In a large bowl, combine pumpkin, apple butter, ¼ cup brown sugar, cinnamon, nutmeg, and salt. Stir in eggs and evaporated milk. Pour into pie crust.
4. To make the streusel topping, combine flour, butter, and ⅓ cup brown sugar in a small bowl. Stir until mixture resembles coarse crumbs. Stir in pecans; set aside.
5. Bake pie in the preheated oven for 50 minutes to 1 hour or until a knife inserted 2 inches from the center comes out clean. Sprinkle streusel topping over the pie and bake for 15 more minutes.
Yield: 8 servings.

Per serving: 420 calories, 8g protein, 50g carbohydrate, 22g fat, 3g fiber, 101mg cholesterol, 402mg sodium

Kentucky Pecan Pie *(pictured on page 1)*

Submitted by: **Laurie Nanni**

"This pie is a family favorite. I get many requests to make this for our church bake sales."

MAKE-AHEAD ▶

Prep Time: 15 minutes

Cook Time: 50 minutes

Average Rating: ★★★★★

What other cooks have done:

"This was my first time to make a pecan pie, and I was very pleased with the results. I liked the fact that most of the ingredients were already in my pantry. My pie crust was frozen, and I thought I had messed up by not thawing it, but it turned out wonderfully."

Pastry for a 9 inch single-crust pie		¼	teaspoon salt
		⅓	cup butter, melted
1	cup white corn syrup	3	eggs
1	cup packed brown sugar	1	cup chopped pecans

1. Preheat oven to 350°F (175°C).
2. Line a 9 inch pie plate with crust.
3. In a medium bowl, combine syrup, sugar, salt, and melted butter. Slightly beat the eggs and add to sugar mixture. Beat well. Stir in pecans and pour into unbaked pie crust.
4. Bake in the preheated oven for 50 minutes. Shield edges with aluminum foil after 35 minutes. **Yield:** 8 servings.

Per serving: 531 calories, 5g protein, 71g carbohydrate, 28g fat, 2g fiber, 100mg cholesterol, 376mg sodium

Chocolate Cobbler

Submitted by: **KRice1123**

"This rich, wonderful, old-fashioned cobbler is great for potlucks and get-togethers. Fast, easy, and always a hit! Serve it with ice cream for extra decadence."

6	tablespoons butter		1	teaspoon vanilla extract
1	cup self-rising flour		1	cup white sugar
¾	cup white sugar		¼	cup unsweetened cocoa powder
1½	tablespoons unsweetened cocoa powder		1½	cups boiling water
½	cup milk			

1. Preheat oven to 350°F (175°C). Melt butter in an 8x8 inch baking dish while the oven preheats.
2. In a medium bowl, stir together the flour, ¾ cup sugar, and 1½ tablespoons cocoa. Stir in milk and vanilla until smooth. Spoon batter over the melted butter in the baking dish.
3. Stir together 1 cup sugar and ¼ cup cocoa powder. Sprinkle over the batter. Slowly pour boiling water over the top of the mixture.
4. Bake in the preheated oven for 30 minutes or until set. Serve slightly warm. **Yield:** 8 servings.

Per serving: 319 calories, 3g protein, 58g carbohydrate, 10g fat, 2g fiber, 25mg cholesterol, 297mg sodium

◀ COVERED-DISH FAVORITE

Prep Time: 15 minutes

Cook Time: 30 minutes

Average Rating: ★★★★★

What other cooks have done:

"Loved it! It's a little liquidy as is, but I fixed it by making a batch and a half in a 9x13 inch pan but only using the original amounts called for of water and butter. It cooked 10 minutes longer. It was cakelike on top, fudgy on the bottom, and crusty around the edges (my favorite part). Everyone went back for seconds and thirds. Great with vanilla ice cream."

Nana's Apple Crisp

Submitted by: **Keri C.**

"This quick and easy recipe is perfect with vanilla ice cream."

6	tart apples, peeled, cored, and sliced		1	cup quick cooking oats
½	cup butter, melted		2	tablespoons ground cinnamon, divided
1	cup all-purpose flour		¼	cup butter, cut into pieces
1	cup white sugar			

1. Preheat oven to 350°F (175°C).
2. Place apples in a 9x13 inch baking dish. In a bowl, mix together ½ cup melted butter, flour, sugar, oats, and 1 tablespoon cinnamon to form a crumbly mixture. Sprinkle over apples. Dot with ¼ cup butter and sprinkle with remaining 1 tablespoon cinnamon.
3. Bake in the preheated oven for 50 minutes or until lightly browned and apples are tender. **Yield:** 8 servings.

Per serving: 411 calories, 4g protein, 61g carbohydrate, 19g fat, 5g fiber, 47mg cholesterol, 177mg sodium

◀ MAKE-AHEAD

Prep Time: 15 minutes

Cook Time: 50 minutes

Average Rating: ★★★★★

What other cooks have done:

"This is an easy alternative to a time-consuming apple pie. I baked this in a 9x9 inch pan, and it fit perfectly. I sprinkled the last 1 tablespoon cinnamon over the apples instead of on the topping. I sprinkled ½ teaspoon nutmeg and ¼ cup brown sugar on top of the apples, too. Came out delicious!"

Apple Dumpling Cake

Submitted by: **Amy S.**

"This recipe tastes like apple dumplings—without all the work."

3 pounds apples, peeled, cored, and sliced	1 teaspoon salt
2 cups all-purpose flour	2 eggs, lightly beaten
1½ cups white sugar	1 cup vegetable oil
2 teaspoons baking powder	1 teaspoon ground cinnamon

1. Preheat oven to 350°F (175°C). Lightly grease a 9x13 inch baking dish.
2. Place sliced apples in prepared baking dish. In a medium bowl, mix together the flour, sugar, baking powder, and salt. Stir in eggs and oil; pour on top of apples. Sprinkle with cinnamon.
3. Bake in the preheated oven for 40 to 45 minutes or until topping is puffed and golden brown. **Yield:** 12 servings.

Per serving: 415 calories, 3g protein, 59g carbohydrate, 20g fat, 4g fiber, 35mg cholesterol, 286mg sodium

Zucchini Cobbler

Submitted by: **Don and Mary**

"This delicious dessert tastes almost like apple cobbler. In fact, we can't tell the difference."

8 cups peeled, chopped zucchini	½ teaspoon ground nutmeg
⅔ cup lemon juice	4 cups all-purpose flour
1 cup white sugar	2 cups white sugar
1 teaspoon ground cinnamon	1½ cups butter, chilled
	1 teaspoon ground cinnamon

1. In a large saucepan over medium heat, cook and stir zucchini and lemon juice until zucchini is tender, about 15 to 20 minutes. Stir in 1 cup sugar, 1 teaspoon cinnamon, and nutmeg; cook 1 minute. Remove from heat and set aside.
2. Preheat oven to 375°F (190°C). Grease a 10x15 inch baking dish.
3. In a large bowl, combine flour and 2 cups sugar. Cut in butter with a pastry blender or 2 knives until mixture resembles coarse crumbs. Stir ½ cup of butter mixture into zucchini mixture; set aside. Press half of remaining butter mixture into bottom of prepared dish. Spread zucchini mixture over top of crust. Sprinkle remaining butter mixture over zucchini. Sprinkle with 1 teaspoon cinnamon.
4. Bake in the preheated oven for 35 to 40 minutes or until top is golden. Serve warm or cold. **Yield:** 25 servings.

Per serving: 271 calories, 3g protein, 41g carbohydrate, 11g fat, 1g fiber, 30mg cholesterol, 114mg sodium

Old-Fashioned Peach Cobbler

Submitted by: **Eleta**

"I was searching for a peach cobbler recipe that reminded me of the yummy dessert I ate as a young girl in southeast Missouri. No shortcuts here, but it's worth every minute!"

2½	cups all-purpose flour	¾	cup orange juice
3	tablespoons white sugar	½	cup butter
1	teaspoon salt	2	cups white sugar
1	cup shortening	½	teaspoon ground nutmeg
1	egg	1	teaspoon ground cinnamon
¼	cup cold water	1	tablespoon cornstarch
3	pounds fresh peaches, peeled, pitted, and sliced	1	tablespoon white sugar
¼	cup lemon juice	1	tablespoon butter, melted

1. In a medium bowl, sift together the flour, 3 tablespoons sugar, and salt. Cut in the shortening with a pastry blender or 2 knives until the mixture resembles coarse crumbs. In a small bowl, whisk together the egg and cold water. Sprinkle over flour mixture and work with hands to form dough into a ball. Chill 30 minutes.
2. Preheat oven to 350°F (175°C).
3. Roll out half of dough to ⅛ inch thickness. Place in a 9x13 inch baking dish, covering bottom and halfway up sides.
4. Bake in the preheated oven for 20 minutes or until golden brown.
5. Meanwhile, in a large saucepan, mix the peaches, lemon juice, and orange juice. Add ½ cup butter and cook over medium-low heat until butter is melted. In a mixing bowl, stir together 2 cups sugar, nutmeg, cinnamon, and cornstarch; stir into peach mixture. Remove from heat and pour into baked crust.
6. Roll remaining dough to ¼ inch thickness. Cut into ½ inch wide strips. Weave strips into a lattice pattern over peaches. Sprinkle with 1 tablespoon sugar and drizzle with 1 tablespoon melted butter.
7. Bake in the preheated oven for 35 to 40 minutes or until top crust is golden brown. **Yield:** 18 servings.

Per serving: 338 calories, 2g protein, 44g carbohydrate, 18g fat, 1g fiber, 27mg cholesterol, 194mg sodium

◀ COVERED-DISH FAVORITE

Prep Time: 30 minutes

Chill Time: 30 minutes

Cook Time: 1 hour

Average Rating: ★★★★★

What other cooks have done:

"I cut the sugar in half, as it is awfully sweet. Also, I add 1 tablespoon of cornstarch to make it thicker. You need to make sure you roll the dough until it's really thin so you'll have enough to cover the bottom of the pan and make the latticework. This recipe is great for just the crust alone."

Éclairs II

Submitted by: **Patty Stockton**

"My family loves these éclairs and requests them all the time. I usually make them for dessert whenever we have company coming, and they are always a hit!"

½	cup butter	¼	cup confectioners' sugar
1	cup water	1	teaspoon vanilla extract
1	cup all-purpose flour	2	(1 ounce) squares
¼	teaspoon salt		semisweet chocolate
4	eggs	2	tablespoons butter
1	(5.1 ounce) package instant	1	cup confectioners' sugar
	vanilla pudding mix	1	teaspoon vanilla extract
2½	cups cold milk	3	tablespoons hot water
1	cup whipping cream		

1. Preheat oven to 450°F (230°C). Grease a baking sheet.
2. In a medium saucepan, combine ½ cup butter and 1 cup water. Bring to a boil, stirring until butter melts completely. Reduce heat to low; stir in flour and salt. Stir vigorously until mixture leaves the sides of the pan and begins to form a stiff ball. Remove from heat. Add eggs, 1 at a time, beating well after each addition. With a spoon or a pastry bag fitted with a number 10 or larger tip, spoon or pipe dough onto prepared baking sheet in 1½x4 inch strips.
3. Bake in the preheated oven for 15 minutes. Reduce heat to 325°F (165°C) and bake 20 more minutes or until pastries sound hollow when lightly tapped on the bottom. Cool completely on a wire rack.
4. To make filling, combine pudding mix and milk in medium bowl according to package directions. In a separate bowl, beat the whipping cream with an electric mixer until soft peaks form. Beat in ¼ cup confectioners' sugar and 1 teaspoon vanilla. Fold into pudding. Cut tops off cooled pastry shells with a sharp knife. Fill shells with pudding mixture and replace tops.
5. To make icing, melt semisweet chocolate and 2 tablespoons butter in a medium saucepan over low heat. Stir in 1 cup confectioners' sugar and 1 teaspoon vanilla. Stir in hot water, 1 tablespoon at a time, until icing is smooth and has reached desired consistency. Remove from heat, cool slightly, and drizzle over filled éclairs. Refrigerate until ready to serve. **Yield:** 9 servings.

Per serving: 478 calories, 8g protein, 50g carbohydrate, 28g fat, 1g fiber, 170mg cholesterol, 527mg sodium

Easy Baklava *(pictured on page 297)*

Submitted by: **Arvilla**

"This exotic dessert is simple and easy. It freezes well, too. Serve it in paper cupcake liners, if desired."

1	teaspoon ground cinnamon		1	cup white sugar
1	pound finely chopped mixed nuts		1	cup water
1	(16 ounce) package phyllo dough		½	cup honey
			1	teaspoon vanilla extract
1	cup butter, melted		1	teaspoon grated lemon zest

1. Preheat oven to 350°F (175°C). Butter a 9x13 inch pan.
2. Toss together cinnamon and nuts. Unroll phyllo and cover with a damp cloth to keep it from drying out while assembling the baklava. Place 4 sheets of phyllo in the bottom of prepared pan. Brush generously with butter. Sprinkle about 3 tablespoons of the nut mixture on top. Repeat layers until all nut mixture is used, ending with about 4 sheets of phyllo.
3. Using a sharp knife, cut baklava into diamond shapes, being sure to cut all the way through to the bottom of the pan.
4. Bake in the preheated oven 50 minutes or until golden and crisp.
5. Meanwhile, combine sugar and water in a small saucepan over medium heat and bring to a boil. Stir in honey, vanilla, and lemon zest. Reduce heat and simmer for 20 minutes.
6. Remove the baklava from the oven and immediately spoon the syrup over it. Let cool completely before serving. Store uncovered.

Yield: 36 servings.

Per serving: 194 calories, 3g protein, 19g carbohydrate, 12g fat, 1g fiber, 14mg cholesterol, 197mg sodium

◄ AROUND-THE-WORLD CUISINE

Prep Time: 30 minutes

Cook Time: 50 minutes

Average Rating: ★★★★★

What other cooks have done:

"Wonderful! I used pecans and added ¼ teaspoon ground cloves. I also increased the honey to 1 cup. I let the syrup cool completely. I made the syrup first and then did the pastry. I was really happy with the results!"

Caramel-Glazed Flan

Submitted by: **Mogirimi**

"This is a reduced-fat version of a delicious Spanish dessert. My family did not notice the difference from the original fatty version."

¾ cup white sugar
2 egg yolks
6 egg whites
1¾ cups water
1 (14 ounce) can low-fat sweetened condensed milk

½ teaspoon vanilla extract
Pinch salt

1. Preheat oven to 350°F (175°C).
2. In a heavy skillet over medium-low heat, melt sugar and cook until light brown. Carefully pour into a 9 inch round baking dish, tilting the dish to coat the bottom completely.
3. In a medium bowl, beat egg yolks and egg whites. Stir in water, condensed milk, vanilla, and salt; mix until smooth. Pour into prepared dish. Place dish in a roasting pan and place roasting pan on oven rack. Fill roasting pan with boiling water to reach halfway up the sides of the dish.
4. Bake in the preheated oven for 1 hour or until center is just set but still a bit jiggly. Remove dish to a wire rack to cool. Refrigerate several hours or overnight.
5. To unmold, run a knife around the edge of the dish and invert onto a rimmed serving platter. **Yield:** 8 servings.

Per serving: 306 calories, 9g protein, 59g carbohydrate, 4g fat, 0g fiber, 64mg cholesterol, 161mg sodium

Chocolate Cream Pudding

Submitted by: **Mimi**

"Chill this pudding before serving to let the flavors develop."

1	cup white sugar	2	egg yolks
2	tablespoons cornstarch	2	tablespoons butter
¼	teaspoon salt	2	teaspoons vanilla extract
2	cups milk		
2	(1 ounce) squares unsweetened chocolate, chopped		

1. In a medium saucepan over medium heat, combine sugar, cornstarch, and salt. Stir in milk and chocolate. Cook, stirring constantly, until chocolate melts and mixture thickens. Remove from heat; stir in egg yolks. Return to heat and cook 2 more minutes. Remove from heat; stir in butter and vanilla. Chill before serving. **Yield:** 6 servings.

Per serving: 286 calories, 5g protein, 43g carbohydrate, 12g fat, 2g fiber, 88mg cholesterol, 181mg sodium

◀ QUICK & EASY

Prep Time: 15 minutes

Cook Time: 15 minutes

Average Rating: ★★★★☆

What other cooks have done:

"I served this at a dinner party and got loads of compliments. Destroy every lump in the mixture or risk lumpy pudding. Stir a few spoonfuls of the hot chocolate mixture into the egg yolks to warm them up before putting the egg yolks into the pan."

Coconut Bread Pudding

Submitted by: **Yoda**

"The classic bread pudding is enhanced with coconut flakes and coconut milk."

2	tablespoons butter	¼	teaspoon salt
⅓	cup confectioners' sugar	2	tablespoons coconut extract
1	cup white sugar	1½	cups flaked coconut, divided
4	eggs	½	cup grated fresh coconut
1	egg yolk	1	(1 pound) loaf French bread, cut into 1 inch cubes
2	(14 ounce) cans coconut milk		
1	teaspoon ground cinnamon		
¼	teaspoon ground nutmeg		

1. Preheat oven to 325°F (165°C). Grease a 9x13 inch baking dish with butter and dust with confectioners' sugar.
2. In a large bowl, combine white sugar, eggs, egg yolk, coconut milk, cinnamon, nutmeg, salt, and coconut extract. Mix until smooth. Stir in 1 cup flaked coconut and ½ cup fresh coconut. Fold in bread cubes until evenly coated. Pour into prepared baking dish. Let stand for 30 minutes.
3. Bake in the preheated oven for 25 minutes. Sprinkle top with remaining ½ cup flaked coconut. Continue baking for 25 to 30 more minutes or until center springs back when lightly tapped. **Yield:** 12 servings.

Per serving: 417 calories, 7g protein, 47g carbohydrate, 23g fat, 3g fiber, 94mg cholesterol, 350mg sodium

◀ CROWD-PLEASER

Prep Time: 20 minutes

Stand Time: 30 minutes

Cook Time: 55 minutes

Average Rating: ★★★★★

What other cooks have done:

"I layered cinnamon bread cubes; dried fruits, including raisins and diced apricots; and flaked coconut in about 3 layers in a greased casserole dish. I substituted buttermilk for the coconut milk and cut the sugar in half. I poured the egg mixture over the bread cubes and let it sit 30 minutes, pressing the bread cubes down into the liquid every 10 minutes or so. I dotted the mixture with butter and baked as directed."

Butterscotch Bread Pudding

(pictured on page 302)

Submitted by: **Margaret Burger**

"Here's a versatile bread pudding that is easy to make. You can also use chocolate milk and any candy bar of your choice for a variation."

COMPANY IS COMING ▶

Prep Time: 10 minutes

Cook Time: 1 hour

Average Rating: ★★★★★

What other cooks have done:

"I have made this many times. I use raisin bread and cinnamon chips. I also add cinnamon and a generous amount of nutmeg. This is one of the best things I have ever made or eaten. I don't really recommend reheating it the next day—it tastes much better cold after it has been in the fridge overnight."

1	(10.75 ounce) loaf day-old bread, torn into small pieces	½	cup butter, melted
4	cups milk	3	eggs, lightly beaten
2	cups packed brown sugar	2	teaspoons vanilla extract
		1	cup butterscotch chips
			Whipped cream (optional)

1. Preheat oven to 350°F (175°C). Grease a 9x13 inch pan.

2. In a large bowl, combine bread, milk, sugar, butter, eggs, vanilla, and butterscotch chips (mixture should be the consistency of oatmeal). Pour into prepared pan.

3. Bake in the preheated oven for 1 hour or until center is just set but still jiggly. Serve warm or cold. Garnish with whipped cream, if desired. **Yield:** 8 servings.

Per serving: 622 calories, 10g protein, 92g carbohydrate, 23g fat, 1g fiber, 121mg cholesterol, 448mg sodium

Creamiest Rice Pudding

Submitted by: **Bonnie Quinn**

"For a real fan of rice pudding, this recipe is worth every minute. My husband says it reminds him of the rice pudding he used to get as a child at a restaurant."

MAKE-AHEAD ▶

Prep Time: 10 minutes

Cook Time: 1 hour 10 minutes

Stand Time: 10 minutes

Chill Time: overnight

Average Rating: ★★★★★

What other cooks have done:

"I substituted whipping cream for the ¼ cup milk that was added to the eggs. The pudding thickened a lot after it cooled. I also used Arborio rice, which is much better than long-grain rice. It was excellent!"

½	gallon milk	¼	cup milk
1	cup white sugar	¼	teaspoon salt
1	cup uncooked long-grain white rice	2	teaspoons vanilla extract
3	eggs, lightly beaten		Ground cinnamon to taste

1. In a large saucepan over medium-low heat, combine ½ gallon milk, sugar, and rice. Simmer, covered, for 1 hour, stirring frequently. Remove from heat and let stand 10 minutes.

2. In a small bowl, combine eggs, ¼ cup milk, salt, and vanilla. Stir into rice mixture and return pan to low heat, stirring constantly, for 2 minutes. Pour into a 9x13 inch baking dish and cover with plastic wrap, folding back the corners to allow the steam to escape.

3. When pudding has cooled to room temperature, remove plastic wrap and sprinkle surface of pudding with cinnamon. Cover tightly and refrigerate 8 hours or overnight before serving. **Yield:** 12 servings.

Per serving: 229 calories, 8g protein, 38g carbohydrate, 5g fat, 0g fiber, 66mg cholesterol, 148mg sodium

Easy Mint-Chocolate Chip Ice Cream

Submitted by: **Darryn M. Briggs**

"This is a great mint-chocolate chip ice cream that I discovered by accident. The 2% milk makes the ice cream taste 'lighter,' I think."

2   cups 2% milk
2   cups whipping cream
1   cup sugar
½   teaspoon salt
1   teaspoon vanilla extract
1   teaspoon peppermint
       extract

3   drops green food coloring
       (optional)
1   cup miniature semisweet
       chocolate chips

1. In a large bowl, mix together the milk, cream, sugar, salt, vanilla, and peppermint extract, stirring until the sugar has dissolved. Add green food coloring, if desired.
2. Pour the mixture into an ice cream maker and freeze according to the manufacturer's instructions. After about 10 minutes into the freezing process, add the chocolate chips. After the ice cream has thickened (about 30 minutes), spoon into a container and freeze for 2 hours. **Yield:** 8 servings.

Per serving: 455 calories, 4g protein, 45g carbohydrate, 31g fat, 2g fiber, 86mg cholesterol, 201mg sodium

◄ KID-FRIENDLY

Prep Time: 5 minutes

Freeze Time: 2 hours 40 minutes

Average Rating: ★★★★★

What other cooks have done:

"This ice cream has a great texture. Grate some chocolate instead of using chocolate chips. Also, I would halve the peppermint extract—as is, it's just too strong for me."

Cinnamon Ice Cream *(pictured on page 301)*

Submitted by: **Elizabeth**

"This is a delicious treat. It reminds me of the cinnamon ice cream I used to get at Ray's Ice Cream in Detroit!"

4   eggs, lightly beaten
2   cups white sugar
3   cups half-and-half
2   cups whipping cream
2   teaspoons vanilla extract

4   teaspoons ground
       cinnamon
Cinnamon sticks (optional)
Ground cinnamon

1. In a saucepan over medium heat, whisk together eggs, sugar, half-and-half, and whipping cream. Cook 20 minutes or until slightly thickened. Stir in vanilla and cinnamon.
2. Pour cooled mixture into an ice cream maker and freeze according to the manufacturer's instructions. Transfer to a container and freeze overnight. If desired, garnish each serving with cinnamon sticks and sprinkle lightly with ground cinnamon. **Yield:** 8 servings.

Per serving: 560 calories, 7g protein, 57g carbohydrate, 35g fat, 1g fiber, 222mg cholesterol, 92mg sodium

◄ RESTAURANT FARE

Prep Time: 5 minutes

Cook Time: 20 minutes

Freeze Time: overnight

Average Rating: ★★★★★

What other cooks have done:

"I wanted a cinnamon ice cream to go with apple pie or cookies, and this fit the bill perfectly. I could not believe how easy it was to make and what an outstanding flavor it had."

Pumpkin Pie Squares *(pictured on page 304)*

Submitted by: **JRR**

"A great snack and Halloween treat, these bars have the taste of a delicious pumpkin pie without having to roll out a crust. Eat them with a fork."

½	cup butter, softened	½	teaspoon salt
½	cup packed brown sugar	1	teaspoon ground cinnamon
1	cup all-purpose flour	½	teaspoon ground ginger
½	cup rolled oats	¼	teaspoon ground cloves
2	eggs		Confectioners' sugar
¾	cup white sugar		Frozen whipped topping, thawed
1	(15 ounce) can pumpkin		Ground cinnamon
1	(12 ounce) can evaporated milk		

1. Preheat oven to 350°F (175°C).

2. In a medium bowl, cream together butter and brown sugar. Mix in flour. Fold in oats. Press into a 9x13 inch pan.

3. Bake in the preheated oven for 15 minutes or until set.

4. In a large bowl, beat eggs with white sugar. Beat in pumpkin, evaporated milk, salt, 1 teaspoon cinnamon, ginger, and cloves. Pour over baked crust.

5. Bake in the preheated oven for 20 to 25 minutes or just until set. Let cool before cutting into squares. Sprinkle with confectioners' sugar, top with a dollop of whipped topping, and sprinkle with ground cinnamon. **Yield:** 24 servings.

Per serving: 132 calories, 3g protein, 19g carbohydrate, 6g fat, 1g fiber, 32mg cholesterol, 110mg sodium

Snickerdoodles V

Submitted by: **Amy**

"There isn't anyone who doesn't like snickerdoodles. This recipe is a classic."

1	cup shortening	2	teaspoons cream of tartar
1½	cups white sugar	½	teaspoon salt
2	eggs	2	tablespoons white sugar
2¾	cups sifted all-purpose flour	2	teaspoons ground cinnamon
1	teaspoon baking soda		

1. Preheat oven to 375°F (190°C). Grease baking sheets.

2. In a medium bowl, cream together the shortening and 1½ cups sugar. Add eggs, 1 at a time, mixing after each addition. Sift together the flour, baking soda, cream of tartar, and salt; stir into the creamed mixture until well blended.

3. In a small, shallow bowl, stir together 2 tablespoons sugar and cinnamon. Roll the dough into walnut-size balls; roll the balls in the sugar mixture. Place cookies 2 inches apart on prepared baking sheets.

4. Bake in the preheated oven for 8 to 10 minutes or until slightly golden at the edges. Remove to cool on wire racks.
Yield: 3 dozen cookies.

Per 2 cookies: 250 calories, 3g protein, 33g carbohydrate, 12g fat, 1g fiber, 24mg cholesterol, 142mg sodium

Scarlett's Best-Ever Sugar Cookies

Submitted by: **Scarlett Thornley**
"These cookies will melt in your mouth. This recipe can be halved if you only want 50 cookies, but they will disappear quickly!"

1	cup confectioners' sugar	4¼	cups all-purpose flour
1	cup packed brown sugar	1	teaspoon baking soda
1	cup butter, softened	1	teaspoon salt
1	cup vegetable oil	1	teaspoon cream of tartar
2	eggs	1	cup chopped pecans
2	teaspoons vanilla extract		White sugar

1. Preheat oven to 350°F (175°C).
2. In a large bowl, cream together confectioners' sugar, brown sugar, butter, and oil. Stir in eggs and vanilla.
3. In a separate bowl, combine the flour, baking soda, salt, and cream of tartar; stir into the creamed mixture. Mix in the pecans. Roll dough into walnut-size balls. Place balls on ungreased baking sheets. Press each ball down with the bottom of a glass dipped in white sugar (use a glass with a decorative bottom to give cookies a pattern).
4. Bake in the preheated oven for 10 minutes or until golden brown around the edges. **Yield:** 100 cookies.

Per cookie: 81 calories, 1g protein, 8g carbohydrate, 5g fat, 0g fiber, 9mg cholesterol, 57mg sodium

◄ HOLIDAY GIFT GIVING
Prep Time: 16 minutes

Cook Time: 10 minutes per batch

Average Rating: ★★★★☆

What other cooks have done:
"Great recipe! It made a great deal of dough, and I froze half for another day. I rolled the cookies in cinnamon sugar and didn't use the pecans because my hubby dislikes them. A definite keeper!"

Beth's Orange Cookies

Submitted by: **Beth Sigworth**

"These soft, frosted orange cookies are another one of my own recipes. Serve these at your next tea or luncheon party and watch them disappear!"

HOLIDAY GIFT GIVING ▶

Prep Time: 20 minutes

Cook Time: 10 minutes per batch

Average Rating: ★★★★★

What other cooks have done:

"Excellent, soft orange cookies. I used fresh orange zest for maximum orange flavor. I also used an orange-flavored cream cheese icing rather than the glaze; I loved the richness of the cream cheese with these cookies."

2 cups white sugar
1 cup shortening
2 eggs
1 cup sour cream
1 teaspoon vanilla extract
5 cups all-purpose flour
2 teaspoons baking powder
1 teaspoon baking soda
1 teaspoon salt
¾ cup frozen orange juice concentrate, thawed

2 tablespoons grated orange zest
½ teaspoon grated orange zest
2 tablespoons frozen orange juice concentrate, thawed
1 teaspoon vanilla extract
4 tablespoons butter, melted
1½ cups confectioners' sugar

1. Preheat oven to 375°F (190°C). Grease baking sheets.
2. Cream white sugar and shortening; add eggs and stir. Add sour cream and 1 teaspoon vanilla; stir and set aside. In a separate bowl, sift together flour, baking powder, baking soda, and salt. Add little by little to the creamed mixture and stir well. Add ¾ cup orange juice concentrate and 2 tablespoons orange zest. Drop onto prepared baking sheets by teaspoonfuls.
3. Bake in the preheated oven for about 10 minutes. Frost cookies when they are cool.
4. To make frosting, mix together ½ teaspoon orange zest, 2 tablespoons thawed orange juice concentrate, 1 teaspoon vanilla, butter, and confectioners' sugar (add additional confectioners' sugar, if necessary, to reach desired spreading consistency). **Yield:** 6 dozen cookies.

Per cookie: 109 calories, 1g protein, 16g carbohydrate, 4g fat, 0g fiber, 9mg cholesterol, 74mg sodium

Soft Molasses Cookies V

Submitted by: **Sara**

"Celebrate the winter months with spicy and soft molasses cookies. Enjoy them with a cup of hot coffee."

1	cup butter, softened	3	cups all-purpose flour
½	cup packed brown sugar	2	teaspoons baking soda
1	egg	½	teaspoon ground cinnamon
¾	cup molasses	1	teaspoon ground ginger

1. In a large bowl, cream together the butter, brown sugar, and egg until well blended. Stir in the molasses. In a separate bowl, combine the flour, baking soda, cinnamon, and ginger; stir into the molasses mixture. Cover the dough and chill for at least 1 hour.
2. Preheat oven to 350°F (175°C). Grease baking sheets.
3. Roll the dough into walnut-size balls. Place the cookies 2 inches apart on prepared baking sheets.
4. Bake in the preheated oven for 8 to 10 minutes. Allow cookies to cool on the baking sheets for 5 minutes before removing to wire racks to cool completely. **Yield:** 3 dozen cookies.

Per cookie: 111 calories, 1g protein, 15g carbohydrate, 5g fat, 0g fiber, 20mg cholesterol, 127mg sodium

◀ HOLIDAY GIFT GIVING

Prep Time: 10 minutes

Chill Time: 1 hour

Cook Time: 10 minutes per batch

Average Rating: ★★★★☆

What other cooks have done:

"These cookies were good, but I felt the need to spice up the dough a bit. I added more ground ginger and cinnamon, and I rolled the balls in coarse sugar before baking them. The sugar gave them some crunch, while the cookies stayed chewy."

Grandma's Gingersnap Cookies

Submitted by: **Marie Ayers**

"These melt-in-your-mouth cookies come from my grandmother's recipe, which has been in my family since 1899."

2	cups sifted all-purpose flour	¾	cup shortening
1	tablespoon ground ginger	1	cup white sugar
2	teaspoons baking soda	1	egg
1	teaspoon ground cinnamon	¼	cup dark molasses
½	teaspoon salt	⅓	cup cinnamon sugar

1. Preheat oven to 350°F (175°C).
2. Sift together the first 5 ingredients. Sift again and set aside.
3. In a separate bowl, beat the shortening until creamy. Add white sugar gradually and continue beating. Beat in egg and molasses.
4. Sift about one-third of the flour mixture into the shortening mixture; blend well. Repeat until all of the flour mixture is added. Roll the dough into tiny balls by hand; roll each ball in cinnamon sugar. Place 2 inches apart on ungreased baking sheets.
5. Bake in the preheated oven for 10 minutes or until the tops are rounded and slightly cracked. Cool on wire racks. Store in an airtight container. **Yield:** 5 dozen cookies.

Per 2 cookies: 121 calories, 1g protein, 17g carbohydrate, 5g fat, 0g fiber, 7mg cholesterol, 126mg sodium

◀ HOLIDAY GIFT GIVING

Prep Time: 20 minutes

Cook Time: 10 minutes per batch

Average Rating: ★★★★★

What other cooks have done:

"These are wonderful cookies. I like to make them sandwich cookies by adding my own filling. Combine 2 tablespoons instant pudding mix and ¼ cup milk; add ¼ cup butter, 2 cups confectioners' sugar, and ¼ teaspoon almond extract. I also bake the cookies for a little less than 10 minutes so they'll be chewier. They're perfect with a glass of milk."

Better-Than-Sex Cookies

Submitted by: **Mike Warot**

"Here is a recipe for some very good cookies. These cookies were once described as 'better than sex' by a friend."

Prep Time: 15 minutes

Cook Time: 9 minutes per batch

Average Rating: ★★★★★

What other cooks have done:

"I just made these cookies. Make your dough into balls that are a little higher than flat because the cookies spread in the oven. Bake about 10 minutes in a 375°F (190°C) oven. They are good!"

1	cup butter, softened	1	teaspoon baking soda
2	cups white sugar	½	teaspoon salt
2	eggs	1⅔	cups vanilla baking chips
1	teaspoon vanilla extract	4	ounces macadamia nuts,
2½	cups all-purpose flour		chopped

1. Preheat oven to 350°F (175°C).
2. In a large bowl, beat together butter and sugar until creamy. Add eggs and vanilla; beat until light and fluffy.
3. In a separate bowl, stir together flour, baking soda, and salt; gradually blend into butter mixture. Stir in vanilla chips and macadamia nuts and drop by rounded tablespoonfuls onto ungreased baking sheets.
4. Bake in the preheated oven for 9 minutes (do not overbake). Cookies will be soft. They will puff while baking and flatten upon cooling. Cool slightly; remove to a wire rack to cool completely.
Yield: 4 dozen cookies.

Per cookie: 157 calories, 2g protein, 19g carbohydrate, 8g fat, 0g fiber, 20mg cholesterol, 112mg sodium

Apple Hermits

Submitted by: **Aunt Mikie**

"This spicy, nutty apple cookie is moist and cakelike."

2	cups all-purpose flour	1½	cups packed brown sugar
1	teaspoon baking soda	1	egg, lightly beaten
1	teaspoon ground cinnamon	1	cup chopped walnuts
1	teaspoon ground cloves	1	cup chopped apple
½	teaspoon ground nutmeg	1	cup raisins
½	teaspoon salt	⅔	cup confectioners' sugar
½	cup butter, softened	1	tablespoon milk

1. Preheat oven to 350°F (175°C). Line baking sheets with parchment paper.

2. In a medium bowl, sift together flour, baking soda, cinnamon, cloves, nutmeg, and salt.

3. In a large mixing bowl, cream butter until light and fluffy. Mix in brown sugar and egg. Stir in flour mixture and mix thoroughly. Fold in nuts, apple, and raisins. Drop by rounded teaspoonfuls about 1½ inches apart onto prepared baking sheets.

4. Bake in the preheated oven for 12 to 14 minutes. Cool on wire racks.

5. In a small bowl, mix confectioners' sugar with milk to make a thin glaze. Drizzle over cooled cookies. **Yield:** 5 dozen cookies.

Per cookie: 77 calories, 1g protein, 13g carbohydrate, 3g fat, 0g fiber, 8mg cholesterol, 60mg sodium

◄ QUICK & EASY

Prep Time: 30 minutes

Cook Time: 14 minutes per batch

Average Rating: ★★★★★

What other cooks have done:

"These cookies are delicious! Because I am not wild about cloves, I cut the amount called for by half, and I used dark brown sugar. A wonderful cookie for the fall season!"

Pecan Praline Cookies

Submitted by: **Debbie Evans**

"These are simple, but they're out of this world!"

35	graham crackers	¼	teaspoon cream of tartar
1	cup packed brown sugar	1	cup chopped pecans
1	cup butter		

1. Preheat oven to 325°F (165°C).

2. Place crackers on an ungreased 10x15 inch jellyroll pan, covering bottom of pan.

3. In a small saucepan over medium heat, bring sugar, butter, and cream of tartar to a boil. Add nuts. Pour mixture over the top of the crackers.

4. Bake in the preheated oven for 10 minutes. Cool for a few minutes; remove from pan while still warm. **Yield:** 35 cookies.

Per cookie: 124 calories, 1g protein, 12g carbohydrate, 8g fat, 1g fiber, 14mg cholesterol, 77mg sodium

◄ 5 INGREDIENTS OR LESS

Prep Time: 10 minutes

Cook Time: 10 minutes

Average Rating: ★★★★★

What other cooks have done:

"Excellent cookies! I've made this recipe several times and have gotten nothing but compliments. I skip the cream of tartar. I sprinkle chocolate chips over the hot mixture and spread them when they're melted."

Absolutely the Best Chocolate Chip Cookies

Submitted by: **Nicole Faust Hunt**

"This is a secret family recipe for chocolate chip cookies. Everyone who tries them begs for more."

1 cup butter-flavored shortening	2¼ cups all-purpose flour
¾ cup packed brown sugar	1 teaspoon baking soda
¾ cup white sugar	1 teaspoon salt
2 eggs	2 cups milk chocolate chips
2 teaspoons Mexican vanilla extract	

1. Preheat oven to 350°F (175°C). Grease baking sheets.
2. In a large bowl, cream together the butter-flavored shortening, brown sugar, and white sugar until light and fluffy. Add eggs, 1 at a time, beating well after each addition; stir in vanilla.
3. In a separate bowl, combine the flour, baking soda, and salt; gradually stir into the creamed mixture. Fold in the chocolate chips. Drop by rounded spoonfuls onto prepared baking sheets.
4. Bake in the preheated oven for 8 to 10 minutes or until light brown. Allow cookies to cool on baking sheets for 5 minutes before removing to wire racks to cool completely.

Yield: 2 dozen cookies.

Per cookie: 236 calories, 3g protein, 29g carbohydrate, 13g fat, 0g fiber, 18mg cholesterol, 167mg sodium

Chocolate-Chocolate Chip Cookies I

Submitted by: **Kathy Brandt**

"You get a double dose of chocolate with these cookies. Kids and adults love them."

1 cup butter, softened	¾ teaspoon baking soda
1½ cups white sugar	¼ teaspoon salt
2 eggs	2 cups semisweet chocolate chips
2 teaspoons vanilla extract	½ cup chopped walnuts (optional)
2 cups all-purpose flour	
⅔ cup unsweetened cocoa powder	

1. Preheat oven to 350°F (175°C).
2. In a large bowl, beat together butter, sugar, eggs, and vanilla until light and fluffy.
3. In a separate bowl, combine the flour, cocoa, baking soda, and salt; stir into the butter mixture until well blended. Mix in the chocolate chips; mix in walnuts, if desired. Drop by rounded teaspoonfuls onto ungreased baking sheets.

4. Bake in the preheated oven for 8 to 10 minutes or just until set. Cool cookies slightly on baking sheets before transferring to wire racks to cool completely. **Yield:** 4 dozen cookies.

Per cookie: 125 calories, 2g protein, 16g carbohydrate, 7g fat, 1g fiber, 19mg cholesterol, 75mg sodium

Peanut Butter Chip Chocolate Cookies
(pictured on page 4)

Submitted by: **Michelle Laverdiere**

"My best friend's mom made these when we were kids. They are the best cookies I have ever eaten, and I have yet to screw up a batch. Warning: You may be tempted to eat the entire batch!"

1 cup butter, softened	⅔ cup unsweetened cocoa powder
1½ cups white sugar	
2 eggs	¾ teaspoon baking soda
2 teaspoons vanilla extract	½ teaspoon salt
2 cups all-purpose flour	2 cups peanut butter chips

1. Preheat oven to 350°F (175°C). Grease baking sheets.
2. In a medium bowl, cream together the butter and sugar. Stir in the eggs and vanilla.
3. In a separate bowl, combine the flour, cocoa, baking soda, and salt; stir into the creamed mixture. Fold in the peanut butter chips. Drop cookies by teaspoonfuls onto prepared baking sheets.
4. Bake in the preheated oven for 8 to 10 minutes or until set. Cool on wire racks. **Yield:** 2 dozen cookies.

Per cookie: 278 calories, 7g protein, 32g carbohydrate, 15g fat, 2g fiber, 39mg cholesterol, 218mg sodium

◀ QUICK & EASY

Prep Time: 10 minutes

Cook Time: 10 minutes per batch

Average Rating: ★★★★

What other cooks have done:

"These cookies were a delight! I didn't have peanut butter chips, so I substituted orange-and-black candy-coated peanut butter morsels. They were delicious and even better the day after baking. They had the consistency of brownies packed with peanut butter chips."

Wilderness Place Lodge Cookies

Submitted by: **Kim Brittain**

"These cookies were created by the owners of Wilderness Place Lodge in Lake Creek, Alaska. The owners are very good friends of mine, and the culinary creations at this fishing lodge are out of this world! I promise that one of these cookies will fill you as much as a cheeseburger and fries would."

FREEZER FRESH ▶

Prep Time: 20 minutes

Cook Time: 12 minutes per batch

Average Rating: ★★★★★

What other cooks have done:

"I make a batch of the dough, roll it in plastic wrap, and freeze it. When I want cookies, I just slice and bake. There is absolutely no difference in flavor, and the texture is perfect. These cookies rock! If you make them with heaping table-spoonfuls, the cookies will be very large, but if you want to freeze them, you can make the rolls of dough whatever size you want."

2	cups butter, softened	2	teaspoons baking soda
2	cups packed brown sugar	6	cups quick cooking oats
2	cups white sugar	2	cups chocolate chips
4	eggs	2	cups chopped and toasted walnuts
2	teaspoons vanilla extract		
3	cups all-purpose flour	1	cup coconut
2	teaspoons salt	1	cup raisins

1. Preheat oven to 350°F (175°C). Grease baking sheets.
2. In a very large bowl, cream together the butter, brown sugar, and white sugar until smooth. Beat in the eggs, 1 at a time; stir in the vanilla.
3. In a separate bowl, combine the flour, salt, and baking soda; stir into the sugar mixture until well incorporated. Mix in oats; stir in the chocolate chips, nuts, coconut, and raisins. Drop by heaping teaspoonfuls onto prepared baking sheets.
4. Bake in the preheated oven for 10 to 12 minutes or until golden brown. Let cookies cool for a few minutes on the baking sheets before removing to wire racks to cool completely.

Yield: 5 dozen cookies.

Note: Make sure to soften the butter and get the eggs to room temperature before starting. For plumper raisins, boil them in water for a few minutes and cool before adding to batter. If you want to play around with different flavors of chips, feel free. I've found I like milk chocolate chips best.

Per cookie: 229 calories, 4g protein, 28g carbohydrate, 12g fat, 2g fiber, 31mg cholesterol, 190mg sodium

Oatmeal-Toffee Cookies *(pictured on page 4)*

Submitted by: **Lori**
"These prizewinning oatmeal cookies are full of rich toffee flavor."

¾ cup butter, softened	¼ teaspoon salt
½ cup packed light brown sugar	½ teaspoon baking soda
1 egg	1½ cups rolled oats
1 teaspoon vanilla extract	½ cup chopped pecans
1 cup all-purpose flour	2 cups toffee baking bits

1. Preheat oven to 350°F (175°C). Line baking sheets with parchment paper.

2. In a medium bowl, cream together the butter and brown sugar. Stir in egg and vanilla until smooth. In a separate bowl, sift together flour, salt, and baking soda; stir into the creamed mixture. Stir in rolled oats, pecans, and toffee bits. Drop dough by rounded tablespoonfuls onto prepared baking sheets and flatten slightly.

3. Bake in the preheated oven for 10 to 15 minutes (cookies will have a dry appearance when finished baking). **Yield:** 3 dozen cookies.

Per cookie: 160 calories, 2g protein, 16g carbohydrate, 10g fat, 1g fiber, 28mg cholesterol, 139mg sodium

◀ **BLUE RIBBON WINNER**

Prep Time: 15 minutes

Cook Time: 15 minutes per batch

Average Rating: ★★★★★

What other cooks have done:

"I wanted to add a little chocolate to this recipe, so after cooling the cookies completely, I dipped half of each cookie into chocolate and allowed them to cool. They were extra special!"

Minnesota's Favorite Cookie

Submitted by: **Barb**
"Try this luscious brown sugar butter cookie made with toffee bits and two kinds of chocolate chips. Yummy!"

1 cup butter, softened	¼ teaspoon salt
1½ cups packed brown sugar	1 cup milk chocolate chips
2 eggs	½ cup semisweet chocolate chips
2 teaspoons vanilla extract	
2½ cups all-purpose flour	⅔ cup toffee baking bits
1 teaspoon baking powder	1 cup chopped pecans

1. Preheat oven to 350°F (175°C). Grease baking sheets.

2. In a medium bowl, cream together the butter and sugar. Beat in eggs, 1 at a time; stir in the vanilla.

3. In a separate bowl, combine the flour, baking powder, and salt; stir into the creamed mixture. Stir in the milk chocolate and semisweet chocolate chips, toffee bits, and pecans. Drop by tablespoonfuls onto prepared baking sheets.

4. Bake in the preheated oven for 10 to 12 minutes. Cool on the baking sheets before transferring to wire racks to cool completely. **Yield:** 4 dozen cookies.

Per cookie: 140 calories, 2g protein, 15g carbohydrate, 9g fat, 1g fiber, 22mg cholesterol, 84mg sodium

◀ **QUICK & EASY**

Prep Time: 15 minutes

Cook Time: 12 minutes per batch

Average Rating: ★★★★☆

What other cooks have done:

"These were so good! Very rich tasting. I undercooked them a little because I like softer cookies. I also used a combination of semisweet and white chocolate chips because I didn't have milk chocolate ones."

Kay's Shortbread

Submitted by: **k. johnston**

"This simple shortbread cookie is baked in a 9 inch round cake pan and cut into wedges."

FROM THE PANTRY ▶

Prep Time: 15 minutes

Cook Time: 35 minutes

Average Rating: ★★★★★

What other cooks have done:

"Absolutely the best shortbread, hands down. I cut the dough in half and rolled each half into a log. You can roll the logs in sliced almonds, poppy seeds, or crushed peppermints for the holidays and then slice them and place them on baking sheets for cooking."

2	cups all-purpose flour	1	cup butter, softened
¼	teaspoon baking powder	1	teaspoon vanilla extract
¼	teaspoon salt	2	tablespoons white sugar
½	cup confectioners' sugar		

1. Preheat oven to 350°F (175°C).

2. In a medium bowl, stir together the flour, baking powder, salt, and confectioners' sugar. Stir in the butter and vanilla until a stiff dough forms. Pat dough into a 9 inch round cake pan and prick well with a fork. Sprinkle 2 tablespoons white sugar over dough.

3. Bake in the preheated oven for 30 to 35 minutes or until golden. Score into wedges while warm. Cool on wire rack; separate wedges.

Yield: 14 servings.

Per serving: 206 calories, 2g protein, 20g carbohydrate, 13g fat, 1g fiber, 36mg cholesterol, 185mg sodium

Shortbread Tips

Originally associated with Christmas and New Year's Eve, shortbread is a tender, rich pastry of Scottish origin. Made from butter, flour, and sugar, shortbread dough is traditionally formed into a circle and cut into pie-shaped wedges called petticoat tails. Another way of making shortbread is to press the dough into a round, shallow, carved earthenware mold. After baking, the large shortbread cookie is turned out of the mold and cut into wedges.

The term "short" simply refers to pastry that contains a high proportion of shortening, margarine, butter, or cooking oil to flour. Baked goods that are short are tender, rich, flaky, and crisp. Shortbread's basic blend of butter, sugar, and flour results in a taste that's far more than the sum of its parts. This simplicity is what produces the cookie's famous buttery crumb.

Careful handling and precise baking produce the optimum results, and the key to successful shortbread comes from baking it slowly so that it turns a golden color but doesn't brown. Of course, you don't have to limit yourself to basic shortbread. Almost anything can be stirred into your batter, including chocolate cookie crumbs, toffee bits, coffee, and peanut butter.

Shortbread also makes an excellent gift. Use cookie cutters to produce circles, stars, or any other favorite shape. Give a stack of shortbread in a variety of flavors or use graduated cookie cutters in a range of sizes to create a fun pyramid of cookies made from a single flavor of shortbread. Either way, shortbread is sure to please.

For more information, visit **Allrecipes.com**

Caramel Shortbread

Submitted by: **Mary**

"I got this recipe from a Scottish friend."

½ cup butter, softened
¼ cup white sugar
1 cup all-purpose flour
¼ cup ground almonds
¾ cup butter
⅜ cup white sugar
3 tablespoons golden syrup

1 (14 ounce) can sweetened condensed milk
8 (1 ounce) squares high-quality milk chocolate
⅓ cup toasted and sliced almonds

1. Preheat oven to 350°F (175°C). Grease an 8x8 inch pan and line with parchment paper.

2. Beat together ½ cup butter and ¼ cup sugar until pale. Add the flour and ground almonds to form a soft dough. Press dough into the prepared pan.

3. Bake in the preheated oven for 20 to 25 minutes or until pale golden brown. Leave in pan until cool.

4. To make topping, cook ¾ cup butter, ⅜ cup sugar, syrup, and sweetened condensed milk in a saucepan over low heat. Bring to a boil, stirring constantly. Boil for 5 to 7 minutes or until mixture has thickened and has a pale caramel color.

5. Spread caramel on cooled shortbread and let stand about 40 minutes to set. Melt chocolate over low heat. Spread melted chocolate on top of caramel and sprinkle with toasted almonds. **Yield:** 16 servings.

Per serving: 377 calories, 5g protein, 39g carbohydrate, 24g fat, 1g fiber, 50mg cholesterol, 194mg sodium

◄ AROUND-THE-WORLD CUISINE

Prep Time: 15 minutes

Cook Time: 35 minutes

Stand Time: 40 minutes

Average Rating: ★★★★★

What other cooks have done:

"I first tried caramel shortbread while living in Northern Ireland. I've wanted the recipe for years! This recipe is delicious and so easy. Everyone who tries it raves about how rich and yummy this dessert is."

Orange-Almond Biscotti II

Submitted by: **Karen**

"These biscotti are very low in fat, but they are delicious. You can substitute ¾ cup cranberries for the almonds."

HOLIDAY GIFT GIVING ▶

Prep Time: 15 minutes

Cook Time: 40 minutes

Average Rating: ★★★★★

What other cooks have done:

"Absolutely delicious! I found mixing the dough into a ball on the countertop to be easier. Using the serrated knife was easy—I just sawed across the top and then applied pressure to slice. After they cooled, I dipped the tops in melted semi-sweet chocolate."

2¼	cups all-purpose flour	1	tablespoon orange zest
1¼	cups white sugar	3	eggs, beaten
2	teaspoons baking powder	1	tablespoon vegetable oil
	Pinch salt	¼	teaspoon almond extract
½	cup sliced almonds		

1. Preheat oven to 350°F (175°C). Grease and flour a baking sheet.
2. In a large bowl, stir together flour, sugar, baking powder, salt, almonds, and orange zest. Make a well in the center and add the eggs, oil, and almond extract. Stir by hand until the mixture forms a ball.
3. Separate dough into 2 pieces and roll each one into a log about 8 inches long. Place logs on prepared baking sheet and flatten so they are about ¾ inch thick.
4. Bake in the preheated oven for 20 to 25 minutes. Cool slightly and remove from baking sheet. Using a serrated knife, slice diagonally into ½ inch slices. Set cookies, cut side down, on baking sheet and bake for 5 more minutes. Turn cookies over and bake for 5 to 10 more minutes. Finished cookies should be hard and crunchy.

Yield: 2 dozen cookies.

Per 2 cookies: 220 calories, 5g protein, 40g carbohydrate, 5g fat, 1g fiber, 53mg cholesterol, 130mg sodium

Double-Chocolate Biscotti

Submitted by: **Janet Allen**

"A crisp chocolate cookie that's not too sweet. These are wonderful with coffee, and they store very well."

½	cup butter, softened	1¾	cups all-purpose flour
⅔	cup white sugar	4	(1 ounce) squares white
¼	cup unsweetened cocoa		chocolate, chopped
	powder	¾	cup semisweet chocolate
2	teaspoons baking powder		chips
2	eggs		

1. In a large mixing bowl, cream together butter and sugar with an electric mixer until light and fluffy. Gradually beat in cocoa and baking powder. Beat for 2 minutes. Beat in the eggs, 1 at a time. Stir in flour by hand. Mix in white chocolate and semisweet chocolate chips. Cover dough and chill for about 10 minutes.
2. Preheat oven to 375°F (190°C). Lightly grease a baking sheet. Divide dough into 2 parts; roll each part into a 9 inch log. Place logs about 4 inches apart on prepared baking sheet. Flatten slightly.
3. Bake in the preheated oven for 20 to 25 minutes or until a toothpick inserted into the center comes out clean. Cool on baking sheet for 5 minutes before carefully transferring to wire rack to cool for 1 hour.
4. Preheat the oven to 325°F (165°C). Using a serrated knife, cut each loaf into ½ inch wide diagonal slices. Place slices on ungreased baking sheets.
5. Bake in the preheated oven for 9 minutes. Turn cookies over and bake for 7 to 9 more minutes. Cool completely and store in an airtight container. **Yield:** 3 dozen cookies.

Per cookie: 99 calories, 2g protein, 13g carbohydrate, 5g fat, 1g fiber, 19mg cholesterol, 61mg sodium

◄ HOLIDAY GIFT GIVING

Prep Time: 25 minutes

Chill Time: 10 minutes

Cook Time: 43 minutes

Cool Time: 1 hour 5 minutes

Average Rating: ★★★★★

What other cooks have done:

"These baked up very nicely. For the second baking, I left them in for the specified time and then turned the oven off and left them in for about another 15 minutes. Crisp, beautiful cookies. Serve two cookies in a fancy glass with a scoop of vanilla ice cream for a very elegant dessert."

Frosted Banana Bars

Submitted by: **Delta**

"These are a big hit for snack days at work. They're very moist and easy to make."

½	cup butter, softened	1	teaspoon baking soda
1½	cups white sugar	¼	teaspoon salt
2	eggs	1	cup mashed ripe banana
1	cup sour cream	1	(16 ounce) container cream
1	teaspoon vanilla extract		cheese frosting
2	cups all-purpose flour		

1. Preheat oven to 350°F (175°C). Grease a 10x15 inch jellyroll pan.

2. In a large bowl, cream together the butter and sugar until smooth. Beat in the eggs, 1 at a time; stir in the sour cream and vanilla.

3. In a separate bowl, combine the flour, baking soda, and salt; stir into butter mixture. Mix in the mashed banana. Spread evenly into prepared pan.

4. Bake in the preheated oven for 20 to 25 minutes or until a toothpick inserted into the center of the pan comes out clean. Allow bars to cool completely before frosting with the cream cheese frosting.

Yield: 3 dozen bars.

Per bar: 157 calories, 1g protein, 24g carbohydrate, 6g fat, 0g fiber, 22mg cholesterol, 109mg sodium

Chocolate Revel Bars

Submitted by: **Holly**

"These chewy bar cookies are loaded with fudgy filling. My family really loves them."

1	cup butter, softened	1	teaspoon salt
2	cups packed brown sugar	1	(14 ounce) can sweetened condensed milk
2	eggs		
4	teaspoons vanilla extract, divided	1½	cups semisweet chocolate chips
3	cups quick cooking oats	2	tablespoons butter
2½	cups all-purpose flour	½	teaspoon salt
1	teaspoon baking soda	½	cup chopped walnuts

1. Preheat oven to 350°F (175°C). Lightly grease a 9x13 inch pan.
2. In a large bowl, beat together 1 cup butter and brown sugar until fluffy. Mix in eggs and 2 teaspoons vanilla. In a separate bowl, combine oats, flour, baking soda, and 1 teaspoon salt; stir into butter mixture. Set aside.
3. In a medium saucepan, heat sweetened condensed milk, chocolate chips, 2 tablespoons butter, and ½ teaspoon salt over low heat, stirring until smooth. Remove from heat. Stir in walnuts and remaining 2 teaspoons vanilla.
4. Pat two-thirds of the oat mixture into the bottom of prepared pan. Spread chocolate mixture evenly over the top; dot with remaining oat mixture.
5. Bake in the preheated oven for 30 to 35 minutes. Cool on a wire rack. Cut into bars. **Yield:** 2 dozen bars.

Per bar: 359 calories, 6g protein, 51g carbohydrate, 16g fat, 2g fiber, 47mg cholesterol, 321mg sodium

◄ MAKE-AHEAD

Prep Time: 30 minutes

Cook Time: 40 minutes

Average Rating: ★★★★★

What other cooks have done:

"My mom had a similar recipe in the 1970s. She made hers in a jellyroll pan, which makes a big difference. Once the bars are cut, separate them with wax paper and keep them in a cookie tin to keep them fresh."

The Best Lemon Bars

Submitted by: **Patty Schenck**

"Tart, rich, and perfect, this simple recipe will wow your friends. For a festive tray, make another pan using limes instead of lemons and adding a drop of green food coloring to give the bars a very pale green color. After both pans have cooled, cut into uniform 2 inch squares and arrange in a checkerboard fashion."

5 INGREDIENTS OR LESS ▶

Prep Time: 15 minutes

Cook Time: 40 minutes

Average Rating: ★★★★☆

What other cooks have done:

"These are really good. I gave the recipe a twist, though. I put a lemon glaze on top after the bars were done. I stirred together 2 cups confectioners' sugar, juice from a lemon, and 2 tablespoons butter. Really lemony!"

1	cup butter, softened	2	cups white sugar, divided
2¼	cups all-purpose flour, divided	4	eggs
		2	lemons, juiced

1. Preheat oven to 350°F (175°C).

2. In a medium bowl, blend together softened butter, 2 cups flour, and ½ cup sugar. Press mixture into the bottom of an ungreased 9x13 inch pan.

3. Bake in the preheated oven for 15 to 20 minutes or until firm and golden.

4. In a medium bowl, whisk together remaining 1½ cups sugar and remaining ¼ cup flour. Whisk in the eggs and lemon juice. Pour over the baked crust.

5. Bake for 20 more minutes. Cool completely to firm; cut into bars.

Yield: 3 dozen bars.

Per bar: 126 calories, 2g protein, 18g carbohydrate, 6g fat, 1g fiber, 37mg cholesterol, 60mg sodium

Tart Lemon Triangles

Submitted by: **Melissa**

"This makes a lovely conclusion to an elegant spring dinner. I garnish these with whipped cream, a strawberry fan, and a sprig of mint."

⅜ cup butter
¼ cup confectioners' sugar
1 cup all-purpose flour
3 eggs
1 cup white sugar
1 tablespoon lemon zest

¼ cup lemon juice
3 tablespoons all-purpose flour
2 tablespoons confectioners' sugar

1. Preheat oven to 350°F (175°C).
2. Process butter, ¼ cup confectioners' sugar, and 1 cup flour in a food processor for 10 seconds or blend with a pastry blender. Pat dough evenly into a 9 inch round pie plate.
3. Bake in the preheated oven for 12 to 15 minutes or until golden.
4. Combine eggs, white sugar, lemon zest, lemon juice, and 3 tablespoons flour. Mix until smooth; pour mixture over hot crust.
5. Bake 14 to 18 more minutes or until firm. Let cool completely. Cut into 12 triangles and sprinkle with 2 tablespoons confectioners' sugar. **Yield:** 12 servings.

Per serving: 195 calories, 3g protein, 31g carbohydrate, 7g fat, 0g fiber, 69mg cholesterol, 75mg sodium

◀ COMPANY IS COMING

Prep Time: 10 minutes

Cook Time: 33 minutes

Average Rating: ★★★★★

What other cooks have done:

"Instead of making this in a pie plate, I poured the mixture into a bunch of mini phyllo pastry shells—they turned out wonderfully!"

Raspberry Oat Bars

Submitted by: **Corwynn Darkholme**

"Quick and easy! These bars are great for breakfast, Sunday brunch, or a snack."

¾ cup butter, softened
1 cup packed light brown sugar
1½ cups rolled oats
1½ cups all-purpose flour

1 teaspoon salt
½ teaspoon baking powder
1 (10 ounce) jar raspberry preserves

1. Preheat the oven to 400°F (200°C). Grease a 9x13 inch pan.
2. In a large bowl, cream together the butter and brown sugar until smooth. In a separate bowl, combine the oats, flour, salt, and baking powder; stir into the creamed mixture. Press half of the crust mixture into the bottom of prepared pan. Spread the preserves over the crust. Crumble the remaining crust mixture over the raspberry layer.
3. Bake in the preheated oven for 20 to 25 minutes or until light brown. Cool completely before cutting into bars.
Yield: 2 dozen bars.

Per bar: 162 calories, 2g protein, 26g carbohydrate, 6g fat, 1g fiber, 16mg cholesterol, 165mg sodium

◀ PARTY FOOD

Prep Time: 30 minutes

Cook Time: 25 minutes

Average Rating: ★★★★★

What other cooks have done:

"These bars are fabulous! I made mine with strawberry jam, and they were great. The recipe was so quick and easy. These could probably even be made in an 8x8 inch pan for a thicker bar."

Raisin-Sour Cream Bars

Submitted by: **Prudence N.**

"Try these very moist bars that are filled with a delicious raisin mixture."

KID-FRIENDLY ▶

Prep Time: 10 minutes

Cook Time: 25 minutes

Average Rating: ★★★★★

What other cooks have done:

"I loved this, and my family raved about it. These bars weren't too sweet, and the 'crumble' was just right. I'm going to try this using a date filling next time. Refrigerate before cutting for nice, clean squares. I have added this to my recipe book, and it will be passed on to my daughters and daughters-in-law."

2	cups raisins	1	cup packed brown sugar
1	cup white sugar	1¾	cups rolled oats
3	eggs	1	teaspoon baking soda
2½	tablespoons cornstarch	1	cup butter, softened
1½	cups sour cream	1¾	cups all-purpose flour
1	teaspoon ground cinnamon	½	teaspoon salt

1. Preheat oven to 350°F (175°C). Grease and flour a 9x13 inch pan.
2. Stir together raisins, white sugar, eggs, cornstarch, sour cream, and cinnamon in a saucepan over low heat until well blended. Set aside to cool.
3. In a separate bowl, mix together brown sugar, oats, baking soda, butter, flour, and salt until crumbly. Press half of oat mixture into prepared pan.
4. Pour raisin mixture over crust. Crumble remaining oat mixture over the top.
5. Bake in the preheated oven for 20 minutes. Cool on a wire rack and cut into bars. **Yield:** 30 bars.

Per bar: 216 calories, 3g protein, 31g carbohydrate, 10g fat, 1g fiber, 43mg cholesterol, 160mg sodium

Granola Bars III

Submitted by: **Ilene**
"These absolutely delicious granola bars made with honey, nuts, and raisins make a great snack."

2	cups quick cooking oats	½	cup chopped English walnuts
1	cup all-purpose flour	½	cup vegetable oil
¾	cup packed brown sugar	½	cup honey
¾	cup raisins	1	egg
½	cup wheat germ	2	teaspoons vanilla extract
½	teaspoon salt		
½	teaspoon ground cinnamon		

1. Preheat oven to 350°F (175°C). Line a 9x13 inch pan with aluminum foil or parchment paper and spray with cooking spray.
2. In a large bowl, stir together oats, flour, brown sugar, raisins, wheat germ, salt, cinnamon, and walnuts. In a separate bowl, thoroughly blend oil, honey, egg, and vanilla; add to the flour mixture and mix by hand until evenly distributed. Press evenly into prepared pan.
3. Bake in the preheated oven for 25 to 30 minutes or until edges are golden. Cool completely in pan before turning out onto a cutting board and cutting into bars. **Yield:** 20 bars.

Per bar: 213 calories, 4g protein, 32g carbohydrate, 9g fat, 2g fiber, 11mg cholesterol, 66mg sodium

◀ KID-FRIENDLY

Prep Time: 15 minutes

Cook Time: 30 minutes

Average Rating: ★★★★☆

What other cooks have done:
"These were wonderful! A hit at our house! I made one batch with dried cranberries and almonds and one with miniature chocolate and peanut butter chips. Very handy to grab along with an apple on the way out the door for work. Great travel food. Roll these out in the pan using a small hand-held rolling pin—it works like a dream."

Granny's Brownies

Submitted by: **Carl T. Erickson**
"This recipe has been in our family since the late 1800s. I am 70 now, and my grandnephew enjoys these brownies. Keep them under lock and key, or they will disappear in a trice!"

¾	cup butter, softened	1	teaspoon vanilla extract
2	cups packed brown sugar	1	cup all-purpose flour
3	eggs	1	cup chopped walnuts
4	(1 ounce) squares unsweetened chocolate, melted		

1. Preheat oven to 250°F (120°C). Grease an 8x8 inch pan.
2. In a large bowl, cream together butter, brown sugar, and eggs until light and fluffy. Stir in chocolate and vanilla until well blended. Mix in flour and then the walnuts. Spread batter evenly into prepared pan.
3. Bake in the preheated oven for 1 hour or until a toothpick inserted into the center comes out clean. Cool in the pan on a wire rack before cutting into squares. **Yield:** 16 brownies.

Per brownie: 308 calories, 4g protein, 36g carbohydrate, 18g fat, 2g fiber, 63mg cholesterol, 112mg sodium

◀ FROM THE PANTRY

Prep Time: 15 minutes

Cook Time: 1 hour

Average Rating: ★★★★☆

What other cooks have done:
"These had the perfect consistency—just what I was looking for in brownies. Since I didn't have unsweetened chocolate baking squares, I used 3 tablespoons cocoa and 1 tablespoon butter. I skipped the walnuts but added milk chocolate chunks for a bit of flavor. I served these with vanilla ice cream for dessert at a dinner I hosted, and they were a hit."

Chocolate Chip-Cheesecake Brownies

Submitted by: **Barb W.**

"Here's a scrumptious recipe that combines a blonde brownie and cheesecake."

Prep Time: 25 minutes

Cook Time: 45 minutes

Average Rating: ★★★★★

What other cooks have done:

"In my oven, these were done on top in about 35 to 40 minutes, but they were not done in the middle in just one or two very small areas. Next time, I will turn my oven down just a tad and keep a close eye on them. For those of you who need to bake longer, just cover with foil to prevent excess browning and test with a knife until done. The mix of chocolate chip cookie and cheesecake is perfect. Although they are not kind to the waistline, these will definitely fix any sweet tooth cravings."

1	cup shortening	1½ cups semisweet chocolate chips
1	cup packed brown sugar	
½	cup white sugar	2 (8 ounce) packages cream cheese, softened
3	eggs	
1	teaspoon vanilla extract	¼ cup white sugar
2	cups all-purpose flour	2 eggs
1	teaspoon baking soda	1 cup chopped pecans
½	teaspoon salt	

1. Preheat oven to 350°F (175°C). Grease a 9x13 inch pan.

2. In a large bowl, cream together shortening, brown sugar, and ½ cup white sugar. Beat in 3 eggs, 1 at a time; stir in the vanilla.

3. In a separate bowl, combine the flour, baking soda, and salt; blend into the sugar mixture. Stir in chocolate chips and set aside.

4. In a separate bowl, mix together the cream cheese and ¼ cup white sugar. Mix in 2 eggs.

5. Spread half of chocolate chip dough in bottom of prepared pan. Pour cream cheese batter on top of dough. Sprinkle with pecans. Drop pieces of remaining chocolate chip dough over filling (don't worry if there are gaps; the dough will spread).

6. Bake in the preheated oven for 45 minutes or until lightly browned on the top. Let brownies cool in the pan before cutting into bars.

Yield: 2 dozen brownies.

Per brownie: 338 calories, 5g protein, 31g carbohydrate, 23g fat, 1g fiber, 65mg cholesterol, 174mg sodium

Crispy Rice Candy

Submitted by: **Patty**

"I received this recipe from a friend at work, and it has quickly become a family favorite."

2 cups crispy rice cereal	1 cup crunchy peanut butter
2 cups dry-roasted peanuts	2 pounds white chocolate, chopped
2 cups miniature marshmallows	

1. In a large bowl, combine cereal, peanuts, marshmallows, and peanut butter. Stir until evenly mixed.

2. In a microwave-safe bowl or in a heavy saucepan, heat white chocolate until melted, stirring occasionally until chocolate is smooth. Stir chocolate into cereal mixture. Mixture will be slightly runny.

3. Drop by tablespoonfuls onto wax paper. Let set until firm, about 2 hours. Store in an airtight container. **Yield:** 7 dozen candies.

Per candy: 104 calories, 2g protein, 10g carbohydrate, 7g fat, 1g fiber, 2mg cholesterol, 31mg sodium

◀ **5 INGREDIENTS OR LESS**

Prep Time: 15 minutes

Cook Time: 5 minutes

Stand Time: 2 hours

Average Rating: ★★★★★

What other cooks have done:

"This is a quick and easy candy that should cure even the most raging sweet tooth! For variation, I made a batch with raisins mixed in. I dropped the candy by half teaspoonfuls into little foil candy cups for ease of serving and eating."

Metric Equivalents

The recipes that appear in this cookbook use the standard United States method for measuring liquid and dry or solid ingredients (teaspoons, tablespoons, and cups). The information on this chart is provided to help cooks outside the U.S. successfully use these recipes. All equivalents are approximate.

METRIC EQUIVALENTS FOR DIFFERENT TYPES OF INGREDIENTS

A standard cup measure of a dry or solid ingredient will vary in weight depending on the type of ingredient.
A standard cup of liquid is the same volume for any type of liquid. Use the following chart when converting standard cup measures to grams (weight) or milliliters (volume).

Standard Cup	Fine Powder	Grain	Granular	Liquid Solids	Liquid
	(ex. flour)	(ex. rice)	(ex. sugar)	(ex. butter)	(ex. milk)
1	140 g	150 g	190 g	200 g	240 ml
¾	105 g	113 g	143 g	150 g	180 ml
⅔	93 g	100 g	125 g	133 g	160 ml
½	70 g	75 g	95 g	100 g	120 ml
⅓	47 g	50 g	63 g	67 g	80 ml
¼	35 g	38 g	48 g	50 g	60 ml
⅛	18 g	19 g	24 g	25 g	30 ml

USEFUL EQUIVALENTS FOR DRY INGREDIENTS BY WEIGHT

(To convert ounces to grams, multiply the number of ounces by 30.)

1 oz	=	¹⁄₁₆ lb	=	30 g
4 oz	=	¼ lb	=	120 g
8 oz	=	½ lb	=	240 g
12 oz	=	¾ lb	=	360 g
16 oz	=	1 lb	=	480 g

USEFUL EQUIVALENTS FOR LENGTH

(To convert inches to centimeters, multiply the number of inches by 2.5.)

1 in					=	2.5 cm		
6 in	=	½ ft			=	15 cm		
12 in	=	1 ft			=	30 cm		
36 in	=	3 ft	=	1 yd	=	90 cm		
40 in					=	100 cm	=	1 m

USEFUL EQUIVALENTS FOR LIQUID INGREDIENTS BY VOLUME

¼ tsp							=	1 ml	
½ tsp							=	2 ml	
1 tsp							=	5 ml	
3 tsp	=	1 tbls			=	½ fl oz	=	15 ml	
		2 tbls	=	⅛ cup	=	1 fl oz	=	30 ml	
		4 tbls	=	¼ cup	=	2 fl oz	=	60 ml	
		5⅓ tbls	=	⅓ cup	=	3 fl oz	=	80 ml	
		8 tbls	=	½ cup	=	4 fl oz	=	120 ml	
		10⅔ tbls	=	⅔ cup	=	5 fl oz	=	160 ml	
		12 tbls	=	¾ cup	=	6 fl oz	=	180 ml	
		16 tbls	=	1 cup	=	8 fl oz	=	240 ml	
	1 pt	=	2 cups	=	16 fl oz	=	480 ml		
	1 qt	=	4 cups	=	32 fl oz	=	960 ml		
					33 fl oz	=	1000 ml	= 1 liter	

USEFUL EQUIVALENTS FOR COOKING/OVEN TEMPERATURES

	Fahrenheit	Celsius	Gas Mark
Freeze Water	32° F	0° C	
Room Temperature	68° F	20° C	
Boil Water	212° F	100° C	
Bake	325° F	165° C	3
	350° F	175° C	4
	375° F	190° C	5
	400° F	200° C	6
	425° F	220° C	7
	450° F	230° C	8
Broil			Grill

Common Substitutions

Ingredient	Amount	Substitution
Allspice	1 teaspoon	• ½ teaspoon ground cinnamon, ¼ teaspoon ground ginger, and ¼ teaspoon ground cloves
Arrowroot starch	1 teaspoon	• 1 tablespoon flour OR 1 teaspoon cornstarch
Baking powder	1 teaspoon	• ¼ teaspoon baking soda plus ½ teaspoon cream of tartar OR ¼ teaspoon baking soda plus ½ cup buttermilk (decrease liquid in recipe by ½ cup)
Beer	1 cup	• 1 cup nonalcoholic beer OR 1 cup chicken broth
Brandy	¼ cup	• 1 teaspoon imitation brandy extract plus enough water to make ¼ cup
Breadcrumbs	1 cup	• 1 cup cracker crumbs OR 1 cup matzo meal OR 1 cup ground oats
Broth (beef or chicken)	1 cup	• 1 bouillon cube plus 1 cup boiling water OR 1 tablespoon soy sauce plus enough water to make 1 cup OR 1 cup vegetable broth
Brown sugar	1 cup, packed	• 1 cup white sugar plus ¼ cup molasses and decrease the liquid in recipe by ¼ cup OR 1 cup white sugar OR 1¼ cups confectioners' sugar
Butter (salted)	1 cup	• 1 cup margarine OR 1 cup shortening plus ½ teaspoon salt OR ⅞ cup vegetable oil plus ½ teaspoon salt OR ⅞ cup lard plus ½ teaspoon salt
Butter (unsalted)	1 cup	• 1 cup shortening OR ⅞ cup vegetable oil OR ⅞ cup lard
Buttermilk	1 cup	• 1 cup yogurt OR 1 tablespoon lemon juice or vinegar plus enough milk to make 1 cup
Cheddar cheese	1 cup, shredded	• 1 cup shredded Colby Cheddar OR 1 cup shredded Monterey Jack cheese
Chervil	1 tablespoon, fresh	• 1 tablespoon fresh parsley
Chicken base	1 tablespoon	• 1 cup canned or homemade chicken broth or stock. Reduce liquid in recipe by 1 cup.
Chocolate (semisweet)	1 ounce	• 1 (1 ounce) square of unsweetened chocolate plus 4 teaspoons sugar OR 1 ounce semisweet chocolate chips plus 1 teaspoon shortening
Chocolate (unsweetened)	1 ounce	• 3 tablespoons unsweetened cocoa plus 1 tablespoon shortening or vegetable oil
Cocoa	¼ cup	• 1 (1 ounce) square unsweetened chocolate
Corn syrup	1 cup	• 1¼ cup white sugar plus ⅓ cup water OR 1 cup honey OR 1 cup light treacle syrup
Cottage cheese	1 cup	• 1 cup farmers cheese OR 1 cup ricotta cheese
Cracker crumbs	1 cup	• 1 cup breadcrumbs OR 1 cup matzo meal OR 1 cup ground oats
Cream (half-and-half)	1 cup	• ⅞ cup milk plus 1 tablespoon butter
Cream (heavy)	1 cup	• 1 cup evaporated milk OR ¾ cup milk plus ⅓ cup butter

Ingredient	Amount	Substitution
Cream (light)	1 cup	•1 cup evaporated milk OR ¾ cup milk plus 3 tablespoons butter
Cream (whipped)	1 cup	•1 cup frozen whipped topping, thawed
Cream cheese	1 cup	•1 cup pureed cottage cheese OR 1 cup plain yogurt, strained overnight in cheesecloth
Cream of tartar	1 teaspoon	•2 teaspoons lemon juice or vinegar
Crème fraîche	1 cup	•Combine 1 cup heavy cream and 1 tablespoon plain yogurt. Let stand for 6 hours at room temperature.
Egg	1 whole (3 tablespoons)	•2½ tablespoons powdered egg substitute plus 2½ tablespoons water OR ¼ cup liquid egg substitute OR ¼ cup silken tofu pureed OR 3 tablespoons mayonnaise OR ½ banana mashed with ½ teaspoon baking powder OR 1 tablespoon powdered flax seed soaked in 3 tablespoons water
Evaporated milk	1 cup	•1 cup light cream
Farmers cheese	8 ounces	•8 ounces dry cottage cheese OR 8 ounces creamed cottage cheese, drained
Fats for baking	1 cup	•1 cup applesauce OR 1 cup fruit puree
Flour (bread)	1 cup	•1 cup all-purpose flour plus 1 teaspoon wheat gluten
Flour (cake)	1 cup	•1 cup all-purpose flour minus 2 tablespoons
Flour (self-rising)	1 cup	•⅞ cup all-purpose flour plus 1½ teaspoons baking powder and ½ teaspoon salt
Garlic	1 clove	•⅛ teaspoon garlic powder OR ½ teaspoon granulated garlic OR ½ teaspoon garlic salt (reduce salt in recipe)
Ginger (dry)	1 teaspoon, ground	•2 teaspoons chopped fresh ginger
Ginger (fresh)	1 teaspoon, minced	•½ teaspoon ground dried ginger
Green onion	½ cup, chopped	•½ cup chopped onion OR ½ cup chopped leek OR ½ cup chopped shallots
Hazelnuts	1 cup whole	•1 cup macadamia nuts OR 1 cup almonds
Herbs (fresh)	1 tablespoon, chopped	•1 teaspoon chopped dried herbs
Honey	1 cup	•1¼ cups white sugar plus ⅓ cup water OR 1 cup corn syrup OR 1 cup light treacle syrup
Hot sauce	1 teaspoon	•¾ teaspoon cayenne pepper plus 1 teaspoon vinegar
Ketchup	1 cup	•1 cup tomato sauce plus 1 teaspoon vinegar plus 1 tablespoon sugar
Lemon grass	2 fresh stalks	•1 tablespoon lemon zest
Lemon juice	1 teaspoon	•½ teaspoon vinegar OR 1 teaspoon white wine OR 1 teaspoon lime juice
Lemon zest	1 teaspoon, grated	•½ teaspoon lemon extract OR 2 tablespoons lemon juice
Lime juice	1 teaspoon	•1 teaspoon vinegar OR 1 teaspoon white wine OR 1 teaspoon lemon juice
Lime zest	1 teaspoon, grated	•1 teaspoon grated lemon zest
Macadamia nuts	1 cup	•1 cup almonds OR 1 cup hazelnuts
Mace	1 teaspoon	•1 teaspoon ground nutmeg
Margarine	1 cup	•1 cup shortening plus ½ teaspoon salt OR 1 cup butter OR ⅞ cup vegetable oil plus ½ teaspoon salt OR ⅞ cup lard plus ½ teaspoon salt
Mayonnaise	1 cup	•1 cup sour cream OR 1 cup plain yogurt

Ingredient	Amount	Substitution
Milk (whole)	1 cup	•1 cup soy milk OR 1 cup rice milk OR 1 cup water or juice OR ¼ cup dry milk powder plus 1 cup water OR ⅔ cup evaporated milk plus ⅓ cup water
Mint (fresh)	¼ cup, chopped	•1 tablespoon dried mint leaves
Mustard (prepared)	1 tablespoon	•Mix together 1 tablespoon dried mustard, 1 teaspoon water, 1 teaspoon vinegar, and 1 teaspoon sugar.
Onion	1 cup, chopped	•1 cup chopped green onions OR 1 cup chopped shallots OR 1 cup chopped leek OR ¼ cup dried minced onion
Orange zest	1 tablespoon, grated	•½ teaspoon orange extract OR 1 teaspoon lemon juice
Parmesan cheese	½ cup, grated	•½ cup grated Asiago cheese OR ½ cup grated Romano cheese
Parsley (fresh)	1 tablespoon, chopped	•1 tablespoon chopped fresh chervil OR 1 teaspoon dried parsley
Pepperoni	1 ounce	•1 ounce salami
Raisins	1 cup	•1 cup dried currants OR 1 cup dried cranberries OR 1 cup chopped pitted prunes
Rice (white)	1 cup, cooked	•1 cup cooked barley OR 1 cup cooked bulgur OR 1 cup cooked brown or wild rice
Ricotta	1 cup	•1 cup dry cottage cheese OR 1 cup silken tofu
Rum	1 tablespoon	•½ teaspoon rum extract plus enough water to make 1 tablespoon
Saffron	¼ teaspoon	•¼ teaspoon turmeric
Semisweet chocolate chips	1 cup	•1 cup chocolate candies OR 1 cup peanut butter or other flavored chips OR 1 cup chopped nuts OR 1 cup chopped dried fruit
Shallots (fresh)	½ cup, chopped	•½ cup chopped onion OR ½ cup chopped leek OR ½ cup chopped green onions
Shortening	1 cup	•1 cup butter OR 1 cup margarine minus ½ teaspoon salt from recipe
Sour cream	1 cup	•1 cup plain yogurt OR 1 tablespoon lemon juice or vinegar plus enough cream to make 1 cup OR ¾ cup buttermilk mixed with ⅓ cup butter
Soy sauce	½ cup	•¼ cup Worcestershire sauce mixed with ¼ cup water
Stock (beef or chicken)	1 cup	•1 beef or chicken bouillon cube dissolved in 1 cup water
Sweetened condensed milk	1 (14 ounce) can	•¾ cup white sugar mixed with ½ cup water and 1⅛ cups dry powdered milk (Bring to a boil, and cook, stirring frequently, until thickened, about 20 minutes.)
Vegetable oil (for baking)	1 cup	•1 cup applesauce OR 1 cup fruit puree
Vegetable oil (for frying)	1 cup	•1 cup lard OR 1 cup vegetable shortening
Vinegar	1 teaspoon	•1 teaspoon lemon or lime juice OR 2 teaspoons white wine
White sugar	1 cup	•1 cup brown sugar OR 1¼ cups confectioners' sugar OR ¾ cup honey OR ¾ cup corn syrup
Wine	1 cup	•1 cup chicken or beef broth OR 1 cup fruit juice mixed with 2 teaspoons vinegar OR 1 cup water
Yeast (active dry)	1 (0.25 ounce) package	•1 cake compressed yeast OR 2½ teaspoons active dry yeast OR 2½ teaspoons rapid rise yeast
Yogurt	1 cup	•1 cup sour cream OR 1 cup buttermilk

Recommended Storage Guide

IN THE PANTRY

Baking powder and soda	1 year
Flour, all-purpose	10 to 15 months
Milk, evaporated and sweetened condensed	1 year
Mixes	
cake	1 year
pancake	6 months
Peanut butter	6 months
Salt and pepper	18 months
Shortening	8 months
Spices (discard if aroma fades)	
ground	6 months
whole	1 year
Sugar	18 months

IN THE REFRIGERATOR

Butter and margarine	1 month
Buttermilk	1 to 2 weeks
Eggs (fresh in shell)	3 to 5 weeks
Half-and-half	7 to 10 days
Meat	
casseroles, cooked	3 to 4 days
steaks, chops, roasts, uncooked	3 to 5 days
Milk, whole or fat-free	1 week
Poultry, uncooked	1 to 2 days
Sour cream	3 to 4 weeks
Whipping cream	10 days

IN THE FREEZER

Breads	
quick	2 to 3 months
yeast	3 to 6 months
Butter	6 months
Cakes	
cheesecakes and pound cakes	2 to 3 months
unfrosted	2 to 5 months
with cooked frosting	not recommended
with creamy-type frosting	3 months
Candy and fudge	6 months
Casseroles	1 to 2 months
Cheese	4 months
Cookies	
baked, unfrosted	8 to 12 months
dough	1 month
Eggs (not in shell)	
whites	1 year
yolks	8 months
Ice cream	1 to 3 months
Meat	
cooked	2 to 3 months
ground, uncooked	3 to 4 months
roasts, uncooked	9 months
steaks or chops, uncooked	4 to 6 months
Nuts	8 months
Pies	
pastry shell	2 to 3 months
fruit	1 to 2 months
pumpkin	2 to 4 months
custard, cream, meringue	not recommended
Poultry	
cooked	3 to 4 months
parts, uncooked	9 months
whole, uncooked	12 months
Soups and stews	2 to 3 months

Nutritional Analysis

Nutrition Analyses Based on Premier Databases

Allrecipes.com is proud to provide ESHA Research's nutrient databases for recipe nutrition analysis. ESHA Research is the premier nutrition analysis provider for the world's nutrition and health industries, having provided nutrient information to health care providers and the world's top food manufacturing firms for more than 15 years. Its nutrient databases total more than 22,000 foods, track 165 nutrient factors, and combine nutrient data from over 1,200 scientific sources of information. For more information about ESHA Research, visit the website at **http://www.esha.com.**

Using Allrecipes.com Information with Care

Allrecipes.com is committed to providing recipe-based nutritional information so that individuals may, by choice or under a doctor's advice, adhere to specific dietary requirements and make healthful recipe choices. The nutrition values that appear in this book and on **Allrecipes.com** nutrition pages are based on individual recipe ingredients. When a recipe calls for "salt to taste," we calculate sodium based on ¼ teaspoon or 1 gram of salt. While we have taken the utmost care in providing you with the most accurate nutritional values possible, please note that this information is not intended for medical nutrition therapy. If you are following a strict diet for medical or dietary reasons, it's important that you, first, consult your physician or registered dietitian before planning your meals based on recipes at **Allrecipes.com,** and, second, remain under appropriate medical supervision while using the nutrition information at **Allrecipes.com.**

Microwave Vegetable Chart

Cooking vegetables in the microwave is the best way to preserve nutrients and flavor, and it is often the quickest way to cook them. Cook all vegetables on High power in a baking dish covered with dish lid. If you use heavy-duty plastic wrap to cover the dish, be sure to turn back one corner to allow steam to escape.

Food	Microwave Time*	Special Instructions
Asparagus, 1 pound	2 to 4 minutes	Snap off tough ends of spears. Add 2 tablespoons water.
Beans, green, 1 pound	10 minutes; stand 5 minutes	Trim ends; cut beans into 1-inch pieces. Add ½ cup water.
Broccoli spears, 1 pound	6 to 7 minutes	Arrange in a circle, spoke-fashion, with florets in center; add ¼ cup water.
Carrots, baby, 1 pound	6 minutes; stand 2 minutes	Add ¼ cup water.
Cauliflower florets, 1 pound	6 to 7 minutes; stand 2 minutes	Add ¼ cup water.
Corn on the cob, 2 (large) ears / 3 ears / 4 ears	6 to 7 minutes / 7 to 8 minutes / 8 to 9 minutes	Cut ears in half. Arrange end-to-end in a circle; add ¼ cup water.
Onions, 1 pound, peeled and quartered (2 medium)	4 minutes; stand 2 minutes	Add 2 tablespoons water.
Potatoes, sweet/baking (9-ounce) 1 potato / 2 potatoes / 4 potatoes	3 to 5 minutes / 5 to 7 minutes / 10 to 12 minutes	Pierce skins and arrange end-to-end in a circle; let stand 5 minutes after cooking.
New potatoes, 1 pound	6 to 8 minutes	Pierce if unpeeled; add ¼ cup water.
Spinach, 10-ounce package fresh leaves	2 to 3 minutes	Rinse leaves before cooking; leave leaves damp.
Squash, yellow/zucchini, 1 pound, sliced (4 medium)	6 minutes	Add ¼ cup water.
Squash, acorn, 1 pound, (1 medium)	4 minutes	Pierce skin.
Turnips, 1 pound, peeled and cubed (3 medium)	6 to 7 minutes	Add ¼ cup water.

✻ These times are based on times in a 1,000 watt microwave oven. Your times may vary if your oven has a different wattage.

Equivalent Weights and Yields

Food	Weight or Count	Yield
Apples	1 pound (3 medium)	•3 cups sliced
Bacon	8 slices cooked	•½ cup crumbled
Bananas	1 pound (3 medium)	•2½ cups sliced or about 2 cups mashed
Bread	1 pound	•12 to 16 slices
	1½ slices	•1 cup soft crumbs
Butter or margarine	1 pound	•2 cups (4 sticks)
	¼ pound stick	•½ cup (1 stick)
Cabbage	1 pound head	•4½ cups shredded
Candied fruit or peels	½ pound	•1¼ cups chopped
Carrots	1 pound	•3 cups shredded
Cheese		
American or Cheddar	1 pound	•about 4 cups shredded
cottage	1 pound	•2 cups
cream	3 ounce package	•6 tablespoons
Chocolate morsels	6 ounce package	•1 cup
Cocoa	16 ounce can	•5 cups
Coconut,		
flaked or shredded	1 pound	•5 cups
Coffee	1 pound	•80 tablespoons (40 cups brewed)
Corn	2 medium ears	•1 cup kernels
Cornmeal	1 pound	•3 cups
Crab, in shell	1 pound	•¾ to 1 cup flaked
Crackers		
chocolate wafers	19 wafers	•1 cup crumbs
graham crackers	14 squares	•1 cup fine crumbs
saltine crackers	28 crackers	•1 cup finely crushed
vanilla wafers	22 wafers	•1 cup finely crushed
Cream, whipping	1 cup (½ pint)	•2 cups whipped
Dates, pitted	1 pound	•3 cups chopped
	8 ounce package	•1½ cups chopped
Eggs	5 large	•1 cup
whites	8 to 11	•1 cup
yolks	12 to 14	•1 cup
Flour		
all-purpose	1 pound	•3½ cups unsifted
cake	1 pound	•4¾ to 5 cups sifted
whole wheat	1 pound	•3½ cups unsifted
Green pepper	1 large	•1 cup diced
Lemon	1 medium	•2 to 3 tablespoons juice; 2 teaspoons grated rind

Food	Weight or Count	Yield
Lettuce	1 pound head	•6¼ cups torn
Lime	1 medium	•1½ to 2 tablespoons juice; 1½ teaspoons grated rind
Macaroni	4 ounces dry (1 cup)	•2 cups cooked
Marshmallows		
large	10	•1 cup
miniature	10	•1 large marshmallow
	½ pound	•4½ cups
Milk		
evaporated	5 ounce can	•about ⅔ cup
	12 ounce can	•1½ cups
sweetened condensed	14 ounce can	•1¼ cups
Mushrooms	3 cups raw (8 ounces)	•1 cup sliced, cooked
Nuts		
almonds	1 pound	•1¾ cups nutmeats
	1 pound shelled	•3½ cups
peanuts	1 pound	•2¼ cups nutmeats
	1 pound shelled	•3 cups
pecans	1 pound	•2¼ cups nutmeats
	1 pound shelled	•4 cups
walnuts	1 pound	•1⅔ cups nutmeats
	1 pound shelled	•4 cups
Oats, quick cooking	1 cup	•1¾ cups cooked
Onion	1 medium	•½ cup chopped
Orange	1 medium	•½ cup juice; 2 tablespoons grated rind
Peaches	2 medium	•1 cup sliced
Pears	2 medium	•1 cup sliced
Potatoes		
white	3 medium	•2 cups cubed cooked or 1¾ cups mashed
sweet	3 medium	•3 cups sliced
Raisins, seedless	1 pound	•3 cups
Rice		
long-grain	1 cup	•3 to 4 cups cooked
precooked	1 cup	•2 cups cooked
Shrimp, raw, unpeeled	1 pound	•8 to 9 ounces cooked, peeled, deveined
Spaghetti	7 ounces	•about 4 cups cooked
Strawberries	1 quart	•4 cups sliced
Sugar		
brown	1 pound	•2⅓ cups firmly packed
powdered	1 pound	•3½ cups unsifted
granulated white	1 pound	•2 cups

Recipe Title Index

This index alphabetically lists every recipe by exact title.

General Recipe Index

This index lists every recipe by food category and/or major ingredient.

Favorite Recipes Journal

Jot down your family's and your favorite recipes for quick and handy reference.
Remember to include the dishes that drew rave reviews when company came for dinner.

Recipe	Source/Page	Remarks